# SUPREME COURT JUSTICE TOM C. CLARK

# TEXAS LEGAL STUDIES SERIES

*Jason A. Gillmer and William S. Pugsley, Editors*

Texas's rich legal heritage spans more than three centuries and has roots in both Spanish law and English common law, but this dimension of the state's history is relatively unexplored. Books in the Texas Legal Studies Series will examine a range of topics, including state-specific studies and those with a regional or national focus.

SUPREME COURT JUSTICE

# TOM C. CLARK

*A Life of Service*

## MIMI CLARK GRONLUND

FOREWORD BY RAMSEY CLARK

University of Texas Press ❦ Austin

*To his grandchildren:*
*Ronda, Tom, Gail, Laurie, Mary, Julie, and Susie*

*A generous gift from the Jess and Betty Jo Hay Endowment*
*supported the publication of this book.*

Library of Congress Cataloging-in-Publication Data

Gronlund, Mimi Clark, 1933–
Supreme Court Justice Tom C. Clark : a life of service / Mimi Clark Gronlund ; foreword by Ramsey Clark. — 1st ed.
    p.    cm. — (Texas legal studies series)
Includes bibliographical references and index.
   ISBN 978-0-292-71990-3 (cloth : alk. paper) — ISBN 978-0-292-71991-0 (pbk. : alk. paper)
   1. Clark, Tom C. (Tom Campbell), 1899–1977   2. United States. Supreme Court—Biography.   3. Judges—United States—Biography.   I. Clark, Ramsey, 1927–   II. Title.
   KF8745.C54G76 2010
   347.73'2634—dc22
   [B]

                  2009013811

# Contents

# Foreword

M Y SISTER AND I REMEMBER STILL, and always will, the joy that best defines the years we shared with our father, Tom Clark, and mother, Mary Ramsey. We were a happy family, but not in the same way as all happy families.

The principal source of our happiness, if I can identify it, was a sense felt by all four that we were involved, each in our own way, in a cause that was of overriding importance to other interests we might have. That cause, even when we didn't know what he was doing, was Dad's career. And apparently the major reason, entirely subjective, we felt the cause was of such great importance was the diligence with which Dad pursued it. That pursuit, in our case, was tempered by his clear and excessive love for each of us and by his always good nature, which tended to bring out the same in us.

Indeed, all our years were afflicted by only one profound—and for our parents, enduring—sadness, the death of their firstborn, Tommy, at age six. Mother was devastated. One of my earliest (I was three) and most troubling memories is of mother's absence for what seemed a long time, their bedroom darkened and empty in the daytime, then later still darkened in the daytime with mother in bed. Mother often said to me, even in her last years, that Mimi's birth some fifteen months after Tommy's death saved her life. The birth of a healthy baby is a source of joy that makes the deepest sorrow seem selfish.

Our happiness was free of anger. I do not recall a single family incident or disagreement that brought distress, shouts, tears, punishment, or even a sense of unfairness. Important decisions were the prerogative of the parents. We seemed to resolve differences, which involved only minor matters—where to eat on the rare occasions when we went out, or what to do on a free weekend—by who was most determined to have his or her way. Mimi, though the smallest, was a tenacious contender when she asserted herself. By some family osmosis, the process seemed to work democratically, achieving a common appreciation that the issue was most important to that character, and when equally important to others, that it was her turn. The highest accolade our family gave was the designation "most determined character we've ever met."

After birthing five beautiful daughters, Mimi went on to become a professional. She married at age twenty, after only two years of college. She obtained her bachelor's degree some twenty years later, followed by master's degrees in library science and English, and then twenty-two years as a college reference librarian. These last were the years in which she prepared for and began researching and writing the labor of love that possessed her for so many years. This book is the fruit of that careful effort.

One of the great values of the book is that, beyond displaying the skills of an experienced professional in research and writing about important history and a major player, it is imbued, however subjectively, with an understanding, nurtured by years of direct exposure, of the character of its subject, and with both direct, personal perception of his role in many of the events described and reflection about them in later years.

As a single illustration: being present in a closely knit family, Mimi felt the urgency and exhausting intensity with which our father addressed his major duties in the relocation of Japanese and Japanese Americans in the frenetic months after the attack on Pearl Harbor in December 1941. She observed Mother's role and equipment as air raid warden for our block, which was located near a Lockheed aircraft plant in west Los Angeles, six miles from the Pacific Ocean. She felt the awe and fear caused by searchlights, antiaircraft fire, and planes in the sky. Suddenly there was an enormous task to be done: tens of thousands of people to be identified, located, rounded up, and transported to secure detention camps not yet in existence, and their property seized and secured.

The challenge was complex, controversial, unprecedented, determined by the president to be of urgent importance to national security—with a major civilian role for our father, a forty-one-year-old lawyer in the West Coast office of the Antitrust Division of the Department of Justice, who had never before been mentioned in the national press and who could never have dreamed such a task would be his. Thereafter, Tom Clark was appointed an assistant attorney general by President Roosevelt in 1943, attorney general in 1945, and then a justice of the Supreme Court in 1949 by President Truman. Years later, Mimi observed her father publicly avow, without qualification or equivocation, that the relocation of the Japanese had been a mistake and had violated the most precious principles of law

# ERNEST RUBENSTEIN

March 10, 2010

Malachy —

Here is the TCC biography, as promised. I hope you enjoy it.

I am also enclosing a copy of the letter I sent to Mimi and Tom Marten (the law clerk organizer of the event) after that weekend. It's a little like a mini-memoir of my year at the Court.

As always, you have my warmest wishes!

Ernie

## CARL MARKS & CO. LP

900 THIRD AVENUE   NEW YORK, NY 10022-4775
TELEPHONE: (212) 909-8414   FAX: (212) 980-2631
EMAIL: ERUBENSTEIN@CARLMARKS.COM

and human dignity. And yet she understood that this had been the only possible action at that time for this man she knew as her father.

Mimi had the good fortune to be at home with our parents during the most vital and revealing periods of Dad's career, when he was also of necessity home most. She was twelve when he became attorney general, on July 1, 1945, and remained there throughout his four years as attorney general and his first two terms on the Supreme Court, 1949 and 1950. For me, Mimi's love for our father greatly enriches her book about him. It is a part of his story, a part I have known well since childhood. While still a toddler, even before she named herself Mimi, my sister fell on the hot iron grille of the floor furnace in our small house in Dallas. The skin on her plump little forearm, hand, and the outside of one knee stuck to the grille and were badly burned. Dad seemed to feel responsible. For hours on end over a period of months he patiently held Mimi in his lap and rubbed a soft buttery substance on the scars trying to make them go away. He had great difficulty giving up on anything he cared about. And his efforts made her scars nearly unnoticeable in later years. Mimi observed such qualities of our father in many circumstances.

Too often we feel, after reading even the best biographies and histories, that we have learned a great deal, but only about events, what happened, and about the role of featured personalities; this feeling is due in part to our cultural proclivity to prize celebrity and to overstate the role of the individual. We realize we have no sense of the real character of the person's heroic stature, or only a caricature of it, if that, whether it be George Washington or Thomas Jefferson, Theodore Roosevelt or Woodrow Wilson, George Custer or Geronimo.

The problem that a failure to communicate character creates for the identification of important truth and thus for the value of biography and history is suggested by Lincoln's frank acknowledgment that he did not shape events, but rather events shaped him, though Lincoln surely did more to shape events than most U.S. presidents. If the principal participants do not shape events, what is the worth of most history and biography, which attribute events to a leading cast of characters, but too often ignore the role of character and chance? Character is destiny, but chance has the last and featuring blow at events, as we are told in *Moby-Dick*.

A consideration of Nathaniel Hawthorne's story "The Great Stone Face" may help. Here is a rugged, rocky mountain with the appearance of a human face that has an expression "at once grand and sweet, as if it were the glow of a vast, warm heart, that embraced all mankind in its affections." Famous people, Mr. Gathergold, General Blood and Thunder, a candidate for president, and a famous poet, each successful in the most important walks of life, came from the world over to claim the face was theirs. Why would they bother? Their accomplishments had earned them fame. Because each recognized that mere deeds could never earn the respect that recognition of great character does. Envy, perhaps, but not love. Each wanted respect as a person of noble character; each failed because of some weakness. A local man who grew up in the presence of the Great Stone Face, Ernest, was recognized by the poet as the true likeness, "whose words had power because they accorded with his thoughts and whose thoughts had reality and depth because they harmonized with the life which he had always lived."

From his life as reported by a professional who also observed him up close and unguarded through many vital years, Tom Clark can be seen to have met the test of the Great Stone Face. His appointment to the Supreme Court would have seemed miraculous before 1945. No Texan had ever reached that height in law (and as of this writing, none has since). After graduation from law school at the University of Texas, Tom Clark first practiced law with his father and brother, barely making a living. Then for six vital years he worked in the office of Bill McCraw, a friend and mentor, the fierce prosecutor and district attorney of Dallas County, primarily handling civil cases but exposed daily to the constant stream of criminal prosecutions. Back in private practice, he began achieving financial success, and then, for whatever reason, he decided at age thirty-seven to move his young family to Washington, D.C., to take a job in the U.S. Department of Justice.

The move was traumatic, relieved for both parents only by the belief it was temporary. The position Dad thought he was to take, assistant attorney general for the Claims Division, now called the Civil Division, a presidential appointment, was not realized, and he became a trial attorney in the War Risk Litigation Section of the division, trying claims brought by World War I veterans. He transferred to the Antitrust Division, where his Texas populism was resonant with the policies of Assistant Attorney General Thurman Arnold, and by 1940 his hard work and litigation successes had earned him the position of head of the West Coast office of the division, which was based in Los Angeles.

The chance of geography caused Dad to be selected as civilian coordinator for the Japanese relocation and internment in the early months of 1942, bringing him his first national attention. In the fall of 1942, he was called back to Washington to head the new War Frauds Unit, a promotion that was the result of his work with the military in the Japanese relocation and to some degree stemmed from his litigation successes in War Risk Litigation and Antitrust Division cases. There he prosecuted American companies for fraud in connection with military contracts in World War II, working closely with Senator Harry Truman, who chaired a Senate investigating committee pursuing the same war frauds.

In the spring of 1943, more than six years after he joined the Department of Justice, he was appointed assistant attorney general for the Antitrust Division. The division was restrained from active enforcement of antitrust laws because of the impact such litigation had on the war effort, in which most major corporations had some role. In September of that year, Dad was transferred to head the Criminal Division, where his relationship with the Truman Committee (as the Senate Special Committee to Investigate the National Defense Program was known) was strengthened. Senator Truman was chosen to be President Roosevelt's vice presidential running mate at the 1944 Democratic National Convention, and became vice president in early 1945.

With President Roosevelt's death on April 12, 1945, Truman became president. He made four cabinet changes, effective July 1, 1945, which included making Tom Clark attorney general, a position that had been beyond his imagination three years earlier. To a unique degree, Dad earned the appointment on the merits of his legal skills and his effective performance within the Department of Justice, including his working relationship with then-senator Truman.

Service as attorney general in the postwar period, a time so difficult that President Truman seemed to be an unlikely candidate for election to a full term, placed my father in an advantageous position for appointment to the Supreme Court, which followed four years later. The positions Tom Clark held as attorney general and Supreme Court justice were earned by hard and effective work, but chance had the last and featured blow at events. An earned position is hardest to relinquish. And though for several years he found the Court too isolated and quiet for his restless energies, even if it was the quiet in the eye of the storm, he came to love the Court's work before the midfifties.

I will describe the circumstances of his retirement insofar as I know them, because they are a powerful revelation of his character. I joined the Kennedy administration in 1961 as an assistant attorney general. I was appointed deputy attorney general in early 1965 by President Johnson, after the assassination of President Kennedy, when Nicholas Katzenbach was promoted to attorney general, nearly six months after Robert Kennedy resigned. Unexpectedly, in September 1966, President Johnson asked Nick Katzenbach to take the position of deputy secretary of state to replace George Ball, who had differed publicly with the president's Vietnam policies, in part to provide support for the legality of the war with Congress. Nick accepted. That day I became acting attorney general by law. Within a day or so, President Johnson called me on the telephone and said in the strongest terms that he would not appoint me attorney general, that he wanted me to remain in his administration, but that I must clearly understand he could not appoint me attorney general. He gave as his reason that there were too many Texans in high positions, and the office of attorney general was too sensitive politically for another one. I believed him, and still think that was his opinion at that time.

I was not disappointed. I had been in the department for nearly six fulfilling years. I had never sought higher office. I passionately supported the president's crusades against poverty and for civil rights. But, as was known, I was deeply distressed by the war in Vietnam. I nonetheless believed it was my duty to steer the department full speed ahead until a new attorney general was confirmed. This caused President Johnson some political discomfort. On my strong recommendation, he vetoed the District of Columbia crime bill in December, which assaulted the Constitution by authorizing wiretapping and other intrusions on the Bill of Rights and human dignity. The immediate and widespread hostile reaction to that veto signaled the growing fear of crime as a major political issue in the 1968 elections.

Though I do not recall the conversation and was completely unaware that conversations with the president were tape-recorded, and have not read my recorded conversations, I now know the president called me in January 1967 and, apparently seeking my comment, stated out of the blue that my father would have to retire from the Court if I were appointed attorney general. I had argued a case before the Supreme Court in the 1950s; Dad did not participate. Scores of cases from the Lands Division, where I served as assistant attorney general and while I was deputy, and from the entire Department of Justice were decided by the Court while I was in office, and Dad had participated in the proceedings. We knew each other well, and each knew the other would exercise a completely independent judgment, whatever the subject, as we always had. Appearance, however, would be a great problem. The interests of justice would clearly be best served if the attorney general were someone other than the offspring of a sitting justice.

I paid little attention to the president's inquiry. During the four months that I was acting attorney general, I heard of more than half a dozen prospects for the job, and my name came up from time to time. I knew the president played games about such things, and believed he would not consider me, as he had said.

Then at the end of February 1967, I was asked to come to the White House to meet with the president for no stated purpose—a frequent request. When I arrived, I was sent into the Oval Office, where I found the president sitting at his desk alone. We chatted briefly, then the president said he had changed his mind and was announcing my appointment as attorney general. He then reached under his desk and pressed a button, and the press poured in.

After an impromptu press conference, as I was leaving the Oval Office, I was told the Supreme Court had announced my father's retirement at the end of the Court's term, usually in June. My father and I had not discussed the subject before and did not discuss it after my appointment. This is difficult for many, particularly nonlawyers, to understand. But from the time I started law school, we never discussed his activity in the Department of Justice or on the Court, or my duties in the Department of Justice. The appearance or fact of having inside information—much less any advantage gained from family relationships to obtain information—would be devastating to the integrity of the law and to our individual reputations. Without honorable servants, the rule of law is lost.

The burden of judgment both for an attorney general and a justice of the U.S. Supreme Court is heavy and can be extremely alienating, adding to the isolation of judicial life. In case after case, Tom Clark applied the law as he found it, however hostile doing so may have been to the beliefs and interests of those he knew best and loved most. At times, my father's judgments hurt, angered, or alienated nearly every person or group dear to him, further adding to the isolation of judicial life. For example, as World War II ended, the offshore tidal lands and marginal seas were known to contain valuable deposits of oil, some already in production off California, Louisiana, and Texas. Both the states and the federal government claimed title. As attorney general, Dad chose to argue the first tidelands case against California, followed by suits against Texas and Louisiana. He was attacked viciously in Texas by politicians and the press as having violated the rights of states and as being a traitor to his own state. The attacks were unrelenting for several years.

With *Brown v. Board of Education*, the attacks were passionate against the entire Supreme Court and focused on Earl Warren, who wrote the unanimous opinion. "Impeach Earl Warren" ads were placed on highway billboards through the South. Dad knew his father and mother and many friends in Texas would feel betrayed by his vote. I had learned by the time I was ten not to discuss Lincoln with Grandmother Clark.

When Dad wrote the majority opinion in the first school prayer case, his sisters (except for the youngest), who had worked in their father's law office, wondered what had happened to Tom. They thought Christianity should be taught and lived everywhere. His mother would have wondered, too.

The lawyers with whom he worked in the Dallas district attorney's office, including his old friend Bill McCraw, must have been astounded by his 5–4 opinion for the majority in *Mapp v. Ohio*, which applied the Fourth Amendment to searches and seizures by state and local officers in addition to federal agents, thereby reversing a series of Supreme Court precedents dating to 1914.

The lawyers in the Criminal and Internal Security Divisions of the Department of Justice, for whom he (as attorney general) had authorized many wiretaps, were distressed when they read his opinion in *Berger v. New York*. *Berger* held that the Fourth Amendment applies to wiretapping and requires a judicial warrant supported by probable cause with a description of the phones to be tapped and the criminal information to be obtained. I was at Justice at the time, and though a minority of close to one, I agreed with Dad.

My father revered President Truman as a man of great courage, morality, and wisdom, to whom he was personally indebted for his appointments both as attorney general and justice. And Dad was loyal to a fault, except when loyalty conflicted with the faithful upholding of the rule of law. When President Truman seized steel mills to ensure production for the war in Korea, the resulting court case, *Youngstown Steel v. Sawyer*, came before the Court and Dad voted with the majority, which held that the president did not have the power under law to seize the mills. President Truman was apparently upset that his friend and former attorney general, whom he had appointed a justice, would rule against something he felt essential to our war effort. Dad was clearly distressed by the apparent hurt he caused his president, and remained so, but never wavered in his decision.

Tom Clark faced many highly emotional and profoundly important issues, ranging from the most private family values to the most far-reaching constitutional questions of legislative, executive, and judicial power in war and in peace, and sometimes his judgment offended family, friends, and associates. He faced them as they came. He decided them as his experience and understanding of law, government, and life told him the rule of law required. And he went on to the next tasks his hand, heart, and mind found to do, and he did them with all his might.

I can easily recall a dozen kitchens—our homes in Dallas, Washington, Los Angeles, and New York as well as vacation apartments with kitchens in Ocean City and the Virgin Islands—in which I saw Dad scrubbing pots and pans. If the task was easy, he would use soap and water. If more was needed, he would use a dishcloth and, importantly, Old Dutch Cleanser. Beyond that, steel wool or, later, Brillo pads. It was nothing for him to spend ten minutes restoring a pot or pan to a nearer pristine condition. Later that evening, long after we all went to bed, if you came out for a drink of water, you would probably find Dad working on a case, reading briefs, preparing an opinion, or writing letters with total concentration.

Two qualities seemed always to accompany Tom Clark's actions. To a higher degree than anyone I have known, he was always kind and true. In my haste to get out of Sunday-school classes taught by one of Dad's sisters, I rarely sang but never forgot the parting song: "Sunday school is over and we are going home / Goodbye, goodbye, be always kind and true." Considering the words later and even now, I have been unable to find a better way to achieve understanding, resolve disputes, reach agreement, "insure domestic tranquility," or "save succeeding generations from the scourge of war"—interpersonal and international—than by being always kind and true. Work is the essential activity to make a better world. Kindness and truth are essential to resolve differences and reach agreement about what that work ought to be and make the work go well.

Tom Clark was a superb lawyer, widely experienced, extremely diligent, versatile, and practical. He worked harder on his cases and legal matters than he did on the kitchen pots and pans, but he never neglected either. From his earliest days in Dallas, he was a doer. He had stunning reservoirs of energy under total control. In company, he was always relaxed, amiable, and focused on what was being said and done, but when the party was over, he was back at work without dropping a stitch.

He loved his family excessively, and none of us were ever able to doubt it. But he thrived on his work and seemed in his post-Court years to feel some duty to action, both because his experience and position had exposed him to urgent human need and because his own good fortune created an obligation to give all he could to the justice systems of the nation, judicial administration, the Federal Judicial Center, the education of state trial judges, and even traffic courts. And all felt the impact of his energies.

Judges rarely enjoy administration. They like to try cases and decide legal issues. Dad saw our courts failing through their failure to address the necessity for efficient handling of ever-increasing caseloads. He believed that meeting this irreversible fact with merely more judges and personnel depreciated the role of the judge and the development of law, since such actions led to the proliferation of decisions, inconsistencies, conflicts, and the denial of justice by delay and uncertainty. Few judges in our history have had the impact on judicial administration and the quality of judicial service that Tom Clark had.

If, over the years, it seemed that Tom Clark neglected his family because of his fierce devotion to his work—and it was sometimes hard on Mother, particularly in later years, when she worried about his health and was often alone at home—it was not because he was selfish or thoughtless. Just as he reacted to his father's efforts to determine the lives of his children, he consciously believed that we must each find our own way and work in life, wisely counseled where possible, but uncoerced and independent above all, and that having found that way and work, we were to do it with all our might.

In June 1977, my wife and I were returning from Tunisia, where we had participated in a human-rights support effort, and stopped in London, where I planned to meet with a client. We were barely into our hotel room late in the evening when the phone rang and a frantic voice I could barely understand was screaming, "Your father died." It was my client's mother, who had been called by my office, hoping to reach me. We caught an early flight out the next morning, and by noon entered our apartment in Greenwich Village. Only Kenny Jackson, a friend who was president of the Fortune Society, a prisoner-support and prison-reform organization, was there waiting for us.

Dad had come to New York to sit on the Second Circuit Court of Appeals. He died peacefully in his sleep, in the bed of our handicapped daughter, Ronda. He worried most about Ronda. She could not find her own way. In the kitchen was an empty Ray's Pizza box in which he had brought his late dinner home.

On the coffee table by the front window—the top of a slab of marble cut from the east face of the U.S. Capitol, a gift from Dad—were several law books from the Second Circuit library, a stack of legal briefs, and notes in green ink on a yellow pad in Dad's small, clear handwriting, made in preparation for hearings to be held the next day. He was ready for court.

Read this wonderful story, beautifully told by a loving daughter, the most determined character I have ever met; it is the story of a good man's life, the best man I have ever known. It tells a great deal about the successes and failures of our country's quest for justice in the runaway twentieth century and more of the strength and character we will need if we are to overcome the many challenges we face today.

RAMSEY CLARK
NEW YORK, NEW YORK
JULY 2008

# Preface

I T HAS BEEN MORE THAN THIRTY YEARS since my brother, Ramsey, suggested that I write a biography of our father, Tom C. Clark. Ramsey made the suggestion in June 1977, just a few days after our father's death. We were attending his burial and memorial service in Dallas, and grieving for the man who had been such an important part of our lives. I suspect that Ramsey was merely making a passing remark and did not anticipate the impact that it had on me. But the seed of an idea was planted, and though the road to completion has been long, and at times bumpy, I have persisted, motivated by the desire to leave a portrait of this remarkable man for future generations of my family as well as for the public at large.

I did not immediately plunge into the task of writing a biography. In 1977, the year of my father's death, my life was full and not conducive to taking on another major commitment. My husband and I had moved back to the Washington, D.C., area from Buffalo, New York, the previous year. I had received a master's in library science that summer and was working as a reference librarian at Northern Virginia Community College. Two of our five daughters were in college, and the remaining three were still living at home. Writing a biography seemed a formidable task, but I realized that it was important to begin immediately by contacting my father's contemporaries, who were elderly. Many had already passed on. In 1978, I interviewed my father's two surviving sisters, a sister-in-law, and his former secretaries. I began a series of conversations with my brother and my mother, who wrote a journal intended to help me with my research. I was privileged in 1981 to interview the three living justices who served on the Supreme Court with my father: William J. Brennan, Potter Stewart, and Byron White. In 1980, I enrolled in George Mason University in a master's degree program in English, with a specialization in writing. My purpose was to begin work on the biography by writing a master's thesis covering the first thirty-six years of my father's life. The first section of this biography is based on that thesis, which I completed in 1984.

For the next fifteen years, I continued to work on the biography piece-meal, fitting in research and writing between work and family responsibilities. I traveled to the Harry S. Truman Presidential Library, where my father's attorney general papers are located, and to the University of Texas Law School library, which holds his Supreme Court papers. I spent hours at the Library of Congress, going through microfilmed copies of old newspapers, primarily ones from Dallas, New Orleans, Los Angeles, and Washington, D.C. I perused FBI files obtained through the Freedom of Information Act and dug through family scrapbooks and old newspaper clippings that my mother had saved. I sent questionnaires to my fathers' former law clerks. In 1999, I retired as an associate professor and librarian at Northern Virginia Community College and vowed to immerse myself in writing and completing the biography.

Then, in 2001, my husband of forty-eight years died unexpectedly of pancreatic cancer. I dropped the biography completely during his illness. A year later, my mother died at the age of one hundred. Another year passed before I was able, mentally and emotionally, to return to the biography. I deeply regret that my husband, without whose patient support I could not have succeeded, and my mother, for whom this biography would have meant so much, did not live to see its completion.

My account is clearly from the perspective of a loving daughter, and much of the information in it is based on personal knowledge and experience. I have not attempted to write a comprehensive analysis of my father's professional career, but have chosen events, policies, and cases that continue to be of interest and that show his growth and development. I am hopeful that my biography, the first to be written of Tom Clark, will stimulate legal scholars to study and write about him from a professional viewpoint. I have tried to paint a portrait of my father as I knew him—a dedicated public servant, a wonderful husband, father, grandfather, and friend, and a delightful human being who remained humble despite his impressive success.

# Acknowledgments

THE WRITING OF THIS BIOGRAPHY stretched out for more than twenty-five years, and during that time, many of the people to whom I am deeply indebted passed on. They include my mother, Mary Ramsey Clark, whose knowledge, insights, and love were crucial to the portrayal of my father; my husband, Tom Gronlund, who never lost faith in my ability to complete the work and without whose support I could not have succeeded; my father's sisters Elizabeth Clark Capers and Mary Clark Burchfield, who provided unique perspectives as siblings of my father; three of his colleagues on the Supreme Court—Associate Justices William Brennan, Potter Stewart, and Byron White—who, because of their respect and friendship for my father, granted me the privilege of interviewing them; Alice O'Donnell, his devoted secretary and right-hand assistant during most of his years at the Department of Justice and throughout his tenure on the Supreme Court; and Grace Stewart, later a judge, who was his secretary during his years as attorney general. I regret that all of these family members, friends, and colleagues who loved Tom Clark are not here to see the final product of an effort that they contributed to in important ways.

I am indebted to English professor Jeffrey Hammond for helping me improve my writing skills through a course he taught at George Mason University while I was working on my master's in English, and to my colleagues at Northern Virginia Community College, who selected me to receive the Cecil Shuler Open Moment Fellowship. This award, established by NVCC dean Cecil Shuler at the time of his retirement, allowed me to travel to the Harry S. Truman Presidential Library in Independence, Missouri, where Tom Clark's attorney general papers are kept. I am also indebted to Vincent R. Johnson, professor of law at St. Mary's University in San Antonio, for his suggestions about and support of the biography.

My thanks go to the librarians at the Truman Library for their able assistance and also to those at the Tarlton Law Library at the University of Texas Law School, where my father's Supreme Court papers are housed. I regret that the director of the Tarlton Law Library, Professor Roy Mersky, whose unfailing help, and that of his staff, greatly facilitated my research, passed away recently, in May 2008.

The Biography Group of Washington, D.C., which I joined at its inception more than twenty years ago, under the inspiring leadership of Marc Pachter, former director of the National Portrait Gallery, has served as both a support group during times of discouragement and a source of practical advice when questions arose.

A number of my father's former law clerks are now deceased, but I am most indebted to those who provided outstanding responses to a questionnaire and gave unique perspectives that have enriched the biography. My thanks go to Percy Williams, Vester Hughes, Fred Rowe, Ellis McKay (now deceased), Ernest Rubenstein, Robert Hamilton, John Nolan, Larry Temple, James Knox, Raymond Brown, Lee Freeman, Charles Reed, Marshall Groce, Theodore Garrett, William Hannay, and Tom Marten.

My five daughters have been a source of moral support and practical assistance. If they tired of hearing about the project during the many years that it was a work in progress, they never complained. They were willing readers who always offered encouragement. Furthermore, their computer and word-processing skills far surpass mine, and they have come to my rescue with technical support on a number of occasions.

My brother, Ramsey, contributed in major ways despite an extraordinarily busy schedule. He not only wrote an outstanding foreword for the biography, but also went through the entire manuscript, making suggestions and correcting minor inaccuracies.

Finally, I am grateful to Joanna Hitchcock, director of the University of Texas Press; William Bishel, the sponsoring editor; and their excellent staff for making my dream come true by publishing the biography. Tom Clark, a devoted Texan and an alumnus of the University of Texas, would be pleased!

# Prologue

He is a great man and was a great Justice.

Stanley M. Barnes, judge of the
Court of Appeals for the Ninth Circuit, 1967

"OYEZ! OYEZ! OYEZ! All persons having business before the Honorable, the Supreme Court of the United States, are admonished to draw near and give their attention, for the Court is now sitting. God save the United States and this Honorable Court!" The marshal of the U.S. Supreme Court sang out the traditional chant on June 12, 1967, the last day of the 1966–1967 term. The moment, as always, was charged with reverence and awe as the nine justices took their seats and a silent courtroom waited for the session to begin.

First on the agenda was the traditional introduction of almost one hundred lawyers who were admitted to practice before the Court. Next came the most important part of the session—the handing down of decisions. Thirteen opinions were handed down that day, four by a 5–4 vote. My father, Tom Clark, often a swing voter, joined the majority in three of the four cases but delivered a vehement dissent in the fourth. He also joined a unanimous opinion that struck down Virginia's miscegenation law. After the decisions were handed down, Chief Justice Warren made an important announcement: it was the last time that Tom Clark would sit on the highest court of the land.

The circumstances of my father's retirement were unprecedented. He was stepping down from the Court in good health, still in his prime at sixty-seven years old, in order to avoid any appearance of conflict of interest after his son, my brother Ramsey, was appointed U.S. attorney general by President Lyndon Johnson. The only other father-son appointment affecting the Court occurred in 1930 and led to the opposite exchange.

The son, Charles Evans Hughes, Jr., resigned as solicitor general of the United States after his father, Charles Evans Hughes, was appointed chief justice by President Herbert Hoover.

The reaction to my father's retirement contrasted sharply with the reaction that had occurred eighteen years earlier when Attorney General Tom Clark, described by *Time* magazine as "the storm center of the Truman Administration" was appointed to the Supreme Court.[1] Cries of cronyism came from a variety of sources as critics complained that Truman had selected a loyal friend rather than a respected jurist. Opposition came from both ends of the political spectrum. On the liberal side, former secretary of the interior and renowned curmudgeon Harold Ickes described Clark as "a second-rate political hack."[2] Ickes and many other liberals opposed my father because of the Truman administration's anticommunist policies, which included the attorney general's list of subversive organizations and the FBI's use of wiretapping. Civil libertarians worried that as an associate justice, Clark could have a negative impact on individual rights. The far left was especially distressed. An article that appeared in the communist newspaper the *Daily Worker* on September 19, 1949, was headlined "Witchhunter Gets Bid to High Court."

The far right also expressed dismay. The National Blue Star Mothers of America, describing itself as an organization "chiefly concerned with the preservation of constitutional Republican form of government," charged Clark with being "definitely of communistic tendencies," and requested that a representative from their group be invited to testify against him.[3] Conservative Republicans under the leadership of Senator Homer Ferguson of Michigan fought the nomination, although, in the end, only eight Republicans voted against confirmation. Big business entered the fray because of Clark's strong antitrust record, and accused him of taking "a sadistic sort of delight in bringing government lawsuits aimed at breaking up large businesses into smaller and less potent units."[4]

"Oh, no!" wrote Lynn Landrum, a columnist for the conservative *Dallas Morning News*.[5] The piece criticized Truman for appointing a politician rather than a jurist and expressed the anger many Texans felt over the tidelands oil case, in which the attorney general argued for federal rather than state ownership of offshore oil-rich lands.

Eighteen years later, the "Oh, no!" headline was repeated, but the editorial that followed carried a very different message. It praised Tom Clark and expressed regret over his retirement, which it described as "a loss to the Court and to the country." Clark, the editorial continued, had been "one of the strongest voices of responsibility on the Court."[6] Praise came from every corner. *Time* magazine wrote that Clark was "the author of some of the Court's most lucid and precise opinions."[7] Journalist John MacKenzie of the *Washington Post* described Clark as a "peacemaker among the justices ... whose work off the Court to improve the administration of justice had earned him the title 'the traveling salesman of justice.'" According to MacKenzie, the only negative reaction from Congress to Ramsey Clark's appointment was that it entailed "the elder Clark's impending retirement from the Supreme Court."[8] The words of Stanley M. Barnes, judge of the Court of Appeals for the Ninth Circuit, summed up the changed perception of Tom Clark best: "He is a great man and was a great Justice. I would not have said so twenty years ago, but I do now, and I'm certain of it."[9]

The image of the controversial, political attorney general was no more. He had grown enormously since he moved our family from Dallas, Texas, to Washington, D.C., in 1937—a thirty-seven-year-old lawyer who had rarely been outside the state of Texas and who intended to remain in the nation's capital for no more than two years. But circumstances, hard work, and luck changed all that. Tom Clark's accomplishments surpassed his highest ambitions and did not end when he retired from the Supreme Court, for his retirement years—the last ten of his life—were as productive as any previous ones. Still, he never forgot where he came from. His love for his home state remained with him always, and though he lived more than half his life outside its borders and experienced personal growth that took him far beyond its confines, he remained a Texan, shaped by his beginnings in turn-of-the-century Dallas.

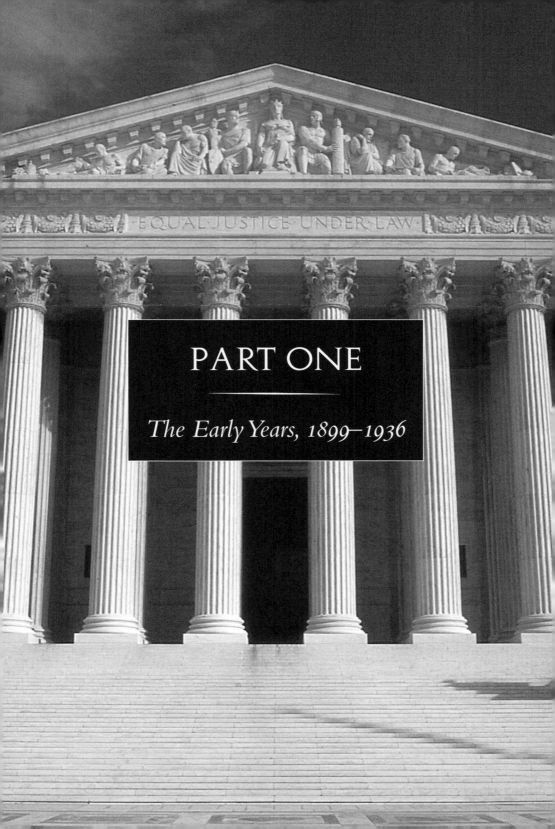

# PART ONE

---

*The Early Years, 1899–1936*

## CHAPTER 1

# Early Influences

'Tis a countenance whose spell
Sheds balm over mead and dell.

Anonymous verse in Tom Clark's
Bryan Street High School yearbook, 1917

T HE AFFECTION MY FAMILY FELT FOR TEXAS, especially during the years that followed our move east in 1937, was unstated but pervasive. It exhibited itself in small ways, such as my surprise at the age of eight or nine at learning that a favorite song, "The Eyes of Texas," was known to most people as "I've Been Working on the Railroad." My romantic perception of the state was based on secondhand knowledge rather than actual experience, for I was only four years old when my father, Tom Clark, left his private law practice in Dallas for a job in Washington, D.C., with the federal government. My brother, Ramsey, dubbed me the family's Yankee, a term that made me instinctively defensive without knowing exactly why.

I sensed a disadvantage at being somewhat less a Texan than other family members. Being a Texan was special. I felt a surge of pride when I responded "Texas" to the familiar question "And where are you from?"— never doubting that everyone shared my lofty esteem of the state. "Mimi looks like a Texan," my father would declare, and I would beam, understanding the significance of the compliment. Looking back, I realize my eastern friends could not have fully appreciated the tribute when my father told them they were "pretty enough to be a Texan."

Tom Clark was a Texan. Even his physical appearance, aided by the Stetson hats and jaunty bow ties he loved to wear, fit the popular image of how a Texan should look. The six-foot frame, lean for most of his life, was topped by a full, thick head of hair that was even more striking in his later years, after it had turned white. "Hi, I'm Tom Clark," he would declare, and the broad smile that lit up his face put people at ease immediately. Only the brisk, light walk hinted at the remarkable energy beneath the easygoing manner. My father's Texas heritage was more than physical, however, for throughout his life, his character retained an imprint that was the result of growing up at a unique time in a unique place—the early 1900s in Dallas.

• • •

Dallas, according to Texas historian Herbert Gambrell, "is an example of a city that man made with a little help from nature and practically none from Providence."[1] Certainly, the spot on the banks of the Trinity River where Dallas's founder, John Neely Bryan, settled in 1839 had no significant natural advantages. Bryan's dream, passed down through generations of Dallasites, that the river would one day be navigable to the Gulf of Mexico, making Dallas a great inland port, has remained unfulfilled. Dallas's strength resided in its people—a hard-working, vigorous group of men and women who believed they could create a great city out of a dusty village. One early settler, whose family established Sanger Brothers, Dallas's first department store, provided the following characterization of the city's early residents:

> While everything was different from what I had been accustomed to, I never felt the least touch of homesickness. I believe it was because I was associated with a jolly crowd of businessmen; some were single, some were married, but all were united on all questions that affected the prosperity of Dallas. Indifference was unknown; all were ready to do their share for the upbuilding of the city . . . Back in the [18]70's there were no *Classes*. I knew every man, woman, and child in the village.[2]

As railroads multiplied throughout the nation, Dallas competed with other towns in the area for a station. Community leaders worked long and hard to persuade officials of the Houston and Texas Central Railroad to route tracks through the city. They finally succeeded, and on July 16, 1872, an excited crowd gathered to witness the arrival of the first train. A visitor to the city provided the following account of the momentous event: "First a wisp of smoke, and then the outlines of the engine shaping up, growing larger, whizzing toward us. The crowd went wild, men whooped, women screamed or even sobbed, and children yelped in fright and amazement."[3]

Excitement and city pride were so extreme that a newspaper in neighboring Fort Worth wryly commented, "The first [words] the children are taught is 'Hurrah for Dallas!'"[4] The town became so well known for its healthy ego that the 1872 *Texas Almanac* gently chided it for "putting on the airs of a city."[5] By 1899, the year Tom Clark was born, Dallas numbered approximately 42,000 people. In 1906, ambitious citizens formed the 150,000 Club with the aim of significantly increasing the city's population by 1910. They fell short, but had surpassed that goal by 1920.[6]

The first two decades of the twentieth century were a special time in the history of Dallas. A. C. Greene, in *Dallas, the Deciding Years*, describes them as a time that reflected "the contentment of security, of understanding without frustration what you could do, what you should do." Dallas, according to Greene, was a "place": "A place is where the individual is still recognized, known to all, or a great many of the fellow citizens. A place has certain characteristics just like a person, recognizable traits, unique attitudes, and actions."[7]

Children grew up in a simple and secure environment. Differences between right and wrong were clear-cut. Religion was an integral part of life, and a belief in the rewards of hard work was a basic part of religion. Boundless optimism prevailed as citizens saw their efforts bring great things to the growing city. In 1900, the city received a $50,000 grant from Andrew Carnegie to build its first public library. That same year, the Dallas Symphony Orchestra performed for the first time. Electric-streetcar tracks sprouted over the city's streets, and in 1902 the first interurban service began between Dallas and Fort Worth, ushering in the growth of the cities' suburbs.

The reign of the automobile was yet to come, but in 1899, the year Tom Clark was born, the first car appeared on Dallas's streets. It was owned by Colonel E. H. R. Greene, whose mother, Hetty, known as "the witch of Wall Street," was reputed to be the richest woman in the country.[8] More cars followed, and soon the first traffic law limited speed to seven miles per hour and imposed fines of up to $200 on violators. Civic pride swelled when Elm Street, the city's main business street, was paved with a new surface—asphalt—previously used only in the large eastern cities.

My father was eight years old when an event of great importance to the city occurred. Herbert Marcus, a fifteen-dollar-a-week shoe salesman at Sanger Brothers department store, along with his sister and brother-in-law, Carrie and Albert Neiman, opened a new shop—Neiman-Marcus. The store introduced the ready-made dress, a radical innovation, to city merchants and established a reputation for excellent taste and outstanding personalized service. Within a few years, Neiman-Marcus had made Dallas a fashion center of national renown.

Although the city exuded the vitality and prosperity of a boomtown, problems also existed. As early as 1882, a newspaper editorial lamented: "Three hundred saloons every minute in the day pour their poisonous compounds down the gullets of their customers."[9] A chapter of the Women's Christian Temperance Union was organized, and members advised mothers to prohibit their children from tasting beer or wine and to avoid the evils of card playing.

Powerful currents of racism churned beneath the town's seemingly congenial surface. The Ku Klux Klan was active during the early 1900s and remained a force until the midtwenties. Stanley Marcus, eldest son of Neiman-Marcus's cofounder, recalls that as a Jewish boy growing up during this era, he was frequently chased home from school by gangs of taunting children. The most frequent victims of virulent racism, however, were black citizens. When my father was ten years old, he was part of a crowd that witnessed the lynching of a black man accused of assaulting a three-year-old white girl. The boy must have shared the shame and anger that afterward engulfed townspeople. Outraged citizens tore down the arch where the man had been hung. It was never rebuilt.[10]

My father's parents, William Henry and Virginia "Jennie" Clark, had come to Dallas from Brandon, Mississippi. Both were descended from aristocratic southern families—a background shared by many Dallas settlers. My father's great-grandfather, General William J. Clark—a rank apparently earned in a North Carolina militia—was married four times and was a young widower when he met and wed Louise Lanier, a second cousin of the famous southern poet Sidney Lanier. They had ten children, five sons and five daughters. General Clark moved the family from North Carolina to Mississippi in 1835 and became a leading figure in that state, serving as state treasurer from 1843 to 1847 and then again from 1851 to 1854. He was also on the board of inspectors for the state penitentiary in Jackson and was involved in bringing public education to Jackson. The general belonged to the Whig Party, one of the precursors to the Republican Party, and was an admirer of Henry Clay. He was also a prohibitionist who did not allow liquor served in his home, although friends recorded that his wife, known for her elegant dinners, occasionally managed to smuggle some in for cooking.

Deeply religious, both General Clark and Louise Lanier Clark were members of the Baptist Church. But the general, upon studying the New Testament, came to disagree with traditionalists in the church, and his outspoken criticism resulted in his expulsion. After moving to Mississippi, he established the Brattle Springs Christian Church, eight miles outside of Jackson, where he preached once a month for a number of years.

General Clark owned a plantation in Madison and Hinds County, Mississippi, that covered more than a thousand acres and was worked by sixty-seven slaves. His family was known for its affluent lifestyle. They traveled to New Orleans for Mardi Gras each year, and the general lavished gifts of jewelry and silver on his daughters. All five sons attended college. One son, James, was valedictorian of his graduating class at Harvard, and later became proctor of the University of Texas. Another son, William Henry Clark, my father's grandfather, served in the Mexican War and was a probate judge in Rankin County, Mississippi, when the Civil War broke out. He joined the Confederate Army, and was captured on July 4, 1863, at the Battle of Vicksburg. He was imprisoned briefly, and then freed as part of a prisoner exchange. His freedom was short-lived. After returning to battle, he was promoted to the rank of colonel, and on October 5, 1864, at the age of thirty-six, was killed at Altoona, Georgia, as he led his men in battle, holding the Confederate flag high in his hand. A note informed his wife of his death:

> Your gallant husband was mortally wounded October 5, 1864, in the assault by French's Division upon the heights of Altoona. I carried him from the field and left him breathing faintly but dying sorely. . . . He requested his sword, pistol and spurs to be given to his "little boys" and expressed hope that they would remind them in after years of a father who had died gloriously in defense of his Country.
>
> He requested me to assure you that he loved you to the last and hoped you would remember him as a gallant soldier who received his death wound in heading a charge upon the enemy's stronghold.

William Clark left a widow, Mary McDowell Clark, and two young sons: James McDowell and William Henry. The second son, the father of Tom Clark, never knew his own father, who was away fighting the war when he was born. The boys were raised by their mother, who came from a distinguished Virginia family. Her uncle James McDowell, a member of the Virginia legislature, gained recognition for a speech denouncing slavery after the Nat Turner uprising. Several years later, in 1843, he was elected governor of Virginia.

Mary McDowell's cousin, Ephraim McDowell, was a physician renowned for his achievements in the field of abdominal surgery. He performed the first ovariotomy in the United States in 1809, removing the ovaries and a twenty-two-and-a-half-pound tumor from Mrs. James Todd Crawford, who survived the surgery without the benefit of anesthesia or antibiotics. The memory of Dr. McDowell remains prominent in his hometown of Danville, Kentucky, where the Ephraim McDowell Regional Medical Center bears his name. His home, where the surgery was performed, was declared a historic site in 1965.[11]

Jennie Clark's father, Captain A.T. Falls, was also an officer in the Confederate Army, and her uncle, Thomas Maxey, was a federal judge in Austin, Texas, for thirty years. By coincidence, the Maxeys' house in Austin was located across the street from the home of William F. Ramsey, whose daughter Mary was destined to marry Jennie's son Tom. The Maxeys and Ramseys were good friends, and Mary had happy memories of going to the Maxeys with her younger sister Dorothy for a dish of homemade ice cream.

William and Jennie Clark grew up during the harsh Reconstruction era that followed the Civil War. Their childhood experiences in Mississippi left them with a strong dislike for Abraham Lincoln and a distrust of Yankees in general. Years later, when my grandmother Jennie visited our family in Washington, D.C., she declined offers to see the Lincoln Memorial. Despite this lasting bitterness, Jennie and William did not approve of the Ku Klux Klan, and no one in their family joined that organization.

William sought greater opportunity than a depressed Mississippi could offer, and moved to Dallas with his mother in 1885, after graduating from the University of Mississippi and Lebanon Law School in Tennessee. His brother, James, seven years his senior and a promising physician, had died two years earlier at the age of twenty-six. Dallas was still more a town than a city, with a population of slightly more than 10,000, but with an economy based on trade and commerce, it was on its way to becoming a major center for the cotton market.[12] In addition, its residents were establishing a "rich cultural life."[13] William practiced law for one year, and then returned to Brandon to marry Jennie and bring her back to Dallas as his bride. At nineteen, Jennie was a lovely, delicate-looking blond. William, five years her senior, had black curly hair, dark eyes, and a large hooked nose. Of all their children, Tom resembled him most physically. Although William was not a tall man, he appeared sturdy and strong next to his petite wife. In the years ahead, however, she would prove to be the stronger of the two.

William and Jennie Clark had ten children. My father, Thomas Campbell, the seventh child, was born on September 23, 1899, and was named for Jennie's uncle, Thomas Maxey, and his wife, Fanny Campbell. Two children died before my father was born: firstborn Joseph McDowell, known as "Mac," stepped on a nail when he was eight years old and died when gangrene developed. That same year, one-year-old William died from an undetermined illness. A third baby died at birth when my father was two years old.

Despite these tragedies, not uncommon among families at that time, William and Jennie's early years of marriage were prosperous and apparently happy. William became known as "Judge," a title of respect frequently bestowed upon prominent southern lawyers, and established himself as a talented and respected lawyer. As one contemporary wrote: "Mr. W. H. Clark of Dallas who was chosen delegate to the American Bar Association is rapidly becoming one of the most favorably known lawyers of Texas . . . he is essentially a lawyer of the people. . . . [His speaking ability has earned him] a sure place among Texas's most effective and brilliant lawyers."[14]

As a lawyer, Judge Clark influenced the development of Texas's legal system in a number of areas. He helped frame the first Railroad Commission laws for the state, and his legal counsel also helped shape the state's insurance laws. Some of the legislation he worked for reflected a decidedly puritanical morality. He helped defeat an ordinance that would have created an area for "bawdy" houses in the city, and tried—unsuccessfully—to establish a law prohibiting divorced parties from ever remarrying. Divorce, he declared, was a greater threat to the nation's well-being than "questions of race, suicide, or foreign armies."[15] At thirty-six, he was elected president of the Texas Bar Association—the youngest man to have held the position up until that time.

Judge Clark was a product of his times and his Mississippi heritage. On July 4, 1925, at the dedication of a new courthouse in Brandon, Mississippi, he made a speech modestly entitled "Brilliant Address of Great Legal and Historical Value." Opening with the statement "Once a Mississippian, always a Mississippian," William praised our forefathers and argued the importance of states' rights.

The Constitution of the United States was based upon and guaranteed to the people the independence and sovereignty of the several states over all local or domestic affairs . . . Upon this sound foundation, the American Republic was built and has prospered—the like of which is not to be found in the History of Nations—ancient or modern; and if you destroy these great principles of States' rights in our government, and in lieu thereof have a central government at Washington, to regulate and control the domestic affairs of the people in the several States, it will surely result in the fall of this great Republic. . . . The greatest danger of our government today is Federal Encroachment on the local and domestic affairs of the several States.

He then moved into the subjects of "The Negro Problem" and "Race Distinctions," expressing views that reflect the deeply embedded racism of that time. Although stating emphatically that "we would not reinstate slavery if we could," he then launched into a lecture on the importance of separation of the black and white races and the inherent inequality of the Negro:

Neither in Asia, nor Africa, nor Europe, nor America, has the white race ever consented to or tolerated either marital relationship or social equality, with the black race. And why? A good and sufficient reason is, because the law of nature or of our Creator does not permit social equality and an amalgamation of the white and black races. . . . We should be hopeful and happy, and not pessimistic . . . that the Mason and Dixon line is wiped from the map of the United States forever, and that as long as the negro sees fit to remain with us, in preference to returning to his native land, the white people of the South will in the future, as in the past, give him work and a home, and treat him kindly, and give him equal rights before the law with the white, as to the protection of his person, liberty, labor and property, in and out of the courthouse, and give him religious and educational advantages with separate churches and schools for the black and white, but the white people will never allow them social equality, or anything that will result in social equality as evidenced by our miscegenation law, "separate coach" law, and separate schools and churches which principles and customs have been upheld and approved . . . by the Supreme Court of the United States.

Despite these clearly racist views—common in both the North and South at that time—William Clark was dedicated to the law, and established a reputation as a "people's" lawyer. An article that appeared in the *Dallas Law Journal* shortly after his death gave the following description: "This notable attorney was always found on the side of the people. . . . He believed that if the people were let alone they would work out their own destiny. He was nearly always found on the side of the people as against the corporation or the city or the state. . . . Judge Clark loved the law. He studied the law. He gave to the law the best he had. And through the law he made his contribution to this new country in the West."[16] He must have conveyed his love of the law to his sons, for three of the four chose to follow him into that profession.

With his law practice flourishing, William moved his growing family a few months after my father was born. He chose a large house on Ross Avenue, a prosperous residential street lined with the handsome homes of many of Dallas's most prominent families. The Clarks' house was known for a profusion of purple wisteria surrounding the front porch, and townspeople strolled or rode by to view the vines when they were in bloom. The family's lifestyle—typical of affluent Dallasites—reflected a southern heritage. Servants helped maintain the large household, and the older children attended private schools. The family went to St. John's Episcopal Church each Sunday. They enjoyed recreational activities together. The children and their father liked to fish on Bachman Lake, a short ride from the house, and brought their catches home for Jennie to fry. She was an exceptional cook, and her fried chicken and angel food cakes were without equal in the opinion of her children and grandchildren. A favorite annual event for the young family was the arrival of the circus. Jennie and the children would ride the streetcar to William's office to watch the parade beforehand. Afterward, they would return home for lunch and wait until he arrived to take them to the circus grounds. He was always late, and the excited children could hardly contain their impatience.

Judge Clark was a loyal Democrat who attended every state party convention for twenty years. His passion for politics developed at a time when the political arena afforded people the sort of entertainment later provided by radio, movies, and television. Men, women, and children traveled long distances to hear candidates speak. Torchlight parades frequently preceded speeches, and an air of festivity prevailed. William enjoyed the drinking that was part of such convivial scenes. Gradually, however, the effect of his drinking upon his personal and professional life became devastating. By the time Tom was of school age, his father's drinking had become a serious problem that drastically altered the family's comfortable lifestyle. Although William continued to practice law until he died in 1931, at the age of seventy, the once-thriving law practice faltered as word of his drinking began to circulate. Good times enjoyed as a family became rare, and the children avoided bringing friends to the house for fear of embarrassment. Adversity drew the children together and instilled in them a strong sense of responsibility for one another. A close family source described William's behavior as increasingly "bossy" and "ugly." The situation was so painful that two surviving daughters were unwilling to discuss it more than sixty years later.

Jennie held the family together. Uncomplaining, strong, yet gentle, she used her love to provide the children with a secure anchor. My father could not recall ever seeing her lose her temper. Pride and loyalty kept her from discussing "the problem" with anyone—even her own children. Her example inspired in them a fierce family loyalty and an exceptional ability to keep their emotions within. Despite her efforts, the once-handsome house began to deteriorate as its upkeep became more and more difficult to afford. The neighborhood grocer allowed Jennie to accumulate bills of up to two hundred dollars before requiring payment. She always managed to come up with the money as the deadline approached. Avoiding open confrontation with William, she learned to work around him in order to manage the household as she thought best.

The puritan work ethic dominated the culture of that time, and the family's personal hardships undoubtedly reinforced that philosophy. Work became their creed. Servants were no longer affordable, so the family made do with occasional help from Zeke, the son of a former slave, who had come from Mississippi with the Clarks. Jennie taught the girls to sew, cook, and care for their younger brothers and sisters. The boys learned to milk cows, tend the garden, and help maintain the house. Everyone was busy. Tom delivered newspapers and worked in a drugstore, where, he firmly believed, the many free Cokes he drank temporarily stunted his growth. He was short for his age until sixteen, when he suddenly shot up to nearly his full six-foot height.

There were also good times. Jennie often played the piano and sang, and as the children gathered round her to join in on favorites such as "Put On Your Old Gray Bonnet," the music temporarily eased the cares that hung over the large house. She could still have fun and be playful with her children. My father's older sister "Danny" recalled waking up one morning to a snow-covered scene—a rare occurrence in Dallas. While Tom ran to an upstairs porch for a better look, his mother stepped outside from a first-floor entrance. Soon the two were throwing snowballs at each other. My father loved the outdoors and spent as much time outside as possible. Hunting and fishing were his favorite pastimes, and he and his friends often biked out to the village of Highland Park, today a fashionable, close-to-town neighborhood, to hunt quail and dove. He also enjoyed working in the large garden that supplied the family with most of its vegetables and that won him a medal as a Boy Scout—an award he prized all his life. The first Boy Scout troop was established in America in 1910, and my father joined the organization shortly afterward. At fourteen he became one of the first Eagle Scouts in the United States. He participated in many Boy Scout jamborees, and loved to brag that at one he broke all previous records for cutting up the greatest number of chickens. He was, in his own words, "the world's greatest chicken cutter."

I don't know how my father became interested in punching bags, but during his teens, he became quite an expert. Not content to work out with a single bag, he practiced until he was able to keep five going at the same time: two with his hands, two with his knees, and one with his head. Years later—without the benefit of punching bags—he demonstrated to his children how he was able to perform this remarkable feat. We laughed uproariously at the sight of his frenzied motions as he lashed out with every part of his body at the imaginary bags.

The name "Thomas Clark" appears frequently in the Bryan Street High School yearbook for 1917. Although Grandmother called him "Thomas" all her life, my father was not comfortable with the formal name and stopped using it after he entered college. He was a good student, but was not listed on the school's honor roll. Oratory and debate were his main extracurricular interests, a reflection of his father's influence, and he appears on the page of class officers with the title "Class Orator." He worked with typical perseverance to improve his speaking ability and to overcome the shyness that made speaking before an audience very difficult. Once, while still in high school, he became so nervous before a speech that he fainted. The occasion was a parent-teacher meeting at an elementary school he had attended. The principal had asked him to speak as part of the program. Several family members were in attendance, and this may have unknowingly increased his apprehension as he nervously awaited his turn at the podium. As he got up to speak, he fainted. Unhurt, he insisted on continuing, even though he was urged to leave the platform and lie down. He was determined, however, and spoke with no further problem.

His perseverance paid off, for he entered the high school's annual speech competition his senior year with a speech entitled "Modern Slavery." The yearbook writer gave this intriguing, though ambivalent, description of the young orator's performance: "The oration of Thomas Clark was characterized by a peculiar delivery. He received closest attention from his hearers by his picturization of the conditions termed by him as modern slavery."

His choice of a topic seems surprising. His family belonged to the white, conservative mainstream, which was still insensitive to the enslaving deprivations of blacks, and his father's views on the social inequality of Negroes must have had some impact on his own thinking. But his father's alcoholism set him apart from his peers. He had experienced financial insecurity and family instability. He had witnessed, and never forgotten, a lynching. These factors may have stirred a special sensitivity within his inherently compassionate nature. The text of the speech has not survived, but it must have contained the seeds of a philosophy that would make this young Texan a lifelong supporter of civil rights. His argument was apparently impressive, for, despite popular, predominantly negative attitudes toward his topic, Thomas Clark won the 1917 George M. Dealy Award for Oratory at Bryan Street High School.

A quotation from an unknown source accompanies his high school write-up:

> 'Tis a countenance whose spell
> Sheds balm over mead and dell.

The lines suggest the pleasing personality and sunny disposition that almost always hid whatever trials he was experiencing.

## CHAPTER 2

# Emerging into Manhood

Big man on campus.

Mrs. Legg,<br>
Pi Beta Phi housemother, 1921

B Y THE TIME MY FATHER GRADUATED from high school, Dallas was a full-fledged city with a population of more than 150,000 and a downtown area, according to an article in *Collier's*, with the "most imposing skyline of any city save New York."[1] When the United States entered World War I, in April 1917, Dallas joined the war effort with typical gusto. The Texas State Fair grounds became Camp Dick, a training center for U.S. Army aviators, who were housed in converted stables. The Army Air Corps established a second training base next to Bachman Lake, where pilots received final instructions before going to Europe. After the war, the base became the site of the city's airport, Love Field, named for an army cadet killed in a training crash. The airport was dedicated with much fanfare in 1927 by renowned aviator Charles Lindbergh.

According to family lore, Judge Clark, who consistently tried to control his children's lives, was inspired by the prevailing surge of patriotism to decide that his son Tom should become a general. Consequently, he enrolled my father at the Virginia Military Institute, widely regarded as the "West Point of the South." My grandfather admired VMI's involvement in the Civil War as well as its academic reputation. The great southern general Thomas "Stonewall" Jackson was an eccentric chemistry professor there when the war broke out, and its corps of cadets gained renown for a pitched battle at New Market, Virginia—a victory that cost ten students their lives. Later, the Union Army burned the institution.

VMI made a deep impression on my father, who at eighteen had never been outside Texas. Discipline was stringent, and "brother rats," as freshmen were affectionately called, received harsh treatment that included physical hazing. At mealtime, the "rats" were required to sit in exaggerated upright positions with their eyes glued to their plates. The "rat" sitting at the foot of the table was responsible for keeping upperclassmen's water tumblers filled. The older cadets would throw their glasses to the unfortunate freshman, who was in for a rough time if he missed the catch. "Rats" were under constant scrutiny, and my father was severely punished on one occasion for making a face at a superior officer. The school year, with only one holiday at Christmas, must have seemed endless to the young Texan. Furthermore, the winter of 1918 was one of the coldest in Virginia history, and my father, who always slept with an open window regardless of the weather, recalled waking some mornings to find that snow had blown into his room.

Despite these harsh conditions, the boys enjoyed good times and formed strong attachments to one another and to the institution. My father was especially fond of the resident physician, Dr. Carpenter, whom he described as "a great physician." The doctor was a popular figure with the young cadets, and they often turned to him for comfort and support. He lived above his office in a modest frame building in Lexington and posted a sign by the stairs that read: "Dr. Carpenter Upstairs." When he died, the entire VMI corps assembled at his graveside to honor him. At the conclusion of the ceremony, the cadet corps commander stepped forward and placed the "Dr. Carpenter Upstairs" sign on his grave.

My father always spoke of VMI with a mixture of affection and awe. In a letter written after speaking at the institution's graduation exercises on June 11, 1947, he referred to the "strong sense of attachment" that was forged during his year at VMI. For him, the "rat system" succeeded in instilling respect for authority, self-control, and orderliness, and at the same time strengthened a self-preserving sense of humor and an abiding humility. He left VMI after one year because of his family's financial difficulties. World War I was drawing to a close, and he was eager to get into the action. He enlisted in the Texas National Guard, serving in the 153rd Infantry Division as a sergeant. His military career was short-lived, however, for five months later, on November 11, 1918, the armistice ending the war was signed and my father, along with thousands of other American soldiers, was released from service.

Two major decisions faced my father as he reentered civilian life: where to attend college and how to pay for it. Practicalities narrowed his choices to Southern Methodist University (SMU), Dallas's first four-year institution, founded only three years earlier, and the University of Texas at Austin, which his brother Bill had attended. He would have to support himself wherever he went, for his father's income was, at best, unpredictable. SMU was his initial choice, since living at home would be an advantage financially. But SMU, unlike the University of Texas, did not have a law school, and a law degree was now his goal. He must have also been reluctant to return to the volatile atmosphere of his father's home and lose the independence he had enjoyed for the past year. Finally—two weeks after the spring semester began—he changed his mind and left for Austin and the University of Texas.

Tom Clark must have been a forlorn figure when he arrived in Austin in January 1919 with few belongings and a scant 129 pounds on his six-foot frame. He felt very much alone. His high school friends were already well established at the university, and the credits he had earned at VMI put him ahead of them academically, creating an even greater separation. With no place to stay, he spent the first few nights at the local YMCA. Then he learned of another student, Sollie Stolaroff, who had an apartment but needed someone to share expenses. Tom jumped at the opportunity. The fact that Sollie, an upperclassman from El Paso, was Jewish was not a problem for him, and he did not anticipate any unpleasant repercussions. He was mistaken, as he learned when he failed to get a bid from any fraternity during rush week. He was blackballed because of his Jewish roommate. He was deeply disappointed. His high school friends were fraternity men, as were his father and his brother Bill. Being a fraternity man was important to him, not only because of family tradition, but because membership offered social and professional advantages that he felt were important. Despite his disappointment, he kept his emotions to himself and focused on his studies. He had little time to worry about fraternities, for survival was his first priority. Because he was on his own financially, he had to find work immediately in order to cover his expenses of approximately thirty-five dollars a week.

Over the next three years, he supported himself through a variety of jobs. He and Sollie sold blotters that carried advertisements by town merchants, and then distributed them to students. The Cactus Tea Room took the center ad in exchange for free meals for the two students. When the blotters ran out, Tom continued to get free meals by washing dishes at the Tea Room. He also earned money by correcting and grading papers for a government professor and by writing biographies for a book about distinguished Texans—one of whom was his future father-in-law, William F. Ramsey.

The apartment my father and Sollie shared was off campus, and they did not have a large number of visitors. My father's grades stayed high as he concentrated on his studies and worked to support himself. But he also became increasingly involved in extracurricular activities and established a name for himself through his involvement in student publications. Consequently, in the fall of 1920—less than a year after he had been "blackballed"—several fraternities offered him membership. There is no indication that the reversal by the fraternities was due to any enlightenment or lessening of prejudice on their part. Sollie had left the university, and so was no longer an issue. My father still wanted to be a fraternity man and had worked to achieve that goal. He was a pragmatist, not a crusader, and put aside any bitterness he may have felt about the intolerance of the fraternities and their treatment of him and Sollie. Sollie, who would become a successful artist and designer, was apparently unaware of the blackballing incident, for he told his daughter years later that he did not experience any anti-Semitism at the university. My father accepted a bid from Delta Tau Delta, and was elected its president his senior year. He remained close to the fraternity throughout his life, serving as national president of the alumni association while an associate justice on the Supreme Court.

My father's involvement in extracurricular activities grew to the point that by the time he was in law school, his class work was suffering. Besides his activities with Delta Tau Delta, he was a member of both Pi Sigma Alpha, the honorary political science fraternity, and Alpha Phi Epsilon, the honorary literary and public speaking fraternity, and he served as chairman of the Texas Student Publications, which included the yearbook (the *Cactus*), a newspaper (the *Daily Texan*), and a magazine (the *Longhorn*). The editor of the newspaper—Tom Pollard—became a close friend and important colleague. Pollard was a well-known figure on campus. He had attended the university from 1915 to 1917, but left to enlist in the Army Air Corps when World War I broke out. He reentered the university at the same time that my father enrolled, and stood out in the Air Corps uniform that he frequently wore around the campus. He also gained renown by being elected a delegate to the Texas House of Representatives and then the Texas Senate while a student.

Pollard was a "barb"—a nonfraternity man—who also had to support himself financially. Pollard and Clark were a dynamic duo. As they devised ways to earn money, they proved to be ingenious, though somewhat devious, entrepreneurs. During student enrollment, they set up a table at the end of the registration line and distributed forms for the students to fill out. The students thought it was part of the registration process and willingly recorded their names, addresses, and phone numbers on the forms. Clark and Pollard then compiled the information and published student directories, which they sold to local businesses.

Another profitable moneymaking project developed through their involvement in college publications. After Tom Clark became chairman of the Student Publications Board, he and Pollard, along with other members, decided that the publications—the *Daily Texan*, the *Cactus*, and the *Longhorn*—should be consolidated under one management. My father appointed Tom Pollard general manager. Both Pollard and Clark received salaries as well as commissions for advertisements they sold. The enterprise greatly improved their financial situations!

The two young men also assisted each other with studies. Tom Pollard helped my father by giving him his used textbooks, and in return, my father gave Pollard a copy of every memo he wrote on cases they were studying—an arrangement approved by their professor. In addition, my father had an unapproved arrangement with another classmate, Allen Clark, who sat next to him in one law class. The two students would take turns preparing briefs on cases. When the professor called upon "Mr. Clark," the one who was prepared for the case at hand would immediately stand up and give the presentation. The system broke down one day when Allen Clark stood to give his report and the professor said, "Not you, I want the other Mr. Clark." Fortunately for my father, the only female student in the law school, Gladys Rountree, was also in the class. Pretty, bright, and eventually a successful Wall Street lawyer, Gladys was the belle of the law school. Whether she knew of my father's dilemma is uncertain, but she stood up and said "Oh, Professor Potts, don't you remember that you asked me to brief that case? And I'd like to make the report." "Saved by the Rountree!" my father declared when telling the story years later.

During his last year at the university, an event of extraordinary importance occurred. Tom Clark met Mary Ramsey, a lovely strawberry blond with large blue-gray eyes and a dazzling smile. Mary lived in Mrs. Legg's boardinghouse, across the street from the Delta Tau Delta house, and her roommate, Susan Higgins, was dating Bill Clark, Tom's brother. Mary had noticed the tall skinny boy coming and going in and out of the Delt house, and Mrs. Legg had described him as a "big man on campus." The two met for the first time shortly before Christmas 1921. Mary and Susan returned home one evening to find a group of young people, including Tom, gathered in the boardinghouse's living room. Mary and Tom were introduced to each other, but nothing else occurred until the Delts' big annual dance a few weeks later. Tom had been dating another student, Marcella Walker, and Marcella had naturally assumed that he would invite her to the dance. Instead, Tom decided that as president of the fraternity, he should, as a courtesy, invite the president of the Pi Beta Phi sorority. Marcella never forgave him. Mary's cousin William Ramsey, also a Delt, asked Mary to the dance—an invitation she felt certain had resulted from Tom's prodding. Tom danced with Mary often that evening. He never went out with the Pi Beta Phi president again—nor with Marcella. Although he would neither confirm nor deny it, the incident appears to have been his way of ending his romance with Marcella and initiating one with Mary. Mary and Tom saw each other frequently that spring, usually attending "germans"—dances for students—every Saturday night at the Knights of Columbus hall. Neither was ready for a serious commitment, however. Mary was dating other young men, and Tom was busy with studies and extracurricular activities.

As graduation from law school approached, Tom's many class absences placed his graduation in jeopardy. At one point, he was called in by the dean of the law school and warned that he might not be allowed to graduate. Fortunately, because of excellent grades on his exams, the faculty waived his absences, and he graduated on schedule in the fall of 1922. He had earned two degrees in the three years he attended the University of Texas: a bachelor of arts in pre-law and a bachelor of laws (LLB).

After graduation, Tom returned to Dallas to practice law with his father and his brother Bill. Mary, who had dropped out of the University of Texas after her sophomore year, was living in Dallas with her family. Tom frequently took the streetcar from his father's small downtown office to the Ramsey's elegant twelve-acre estate in suburban Oak Cliff. Mary's father was usually sitting on the front porch, whittling or reading a book, when he arrived. Tom always claimed that he was "scared to death" of Judge Ramsey, and his nervousness was understandable. Mary's handsome father was an imposing figure at six feet four inches tall and of a scholarly, somewhat stern demeanor. But despite Tom's avowed fear of the dignified jurist, Judge Ramsey liked him immediately and told Mary that Tom's father had once been a "brilliant" lawyer—a remark she did not fully understand at the time.

My parents' families were similar in many ways. Both were descended from Scotch-Irish ancestors who had immigrated to the United States from Ireland. Both had strong bonds to the legal profession. But there were important differences in their backgrounds. While the Clarks first settled in Virginia and then moved to Mississippi, where they were shaped by the culture of the Deep South, the Ramseys migrated to North Carolina, then moved on to Kentucky, a border state during the Civil War. Judge Ramsey's family moved to Texas before he was born, and the Civil War did not have a profound impact on his life. Judge Ramsey was a great admirer of Abraham Lincoln, and Rowena Ramsey, Mary's mother, was a pacifist who strongly opposed the country's entrance into World War I.

Judge Ramsey was a widower with a nine-year-old son when he married nineteen-year-old auburn-haired Rowena Hill. He had built a successful law practice in Cleburne, Texas—the Santa Fe Railroad Company was a major client—and was president of the Cleburne National Bank when Mary was born in 1902, the seventh of their eight children. She was named for her maternal grandmother, Mary Jane Knox Hill, who was the great-grandniece of President James Knox Polk. Mary Jane Hill was buried the day her granddaughter and namesake, Mary Ramsey, was born.

When Mary was six years old, her father was appointed to the Texas Court of Criminal Appeals, so the family moved from Cleburne to Austin. Less than two years later, he was appointed to the Texas Supreme Court—the only man, at that time, to have served on the state's two highest courts. As a judge, he was known for his scrupulous integrity and Victorian morality. He was an avid prohibitionist, and in 1911, friends convinced him that he was the only candidate who could defeat the incumbent, antiprohibitionist governor. Judge Ramsey reluctantly resigned from the Supreme Court to run for governor. After being defeated in the grueling campaign that followed, he returned to private practice in Austin. A few years later, he was appointed head of the Federal Reserve Bank of Dallas. The Federal Reserve System was only three years old when Judge Ramsey was appointed in 1916, and he was one of its directors at a crucial stage in its development.

All of the children were in awe of their distinguished father, who presided over his large, lively family with loving but unquestioned authority. Mother recalled that the family dinner was a formal ritual for which no one dared be late. If his daughters became a little noisy at the dinner table, their father quieted them swiftly with a firm "settle down, girls." Despite his stern demeanor, Judge Ramsey was a devoted family man with a fine sense of humor. He often joked that he was the richest man on earth with "three beautiful daughters—each worth a million dollars—and three fine sons—three for a quarter." He was devastated, as were all family members, when his and Rowena's oldest son, Sam, died suddenly while in an army training camp during World War I, the victim of a vicious flu pandemic that caused millions of deaths in 1918.

Another unexpected tragedy struck the Ramsey family in October 1922. Judge Ramsey, returning from a business trip to Washington, D.C., had an attack of what seemed to be severe indigestion. By the time the train he was traveling on reached Dallas, it was clear that he had suffered a heart attack. He died a few days after he arrived home. Judge Ramsey's death was an enormous personal loss that brought a dramatic economic change to his family. Debts from his disastrous campaign for governor had drained his income for years, and he had also signed debts for several family members. One, for a younger brother who had invested in a bank that failed, involved substantial sums. These obligations, paid from the estate, resulted in a greatly reduced inheritance for his survivors. Mary's mother sold their handsome estate in Oak Cliff and moved to a modest house in Highland Park.

Tom continued to court Mary during this difficult time, but did not want to propose marriage until his financial situation improved. His brother Bill was urging him to take the step, for Mary had other admirers. In January 1923, Mary broke a date with Tom to go out with someone else. Tom, aware of what had happened, did not contact her again for a month. On Valentine's Day, Mary received a large heart-shaped box of candy in the mail with a card signed "A. Brokenheart." She had regretted her action, and was greatly relieved to hear from Tom again. She called to thank him, and the romance was renewed, stronger than ever.

My father was a lifelong romantic, and his behavior toward women was the essence of old-fashioned chivalry. At the same time, he never viewed women as members of "the weaker sex" or as idols to be confined to the pedestal, for his own mother served as a model of strength and competence. He continued to court Mary, and when she visited her half brother, Felix, in California during the summer of 1923, he wrote to her every day, a practice he would continue throughout their marriage whenever they were apart. He also called her on the phone a number of times—an extraordinary action in those days, when the telephone was still relatively new and long-distance calls were expensive. She had not agreed to marry him at this point, but any doubts remaining in her mind about a lifelong commitment were erased by his romantic letters and phone calls. On Christmas 1923, he gave her a ring with a large amethyst stone and two small diamonds. He had chopped wood to earn the $125 needed to buy it, and Mary's mother was shocked when her daughter accepted the expensive gift. Mary's gentleness belied a firm will, and despite her mother's objections, she kept the ring.

Mary met the Clark family for the first time at a picnic at White Rock Lake. She was nervous and especially self-conscious because she had just had her hair bobbed and was unhappy with the way she looked. Despite her fears, the Clarks welcomed her into the family with affection. Judge Clark, who had actively opposed the marriages of three older children, was thrilled that Tom had selected the lovely daughter of Judge William F. Ramsey for his bride. Mother won over all the Clarks, and her relationship with them remained close and warm throughout the years.

Tom Clark and Mary Ramsey were married on the evening of

November 8, 1924. The wedding was small but formal. Mary's brother Knox gave her away, and her sisters Mildred and Dorothy were matron and maid of honor. Tom's brother Bill was his best man. Wedding guests described the groom as nervous as his radiant bride walked down the aisle toward him. A small reception at the Ramseys' home followed the ceremony, and the two left in time to catch an overnight train to New Orleans for a week's honeymoon. The happy couple, immersed in the present, could not have guessed the course of the fifty-two-year adventure that lay ahead.

## CHAPTER 3

# Forging the Steel

I cannot say, and I will not say
That he is dead.—He is just away!

James Whitcomb Riley, "Away"

A LTHOUGH OIL'S REIGN WAS CLOSE AT HAND, cotton was still king when my parents married in 1924. Texas produced a third of the nation's crop, and Dallas enjoyed a growing prosperity as a major cotton center with an international reputation.[1] Recreational activities thrived in the healthy economy—so much so that the city found it necessary to hire a full-time dance hall inspector. Radio, live theater, and sports were also favorite forms of entertainment, but movies were the number one popular pastime, with four theaters located on a single block of downtown Elm Street.

My parents had little cash to spend on such diversions during the first year of their marriage. My father sometimes joked that he married Mother for her money—her wealth consisting of a four-dollar check received each month as her share of a life insurance policy taken out on her brother Sam, who died during World War I. My father's only assured income was a five-dollar-a-week retainer that he received from a black client who ran a barbecue stand. He and Mother collected the money each Saturday, and afterward used it for their weekly grocery shopping. They did manage to buy a used Model T Ford from Bill Clark and a small but comfortable cottage located in a section considered "the wrong side of the tracks" in otherwise fashionable Highland Park. The house was furnished with an assortment of family donations and miscellaneous pieces received as payment for legal services. My father accepted numerous items from clients who were unable to pay their bills, and ultimately accumulated a variety of possessions, including furniture, pictures, and a cemetery plot. Some items became family treasures, such as two oriental rugs given as collateral for an unpaid loan. The borrower, an army captain who had gone AWOL during World War I, saw the rugs being made when he was stationed in China and brought them back to the States. More than fifty years later, they still adorned the Clark apartment in Washington, D.C.

My father devoted a great deal of time and energy to their first home. He refinished furniture, painted the house inside and out, planted flowers and trees, and even raised chickens until the cost of running an electric heater to warm the baby chicks forced him to end the venture. He could repair almost anything, and earned the nickname "Daddy-Fix-It" from his children, who called upon him whenever a broken toy was in need of repair. His skills amazed Mother, whose father, according to her, "never even changed a lightbulb."

Mother's friends felt sorry for her because she could not afford many material possessions or lead the kind of social life they enjoyed. Their pity was misplaced, for Mother considered these early years of marriage among the happiest of her life. A day rarely passed when she did not see her mother, brothers, and sisters. Thursday evenings, the couple had dinner at the Ramseys; Sundays, they ate with the Clarks. They divided their holidays between the two families, eating Christmas and Thanksgiving dinners at noon with Mother's family, and again in the evening with my father's.

The young couple's happiness seemed complete when an eight-pound baby boy, Thomas Campbell Clark, Jr., was born on August 21, 1925. The tiny room at Baylor Hospital was hot and cramped. My father held Mother's hand throughout the delivery, as he did at the births of their two other children. It was an era when doctors used anesthesia freely, and my father, fearful that Mother was going to be asphyxiated, kept removing the gas mask from her face.

Despite a limited income, they had full-time help after the baby arrived, in keeping with the southern traditions to which they were accustomed. Their maid, Annie Lee Jackson, was a client of my father's and was involved in an ugly divorce suit in which her estranged husband was trying to have her committed to a mental institution. Annie Lee lived with my parents and received seven dollars a week plus room and board for cooking, general housecleaning, and helping with the baby. After one year, she left to open a beauty shop, but kept in touch with my parents for many years—even after they had moved away from Dallas.

Professionally, my father was struggling, but he remained optimistic and ambitious. He had joined the family law practice with his father and his brother Bill for lack of any other opportunity. But the Clark law firm did not bring in enough business to support the three men satisfactorily—my father described it as a "hand-to-mouth practice that was neither lucrative nor satisfying."[2] He took a brief excursion into politics soon after joining the firm, when Bill ran for Dallas county judge and a good friend, Maury Hughes, for Dallas district attorney. My father was campaign manager for the two men, but despite great effort, they failed to win election. Their biggest obstacle was the Ku Klux Klan, which was enjoying a resurgence of respectability and a large increase in membership. The rise of the Klan nationwide was a remarkable phenomenon of the 1920s. The organization achieved its greatest power and largest membership during that decade—some estimates claimed that close to five million white Protestant males were recruited.[3] Although Dallas mayor Sewanee Aldredge had called for the dissolution of the Klan, its popularity was so widespread that a women's auxiliary was formed. The 1923 State Fair of Texas, held at Dallas's Fair Park, even had a Ku Klux Klan Day, and the public was invited to witness the largest group ever initiated into Klan membership. The celebration included elaborate fireworks, a concert by a drum and bugle corps billed as the largest in the world, and competitive drills by men and women of the KKK drill team.[4] Despite political pressure, Bill and Maury refused to join the Klan. They were defeated, and Klan members were victorious in all Dallas County races that year.

My father had been practicing in the family firm for more than four years when he received an offer to become assistant district attorney in charge of civil litigation. He jumped at the opportunity. The newly elected district attorney, a redheaded dynamo named Bill McCraw, had attended Bryan Street High School with Bill Clark, and it was through their association that my father was tapped for the job.

Bill McCraw proved to be an important influence on twenty-seven-year-old Tom Clark. McCraw was a colorful personality with a unique background. His mother, Molly Clay, was a great-great-granddaughter of Henry Clay, the Kentucky senator famous for crafting compromise legislation and running three times as a presidential candidate for the Whig Party. His father, a newspaperman from Arlington, Texas, was a Unitarian and a Republican—both rarities in Texas at that time. Although McCraw did not adopt his father's unconventional allegiances—like his mother, he was a Democrat and a Baptist—he exhibited an individualism that must have been forged by his unusual heritage. McCraw's book *Professional Politicians*, published in 1940, extolled men who possessed qualities he admired: Sam Houston, the renowned general and president of the Texas Republic who befriended Indians and became a citizen of the Cherokee tribe; Mirabeau Buonaparte Lamar, who succeeded Houston as president of Texas and whose belief that "a cultivated mind is the guardian of democracy" earned him the title "father of education in Texas";[5] and James Stephen Hogg, whose political career paralleled McCraw's in many respects and whose populist policies strove to "give equal opportunity to all."[6] These Texas heroes were dedicated public servants who were often subjected to unfair and abusive criticism. Despite political persecution, they retained a firm belief in the basic wisdom of the people, in education, and in equal opportunity. Bill McCraw identified with these colorful idealists and espoused their principles—principles that became an integral part of Tom Clark's political philosophy.

The district attorney's office in the 1920s typically attracted two kinds of men: those who were unable or unwilling to compete in the rough-and-tumble world of private practice, or those with political ambitions, who viewed the office as a stepping-stone to greater things. Tom Clark was clearly in the latter category, as was Bill McCraw, whom my father later described as "the greatest natural politician Texas ever saw except [for] Lyndon Johnson." McCraw's three terms as district attorney were characterized by energy, efficiency, and a great deal of showmanship. Under his leadership, Dallas County convicted more criminals than the rest of the counties in the state combined, and McCraw became known as "ninety-nine-year Bill" because of the many life sentences he succeeded in imposing upon convicted robbers.[7]

My father loved his new job, despite the long hours and hard work, and the move to the district attorney's office proved to be a turning point in his career. Besides providing a break with the family law firm, which was dominated by his father's powerful personality, the new position placed him under the tutelage of an enthusiastic politician whose determination to succeed matched his own, and it gave him valuable trial experience that would be helpful in achieving future success. In addition, since Dallas County allowed lawyers to practice on the side, he was able to maintain a small private practice.

While my father was busy and doing well professionally, he was also very involved with his family. A second son, William Ramsey, named for his maternal grandfather, was born on December 18, 1927, and the birth of the almost eleven-pound baby made Christmas that year a special one. Even the weather contributed to the occasion, for Dallas enjoyed a white Christmas—a rare treat for the city's residents. My father decorated the small house from top to bottom with streamers of green and red crepe paper and decked out a large Christmas tree with ornaments. He and Mother were disappointed when the doctor decided she should not leave

Baylor Hospital in time for Christmas Day, and instead of a festive home-coming, they had to celebrate in the small hospital room. Mother watched from her window as my father carried two-year-old Tommy, dressed in a gray knit snowsuit and cap, up the building's ramp. Unable at two years old to pronounce "brother," Tommy called the baby his "little baby bubba." The name stuck, and the family called Ramsey "Bub," a shortened form of "Bubba," for most of his life. My father often helped with the children—an uncommon trait at that time. He walked and rocked crying babies, gave the night bottle when needed, and took older children on outings. He was as busy at home as he was at the office.

My father's high energy level and desire for new experiences resulted in a vacation with Mother that must have been the fulfillment of a dream. Ramsey was less than a year old when he and Mother used their life savings of five hundred dollars to spend a month traveling, leaving the little boys at home with Mother's sister Mildred Walker. It was the first trip east for either of them, except for my father's year at VMI, and it began with a train trip to Chicago, where they stayed at the Stevens Hotel, the largest in the world at that time. Next they journeyed to Niagara Falls and then on to their final destination: New York City. The fall of 1928 was a fabulous time to be in New York City. The Roaring Twenties were at their peak, and Broadway was ablaze with an array of outstanding shows and performers that included the great actress Helen Hayes in *Coquette*, Lynn Fontanne in *Strange Interlude*, and Helen Morgan and Paul Robeson in *Showboat*. George White's *Scandals* featured the most beautiful girls in the world, and Marilyn Miller starred in the *Ziegfeld Follies* with two then-unknown performers, Fanny Brice and Eddie Cantor.

The two young Texans were awed by the big city, which was unlike anything they had ever experienced. The crowds that constantly swarmed the streets amazed them, and on two occasions they stayed up all night to see whether Times Square was ever empty. It never was. Since Prohibition was still in effect, they drank nothing stronger than the fresh orange juice sold at corner stands. They returned home by ship, sailing from New York Harbor to Galveston, where Mary's brother Benton Ramsey met them and drove them back to Dallas. They were happy to be home, yet their adventure undoubtedly stirred a desire within them to expand beyond the limits of their comfortable, family-centered lifestyle. The vacation had been a dream come true, and though they were to visit New York many times in the future, no trip ever matched the first, magical one of 1928.

Less than a year later, the stock market crashed and the Great Depression struck the country. Fortunately, my parents were not seriously affected, but some family members suffered significantly. Knox Ramsey,

Mother's elder brother, was unemployed for several years, and her brother-in-law Del Walker, who had been a prosperous businessman, never fully recovered from the financial losses he experienced at that time. Although Dallas was not as hard hit as other areas of the country, unemployment was high, and the number of people on welfare ranged from 11,000 to 19,000.[8] The city initiated a "work for food" program in 1931, which paid jobless heads of households in food rather than cash for jobs such as cleaning parks, alleys, and other public places. The Depression brought about a wave of lawlessness, and Dallas residents Bonnie and Clyde were among the nation's most notorious criminals. Clyde Barrow had been in the Texas State Penitentiary for two years before he returned to Dallas in 1932 and met Bonnie Parker. They went on a two-year rampage of murders, kidnappings, and robberies—many committed in the Dallas area—before they were killed in Louisiana in 1934. While Bonnie and Clyde were terrorizing the city, young Babe Didrikson was bringing it honors in basketball and track and field before switching her remarkable talents to golf.

In the spring of 1929, my father bought a small farm on the city's outskirts. He loved working the land, and the farm provided an outlet that gave him great pleasure. He built a dam to create a small lake on the property, planted numerous shrubs, trees, and vegetables, and started a small dairy business, Puritan Dairy. He negotiated with a man named Wilson to take care of the dairy and serve as a caretaker for the farm. Wilson built a house there, where he and his family lived. He tended the cows, sold and delivered the milk that was produced, collected from customers once a week, and brought the money to Mary. He delivered a collection the day before President Roosevelt closed the banks (on March 6, 1933), and consequently my parents avoided the critical shortage of cash that faced many families.

The farm provided the family with many good times. On Saturdays, they picked pecans, fished in the lake, and worked in the gardens. Ramsey was still too little to keep up with his older brother and father, so he and Mother, who did not share my father's love of farming, often stayed in the car while the "two Toms" hiked around the property. On Sundays, if they did not go to the farm, the four enjoyed driving to Love Field to watch the airplanes take off and land. Dallas had become an aviation center, and Love Field, with seven passenger lines, was already one of the busiest in the nation.

These family outings were especially important to my father because of his own difficult childhood. He wanted his children to have everything that he had not had as a child. Mother worried that his indulgent ways would spoil us, but though he deferred to her wishes in every other aspect of child rearing, she never succeeded in curbing his sometimes extravagant shopping. He consistently gave his children toys before they were old enough to use or appreciate them. Ramsey once received a handsome two-wheeled bike before his legs were long enough to reach the pedals. On another occasion, he bought a beautiful toy steam engine before Ramsey was able to run it alone. One day as he and Ramsey lay on the floor playing with the steam engine, my father said, "All my life I've wanted a steam engine." "Now you've got one," Mother replied, with a touch of sarcasm.

Bill McCraw became an important part of their lives. Mother had reservations about the cigar-smoking McCraw, whose boisterous manners created a circus-like atmosphere wherever he went. Although she did not openly object, Mother sometimes resented the intrusion of this dominant personality into their lives, and blamed McCraw for my father's increasingly heavy workload and long hours. McCraw contrasted sharply with her aristocratic father and gentlemanly husband. He was always in motion, juggling a variety of activities, including Sunday-school teacher, amateur actor, and pilot. He owned an open-cockpit airplane, and on one occasion my parents flew from Dallas to Corpus Christi with him. Mother was terrified most of the trip, but went along, as she usually did, with my father's wishes. The frequency of their activities with McCraw lessened somewhat after he married in 1931. The two men remained close, however, and my parents gave the newlyweds several acres of their farm as a wedding present.

McCraw ran for district attorney again in 1928 and 1930, and my father was actively involved in the campaigns. Mother and the little boys frequently attended the political rallies, and five-year-old Tommy loved the excitement of campaigning. He often went with my father to post "McCraw for District Attorney" signs and pass out campaign literature to people on the street. Tommy seemed to be a natural politician, and "playing politics" became a favorite game of his gang of neighborhood boys. Tommy was the leader, standing on a box before his admiring audience and making campaign speeches for Bill McCraw. He was once overheard asking his little brother, "Bubba, who is the greatest man in the world?" Bubba, just three years old, paused before he thoughtfully replied, "Santa Claus." "No!" Tommy responded emphatically, "Bill McCraw."

Tommy was a bright, gregarious child—a born leader in the eyes of his adoring parents. My parents had high hopes for their golden-haired son, whose future seemed so promising. They were totally unprepared for the tragedy that shattered that promise in February 1932.

Dallas winters are treacherous. The weather changes rapidly, and beautiful, spring-like days quickly give way to icy cold spells. Old-timers called these wide-ranging shifts in temperature "pneumonia weather," because they were usually accompanied by an outbreak of illness. This was the case during the first week of February 1932, when Tommy and Ramsey came down with the flu. Ramsey was the sicker of the two, and Mother, always cautious about health, kept him in the house for several days. Tommy's fever never went above one hundred degrees, and he snapped back so quickly that the doctor said he could play outside in the invitingly warm weather. The next day, he complained of a headache, and the doctor was summoned again. The doctor believed that Tommy was having a minor recurrence of the flu, and Mother kept him in bed. She spent that day and the next reading to him and helping him make valentines. She and my father attended a concert the following night, and when they returned, they checked on the boys before going to bed. Mother was alarmed when she felt Tommy's hot head, so she slept with him that night. The next morning he was unconscious. They called an ambulance, and the doctor met them at Baylor Hospital. The ominous diagnosis was spinal meningitis. Mother stayed at the hospital for a week. My father remained at the hospital during the day, calling doctors and clinics all over the country in a desperate attempt to find a miracle cure. The prognosis was the same everywhere—there was no known case of a recovery from spinal meningitis. He never regained consciousness, and died on February 15, 1932, at the age of six.

The funeral service was held at home. Mother used her handkerchief to wipe the tears from my father's face. It was the only time she ever saw him cry. He was crushed by Tommy's death, but Mother was devastated. Though family and friends rallied around to comfort her, she suffered severe depression for months. My father dealt with his pain in his typical way—he focused on the well-being of his family and on his work. He tried to help Mother deal with this tragic blow, keeping up a cheerful front for her and for Ramsey.

A few weeks after the funeral, my father insisted that Mother go with him to attend the dedication of the George Washington Masonic Temple in Alexandria, Virginia. An active Mason, he saw the trip as a good excuse to get away from Dallas and help her overcome her grief. They stayed at Washington's most elegant hotel, the Willard, and took in all the city sights. While touring the Capitol, a guard stopped them as nine black-robed justices crossed the hall. Mother was impressed at the sight, never dreaming that my father would one day be part of a similar group.

After the dedication in Alexandria, my parents took the train to New York City. In the depths of the Depression, the city offered a stark contrast to the liveliness they had found so magical two short years before.

Businesses were boarded up; many of their favorite spots had closed. People everywhere looked sad and serious. The major news story was the kidnapping of the Lindbergh baby. My parents joined a crowd gathered in Times Square to watch the news ticker for the latest information. The whole country was gripped in its hero's tragedy, and my parents felt a special bond because of the recent loss of their child.

Mother did not begin to recover from the loss of her first child until after I was born, on May 30, 1933. Growing up, I was only dimly aware of the brother whom I never knew. Our family life was happy and loving, and the death was never discussed. Traces of him remained, however. A portrait painted after his death always hung in a prominent spot, and a family album I often browsed through contained photographs and a poem by James Whitcomb Riley that read:

> I cannot say, and I will not say
> That he is dead.—He is just away!

Still, I did not realize how much I was born from tragedy until my mother confided to me years later, as I prepared to leave for college, that I had once saved her life.

## CHAPTER 4

# Turning Points

An opportunity to give the best of himself to something he believed in.

Mary Clark Burchfield, 1935

CHANGE WAS THE HALLMARK OF THE 1930S for Dallas. The decade began with an event that catapulted the city's solid, cotton-based economy to unprecedented prosperity, bringing relief from the Depression to many Dallas citizens and incredible personal wealth to a few. The man who triggered the transformation was an audacious wild-catter named Columbus Marion ("Dad") Joiner. He would have an important impact on the life of Tom Clark.

Wildcatters—men who drilled for oil, often without supporting scientific data or adequate financial backing—were an unconventional bunch, and Dad Joiner was as colorful a character as any of those drawn to this wildly speculative enterprise. He had made and lost at least two fortunes by the time he came to Texas from Oklahoma in 1927. At seventy, Joiner was a cagey and charming dreamer whose voracious appetite for reading, though not obtained through formal education, had equipped him with a substantial assortment of biblical and Shakespearean quotations. Dad Joiner located his oil venture on the farm of Daisy Bradford, about a hundred miles east of Dallas in an area that most geologists had labeled a "hopeless case" for oil.[1]

By the end of the summer of 1930, after two previous drillings had ended in failure, Joiner was on his third well, the Daisy Bradford No. 3. At this point, Joiner's money was running out, and to support his drillings, he had sold certificates of ownership to hundreds of people.[2] The outlook was poor until September 1930, when signs appeared that a strike might be close at hand. The news spread quickly, and by the first of October, a crowd of almost eight thousand people had gathered to watch the drilling. Among the observers was another, then-unknown wildcatter from El Dorado, Texas, named H. L. Hunt. Anticipation mounted as the days passed, and on October 5, a faint gurgling became audible. The sound swelled to a rumble and finally erupted in a roar as the oil burst forth. The cheering crowd danced in a shower of black rain, and the rush to East Texas was on.[3] Wildcatters, oil company scouts, the unemployed, and dreamers of all kinds raced to the area, hoping for a piece of the wealth. The town of Joinerville, consisting mostly of shacks, hamburger stands, and a few brothels, sprang up instantly on the edge of the Bradford farm. Close by, the sleepy town of Kilgore awoke to find its streets and sidewalks were standing room only. Country roads leading to the area were constantly jammed with traffic, and farmers began to charge tolls to drivers who improvised paths across their lands. So many oil derricks sprang up over the ensuing months that the East Texas Baseball League complained that there wasn't enough space left for baseball diamonds.[4]

The resulting surge in oil production created a worldwide glut that resulted in a collapse in prices—the cost of a barrel of oil plummeted from $1.30 in 1930 to $0.05 or less within another year.[5] A battle formed quickly between the pro-rationists, mainly made up of large oil corporations and conservationists, who believed regulation was essential, on one side, and the anti-rationists, small, independent oil producers who fought any kind of control, on the other.[6] The well-organized pro-rationists were aided by an atmosphere of near panic, which made some kind of regulation seem crucial. Events had become so chaotic by August 1931 that Texas governor Ross Sterling, describing oil operators as being in a state of "insurrection and rebellion," declared martial law.[7] National Guard troops were sent to the area.

The Texas Railroad Commission, a little-understood agency that was charged with regulating state transportation, oil, and other commercial activities,[8] finally stepped in. The Railroad Commission's pro-ration efforts to establish a quota system for the maximum amount of oil that could be legally produced were largely unsuccessful. Despite the quotas, oil production went virtually unchecked—834,000 barrels of oil per day were gushing out of Texas oil wells—and "hot oil," which included both oil produced above the established maximum and oil that was stolen—was rampant.[9] The streets of East Texas towns, which were close to anarchy, were described as being "almost as exciting as a Chicago street during the gang wars."[10] Not until 1935, when the federal government stepped in and Congress passed the Connally "Hot Oil" Act, which regulated interstate commerce in illegal oil, was the Texas Railroad Commission able to enforce its pro-ration laws. The East Texas oil glut made the commission a power in the world of oil regulation, and according to a *Wall Street Journal* article, for many decades "in its quiet way [it] set world oil prices."

Dad Joiner's discovery established Dallas as a major oil center. As the large city closest to the East Texas field, it became the main source for the money and professional services needed for development. During the first two months of 1931, twenty-eight businesses related directly to oil either organized in Dallas or relocated there. Dallas's largest banks quickly formed oil departments and staffed them with geologists.[11]

The major oil companies, following the advice of their experts, remained skeptical about the scope of the find, and as a result, individual drillers were able to buy up the oil leases. More fortunes were made from the East Texas field than from any other in the history of the industry, at least up to that time.[12] H. L. Hunt, whose oil ventures eventually made him one of the world's richest men, was one of the young wildcatters who quickly bought leases on land adjoining the Joiner strike. Joiner felt a fatherly affection toward the younger Hunt, whose daring and ruthless business dealings resembled his own. He sold Hunt his East Texas holding for approximately $1.3 million in a controversial deal that became the keystone of Hunt's vast fortune.[13] Less than three years later, geologists, describing the oil field as a geological "freak," discovered that Dad Joiner had hit upon an expanse of oil covering approximately 240 square miles—at that time the largest in the world.[14]

Joiner's oil boom proved to be a windfall for young Tom Clark. Ironically, Joiner encountered severe financial difficulties as soon as he struck oil. The hundreds of investors who had purchased certificates of ownership that financed Joiner's oil drillings clamored for payment as soon as news of the strike was out. Joiner, unable to raise the cash, found himself on the verge of bankruptcy. During the next four years, 150 lawsuits were brought against him by people claiming to own shares in his field.[15] The cases were transferred to Dallas, where Judge Towne Young was responsible for administering payments to certificate owners. Judge Young appointed Tom Clark master in chancery for the court—a position that required him to examine evidence, hear testimony, and determine the validity of the certificates, many of which were forged. My father was involved with the Joiner case for more than two years and earned close to $20,000 from it—a fortune to him and mother. Even more importantly, however, he came into contact with many rising young oil tycoons, such as Hunt, Sid Richardson of Fort Worth, and Clint Murchison, future owner of the Dallas Cowboys football team. Through these contacts, he became involved in a considerable amount of profitable oil litigation. The

Joiner case was a financial watershed that resulted in substantial economic security for our family—so much so that a few years later my father could afford to accept a low-paying job with the federal government.

In 1932, as the Joiner case was winding down, Tom Clark and Bill McCraw resigned as assistant district attorney and district attorney and established their own law firm, McCraw & Clark. Any pressure that may have existed for my father to return to the family firm was gone. Grandfather Clark had died in September 1931, and Bill Clark, who had continued in the family firm, was practicing law with a new partner, Percy Rice. McCraw & Clark was doing well in 1934 when Bill McCraw decided to return to his first love—politics—and announced that he was running for Texas attorney general. He named Tom Clark as his campaign manager.

Four men were competing for attorney general in the Texas Democratic primary that summer, and in Texas, still a one-party state, the winner of the primary was assured a victory in the general election. If no one received a majority of the votes cast in the primary, a runoff election would be held between the two candidates receiving the greatest number of votes. With four men in the race, a runoff was almost inevitable. The two top vote getters were Bill McCraw and Walter Woodward, a dignified state senator from Coleman, Texas. The McCraw campaign, adopting a populist tone, stressed integrity and competence. Bill McCraw pointed to his record as Dallas County district attorney as proof of his "unquestioned integrity with demonstrated ability."[16] Campaigning as a friend of the workingman, McCraw vowed independence from interest groups and promised to deal impartially and fairly with everyone. Some campaign issues foreshadowed Tom Clark's later priorities and commitments. One was McCraw's pledge to strengthen and expand the state's educational system, in which many school districts offered only five- or seven-month sessions.

As the date of the runoff approached, the heat of the campaign rose, threatening to match the searing July temperatures. The Democratic state chairman endorsed Woodward, who projected himself as a qualified professional and characterized McCraw as a brash politician. Woodward claimed that McCraw had profited as district attorney by prosecuting criminals under a fee system that paid so much per prosecution. McCraw charged that Woodward was a tool of the large public utilities and characterized the race as McCraw and the people versus Woodward and the public utilities. Race became an issue, although not one initiated by either candidate. The Democratic Party had asked the incumbent attorney general, James Allred, to rule whether it could legally prohibit African Americans from voting in its primary election. Allred ruled in favor of the party, and the decision was upheld by the Texas Supreme Court. Although the ruling was eventually overturned by the U.S. Supreme Court, African Americans were not allowed to vote in the 1934 state primary. The usually consrvative *Dallas Morning News* warned in an editorial: ". . . the Democratic Party needs the competent Negro vote. It should not be alienated while it is weak but encouraged against the day it will be strong."[17] It was a politically sensitive issue, however, and the candidates chose to ignore it.

The campaign demanded long hours and frequent travel, and my father was away from home a great deal. It was a difficult time for Mother, not only because of my father's absences, but also because she found herself at odds politically with most of her friends, who favored the dignified Woodward over boisterous Bill McCraw. Although she handled the tension caused by the political differences with remarkable tact and grace, she found the experience difficult and unpleasant and was never able to enjoy the rough-and-tumble of political campaigns. To ease the stress she was experiencing, my father finally convinced her to take Ramsey and me to California for a few weeks, where his brother Bob and his family were vacationing.

Mother hired an African American maid named Carrie Lewis to cook and do laundry for my father while we were gone. Carrie was a handsome six-foot-tall woman with a hearty laugh and a winning personality. She was also a popular "party girl" whose overindulgences kept her in debt most of the time. Even winnings she made betting on her beloved New York Yankees could not alleviate her frequent money crises. She was such a sympathetic and persuasive character, however, that she was able to avoid serious legal consequences by borrowing from her employers, friends, and almost everyone else she came into contact with. By the end of the summer, my father had lent her a substantial amount, and she began working for the family full time to pay back the debt. It was a happy arrangement. Carrie was an exceptional cook, a talented party giver, and a delightful companion. Ramsey and I loved her, and she was devoted to our family for the rest of her life.

When we returned from California in the middle of August, Bill McCraw had won the runoff election for attorney general. His victory meant the end of McCraw & Clark and of the close personal relationship the two men had enjoyed for almost seven years. Although my father retained a special esteem for Bill McCraw, their careers took them in different directions, and they gradually grew apart.

After Bill McCraw left for Austin, two other lawyers joined my father's firm. Their clientele was varied. It included several large corporations, such as the Safeway Stores, on whose behalf my father testified before the

Texas legislature against a chain-store tax bill, and the Southwestern Life Insurance Company, which he assisted in forming the Southwestern Investors Corporation. His involvement with oil litigation continued to grow, and in 1935 he was selected as the attorney for the Texas Petroleum Council.

One oil case involved the former wife of J. F. Marion, president of the Marion Oil Company. Marion had died soon after divorcing his wife of many years, Mary K. Marion, to marry another woman. Under Texas law, the new Mrs. Marion would inherit the bulk of his estate and the former Mrs. Marion would receive nothing. In representing the first Mrs. Marion, my father's only hope was to locate a valid will. He learned that Marion had been a Mason, an organization of which he was also a member, and he knew that new members were required to have wills. After much investigation, a will was found. In it, Marion left everything to "Mary K. Marion," with no reference to her as his wife. A judge declared the will valid, and the first Mrs. Marion won her lawsuit. Tom Clark's persistence was rewarded. The vindicated Mrs. Marion gave him oil leases in exchange for his services, and the income he received from them helped him establish financial independence.

Although my father's firm represented some large corporations and wealthy individuals, the bulk of its business came from moderate- to low-income clients. Most of his poorest clients were African Americans, like a friend's maid who asked him to defend her son in a murder suit. My father's commitment to the case was no less than that given his wealthiest clients. He believed in his client's innocence, but despite his efforts, the young black man was convicted, sentenced to death, and electrocuted. He insisted to the end that he was innocent.

Charlie Ellis was another of my father's African American clients. Charlie owned a dilapidated farmhouse on a small piece of land next to the city ballpark, where he lived with his wife and several small children. The city wanted the spot for the ballpark, but instead of offering to buy it from Charlie, city attorneys attempted to confiscate the land. Charlie needed a lawyer and turned to Tom Clark. Since Charlie could not afford the legal fees, he and my father arranged for Charlie's wife to do our family's laundry in exchange for legal services. Consequently, once a week for several months, Mother, often accompanied by Ramsey, drove ten miles to South Oak Cliff, one of Dallas's poorer suburbs, where the Ellises lived. Charlie, always flanked by one or two small children, would come out to the car to pick up the laundry and greet them with a large grin that displayed several missing teeth. The sight of the tiny run-down house and its poorly dressed occupants made a lasting impression on nine-year-old Ramsey. Years later, he dated his first awareness of poverty from the trips with Mother to take the family's laundry to South Oak Cliff. My father succeeded in defending Charlie against the city's efforts to confiscate the property, and the Ellises were able to keep their home next to the ballpark.

During the five years my father practiced law, his sister Mary was his secretary. Mary lived with my parents for a few months following the death of Tommy, and Mother felt as close to her as she did to her own sisters. Mary's future husband, Doug Burchfield, courted her while she was living with my parents, and their wedding took place in our home. Looking back almost fifty years later, Mary Clark Burchfield regarded that period in her life as uniquely rewarding. To Mary, Tom was an infinitely patient and understanding boss—a view that some who worked for him may not have shared. His patience did not extend to anyone he regarded as "lazy"—a trait virtually nonexistent in the Clark family. He could not understand or sympathize with anyone who did not complete every task to the best of his or her ability, regardless of the time and trouble involved. Those who did not meet his high expectations did not remain in the firm for long. His sister felt, however, that he was never unreasonable and did not ask people to perform beyond their capabilities. The atmosphere of the law office was one of "understanding, thoughtfulness, and love of fellow man," according to Mary. She felt that Tom's respect and love for the law inspired everyone who worked with him. He regarded work as "an opportunity to give the best of himself to something he believed in."[18]

The law firm was flourishing, but political enemies made during Bill McCraw's race for attorney general sought to embarrass McCraw by discrediting his campaign manager. Consequently, Tom Clark became the object of a Texas Senate subcommittee investigation to determine whether he was using his association with McCraw to enhance his law practice. My father testified before the subcommittee in December 1936. Its chairman, state senator Joe Hill, charged that Clark's friendship with McCraw was the source of several lucrative oil accounts. Hill claimed that my father's income had increased dramatically since 1934, the year McCraw was elected attorney general. My father acknowledged the increase, but countered that his 1934 income was low because of the amount of time spent away from his practice while campaigning for McCraw. When Hill insisted that Tom Clark allow the subcommittee to examine his personal bank account records, my father refused, saying they were a "personal matter." He asserted emphatically: "I will tell you point blank there has never been any undue influence on my part."[19] As Hill continued to press about his friendship with McCraw, my father's frustration finally erupted: "I did not know I was supposed to buy a Spanish dictionary and leave Texas when

McCraw was elected Attorney General. . . . Of course it did not hurt me, any more than it hurts your practice to be a Senator."[20]

Subcommittee members also questioned my father at length concerning his work for the oil industry, especially the Texas Petroleum Council. My father, tracing his experience with oil litigation back to the Joiner case, testified that he advised the council only on pro-ration laws concerning the East Texas oil fields. (As mentioned earlier, these were laws that set limits on the amount of oil that could be produced.) He described his achievements as attorney for the Texas Petroleum Council in a typically self-effacing manner: "I do not want to be put in the position of bragging, for my part was very small. But when I started, there was an estimated 100,000 barrels [of oil produced over the legal limit] in East Texas. Today it is estimated at 5000—next to nothing."[21]

A year later, motivated by McCraw's decision to run for governor of Texas, the same subcommittee resurrected the investigation. By that time, our family had moved to Washington, D.C., so my father made a special trip to Austin to testify after the subcommittee attempted to subpoena the bank account records of the McCraw & Clark law firm. Once again, he refused to give the subcommittee access to his financial records, describing the effort as "an illegal search for information that would be used in political campaigns."[22] The subcommittee never obtained the records, and the investigation was permanently dropped. The investigation plagued my father for years, however, for it was revisited every time he was considered for public office and had to be reexamined and explained each time.

Bill McCraw failed to win his bid for governor of Texas in 1938. McCraw, the favorite in the race, was defeated by a flour salesman and popular radio personality from Fort Worth named "Pappy" (W. Lee) O'Daniel, whose flamboyant campaign combined religious exhortations with hillbilly music. Four years later, using similar tactics, the formidable O'Daniel would narrowly defeat Lyndon Johnson in a race for the U.S. Senate—the only election loss in Johnson's long political career. Although McCraw conceded defeat graciously, the experience was disillusioning and disappointing, for many supporters whom he considered good friends deserted him when he no longer held political office. My father, who had backed McCraw in the campaign, sympathized with his former law partner and learned a lesson about political friendships that he would not forget.

Bill Clark was also enjoying a successful law practice, and through it had made some important political connections. His partner, Percy Rice, was active in Democratic politics and had managed Tom Connally's victorious senatorial campaign in 1934. Bill and Senator Connally became friends, and in the fall of 1936, he and Connally discussed an appointment to a position in the federal government for Bill's brother Tom. Until that time, there is no evidence that my father had any ambitions for public office. Like his father, he was a loyal Democrat, but except for serving as campaign manager for his brother Bill when he ran for district attorney and then for Bill McCraw's campaign for attorney general, his energies had always been directed toward building his private practice. Money was not a motive, for the $6,000 federal salary would be a substantial cut from what he was making in private practice. Indeed, my father's government salaries throughout his long and successful career never equaled his earnings as a lawyer in Dallas. The continuing criticism generated by his friendship with McCraw and the resulting Texas Senate investigation may have been factors. A short absence from Texas might end the political sniping and, at the same time, enhance his reputation and strengthen his private practice. Besides, Tom Clark thrived on challenges and relished new experiences. He was ready for a change.

On January 31, 1937, my father's picture appeared on the front page of the *Dallas Morning News*. The accompanying article stated that Texas's two senators had recommended Tom Clark to President Roosevelt as assistant attorney general of the Department of Justice's Claims Division. The outlook for the appointment was good, the article continued, despite the grumblings by some members of the eastern establishment that there was "too much Texas" in the capital. Indeed, Texas was having a political heyday: native son John Nance Garner had just been reelected vice president; Tom Connally was a powerful voice in the Senate; Dallas congressman Hatton Sumners chaired the House Judiciary Committee; and Sam Rayburn, an influential and respected congressman from Bonham, Texas, would soon be Speaker of the House.

By February, the appointment appeared official, and my father left for Washington, D.C. Mother remained behind to rent the house, pack the family's belongings, and ship the furniture. She was not enthusiastic about the move, yet the excitement that the appointment had generated among family and friends was contagious. She felt she could be happy anywhere as long as the four of us were together, and besides, the move was temporary—we would be gone for two years at most.

As time for our departure approached, friends and family regaled my parents with parties and made plans to visit. Our beloved cook, Carrie Lewis, agreed to go with us, and would drive our green Chevrolet to Washington with a friend and our white Persian cat. The mood was festive at the Highland Park train station when Mother, Ramsey, and I departed on that sunny April day in 1937. Friends and relatives gathered to see us off. Bill McCraw was there and joked that the government salary wouldn't cover the cost of Mother's new wardrobe. There was a moment of panic when Mother forgot where she put the train tickets, but high spirits returned when she located them in a suitcase. My father was already settled in Washington and had an apartment ready for us. He promised that the cherry blossoms would be in full bloom by the time we arrived three days later. And so we left for a new life—excited at the prospect of an adventure and comforted by the knowledge that we would return to Dallas and the secure lifestyle we enjoyed there. After all, Dallas was home, and we were Texans. We would be back.

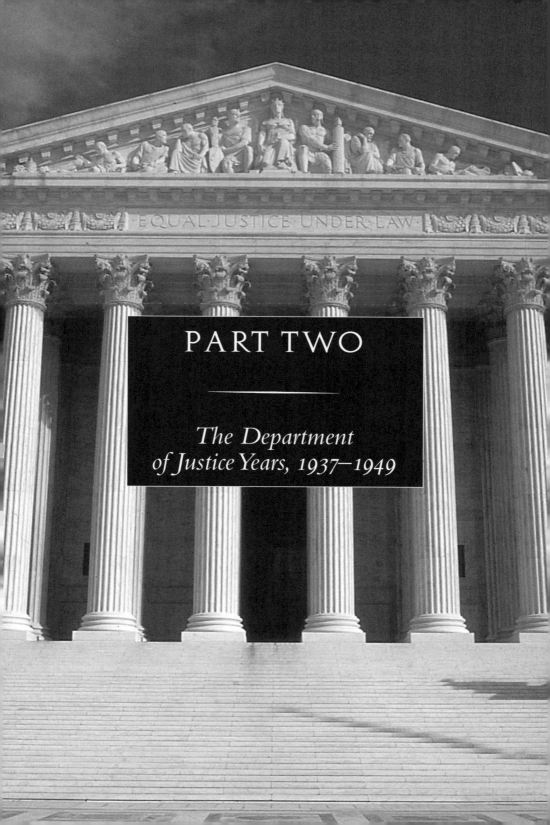

# PART TWO

## The Department
of Justice Years, 1937–1949

## CHAPTER 5

# Some Disruptive Years

Nobody else could have done it.

Assistant Attorney General Thurman Arnold, 1940

W HEN WE ARRIVED IN 1937, Washington, D.C., still resembled a typical quiet southern city. Closer examination, however, revealed a unique environment created by the presence
of its most prominent resident—the federal government. Politics then, as
now, was the lifeblood of the nation's capital, and most residents exhibited
an insatiable appetite for political news ranging from major international
events to the latest White House dinner party.

When our family arrived that spring, the Spanish Civil War dominated
the international scene. Newspapers reported that Germany and Italy
were actively involved in the effort to overthrow Spain's fragile democracy. Still, few Americans were concerned, ignoring the warnings of those
such as New York City's Mayor Fiorello La Guardia, who denounced
Hitler as "that brown shirt fascist who is menacing the peace of the
world."[1]

Locally, a group called the League for Progress in Architecture was
waging a battle against plans to build the Jefferson Memorial. The league
appealed to President Roosevelt to delay construction until a national
competition could be held. Members argued that the proposed site for the
memorial was unacceptable and that the design would render the monu-
ment "dead before it is built."[2] Roosevelt withstood the clamor, for more
important things were on his mind—especially the nation's economy,
which continued to be the major concern of the day. Roosevelt was
locked in a battle with the Supreme Court, whose members were
obstructing his efforts to deal with the Depression. To bypass the Court,
he had devised a scheme, known as the "court-packing plan," that would

increase the number of justices and allow him to choose additional ones. The proposed legislation had a profound effect on Tom Clark's future.

When my father arrived in February 1937, the Department of Justice was immersed in the effort to pass the legislation; Attorney General Homer Cummings and Assistant Attorney General Robert Jackson led the effort. It was not an easy task, especially since the legislation did not enjoy unanimous Democratic support. For example, both senators from Texas opposed the plan, even though polls indicated that 61 percent of Texas voters favored it.[3] Other state officials, including newly elected congressman Lyndon Johnson, worked diligently for its passage.

Tom Clark could not have suspected that the controversy might affect his own position. He and Senator Connally believed that he had been appointed an assistant attorney general of the Department of Justice's Claims Division. Shortly after arriving, my father was shocked to learn the position was not his. Instead, he was a special assistant, a low-ranking job held by at least one hundred others within the department. Furthermore, he was assigned to the War Risk Litigation Section, a neglected unit affectionately known as "the graveyard" of the Department of Justice.

The explanation given at the time was that there had been a misunderstanding between Senator Connally and President Roosevelt. Mother was suspicious, however, and felt that an influx of letters from Texans opposed to the appointment caused the president to change his mind. The letters were a result of written interviews conducted by the FBI as part of a background check, which I obtained through the Freedom of Information Act. They reveal that opposition to the appointment was based on two issues: Tom Clark's close association with Texas attorney general Bill McCraw and his ties to the oil industry. One opponent of the appointment wrote that he considered:

> Thomas C. Clark a very capable civil lawyer at the Dallas Bar; that he was of good moral character and popular with members of the Dallas Bar Association, [but that] he could not endorse him for a Governmental position due to his legal and lobbying activities for certain corporations, and particularly oil companies, who might have matters to come before the Texas Attorney General's department. . . . Clark could not be fair and impartial while occupying a governmental position should the Government's interests and the oil companies and the Attorney General's Department at Austin conflict.

Despite these objections, the majority of letters were highly favorable. One writer, who described my father as "an able lawyer, sober and industrious, highly educated and considered a success in the profession in Dallas," concluded that he "could not understand why he [Tom Clark] would want a governmental departmental position of any kind." That these letters would have influenced Roosevelt seems unlikely, especially since FBI director J. Edgar Hoover described the results of the investigation as "absolutely favorable as far as the FBI was concerned."

During an interview years later, my father gave another explanation, unknown to Mother or other family members, indicating that the president's displeasure with Senator Connally's opposition to the court-packing plan was the reason for the change in the appointment:

> I came here in 1937, and I was just a small time lawyer. Senator Connally asked me to come up and I thought at the time I was going to be an Assistant Attorney General. But when I got here they found out about the Court plan, and I found myself a special assistant. It had been ballyhooed down home that I was going to be an Assistant Attorney General, so I just took it. About 2 or 3 weeks after I had been in the Department, they called me and said they wanted me to talk to Senator Connally about the Court Packing plan. I told him I couldn't do it. One, I was against it, and two, that I wouldn't have any influence with him. While my family was close to Senator Connally, I was not. So they took all of my work away from me in the Department.[4]

My father did not specify who "they" and "him" were, and it seems odd that this version of the incident had not been revealed—even to Mother—at the time it occurred. Still, this lack of communication was not uncharacteristic. Throughout his life, my father kept much within, especially matters of an unpleasant nature. The new explanation was logical, for Senator Connally announced his strong opposition to the court-packing plan on February 9, 1937—only five days after the president proposed it and a short time before my father arrived on the scene. FDR was angry, and Connally felt the president sought to punish him. In his memoirs, Connally cited the rejection of another recommendation he made to the president during this period: "I knew that because of my opposition to Roosevelt's Court bill, my recommendation would be thrown in the wastebasket of the White House."[5] His recommendation of Tom Clark apparently experienced the same fate.

Despite his disappointment, my father decided to stay in Washington, and somehow maintained his usual high spirits. Mother looked back at the early months after the move as an exceptionally happy period. Although she was close to her family and had never been away from them for any length of time, she was not homesick, partly because of the steady flow of visitors from Texas, but even more importantly because my father was spending more time with the family than he had since the early days of their marriage. Since my parents considered their stay in Washington temporary, they immediately began to take advantage of all that the city and the surrounding areas had to offer. They planned numerous weekend trips—first to Lexington, Virginia, for a nostalgic visit to VMI; to Annapolis, Maryland, and the Naval Academy for a lacrosse game; to Gettysburg, Pennsylvania, to see the great Civil War battlefield; and to Rehoboth Beach, Delaware, where my father fell in love with the ocean. A ski trip to Pennsylvania's Pocono Mountains was less successful. My father fell before he descended the first slope, and sprained his wrist. Undaunted, he and Mother switched to what they believed to be a safer sport—bobsledding. Mother, terrified, kept her head buried in my father's back as they hurtled down the winding, treacherous paths at breakneck speed. Mother was a good sport on these excursions. She did not enjoy sports, nor had she any great love for the outdoors. At the beach, she remained under the umbrella or in the cottage so that her fair skin would not burn. She loved to travel, however, and welcomed new experiences. She was also content to go along with my father's plans because of the companionship they offered and the pleasure that the trips brought him.

In the fall of 1937, we moved from the Wardman Park Hotel to the Kennedy-Warren Apartment Building a few blocks away and settled into our new life. Ramsey was a patrol boy at the Oyster School, where his best friend was Joe Cheeseborough. Joe would change his surname to Tydings after becoming the stepson of Senator Millard Tydings of Maryland, and was later elected to the Senate himself. I attended kindergarten and spent most afternoons visiting the National Zoo, which was located next door to our new home. That Christmas, my father arranged photo albums for our two grandmothers. He captioned a picture of me standing by the hotel swimming pool: "Sally Rand [the popular exotic dancer famous for her fan and bubble dance routines] has nothing on Miss Mimi." Under one of Ramsey that was placed next to a picture of the White House, he wrote: "This may be his future home." My father's restless energy produced another move in the spring of 1938—this time because he felt Ramsey and I needed a house and a yard.

Just a few months after the move to a house, an event occurred that gave my father the break he needed at the Department of Justice. Chief Justice Charles Evans Hughes, spurred by the desire to distract the Department of Justice from its efforts to reorganize the Supreme Court, ordered federal trial courts to clear a backlog of cases that included hundreds of war-risk insurance suits. Suddenly, the department's War Risk Litigation Section was overwhelmed with cases. In a 1969 interview, Tom Clark described how this change affected him: "They didn't have many lawyers who had had any trial experience, so when Chief Justice Hughes sent down the word to the trial courts to set the Justice Department cases—there happened to be about 3000 that had been on the books for some time . . . I went from one court to another trying cases. For example we had 600 in the District. I would take a little staff of two or three, and we would try cases day-in and day-out."[6]

Working conditions were somewhat chaotic. The Department of Justice was crowded, and two or three lawyers often shared one office. On several occasions, my father returned from out-of-town trips to find he had been moved out of his office to another one. He had to search for papers and files he had been working on.

A case that brought him special notice involved a veteran who claimed total disability because of a back injury suffered during World War I. My father learned that the man vacationed each year at Owen Sound, a resort area on Lake Huron just northeast of Toronto, Canada. He decided to visit the resort at a time he knew the man would be vacationing there. Mother accompanied him, and when they arrived, the annual bowling-on-the-green competition was being held. The game involves throwing five-pound balls a distance of up to a hundred feet—an act that requires a fair amount of physical strength. The defending champion was the veteran with the bad back. Nothing was said at the time, but a few weeks later the case came to court. Special Assistant Clark began questioning the defendant to establish the nature and extent of his injury. The defendant claimed total disability. My father progressed steadily in the interrogation until he confronted the man with his bowling-on-the-green championship. The veteran was visibly shaken, his case was totally undermined, and Tom Clark and the government were victorious.

My father's success in this and other insurance cases was undoubtedly a major reason he was able to get out of the War Risk Litigation Unit—a necessary step if he were to advance within the Department of Justice. He had been interested in antitrust since he and Bill McCraw had campaigned against the public trusts during McCraw's race for attorney general. The assistant attorney general of the Antitrust Division was Thurman Arnold, a dynamic trustbuster and good friend of Dallas congressman Hatton Sumners. Sumners was chairman of the powerful House Judiciary Committee and a close friend of our family. A bachelor, he shared an apartment with my father at the Wardman Park Hotel before the rest of the family arrived from Dallas. He continued to be a frequent guest in our home, and on May 30, 1937, he and I celebrated our birthdays together—his sixtieth and my fourth. The following year, he stayed with us for six weeks while recuperating from a double hernia operation.

My father sought Congressman Sumners's help in obtaining a position in the Antitrust Division, and Sumners arranged a meeting at Assistant Attorney General Arnold's home in Vienna, Virginia. Arnold was recovering from a bout of jaundice, and his yellow skin was accompanied by a black mood. Although Mrs. Arnold was gracious and hospitable, the meeting was uncomfortable and seemed so unsuccessful to Mother that she predicted on the drive home that Arnold would never give my father a job. She was mistaken. Several weeks later, a position opened up in the Antitrust Division, and Tom Clark was selected to fill it.

The switch to the Antitrust Division ushered in a disruptive period for our family. Special Assistant Clark began traveling a great deal, and in the fall of 1939 was sent to New Orleans for an indefinite period to investigate violations of antitrust laws within the building and construction industry. New Orleans was a hotbed of scandal as numerous federal investigators probed activities that involved colleagues of the late Huey Long. On October 5, 1939, my father's picture appeared on the front page of the *New Orleans Item*, along with that of assistant U.S. attorney Robert Weinstein, as part of an article headlined "Cracking Down on High Building Costs." The article identified my father as Tom C. Sharp. A few days later, the paper printed his correct name and provided additional information about his duties. According to the article, Tom Clark had five assistants in New Orleans and offices in other southern cities. He was quoted as calling the Department of Justice activities "a coast to coast attack on suspected trade restraints in the building industry."[7] According to Clark, residential building costs in New Orleans were 20 to 30 percent higher than in other cities because of building "restraints" such as labor racketeering and price fixing. On October 29, the *New Orleans Item* reported that 117 persons had been indicted on charges that included swindling, forgery, embezzlement, confidence games, and "outright steals."[8] High-ranking public officials were implicated, including former governor Richard Leche, Speaker of the Louisiana House Louis Wimberly, and District Attorney Charles A. Byrne. A forty-four-count indictment was brought against former Louisiana State University president James Monroe Smith, who eventually pleaded guilty to charges of forgery and embezzlement.

On December 3, a federal grand jury indicted the New Orleans chapter of the Associated General Contractors of America and sixteen of its members for illegally adding special fees to construction bids on a hospital. My father presented the case, although it did not involve antitrust violations.[9]

Another major article concerning cases that my father was handling appeared on January 5, 1940, with the headline "42 Reported Ready to Plead Guilty in Indictments on High Building Costs." Within the next two weeks, federal grand juries handed down indictments against the Sheet Metal Association, a Louisiana corporation composed of about twelve firms; the Building and Construction Trades Council of New Orleans; twenty-one American Federation of Labor (AFL) building-trades unions; twenty-two union business agents; the New Orleans chapter of the National Electrical Contractors; and three lumber companies that were members of the huge Southern Pines Association. All were charged with violations of the Sherman Antitrust Act. The lumber companies pleaded nolo contendere (no contest) to the antitrust violations, and were fined $12,000.[10]

During the six months my father was in New Orleans, the rest of the family relocated in Dallas to be closer to him and to visit our Texas relatives. We stayed with Mother's older sister, Mildred (Aunt Mil) Walker; her husband, Del; and son, Bill. Every morning the postman would arrive with a special-delivery letter for Mother from my father. All of us, especially Mother, missed my father, but it never occurred to me as a six-year-old child that the separation from the family was even more difficult for him. An excerpt from a letter Mother received soon after we had arrived in Dallas is revealing:

Dear "Mom,"
After you rest up a few days and see your folks why not come down? This place I am getting will not cost any more for two and we could have a keen time together in "Old Orleans." It's powerful lonesome here without you.

He shared a small apartment in the French Quarter with a young man named George Stinson, who later became president of U.S. Steel. The accommodations were not the best! On October 6, 1939, my father wrote the following account after having just moved in:

Dear Mom,
I'm sitting here on the bed trying to write you. I've moved and I have no table to write on. This place looks like a "dump." It has old furniture but two new iron twin beds with what feels like good mattresses. . . . The place consists of a living room—couch and one chair—bedroom with twin beds and a bureau—no chairs—a bath and a kitchen. It has a lovely porch over-

looking the city but there being no chairs on it you can't sit down. It is on the 3rd floor. You walk up two flights. The floors are carpeted in blue—the best part of the house. I wish you were here to fix it up. I had to buy some sheets so I could sleep here tonight. . . . I got your 2 sweet letters and they saved my life. Thanks a million. They "pepped me up."

He sounded more upbeat in a letter written about a week later:

Well, Stinson and I are all fixed up now. We finally got some covers for the dirty furniture and the apt. looks fairly good. The landlord has agreed to put in some drapes but so far they have not shown up. He has been nice about fixing up—but very slow.

It sure will be keen to see sweet Mom. When are you coming? Stinson can go to the hotel or perhaps some room nearby . . . He is very nice and I'm sure would be glad to move around some. Any day you can come would be perfect. The sooner the better. . . . I think you will like this little apt. It will look swell with you in it.

Mother headed for New Orleans as soon as Ramsey and I had settled in with Aunt Mil, and stayed with my father for two weeks. It was difficult for him to get away, but he managed a short visit to Dallas in early November. We were all disappointed that he wasn't able to get back for Thanksgiving. He wrote the following letter on November 22—the day before Thanksgiving:

Dearest Mom,
I was sure glad to talk with you last night and hear Mimi was OK or rather on the way to being "husky" again. It was quite a relief for your letter yesterday was not favorable. I got your letter and Bub's note this am. I'm glad Mr. Bub is feeling good and enjoying school. We will arrange for the hunt. I hope you can come down.

We are working hard trying to get the cases together—seem to be having a tough time but I guess we will come out OK. I hope so.

There is nothing going on. The folks here are celebrating Thanksgiving tomorrow—wish I was with you. We always had a nice one. I remember the last two—Kennedy and Argyle [our street in D.C.]—wish we were back there. I'm glad my letters are getting there OK now. I try to get them off on the 10 pm every day. That puts them there the next day—special.

Be sweet—take care of our sweethearts—and don't forget me.

My father was able to come to Dallas for Christmas, and afterward

Mother, Ramsey, and Bill Walker returned to New Orleans with him. As usual, my father arranged numerous activities. He and the two boys went goose hunting near Lake Charles while Mother waited for them in the shack of the Cajun family that took care of the hunting grounds. It was a damp, chilling day, and she kept close to the pot-bellied stove that heated the family's small quarters. She was shocked to see that the children were barefoot. The "boys" had a successful outing despite the inclement weather. Afterward, my father commemorated the occasion by ordering a special newspaper front page with the headline "Bub Clark Biggest Goose on Goose Hunt."

On New Year's Eve 1940, the four went to a movie, and then walked around the streets of New Orleans waiting for midnight. Mother and the boys were tired, and she was angry because my father insisted that they stay up to see in the new year. They had tickets for the Sugar Bowl game the next day. Tulane University was playing Texas A&M, and the newspapers described the city as so crowded with "thousands of booted, 10-gallon hatted Texans . . . that standing room only signs should be placed at its entrance."[11]

The weather was fair and mild as they watched Texas A&M beat Tulane 14–13. Mother and the boys drove back to Dallas the next day. They were not feeling well, and came down with the flu soon after returning. A siege of ill health began that lasted several weeks, culminating when I contracted chicken pox just as we were preparing to return to Washington in mid-February.

Since I was unable to travel, my parents decided to take advantage of the delay by driving to Florida. My father had some final business details to complete in New Orleans, so they drove there first and then continued along the Gulf Coast. It was late February, and they followed the blossoming of spring as they traveled. Azaleas, camellias, and other flowering bushes were opening up and blooming everywhere. They eventually crossed over to Miami and then up Florida's east coast to Palm Beach. They thought the Breaker's Hotel was paradise, but the sun proved to be a snake in the grass, for my father burned so badly on a deceptively cool, cloudy day that they called a doctor, who prescribed medication to relieve the pain.

By the time my parents returned to Dallas, the whole family was ready to move back to Washington and settle down in our own home. Grandmother Clark drove back with us, and we stopped in Brandon, Mississippi, to visit her girlhood home. The return to Washington was simplified by our having kept the house we rented before the New Orleans assignment. At last, Mother thought, we would all be together and resume a normal lifestyle.

We had been settled for less than a month when my father returned from work one day and informed Mother that his boss, Thurman Arnold, wanted to send him to the West Coast to head the Antitrust Division's offices there. Mother's response was immediate and unequivocal: "Absolutely no! We're barely settled here. We can't move again so soon." She thought the matter closed until a few days later, when my father broached the subject again: "Thurman really wants me to take the position on the West Coast. It would only be for a year or so. What do you think?" Mother held firm: "No! We can't move again. It would be much too hard on everyone, especially the children." My father retreated once more, but when, a few days later, he brought up the question a third time, Mother was resigned to the inevitable. "When do we go?" she responded.

Once the decision was final, little time was lost. Grandmother returned to Dallas, taking Ramsey with her so that he could complete sixth grade without further interruption. In the meantime, our furniture and all other belongings except the bare necessities were put into storage as my parents prepared for the long drive across the country. The journey began badly when my father locked the keys in the car as he made one last stop at Riggs Bank, but that was only the beginning of a trip that for me, a car-sick six-year-old in the backseat of our Buick, was a nightmare. Nor was it much better for my parents as they listened to radio reports of the Germans' bombing of London and tried to take my mind off my churning stomach. Although we played games, sang songs, including different versions of "California, Here I Come," and did everything conceivable to make me feel better, I was so sick by the time we reached Van Wert, Ohio, that we stopped and sought the aid of a doctor. We stayed in the town for two days, but finally had to continue. The respite helped but did not cure my malady. Other minor incidents, like a flat tire in Idaho, added to our difficulties. My father had packed the car's trunk with great care so that we would not have to unpack it before arriving in California. The flat tire required him to completely unpack and repack the trunk, and then the next day the whole procedure had to be repeated when California border guards inspected the car for smuggled plants or fruit.

The Department of Justice had offices all along the West Coast, so my parents could have chosen a number of cities for their new home. They selected Los Angeles, where Mother's half brother, Felix Ramsey, lived. Besides the advantage of family, the warm climate and beautiful beaches of Southern California made that city an easy choice. The economy in California, like that in the rest of the country, was still depressed, so housing was inexpensive. We found a Spanish-style house in Beverly Hills that had been the residence of several movie stars, including Tony Martin and

Jack Oakie. Rosalind Russell lived on the same block, and Fred MacMurray down the street. We would see George Burns and Gracie Allen drive by almost every day. The monthly rent of $175 included all the furnishings plus a gardener, who took care of a luscious yard replete with lemon, orange, fig, and mulberry trees and huge poinsettia bushes that bloomed at Christmas. A large fishpond with water lilies graced the front yard, and a second one was in the large sunroom inside the house. Ramsey and I occasionally amused ourselves by taking a goldfish from one pond and putting it into the other. Inevitably, the resident fish would chase the intruder until we rescued it.

The public schools were excellent and within easy walking distance. Occasionally, my father drove me to school in a secondhand Dodge convertible that we purchased soon after the move. It was slightly worn-looking, and I remember being somewhat embarrassed because most of my girlfriends were from wealthy families that owned large, luxurious cars. Still, having a convertible was fun, even though automatic tops were not yet available; my father used to say that it took "two men and a little boy" to get the top up or down.

Upon arriving on the West Coast, my father first took a case involving several oil companies. Lawyers there had worked on the case for two years, and my father's success in settling it in sixty days was a major accomplishment.[12] Another important case that he prosecuted successfully involved the Western Pine Association and thirty-five lumber companies. All pleaded nolo contendere to antitrust charges. They were fined $81,500, and agreed to discontinue the practices that led to the suit. Thurman Arnold sent congratulations in a telegram:

Just found out about the verdict. Have been trying to reach you on the phone all day to congratulate you but circuits have been busy so am sending this wire. It was a great triumph and a tough case. Nobody else could have done it.

Regards, Thurman

My father traveled a great deal, since he was responsible for offices in Seattle and San Francisco as well as Los Angeles. Within a few months, he received a citation from United Airlines for having flown 100,000 miles. Several of the young men who had been on his staff in New Orleans also worked with him on the West coast. It was a talented and successful group—two were to become judges, one an assistant attorney general of California, and another, Joe Alioto, mayor of San Francisco. My father's secretary in Seattle was a remarkable young woman named Alice O'Donnell. A few years later, Alice would move to Washington, D.C., to serve again as my father's secretary after he was appointed attorney general. She was dedicated to her boss and to our family.

Although his absences from home were frequent, my father was usually gone for no more than one or two days at a time. When he was home, we would often take weekend trips to one of California's many delightful spots, such as Palm Springs, Lake Arrowhead, or Death Valley, or else simply drive fifteen minutes to the beach in Santa Monica. Sometimes, when no trip was planned and the weather wasn't good for beaching, my father would say, "Let's go look for the sunshine!" We would hop in the Buick and start driving. In the summer of 1941, Mother, Ramsey, and my father sailed up the inland passageway to Alaska. Rather than risk another bout of motion sickness, I stayed behind with Margaret and Charlie Carr. Charlie was the U.S. attorney in Los Angeles, and Margaret was Mother's closest friend in California.

The boat to Alaska was filled with families moving there for job opportunities. The group developed a warm camaraderie as everyone took in the majestic beauty of Alaska and also shared concerns about the world situation. War with Japan was the major topic of conversation, but the threat had existed for so long that many believed it would never happen, and few, if any, could have predicted the disaster that was only a few short months away.

## CHAPTER 6

# His Greatest Mistake

I have made a lot of mistakes in my life, but one I acknowledge publicly is my part in the evacuation of the Japanese from California in 1942.

Tom Clark, 1966

I WAS OUTSIDE PLAYING on that sunny, mild Sunday when Japan bombed Pearl Harbor. My father was in San Francisco, and Mother was in the kitchen of our Beverly Hills home, listening to the radio. Our lives, like those of other Americans, were irrevocably changed. The government moved quickly to protect the country from internal sabotage. Attorney General Francis Biddle identified and designated "restricted" areas, where access was limited and controlled, and "prohibited" areas—ports, harbors, power plants, and other spots considered vulnerable to sabotage—where no access was allowed. He ordered all enemy aliens—that is, all Japanese, German, and Italian citizens—removed from these areas, and on December 11, the *Los Angeles Times* announced that the FBI had 2,300 in custody. People remained calm, and there was no immediate cry for action against Japanese American citizens.

On the West Coast, the army, under the leadership of Lieutenant General John L. DeWitt, the commander of the Fourth Army and the Western Defense Command, assumed responsibility for the area's security. According to my father, President Roosevelt wanted an official civilian voice to balance the military's authority in the handling of enemy aliens, and since the Department of Justice already had offices along the West Coast, it was assigned that task. In a memo to Attorney General Biddle written on January 17, 1942, Assistant Attorney General Thurman Arnold recommended that my father head the project:

I now have a man who has proved himself to be one of the most efficient organizers in the investigation of trial work that I have ever seen. He took the Pacific Coast Offices when they were in the doldrums and made an active, fighting organization out of them. In spite of the aggressive quality of his activities, his public relations were so good that he made friends everywhere. The Antitrust Division has had a remarkably good press on the Pacific Coast even though it has attacked many of the large businesses operating there. Most of this is due to Mr. Clark's ability and tact.[1]

On January 28, Biddle announced the appointment of Thomas C. Clark as coordinator of the Alien Enemy Control Program to the press. It was not surprising that no one sought the position. Deputy Attorney General Jim Rowe, in a letter to Senator Tom Connally, wrote that Tom Clark had been put "on the spot" and assigned the "toughest and nastiest job in the Department." The letter continued, "We do hope that Tom, because of his peculiar combination of tact and toughness, can get away with it."[2]

The coordinator's prime responsibility was to represent the Department of Justice in all matters concerning enemy-alien control that involved cooperation with General Dewitt and Rear Admiral John W. Greenslade, the commandant of the Twelfth Naval District, and to coordinate any activities that included other federal agencies or departments. His staff consisted of thirty-one people whom he already supervised in the Antitrust Division on the West Coast. The *Los Angeles Times*, describing Tom Clark as "a hard-hitting Texas lawyer from Dallas," quoted him as saying, "National defense will be the prime factor behind the enemy control program and all possible measures will be adhered to." Clark also declared that enemy aliens who failed to leave the areas voluntarily by the deadline would be removed by "whatever procedure is necessary."[3]

It was an extraordinarily hectic time, and the responsibilities of the coordinator were not always clearly defined or communicated. My father expressed frustration in a letter written on January 31 to Assistant Attorney General Edward Ennis, the director of Alien Enemy Control in Washington: "I notice in the papers that I am supposed to be placing signs all around these areas that the Attorney General designated. I have no signs, nor do I have any personnel to put them up. I wonder just what the plan was."[4] Somehow, the task was accomplished, and the signs—posters that identified prohibited areas—were put in place. A few days later, Clark announced that two hundred to three hundred Japanese, German, and Italian citizens had received notices to leave the designated areas and that a total of about ten thousand would be moved by February 24.

"I think you had to live it to understand the feeling that Californians had about the people of Japanese descent after Pearl Harbor," my father mused years later.[5] As coordinator, he received hundreds of letters threatening the Japanese. "If you don't get them out of here, you're going to find them dead," went a typical message.[6] Japanese were found murdered, some disappeared. Fearful Chinese citizens began wearing signs that read "I am Chinese" to protect themselves from the violence. Rumors flooded the coordinator's office: Japanese submarines were seen under the Golden Gate Bridge; bombs were found on beaches; Japanese officers were going in and out of certain homes; signals were being sent from Japanese homes to boats at sea. None of these alleged incidents proved to be true, but the rumors continued and raised the fears of an already nervous population. During the weeks and months following Pearl Harbor, the United States suffered one disastrous defeat after another in the Pacific war—the Philippines fell in May 1942, after the battles of Bataan and Corregidor. Singapore and Hong Kong had already been taken over by the Japanese. Fear and distrust of the Japanese, including Japanese Americans, increased dramatically during this difficult period.

Barely latent prejudice toward all Asians was not new to the West Coast and added an ugly element to the anger generated by the attack on Pearl Harbor. Japanese immigrants began arriving in this country toward the end of the nineteenth century. Although forbidden by law from owning land, they eventually obtained property by purchasing it in the names of their children born in the United States; but because of racial bias, the only areas available to them were undesirable, such as land around high-tension wires or under dams. Ironically, when war broke out, these locations appeared vulnerable to sabotage, and the Japanese were accused of deliberately choosing them for that purpose.

Economics also played an ugly role. Through exceptional hard work and perseverance, Japanese farmers converted previously desolate lands into some of the best farmland in California. Consequently, although they comprised only 1 percent of the population, Japanese Americans controlled almost half of the commercial fruit and vegetable market in the state. Farm groups such as the Western Growers Protective Association, the Grower-Fisher Vegetable Association, and the California Farm Bureau Federation actively pressed for the evacuation of Japanese American citizens, thereby eliminating their most successful competitors.[7]

Other powerful groups were increasing the pressure for internment. In Congress, Representative Martin Dies of Texas, the chairman of the House Un-American Activities Committee (HUAC), harshly criticized the administration as "lax, tolerant and soft toward the Japanese who have violated American hospitality."[8] On February 9, 1942, claiming they would soon present evidence of widespread sabotage, HUAC members tentatively recommended the removal of all Japanese aliens and Japanese Americans from the West Coast.

At the same time, a serious rift developed, with state and local officials and the military on one side, and the Department of Justice on the other. Virtually every state and local official, including California governor Culbert Olson, Los Angeles mayor Fletcher Bowron, California attorney general Earl Warren, and liberal Democratic congressman Jerry Voorhis, argued that sabotage was imminent and evacuation necessary for the security of the region. General DeWitt initially took a more moderate stance. He favored a curfew rather than an evacuation—a strategy that failed to satisfy public demand for more drastic action—and asked for the registration of all enemy aliens—a request that the Department of Justice supported. Despite his reluctance to evacuate Japanese citizens, DeWitt and his right-hand man, Colonel Karl Bendetsen, felt the federal government was being "soft" on the Japanese and unrealistic about the threat of sabotage. DeWitt had expressed his distrust of the Japanese in a meeting on January 2: "I have no confidence in their loyalty whatsoever. I am now speaking of the native-born Japanese."[9]

In contrast to the positions taken by state officials and the military, the Department of Justice, under the leadership of Attorney General Biddle, Deputy Attorney General Jim Rowe and Assistant Attorney General Edward Ennis, took a firm stand against mass evacuation. Biddle declared that his hands were tied by the Fourteenth Amendment and that the internment of American citizens would be "profoundly unwise and profoundly un-American."[10] Biddle, known as a committed civil libertarian, trusted the FBI's intelligence assessments of national security. FBI director J. Edgar Hoover, in a memo to Biddle written on February 1, 1942, criticized military intelligence on the West Coast as disorganized and as exhibiting, at times, "hysteria and lack of judgment."[11] According to Jim Rowe, the Department of Justice lawyers felt alone in their opposition to the internment. Biddle tried, but failed, to forge a united front with the War Department, which, under the leadership of Assistant Secretary of War John McCloy, sided with the military in refusing to sign a declaration stating that the evacuation of American citizens was not necessary for the security of the region.

DeWitt and Bendetsen insisted that "military necessity" should determine security policies and that lawyers, ignorant of military matters, could not make that determination. Both men raised negative stereotypes of the Japanese in statements that revealed a deep distrust of all Japanese, including Japanese American citizens. General DeWitt stressed the inability of the Japanese to become assimilated into the American culture and, in a bizarre twist, argued that the absence of sabotage to date was an ominous indicator of future sabotage: "The Japanese race is an enemy race and while many second and third generation born on U.S. soil, possessed of U.S. citizenship have become 'Americanized' the racial strains are undiluted . . . The very fact that no sabotage has taken place to date is a disturbing and confirming indication that such action will be taken."[12] Bendetsen revealed a similar outlook as he invoked the image of the inscrutable "Oriental": "It [mass evacuation] is undoubtedly the safest course to follow. That is to say, as you cannot distinguish or penetrate the Oriental thinking, and as you cannot tell which ones are loyal and which ones are not, it is therefore the easiest course . . . to remove them all from the West Coast and place them in uninhabited areas where they can do no harm under guard."[13]

Tom Clark played the middleman in this three-way tug-of-war. Unlike his superiors in Washington, D.C., he was a resident of California and was inevitably affected by the fearful atmosphere that consumed the West Coast. Still, he did not favor evacuation initially. "I suggested," he recalled years later, "and Mr. Hoover insisted, that we take care of the Japanese in the same manner that we were handling Germans and Italians. That was on the basis of individual prosecutions."[14] Biddle, however, was apparently disappointed that Tom Clark did not present the Justice Department's views more forcefully, and felt that he was too deferential to the military authorities. In his memoirs, Biddle complained that Clark was supposed to "express and explain our views which were far more moderate than the Army's" but instead "construed his assignment as a direction to imply that the Justice Department would patriotically follow the military."[15] In 1981, Jim Rowe testified before the U.S. Commission on Wartime Relocation and Internment of Civilians, formed for the purpose of determining whether compensation should be made to Japanese American citizens who had been interned, that Tom Clark was on the side of the military. Rowe's testimony in 1981 seems to contradict letters he wrote shortly before the decision to intern the Japanese was finalized. In a brief note to my father on February 11, 1942, Rowe stated: "From everything I hear, including a number of sources, you are still on top of the problem. Frankly, I don't think you can keep it up. I'll bet anti-trust looks awfully good to you now."[16] The next day, Rowe attached an article about my father to a memo that he sent Biddle: "Here is the story from Monday's *San Francisco Examiner*," he wrote, "showing how Tom Clark is handling a difficult problem. He is really doing a beautiful job."[17]

My father, clearly influenced by General DeWitt and Colonel Bendetsen, trusted their assessment of the situation. DeWitt was a respected, no-nonsense officer who had served in the Spanish-American War and World War I. In a write-up that appeared in a 1942 issue of *Current Biography*, a close associate of the general described his ability to inspire confidence as being so great that anyone dealing with him came away with the comment: "Whatever the General does is okay with me." Tom Clark's VMI experience had instilled in him a great respect for military authority, and he relied upon the judgment of the older man. His public statements about the federal government's policies were sometimes defensive and indicated that the Department of Justice would comply with the military in handling security: "Let's get this straight!" he declared on February 9, 1942, "The federal government has a certain program, but if at any time the Department of Justice cannot carry out the requests of the Army and Navy, I will recommend that restricted martial law be inaugurated. The people can count on that!"[18]

As dissatisfaction with the government's handling of the situation grew, the press increased its attacks on the administration, and especially on Attorney General Biddle. One *Los Angeles Times* journalist, Henry McLemore, ran a series of vicious articles in his column, ironically named "The Lighter Side." One overtly racist piece began: "Slant my eyes, bow my legs, and hammer me down, I'm turning Japanese. . . . Mr. Biddle does everything but cook rice for the lovely ones."[19] McLemore continued his attack on the attorney general by declaring that Biddle couldn't get elected assistant dogcatcher and was handling the Japanese like "Lord Fauntleroy playing tag with his maiden aunt." "Everyone in California," he wrote, "thinks Mr. Biddle's handling of the bow-legged sons and daughters of the Rising Sun is mighty ridiculous."[20]

On February 10, the executive committee of the Los Angeles County Defense Council presented a resolution to my father, stating that the federal government was moving too slow and its actions were inadequate to meet the threat of possible sabotage. That same day, Los Angeles mayor Fletcher Bowron and California attorney general Earl Warren met with General DeWitt and my father. Bowron and Warren argued for the evacuation of all Japanese—aliens and citizens alike—and DeWitt, though still undecided, was clearly moved. In a conversation with my father after the meeting, DeWitt worried about his own future. "I am not," he declared to my father, "going to be a second General Short."[21] Short was the commanding general in Hawaii when Pearl Harbor was bombed. He and Admiral Husband E. Kimmel, the Pacific Fleet commander, were removed from their posts in disgrace on December 16, 1941. Still, DeWitt was not yet recommending evacuation, nor was my father, who, in a letter to Assistant Attorney General Ennis dated February 10, 1942, stated that despite "the clamor for removal of all Japanese regardless of citizenship. . . . I do not think such drastic steps [that is, evacuation] are necessary."[22]

Each day brought new pressure. On February 12, respected liberal journalist Walter Lippmann wrote in his column that he had received reports of signals being sent from California beaches to Japanese ships at sea and that the West Coast was in "imminent danger of a combined attack from within and without."[23] My father responded to this assertion with uncharacteristic anger:

> I wish Mr. Lippmann would give us the names and places, if anybody is sig-
> naling back and forth. We have heard rumors but haven't intercepted any
> such signaling. We would like to investigate if Mr. Lippmann could tell us
> where his reports come from. As for his report that the coast is in imminent
> danger of invasion, that is gross exaggeration. I am in touch with the Army
> every day. If Mr. Lippmann wants to make California a ghost state, he can
> keep on writing stories like that which have no foundation in fact. This
> does not mean that the goose hangs high and there's nothing to be con-
> cerned about. That's not true. I think we must maintain our alertness as we
> are doing; that is the only way we can combat the danger of sabotage.[24]

The West Coast clamored for more drastic action, and on February 13, members of Congress from California, Oregon, and Washington sent President Roosevelt a communication urging "the immediate evacuation of all persons of Japanese lineage and all other aliens and citizens alike whose presence shall be deemed dangerous to the defense of the United States from all strategic areas."[25]

An incident on February 14 fueled the hysteria even further. Los Angeles residents were awakened in the middle of the night by the sound of antiaircraft fire. I recall looking out my bedroom window and seeing beaded strings of light in the dark sky as the planes were attacked from the ground. I shared the same terror as our German housekeeper, who stood barefoot in the backyard and cried, "My Gott, my Gott, we're raided!" The next day, the headlines in the city's papers screamed "Los Angeles Bombed" and "Los Angeles Raided." Although officials quickly determined that the planes were American and had been mistaken for enemy aircraft, the incident strengthened the public's demand for Japanese internment.[26]

Clearly, my father's views on evacuation changed during these crucial days, for on February 15 he announced that he would "recommend that all persons regarded as inimical to defense efforts be removed from vital areas already designated and from such additional ones as are designated by the War and Navy Departments. This will include citizens as well as aliens." He advocated moving them to interior areas of the western states and establishing "work projects that would not interfere with the local economy."[27]

Two days later, my father and Colonel Bendetsen, standing in for General DeWitt, flew to Washington for a meeting at the home of Attorney General Biddle. My father knew that the army would recommend evacuation, but was unaware that the Department of War was ready to accept this policy. Deputy Attorney General Jim Rowe, Assistant Attorney General Edward Ennis, Provost Marshal General Allen W. Gullion (the army's chief law-enforcement officer), and Assistant Secretary of War John McCloy were all present, along with Bendetsen, Biddle, and my father. Rowe and Ennis, who had no knowledge of the impending proposal, began the meeting by arguing against the mass evacuation of enemy aliens. Suddenly, General Gullion reached into his pocket and pulled out a draft of a presidential order giving the secretary of war authority to move both citizens and enemy aliens from areas designated as strategic. Rowe was amazed—he even laughed at the suggestion. When they realized Gullion was serious, Ennis and Rowe pleaded for evacuation on an individual basis; Ennis seemed close to tears. Biddle barely spoke, apparently resigned to what he perceived as inevitable. Surprisingly, he did not request a presidential review. Nor is there any evidence that he ever personally discussed the issue with the president.[28] My father remained silent, an observer of the unfolding drama. He was not in a position of authority as far as determining policy, and by this time felt internment was inevitable.

President Roosevelt signed Executive Order 9066 on February 19, 1942, but its full meaning was not understood until actual implementation began. The order established strategic areas and gave the military the authority to exclude from them "any or all persons." On March 2, General DeWitt announced that "all persons of Japanese ancestry would be removed from the western half of California, Oregon and Washington and the southern third of Arizona."[29] Initially the evacuation was to be "voluntary": the Japanese were required to leave restricted areas, but were free to go wherever they wished. This strategy was doomed from the beginning because of the unwillingness of other states and localities to accept the evacuees. On March 18, 1942, Roosevelt created the War Relocation Authority (WRA) and appointed Milton Eisenhower, the younger brother of General Dwight Eisenhower, the future president, its director.

The WRA was responsible for assisting the army in evacuating the Japanese from designated areas and relocating them to areas where there were work opportunities. The authority was also responsible for protecting the evacuees from possible violence.

At the same time, General DeWitt organized the Wartime Civil Control Administration to implement the policy and selected Colonel Bendetsen as its head. Tom Clark was asked to serve under Bendetsen as coordinator for the federal civilian agencies and the military. His responsibilities included coordinating the evacuation and identifying locations for the internment camps. The first step was to locate the homes of the Japanese—a task greatly facilitated by the 1940 census, which, barely two years old, was still remarkably accurate. According to my father, "The Census Bureau moved out its raw files . . . they would lay out on the tables various city blocks where Japanese lived and they would tell me how many were living on that block."[30] The evacuees were then removed to "reception centers," where their backgrounds were checked and decisions were made about where they should be sent.

An important goal was to keep families together and to enable the evacuees to be self-supporting. There was also concern that the loss of the productive Japanese farms would severely damage California's economy, and evacuees were pressured to establish farms at the camps. I wonder now whether my father felt a pang of conscience when he called upon Japanese Americans to farm as proof of their patriotism. "There can be no doubt," he was quoted as saying in an article that appeared in the *Los Angeles Times* on March 2, 1942, "that all persons who wish to show their loyalty to this country should continue farming operations to the fullest extent." At the same time, he warned that federal agents would prosecute anyone attempting to defraud the Japanese, who, he promised, would be treated well: "We'll be as tough as needed but none will be persecuted. Places are being prepared for agriculturists. . . . Families will be provided for by the U.S. government with comfortable quarters throughout the war."[31]

My father asked Laurence Hewes of the Farm Security Administration to develop a list of possible sites for the detention camps. Selection was based on the feasibility of establishing the camps within a year in areas that could support agriculture. Racetracks, fairgrounds, an abandoned Civilian Conservation Corps camp, a migrant-worker camp, an unused mill site, and livestock pavilions were among the locations chosen. Saburo Kido of the Japanese American Citizens League described the original concept of the camps as: "havens of refuge. . . . We were supposed to be protected from the outside with free going in and out of the centers. Industry and farming were to be developed so that the residents of the relocation centers would have a trust fund which would help them to relocate after the war. The public hysteria created an atmosphere which made such a friendly haven impossible. We became virtual prisoners contrary to the original understanding and promises."[32]

Opposition from communities where the detention camps were to be located was tremendous. Milton Eisenhower described meeting with the governors of states where relocation centers were sought as "probably the most frustrating experience I ever had."[33] One governor even declared: "If you bring Japanese into my state, I promise you they will be hanging from every tree."[34] On one occasion, my father was actually threatened by an angry crowd. To overcome these objections, and to prevent the potential violence that accompanied them, required enormous patience and perseverance. Tom Clark possessed both, and must have also called upon all the powers of persuasion that he had developed over the years. One cattle rancher who had been a leading opponent of a relocation center in Owens Valley, California, provided the following colorful analysis of my father's negotiating skills: "That young fellow sure was bit by a fox when he was a young 'un down in Texas."[35]

By April 1, the negotiations were completed. Ten "relocation centers" in six states—California, Arizona, Utah, Colorado, Idaho, and Wyoming— had been selected, and the governors of those states had agreed to cooperate with the effort. "The situation looks much improved," my father declared.[36]

My father worked at a frenzied pace, traveling constantly during the weeks he was involved in the evacuation. He occasionally traveled on General DeWitt's plane but usually flew United Airlines. In an interview for the *Eastland (Texas) Telegram,* he described himself as "busier than any six men have any right to be" and referred to his home in Beverly Hills as the place "where he used to live."[37]

I remember this as a time when black curtains covered the windows of our house in compliance with the blackouts that were practiced as security measures. Mother was an air-raid warden for our neighborhood block. She kept the household running smoothly, and as an eight-year-old child, I was not really aware of drastic changes in our family life except for my father's increased absences. On the rare occasions when he was home, we no longer took weekend trips or impromptu Sunday drives, as had been our custom before the war. Still, my father remained as upbeat as ever and, with his exceptional ability to focus on what was at hand, did not allow his awesome responsibilities to intrude upon his private life.

In a *New York Times* article that appeared on March 17, 1942, my father described the evacuation as the "greatest orderly mass hegira in modern history, a forced movement dictated by military necessity." His testimony in February 1942 before the Tolan Committee, a congressional committee formed for the purpose of investigating the decision to intern the Japanese, provides insight into his thoughts at that time:

> If military authorities, in whom I have the utmost confidence, tell me it is necessary to remove from any area the citizens as well as the aliens of a certain nationality or of all nationalities, I would say the best thing to do would be to follow the advice of the doctor. Whenever you go to the doctor, if he tells you to take aspirin, you take aspirin. If he tells you to cut off your leg so you can save your body, you cut off your leg. So I think it is up to the military authorities.[38]

Military necessity was also cited as the rationale for evacuation in the Tolan Committee's final report, which concluded that despite a "profound sense of certain injustices and constitutional doubts concerning evacuation," there were no alternatives to the policy.[39]

Sadly, by the time Executive Order 9066 was signed, support for the internment of Japanese American citizens was overwhelming. Even the American Civil Liberties Union, an established champion of individual rights, had succumbed to the notion that national security required the suspension of the civil rights of more than 100,000 American citizens. In 1944, the policy was given further validation when, in a 6–3 decision, the Supreme Court upheld its constitutionality. Justice Hugo Black wrote the majority opinion in *Korematsu v. U.S.*, with Justices Robert Jackson, Frank Murphy, and Owen J. Roberts dissenting. Black cited a well-established principle that not all discrimination is unconstitutional, and asserted that the president, as commander in chief, had the power to call for the evacuation in time of war in order to protect the nation from espionage and sabotage.

California newspapers reflected the West Coast's satisfaction with the evacuation. An editorial in the *Los Angeles Evening Herald Express*, on April 7, 1942, praised those responsible for implementing the policy:

> All this tremendous job, the greatest mass movement job in American history, is being done with minimum disturbance and with a spirit of tolerance and fair play which is a bright light in the darkness of a great and terrible war. . . . For a tremendous task being so well done under wartime conditions, we congratulate the government at Washington, General DeWitt, and Thomas C. Clark, the special assistant to the Attorney General,

who has so splendidly coordinated the greatest problem that has faced the Pacific Coast since the outbreak of hostilities.

If Tom Clark agonized over his part in the Japanese internment, he did not reveal his emotions to any family member. Neither my brother Ramsey, six years my senior, nor I remember any discussions of the Japanese threat or internment either at the time or later. Looking back, Mother recalled that she and my father considered internment a necessary evil. They were swept along with events that moved so rapidly there was little time for reflection. My father, always a team player, deferred to the decisions of the authorities, whom he trusted. His association with that tragic policy was brief—only four months—and his role was that of implementer rather than decision maker. Yet the impact of the internment remained with him, as it did with the country as a whole. As attorney general, Tom Clark supported the Japanese American citizens who lobbied Congress to provide restitution for the property losses they suffered during the internment. The result was the Japanese Evacuation Claims Act of 1948. Although the compensation provided by the act was pitifully inadequate, it was the first admission on the part of the government of the terrible injustice suffered by loyal Japanese American citizens during World War II.

Years later during an interview, my father cited another reason for his support of mass evacuation—the need to protect the Japanese from violence—and expressed thoughts that clearly reveal he had done some soul-searching and now considered the policy a mistake:

I found the final decision for removal of the Japanese to be based upon the physical dangers then facing 110,000 people of Japanese descent living in California, Oregon and Washington. I did not expect sabotage from Japanese residents; there had been none in Hawaii where the opportunity was greater. The ONI [Office of Naval Intelligence] and FBI had a tight oversight of all nationality groups, especially the Japanese . . . There was little strategic justification for the evacuation. . . . Honestly we didn't have any trouble with the Japanese. As a matter of fact the Japanese were not interned until I'd say April or May 1942, and we never suffered any sabotage either in Hawaii or on the west coast. As I look back on it, it was entirely unnecessary. Indeed the Department of Justice successfully handled a similar problem involving persons of German and Italian extraction, dealing with them on an individual basis rather than by mass incarceration.[40]

Not everyone involved in the policy underwent the same change. John

McCloy, a distinguished public servant and an adviser to every president from Roosevelt to Reagan, was the assistant secretary of war at the time of the internment and a major player in the decision. He continued to believe the policy had been necessary, and defended it in 1981 while testifying before the U.S. Commission on Wartime Relocation and Internment of Civilians. Earl Warren, who as chief justice of the Supreme Court was known as a champion of civil rights, found reexamination of the policy painful and difficult. He remained defensive and reluctant to discuss the subject of internment, and never apologized publicly during his lifetime. He did, however, express regret in his memoirs, published after his death in 1974.[41] Some not involved in formulating the policy have continued to defend it, including the late chief justice William Rehnquist, who in 1988 expressed the view that condemnation of the internment had gone too far and that the policy had been legitimate and appropriate for Japanese nationals.[42]

Clearly, my father felt a need to discuss this disastrous policy, openly expressing his regrets about it both verbally and in writing. In a preface to Frank Chuman's *The Bamboo People* and in an epilogue to Maisie and Richard Conrat's *Executive Order 9066*, he records the change in his views and his hopes that the country would learn from this dark episode in its history:

> As Civilian Coordinator, I found a complete lack of understanding, respect and regard for our fellow Japanese-Americans in the very communities where they were born, where they were reared, and where they worked. Some said they were too clannish, too race-conscious, too Emperor-oriented; that they would not cultivate American ways and could not be assimilated. But mutual understanding and respect are not a one-way street—to be loved and to be respected one must himself love and be respectful. Racial hatred, coupled with economic and political opportunism, kept hearts closed and fear predominant. It was a sad day in our constitutional history. . . .
>
> Let us determine to abide by the lessons that Executive Order 9066 teaches us. Even though malefactors might have been present—which was never proven—the liberty of the many cannot be forfeited because of the guilt of a few. The stubborn fact is our fellow Japanese-American citizens lost their liberty simply and only because of their ancestry.[43]

Looking back today, it is difficult to understand how a policy so clearly in opposition to the principles that this country prizes could have been enacted in the first place, much less subsequently affirmed by the Supreme

Court in *Korematsu* Justice finally prevailed, however, for in a 1984 rehearing of the case, U.S. district judge Marilyn Hall Patel rescinded Korematsu's conviction. (Fred Korematsu, an American-born citizen of Japanese descent, had been convicted of refusing to report to a relocation center.) In her ruling, Judge Patel stated: "As a historical precedent it [*Korematsu v. U.S.*] stands as a constant caution that in times of war or declared military necessity our institutions must be vigilant in protecting constitutional guarantees."[44] It is worth noting, however, that the Supreme Court has never overturned the original decision in *Korematsu* which still stands as a legal precedent and is, therefore, still the law of the land.

The decision for internment was not arrived at easily and can only be understood in the context of its times. Michi Weglyn, in *Years of Infamy: The Untold Story of America's Concentration Camps*, concludes that, for a cruel and unjust policy, it was implemented as humanely as possible: "Our internment camps were not allowed to become hell holes of starvation or death; many concerned Americans, military and civilian, saw to it that this did not happen, and in their hard, persistent work helped salvage our national honor."[45]

It is appropriate, however, that history, unencumbered by the emotions of that time, has rightly judged Executive Order 9066 to be a violation of the principles that this nation stands for. In retrospect, Tom Clark agreed, and was the first public official to openly apologize. "I have made a lot of mistakes in my life," he admitted ruefully in 1966, "but one that I acknowledge publicly is my part in the evacuation of the Japanese from California in 1942."[46]

## CHAPTER 7

# Beyond the Goal

[Tom Clark] has achieved a splendid reputation for efficiency, legal ability, industry and devotion to the high duties of his office.

Senator Tom Connally, 1943

B Y MAY 1942, TOM CLARK'S ROLE in the Japanese internment was completed. More than five years had passed since he moved to Washington in anticipation of becoming an assistant attorney general, yet he had still not achieved that position, despite continuing efforts to do so. A promising opportunity occurred in September 1941 when Matt McGuire, the assistant to the attorney general—the third-highest position in the Department of Justice—was appointed a judge of the U.S. District Court for the District of Columbia. Senator Tom Connally, Speaker of the House Sam Rayburn, Majority Leader John McCormack, and Congressman Lyndon Johnson were among those who recommended Tom Clark for the position. Roosevelt was noncommittal but said he would discuss the matter with Attorney General Biddle. A few weeks later, Jim Rowe, an administrative assistant to the president, was appointed. Rowe enjoyed a close relationship with FDR, and his influence was far greater than his official position indicated.

Tom Clark reacted graciously to the disappointing news. In a letter to Attorney General Biddle, he wrote: "In the appointment of Mr. Rowe, I know that you will have a man that will bring a vast experience to the office that I have not had the privilege of enjoying. He will make you an able 'right hand man' and I wish for both of you every success in your respective offices. If I can be of service to you, I trust that you will command me."[1]

He also sent a congratulatory letter to Jim Rowe, who was a close friend of Lyndon Johnson's. When the opening of the position was first known, Rowe indicated to Johnson that he was not interested. Subsequently, Johnson threw his full support to Tom Clark. Rowe describes Johnson's reaction to his appointment in his response to my father's letter:

I am sorry that I had to be the one to get in your way and I feel particularly badly about it because I do feel I misled you by sending word that I was not interested in the job. As a matter of fact, our mutual friend, Lyndon, had asked me some months ago whether I was interested and I told him flatly I was not. He spent the other evening at my house and had the pleasure of giving me unshirted Hell in his own inimitable fashion about it and I confess I had no ready answer. The only thing I can say is that I changed my mind for what were adequate personal reasons.[2]

My father's reaction to Rowe's appointment brought forth the following letter from Lyndon Johnson:

Dear Tom:

You are a prince. Jim Rowe called me after he had received your letter and told me he wanted to know you better and that he was putting your name on his list. I think the attitude you took in the matter was an extremely generous one, and I hope the next time we go to bat we will get better results.[3]

A great deal had occurred since this exchange of letters. The outbreak of World War II and the Japanese internment took precedence over everything else, and my father had given little thought to becoming an assistant attorney general during this hectic period. When, in the spring of 1942, Attorney General Biddle asked him to head the War Frauds Unit, an office Biddle established soon after Pearl Harbor, he accepted the assignment readily. On May 19, 1942, in an article entitled "Able Tom Clark named as Head of the War Frauds Bureau," the *Los Angeles Times* reported the appointment in glowing terms: "It is a fine thing that a man of his stature has been chosen to the tremendously important office of chief of the War Frauds Bureau, a position requiring calm judgment, expert knowledge and careful analysis of the law and the facts."

Once again the family prepared to move across the country. Mother spent a month in Washington, D.C., staying in Hatton Sumner's apartment while he campaigned in Texas. Housing was extremely difficult, but she found a new house to rent that was owned by a colonel who had been ordered overseas. No one wanted to repeat, in the opposite direction, the nightmarish trip west from two years earlier, so mother's sister Dorothy accompanied me on the train to Dallas, where I stayed with Grandmother Ramsey. Three weeks later I flew, for the first time, from Dallas to Washington, D.C., a flight that required three stops and took approximately eight hours.

My parents had arranged for Ramsey to attend a military school in Carlsbad, California, for a few weeks, so he also arrived in Washington after they had made the long drive across the country. Their trip east was beset with difficulties. The fully packed car held my parents; Betty, our young, attractive African American housekeeper; the family cocker spaniel, Blackie; and numerous boxes and belongings. The car had retreaded tires—new ones were virtually impossible to get because of the war—and was not supposed to be driven over fifty miles per hour. My father had a carbuncle on his back, which made driving extremely uncomfortable. Still, he was determined to take the longer, scenic northern route along what is now called the Buffalo Bill Cody Scenic Byway. As they drove farther east, many motels refused to admit Betty, and those that did accept her were often so dirty that she refused to stay in them. Ironically, but in keeping with the racism of the times, our cocker spaniel was accepted everywhere.

Washington seemed like a different city from the one we had left only two short years before. The war dominated the news and the minds of people everywhere. The outcome seemed far from certain during the summer of 1942. British forces were battling the Nazis in North Africa, and the Soviet Union was taking a beating on the eastern front. News from the Pacific was more encouraging, however. After a series of defeats, U.S. naval forces under Admiral Chester Nimitz turned back the Japanese at Midway Island—a victory that proved to be a turning point in the Pacific war.

Our family life was significantly altered, and the changes were especially difficult for Mother. No more the steady stream of visitors from Texas or the weekend trips to nearby spots of interest. The Washington summer was beastly hot, and Mother wondered whether she would survive without air conditioning, especially since our housekeeper, Betty, quickly returned to California, and Mother found herself without household help. My father worked long hours; we considered it a treat when he was home by seven thirty. Sundays were the one day when we could usually count on his presence. For Sunday breakfasts, my father often treated us to his specialty—silver dollar–sized hotcakes. Sometimes the four of us would play dominoes or work in our Victory Garden, located in the vacant lot two houses down from ours. He had so little free time that maintaining the garden and the yard—something he had always enjoyed—became a real problem, especially since Ramsey spent the summers working in Colorado. The grass would sometimes grow almost a foot high before my father found time to cut it.

We lived in a residential neighborhood considered far out at that time, although it was within the city limits. Transportation was a problem because of gas rationing, but my father bought a dilapidated 1938 Dodge from Thurman Arnold. The car, which the family dubbed "Thurman," had multicolored fenders and could not be relied upon to start each morning. Fortunately, we lived on a hill on the edge of Rock Creek Park, and my father was often able to start the car by coasting downhill and into the park. Mother drove the Buick they had bought before our move to California, but could go only short distances because of the gas rationing. She would drive to Connecticut Avenue, where she could catch a bus to downtown Washington. Ramsey and I walked to school—for me a reasonable eight blocks to the Lafayette School, but for him a hike of more than two miles to Alice Deal Junior High and to Woodrow Wilson High School the following year.

The War Frauds Unit was established within the Department of Justice's Criminal Division in order to avoid repeating the mistakes made during World War I, when no prosecutions were undertaken until after the war ended. The government had been largely unsuccessful in those prosecutions because witnesses disappeared, records were destroyed, and general apathy allowed statutes of limitations to run out. In contrast, the antifraud effort during World War II was aggressive and successful. Cases of war fraud were identified by the FBI, which created special units in key field offices to identify and concentrate on fraudulent activities. Typical cases involved the padding of expense accounts in cost-plus fixed-fee contracts; the filing of collusive bids to prevent competition; and conspiring with procurement officers to approve inferior materials. By December 1, 1943, the War Frauds Unit had handled more than 3,000 complaints, and grand juries throughout the country had handed down 176 indictments, 92 percent of which were successfully prosecuted.[4] In addition, the government prosecuted 135 cases of sabotage, winning all but one. Fines collected from war-fraud cases brought in more than half a million dollars—twice the cost of operating the unit. When complimented on the unit's high rate of success, my father expressed his personal philosophy: "A good lawyer never files a suit unless he's sure he'll win."[5]

Tom Clark's successes as head of the War Frauds Unit strengthened his chances of becoming an assistant attorney general as he once again sought that position. An opportunity arose in January 1943 when Thurman Arnold was appointed a judge on the U.S. Court of Appeals for the District of Columbia Circuit, opening the position of assistant attorney general of the Antitrust Division. Tom Clark's supporters went into action, and on January 16, 1943, Senator Connally wrote the following letter to President Roosevelt:

Since Mr. Clark's first connection with the Department of Justice, he has risen steadily in the esteem of the Department and has achieved a splendid reputation for efficiency, legal ability, industry and devotion to the high duties of his office. . . . It occurs to me that the promotion of worthy assistants contributes to the best possible morale in a department. . . . It would seem most fitting to me that he should be appointed as an Assistant Attorney General in charge of the Antitrust Division. I have known Mr. Clark personally for many years, and I am deeply interested in his service and in his welfare.[6]

This time the effort was successful, and on March 16, 1943, Tom Clark became an assistant attorney general.

No sooner had the appointment gone through than a major reorganization took place within the Department of Justice. The criminal functions of the department were scattered throughout various divisions. Attorney General Biddle decided they should be pulled together and placed under the jurisdiction of the Criminal Division. The attorney general had the authority to switch assistant attorneys general from one division to another without confirmation by the Senate, so Tom Clark was transferred to the Criminal Division—an appropriate choice since the War Frauds cases were within that division—and Wendell Berge became assistant attorney general of the Antitrust Division.

My father immediately began to reorganize the division into six anti-crime units. His purpose was to give more authority to local attorneys and to speed up the legal process. The division received more than 14,000 cases each month, and according to an article in the June 12, 1944, issue of *Newsweek* entitled "Calm Tom," his position was "the hottest legal seat in the country." Clark's telephone, according to the article, rang every three minutes. He gave orders into a "talking box" and showed impatience if they were not executed promptly. No one in the department, however, had ever heard him raise his voice or appear excited. When asked about his long hours, my father made a typically self-deprecating comment: "I have to work long hours," he responded, "because I'm not as smart as some other fellows."[7]

One of the most publicized war-fraud cases involved the Anaconda Wire and Cable Company. The company and some of its officers were charged with manufacturing defective cable and communication wires in its Fort Wayne, Indiana, and Pawtucket, Rhode Island, plants. The problem had come to light because of complaints from the Soviet Union, which had received some of the defective materials. The FBI obtained evidence showing that special circuit breakers, button boxes, and other devices were being used to prevent required Signal Corps resistance tests from picking up the flaws. The army immediately held onto all wire coming from those plants so that it would not be shipped to combat zones. Tom Clark oversaw the successful prosecution of the case. The harshest penalties were given to managers at the Rhode Island plant, where defendants were sent to jail without bond—eighteen months for the two highest officials, fifteen months and a year for others. Subsequently, the company placed new inspection safeguards in the plants to prevent any future fraud.[8]

In January 1945, Attorney General Biddle selected Tom Clark to prosecute two German agents captured by the FBI—William C. Colepaugh, an American citizen who had volunteered his services to Germany, and Erich Gimpel, a native of Germany. The two men stole into the country via a German submarine, entering at Frenchman's Bay, Maine, on November 29, 1944. They were captured by the FBI a few weeks later after Colepaugh, citing a "guilty conscience," turned himself in. The trial was held before a military commission on Governor's Island, New York, and was only the third of its kind in the history of the country. The first followed Lincoln's assassination, and the second, held in 1943, was a case prosecuted by Attorney General Biddle himself against seven Nazi agents. The government's case was strong, and both men were convicted and sentenced to death. After the war in Europe ended, President Truman commuted the death sentences to life imprisonment. In the case of Gimpel, the president cited international law, which states that espionage is an accepted practice in wartime and not a crime. Gimpel was deported to Germany. Colepaugh's commutation was based on the fact that he had turned himself in and provided crucial information to prosecutors. He was paroled in 1960.

Tom Clark worked closely with FBI agents and Director J. Edgar Hoover on the Colepaugh-Gimpel espionage case and on many others. Letters exchanged between the two men indicate a cordial relationship and carry no hint of the tensions that would develop after my father became attorney general. In one note, my father thanked Hoover for "the splendid results we are getting from the Bureau."[9] Hoover replied:"I want you to know that it has been a pleasure for us to work with you . . . and your thoughtful expressions are a real source of encouragement to me during this period when the FBI is shouldering the greatest responsibilities it has ever been called upon to meet."[10]

Hoover sent a personal letter of condolence on October 16, 1943, after my father's forty-six-year-old brother Bill Clark was killed in an airplane accident during takeoff from the Nashville, Tennessee, airport. In his response to Hoover's letter, my father expressed his appreciation and requested any additional information the FBI might have on the crash, which was apparently caused by turbulent weather. Family members turned to my father in times of trouble. We went to Dallas for Christmas that year and stayed with Bill's family, hoping to help his widow, Martha, and their three young sons during this painful period. My father also worked with the airline's insurance representatives to obtain a fair settlement from the accident. A letter from his younger brother Bob Clark reflects the high expectations some family members had of my father:

She [Martha Clark] sees in you a miracle man possessed of greater powers and means and ways of getting people to do the right thing and what you want done and of doing the impossible than any mystic ever to gaze into a crystal ball.

The letter continued in a different vein:

I'm happy to know you're interested in the idea of a partnership with me in the law business. Guess you'll have your mind made up and know pretty well when you can leave up there by the time you get here Christmas. I've been spending all of my time on Martha's affairs and haven't given any attention to my own or the future.[11]

Clearly, my father was contemplating a return to Dallas. He had achieved his goal of becoming an assistant attorney general and felt that his career with the government was at a dead end. He was still not ready to make the break, however. He was deeply committed to his work and did not intend to leave until he felt satisfied that he had completed certain projects to the best of his ability. He had no inkling that his association with the junior senator from Missouri would have a dramatic effect on his future.

Tom Clark first met Harry Truman through his work with the War Frauds Office, and their association continued and broadened after he became an assistant attorney general. Senator Truman was chairman of the Senate Special Committee to Investigate the National Defense Program, known as the Truman Committee—a position that brought him national recognition and was largely responsible for his becoming vice president in 1944. As head of the War Frauds Unit, Tom Clark became the liaison between the committee and the Department of Justice. The two men hit it off immediately. They shared many of the same values and characteristics, such as unpretentiousness, loyalty, and a can-do attitude. My father provided the following description of his relations with the Truman Committee and its chairman:

> As head of the War Fraud Section, I used to go up to see Mr. Truman quite often, beginning about 1942. . . . We worked hand-in-glove. There was tremendous cooperation. . . . Well, we went all over the United States. The Committee did a tremendous job on it [war frauds], and of course it brought Senator Truman notice with the public.[12]

They traveled together on a number of occasions and were once snowed in at the Buffalo, New York, airport. Senator Truman's flight was canceled, but my father had a later reservation. The weather cleared, and since Truman was anxious to get back to Washington for an important Senate vote, my father gave the senator his airline ticket. Senator Truman was most appreciative and did not forget the favor.

The election of 1944 was approaching, and with Roosevelt a shoo-in for the presidential nomination, the competition for the vice presidency provided the greatest interest and activity. The current vice president, Henry Wallace, had become unpopular, and was perceived by many as a leftist and a communist sympathizer. A majority of Democratic leaders opposed a second term for him. Tom Clark supported Sam Rayburn for vice president, although years later he described Wallace as "a very able and honorable man, [who had] served well during Mr. Roosevelt's terms not only as the Secretary [of Agriculture] but as the Vice President."[13] Harry Truman also supported Speaker Rayburn, and Rayburn, according to his private correspondence, wanted the nomination.[14] He was still on the president's short list of acceptable candidates a few days before the convention began, although FDR may have preferred to keep Rayburn in Congress, where his powerful leadership as Speaker would be of more help. The greatest opposition to his nomination came from the Texas delegation. Texas was still a one-party state in 1944, but it was sharply divided into two camps: pro–New Dealers and anti–New Dealers. Wealthy, conservative Texans despised Roosevelt and opposed Rayburn because of his close association with the president. They were able to place like-minded Democrats as delegates to the national convention, and Rayburn, despite his position as Speaker of the House, was not selected. The conservatives also mounted a challenge to Rayburn's congressional seat, forcing him to stay at home to campaign. Rayburn's supporters urged him to come to the convention, and Tom Clark called him in an effort to persuade him to do so, but Rayburn could not be convinced. His fears proved to be unfounded, for he was reelected by a substantial number of votes. Nevertheless, the lack of support from his own state delegation killed his chances for the vice presidential nomination.

As soon as it was clear that he would not get the nomination, Rayburn and his supporters, including Tom Clark, Lyndon Johnson, and Senator Tom Connally, threw their support behind Harry Truman. Subsequently, Truman became FDR's running mate. My father actively campaigned for the Democratic ticket, and in a speech before the Women's National Democratic Club, spoke highly of the vice presidential candidate: "Senator Truman is making a great candidate for the Vice Presidency. His work on the Truman Investigating Committee has been one of the greatest services given our government during the war. Not only millions of dollars have been saved by his watchfulness, but his tremendous activity has, beyond question, saved thousands of American lives . . . The American people are fortunate in having an opportunity to vote for such an outstanding Democrat."[15]

The Roosevelt–Truman ticket was victorious, and with the election over and Francis Biddle still attorney general, my parents planned to return to Dallas as soon as Ramsey graduated from high school that spring. Then the unexpected occurred. On April 12, 1945, my father was speaking at a Jefferson–Jackson Day dinner in Arizona. Ramsey was in the hospital, recuperating from a hernia operation. Mother and I visited him there before going out to dinner with Nash and Lois Adams, good friends of my parents. Mr. Adams picked us up at the hospital and drove us to his home. As soon as we arrived, Mrs. Adams opened the door. It was clear from the expression on her face that something had happened. "Have you heard the news?" she asked. My first thought was that the war was over. "President Roosevelt died," she said, before we could answer. We were stunned. At twelve years old, I had never known another president, and there was a profound sense of loss. The fact that Roosevelt's death would have a major impact on our personal lives did not enter my mind.

## CHAPTER 8

# The President's Lawyer

We are there to see that "simple justice" is done in every case.

Tom C. Clark, 1945

A SHOCKED NATION MOURNED THE PASSING of a president who had led it through two of the most difficult crises in its history: the Great Depression and World War II. In his memoirs, Harry S. Truman described a grieving population: "I shall never forget the sight of so many grief-stricken people. Some wept without restraint. Some shed their tears in silence. Others were grim and stoic, but all were genuine in their mourning."[1]

People were also fearful. The end of the war was in sight but not yet achieved. Truman was relatively unknown, and many doubted his ability to effectively pick up the reins of government and lead the country during this critical juncture. Although a loyal Democrat and New Dealer, Truman was not a member of the eastern establishment that had dominated the Democratic Party for twelve years, and many in that group viewed him as woefully inadequate to follow Roosevelt. Despite these doubts, Harry S. Truman took charge. Within a few weeks he had chosen his cabinet—all men, half of whom were from west of the Mississippi, who reflected his own down-to-earth attitude and basic values.

Neither Ramsey nor I recall any family discussions during the weeks preceding our father's appointment as attorney general. Ramsey knew the appointment was a possibility but understood that it was best not to talk about it. There was no inkling, as far as I was concerned, of the momentous event that was about to occur in our lives, although I did wonder what my father meant when he joked, "Let's put the latch on Hatch," a reference to Senator Carl Hatch of New Mexico, who had served on the Truman Committee and was a good friend and supporter of the president. Hatch, apparently aware that Tom Clark was being considered for attorney general, had misgivings, and sent a memo to FBI director J. Edgar Hoover, inquiring about the 1936 Texas Senate subcommittee investigation. In a phone call to Hatch, Hoover described the FBI investigation of Clark as "entirely favorable."[2] Hatch was one of a small number of detractors, and my father enjoyed strong support from influential politicians including Democratic national chairman Bob Hannegan, Speaker of the House Sam Rayburn, Senator Tom Connally, and Congressman Lyndon Johnson.

Mother was fully aware of the developing situation, but her ability to keep a secret was unsurpassed, and she gave no hint of what must have been a suspenseful time for both her and my father. On May 23, 1945, she was preparing to have lunch with friends at the Mayflower Hotel. Just as she was leaving the house, the phone rang. My father was calling from a public telephone booth to tell her that his appointment as attorney general would be announced that afternoon. Mother went to lunch, but did not divulge any information to the group of good friends who attended, even though they speculated on who would be chosen for the position. Afterward, as Mother left the hotel, she saw newspaper columnist Elizabeth Churchill. Mother waved but did not stop to speak. She was surprised and annoyed a few days later when Churchill claimed in her column, "Town Talk," that Mrs. Clark had told her of the appointment when they saw each other at the Mayflower Hotel.[3] It was Mother's first lesson in the media's ability to stretch the truth.

Despite initial skepticism about his competence, Truman was enjoying the honeymoon stage of his presidency, and his appointees were confirmed with little controversy. Tom Clark's appointment was reported favorably in the newspapers, but Senator Hatch raised questions about the 1936 Texas Senate investigation when the Senate Judiciary Committee reviewed the nomination. Testifying before the committee in two closed sessions, Tom Clark impressed the senators with his frank responses to their questions, which focused largely on the increase in his income during the 1930s. Satisfied, Senator Hatch declared that Clark "made a good witness. The whole matter of the Texas investigation and the Texas Senate report was laid before the committee. . . . Mr. Clark made satisfactory answers to all criticism that had been leveled against him."[4]

The Judiciary Committee approved his nomination unanimously on June 14, 1945. The swearing-in ceremony, held in the great hall of the Department of Justice, was attended by a gathering of 1,500 people, including a large number of Texans who came to see a son of Texas attain the office of attorney general for only the second time. (The first, Thomas

Watt Gregory, served under Woodrow Wilson.) Dallas relatives who traveled to Washington for the ceremony included Grandmother Clark, my father's brother Bob and his family, and another nephew, Whit Clark, the son of his deceased brother Bill. Longtime supporters Congressmen Hatton Sumners and Sam Rayburn also attended, and Senator Tom Connally spoke briefly as part of the ceremony. Those who knew my father well were surprised that he chose a traditional four-in-hand, rather than his trademark bow tie, to wear with his dark blue business suit.

His former boss Thurman Arnold, now a judge on the U.S. Court of Appeals for the District of Columbia, delivered the oath of office, and outgoing attorney general Francis Biddle served as master of ceremonies. In a brief speech following the ceremony, my father attributed his success to his wife and mother and praised his immediate predecessor, Francis Biddle. Fred Vinson, at that time the director of War Mobilization and Reconversion, commented on the congenial relationship between the new attorney general and the former one.[5] The cordial atmosphere of the swearing-in ceremony masked the more complex relationship that had developed between the two men.

President Truman and Attorney General Biddle recorded conflicting versions of the way the change in attorneys general was handled. In his memoirs, Truman wrote that he did not ask Biddle to resign, but that Biddle chose to do so and recommended Tom Clark as his successor. Biddle's recollections were very different from the president's. He described learning that Truman wanted his resignation through presidential secretary Steve Early. Unhappy with the way he was being dismissed, Biddle contacted Truman immediately, and within an hour he was in the president's office. When told that Tom Clark would be the new attorney general, Biddle was not pleased, noting he would not have recommended him. Then, according to Biddle, he asked Truman whether he knew Tom Clark.[6] Biddle's claim that the president responded negatively to this question is clearly incorrect. Truman would never have denied knowing Tom Clark, and Biddle must have known that my father had worked closely with Senator Truman on war-fraud cases. Despite the flawed account, however, Biddle was obviously unhappy with his dismissal and with my father's appointment.

Lawyers close to Biddle within the Department of Justice were also unhappy about his successor. John Frank, who did not know my father personally at the time, described a morose gathering of Biddle loyalists after the appointment was announced. Frank admitted that it was the one time in his professional career that he went home drunk. Years later, after my father was on the Supreme Court, Frank's views changed drastically.

In a 1999 letter to me, he wrote: "When Tom went to the Supreme Court ...I rapidly became acquainted with your father and very quickly became captive, not merely to his charm, but also to his wisdom."[7]

Not all lawyers within the department shared the Biddle loyalists' dismay. On May 27, 1945, a *Washington Star* article by George Kennedy quoted an unnamed Department of Justice lawyer's assessment of Tom Clark:

> I want to tell you, there never was an appointment of an Attorney General that was more popular in the department. This man has come up from the ranks of lawyers here. He has been in the field. He knows their problems. When he hears a lawyer in the Criminal Division has won a tough case, he writes him a congratulatory note. In long hand. He carries on a large correspondence with lawyers in the division who are away in uniform. He walks around, talks to people, asks them how they are doing. The other day he was in the stenographers' pool, asking about their light. One girl said more light would help. A little later a messenger was in with a tube-light desk lamp for her—the kind that are issued here to executives. He took it off his own desk. His secretary could wrestle with the problem of getting him another.

Letters of congratulations poured in from a variety of sources, including at least one well-known New Dealer, Tommy Corcoran, who wrote: "I can think of no one who better knows the Department, who has more of the affection of the people in it, or who has more opportunity for a great life. To be Attorney General at 45 is in the Great Tradition. I know you and Mary will be worthy of it."[8] Former boss Thurman Arnold sent congratulations: "It certainly proves that the boys in the Antitrust Division finally make good." To which my father responded, "Right you are, but I would add *when Arnold trains them.*"

The sheriff of Los Angeles County, Eugene Biscailuz, who had worked with my father during the Japanese internment, wrote: "I remember so well your helpfulness to me when you were here in 1942, when you were directing the arrangements for the Department of Justice in the internment of those Japanese who were in Southern California. Your appointment has been very gratifying, not only to me personally, but to numerous other of Southern Californians who I know feel just as I do." Even FBI Director J. Edgar Hoover seemed pleased:

Dear Tom,
Your appointment as Attorney General is indeed gratifying and I want to

extend my heartfelt congratulations. I know you will fill the position with distinction and will do a grand job. You may be assured of my personal and official cooperation.

And at least one person from the entertainment world joined in the congratulations. Comedian Milton Berle, whom my father knew slightly through Irving Kaufman, a future judge who would become well known for the Rosenberg treason case, wrote: "Mrs. Berle and I were overjoyed at the wonderful news of your appointment. Irving Kaufman had talked so much about your charm and personality within recent weeks that I was just about getting ready to find a part for you in my new show."

Tom Clark immediately strove to bring the office of attorney general closer to the people and to establish the informal work environment that he was comfortable with. He pledged an "open door" policy toward staff members and set up a suggestion box outside his office. On July 14, 1945, he sent the following memo to all employees:

To my Associates in "Justice":
For two weeks I have served as Attorney General. It is my ambition to serve well. To do this each of us must perform the everyday duties as assigned to us. It is the "team work" that gets the job done. You are an important member of that team.

I deeply appreciate your renewed efforts and loyalty. Together we shall meet the problems and solve them. Your suggestions for improvement of our work would be most helpful. A "suggestion box" is being placed in the hall outside my door. I hope you will make suggestions freely thru this box or direct by mail to me.

Yours for the greatest Department of Justice ever,
Tom Clark

One of the department lawyers, who later became a good friend of my father's, expressed his appreciation of the memo in a lengthy letter:

Dear Tom Clark:
Your note of July 14, 1945 which, as one of your fellow-workers, I had the pleasure of receiving, was unique and unprecedented and raised the morale of us all . . .

By raising the self-respect of the average department lawyer, eliminating condescension towards him by persons who enjoy mainly their own company, a new spirit of cooperation will follow. The ineffable memory that I hope always to retain is the look of pride and affection on your face as you presented your mother, Mrs. Clark, and your son and daughter to your fellow workers. Life is so short and so arduous at best. For the first time I have been made to feel that in our chief we have a friend. May we prove worthy of that friendship.

Sincerely yours,<br>
Lewis C. Cassidy[9]

Tom Clark's warm and friendly style was accompanied by high expectations of total commitment by those who worked for him. He made it illegal for federal attorneys to maintain private law practices: "They must give the government their undivided attention. Their hearts, minds and their souls must be in their work."[10] A memo sent to his staff and the assistant attorneys general required that they answer all letters within twenty-four hours if possible, and if not, that they should send an acknowledgment followed by a final reply within five days: "No letters should remain unanswered. As we are public servants, every person writing to this Department is entitled to a courteous acknowledgement or reply."[11] He also suggested that the tone of the letters should be as informal as possible and as personal as appropriate.

During a speech in Dallas in October 1945, Tom Clark described his goals as attorney general:

I hope I can instill in the hearts of the 27,000 persons who work with me in the Department the understanding that as the people's lawyers . . . we are there to see that "simple justice" is done in every case. We represent all the people. We must see that the guilty are punished—and we shall—but with like fervor we must protect the innocent. Constitutional guarantees must be held inviolate, civil liberties must be insured.[12]

He also expressed his high regard for the new president:

And what a president he is—an every day American like you and me—with high purposes, unfailing courage, a quick, well-informed mind, and the stamina of a Missouri mule. He will make a great President. He has but one purpose—to serve you—and that purpose is ignited by an overwhelming passion and determination to serve you well.

The transition from war to peacetime created myriad problems for the new administration, and Truman's handling of the transition was, in my father's view, his most significant accomplishment. One of the first issues dealt with, and one that was agreed upon by all the Allies, was the handling of war-crimes trials. It was agreed that persons responsible for the war should be tried by an international tribunal and punished if found guilty.

My father's involvement in the war-crimes trials was limited, but in the case of Japan, important. He appointed Department of Justice lawyers to prosecute the Tokyo trials and recommended Joseph Keenan, a former assistant attorney general who had been a close adviser of Roosevelt's, as the chief prosecutor. Once he had completed these appointments, he was not directly involved in the Japanese trials and did not attend them. He and Mother did attend the Nuremberg Trials, traveling to Europe in July 1946 to be present at their opening. I remained behind, staying with my close friend Rose Caudle, whose father was assistant attorney general of the Criminal Division. My parents flew from Washington to Paris on an old army plane that had been used to carry troops. The trip took eighteen hours. Ramsey was a marine corporal serving as a courier, and was stationed in Paris at that time. He joined them there, and the three continued on to Berlin and Nuremberg.

In Berlin, they stayed at the army's guesthouse, and were shown around the city by Kay Summersby, General Eisenhower's military aide. They were shocked at the devastation caused by the Allies' bombing. Mother wrote the following description of the city in her diary: "It was the grimmest city I have ever been in. The war was written on their [German people's] faces. . . . It seemed out of place to be enjoying oneself." They stayed at the Grand Hotel in a suite that Hitler had supposedly used; from the hotel window, they could look out at the ruins of the city. My father had brought a supply of cigars, which he smoked at that time, and used them to tip people. Cigars and cigarettes were scarce and expensive in postwar Germany, and one cigar was worth about twenty dollars.

After they returned to Washington, my father sent a memo to President Truman, expressing his support of the trials and powerfully condemning the perpetrators of war:

> The trial for war crimes established . . . that the waging of an international war is an international crime and those responsible for its conduct must be punished. By its judgment the Tribunal repudiated once and for all the doctrine that resort to war is a legitimate instrument of statecraft. . . . Now at last we have recognized that the supreme crime is the murder of innocent peoples by those who lead aggressive wars. . . . The Allied nations and the United States are attempting to apprehend and bring to justice all

German and Japanese war criminals and to mete out to them the punishment which they deserve for the destruction and havoc they have inflicted upon the world.[13]

At the time, he did not express opposition to Associate Justice Robert Jackson's appointment as chief prosecutor of the Nuremberg Trials, but did so years later, after he had retired from the Supreme Court: "He [Jackson] should never have been prosecutor on the Nuremberg Trials. That was a great mistake. Justices should not accept these outside appointments while they are sitting on the court. I love Bob. He carried off his Nuremberg assignment superbly. However, I don't agree with the Nuremberg [appointment]."[14]

The Nuremberg and Japanese trials were an unprecedented effort to establish a just and open means of bringing perpetrators of war to justice. Harry Truman faced other unprecedented issues during the early months of his presidency. Tom Clark agreed with the president's most difficult and still-debated decision—to drop the atomic bomb on Japan—but disagreed with Truman's initial inclinations on a second, related issue: the sharing of scientific information, specifically on atomic energy development, with other nations, especially the Soviet Union. Outgoing secretary of state Henry L. Stimson stressed that scientific knowledge could not be kept secret in the same way that weapon development could, and that the challenge was to develop effective, secure, and mutually beneficial communication between nations. He advocated an exchange of scientific findings between the Soviet Union and the United States, with safeguards to ensure a mutual sharing of knowledge. Robert Patterson, who would succeed Stimson as secretary of state, agreed that an exchange should be established. Secretary of the Treasury Vinson objected strongly to their proposed policy, and Tom Clark and Secretary of the Navy James Forrestal sided with him. Forrestal asked that "no precipitate action" be taken, and pointed out that there was a military aspect to sharing the information. The debate was lively; cabinet members were almost evenly divided on the issue. My father recalled the meeting years later: "I rather think that Mr. Truman was favorable to giving the atomic bomb formula to Russia. I voted against it and so did Vinson. The cabinet voted against it and the president decided not to do it."[15]

As Harry Truman was dealing with these important issues, he was also establishing a style and working relationship with his cabinet members. He held a full cabinet meeting every Friday and lunch once a week with a select group whose membership rotated. My father provided the following descriptions of the cabinet meetings:

A quiet man is seated at the head of the table. He is friendly, and he asks for each of us by name. He asks about the wives and children. Then the business of the day begins. . . . People ask me everywhere what sort of fellow he is. I will say that he is a real American, and he can keep his head when a lot of people all over the world are losing theirs.[16]

I have seen him decide the issues and decide them with that rare judgment, with that uncanny accuracy that comes from one, who, like you and me, is of the people. A great Missourian who has that common ordinary horse sense that today leads us to victory in the peace.[17]

According to my father, President Truman let cabinet officers run their departments without interference: "He never did interfere—never asked me to bring a suit or to slow down on one. He never was critical although I got a lot of criticism otherwise. . . . But at no time . . . did he ever criticize my action."[18]

Criticism from other sources began soon after Tom Clark took office. On May 29, 1945, just a few days after my father's appointment, Attorney General Biddle filed suit against the Pacific Western Oil Corporation, which was extracting oil off the coast of California. This, the first of the tidelands cases, put Tom Clark in immediate trouble with his beloved Texas. The case was on my father's desk his first day in office, and the timing made him suspect that it was a deliberate effort to embarrass him on the part of Biddle loyalists. In a 1972 interview, my father described the tidelands case as "one of the worst experiences I had when I was Attorney General."[19]

The dispute was over the ownership of coastal lands lying between low tide and the three-mile limit that had been traditionally regarded as the beginning of the federal governments' ownership. The case, *United States v. California*, went all the way to the Supreme Court, and was argued on March 13, 1947, by Attorney General Clark. On June 23, 1947, the Supreme Court ruled that the federal government had always had "paramount rights in and full dominion and power" over the tidelands and its resources. Tom Clark would have liked to end the matter in California, but Texas and Louisiana had filed amicus curiae (friend-of-the-court) briefs supporting California, and this forced him to bring suit against those states. Oil was at the center of the controversy, and Texans were distressed and angry that the attorney general, a Texan whom they had considered their friend, would support the federal government's claim over the state's. My father received scurrilous phone calls, and mail poured in from outraged Texans who called him a traitor, a thief, and other derogatory terms. Although he had a few defenders, in 1948 the state Democratic convention, under the leadership of Governor Beauford Jester, rejected him as a delegate to the national convention, and Texas national committeeman Wright Morrow expressed his "hearty approval" because of Clark's position on the tidelands issue.[20] The break with Texas was painful for my father, but he was now "the president's lawyer," and as such he was responsible for the whole nation.

Attorney General Clark received a second flood of outraged letters in the fall of 1946 when he fired John Rogge, a special assistant attorney general. Rogge had been assistant attorney general of the Criminal Division in the late 1930s but had left the government for private practice. He returned in 1943 at the request of Attorney General Biddle, who asked him to investigate two sedition cases, *U.S. v. McWilliams* and *U.S. v. Winrod*. Both involved pro-Nazi Americans. In March 1946, after my father became attorney general, Rogge recommended that the government drop the cases, citing his belief that the Supreme Court would reverse any verdict the government succeeded in obtaining. The new attorney general did not agree, and Rogge was sent to Germany to obtain more evidence and to investigate the German government's involvement with American supporters of Nazi Germany.

In September 1946, Rogge produced a 300-plus-page report alleging that during World War II, the Nazis had attempted to manipulate our country's political system through a number of prominent Americans. The report charged that the Nazis used a group including Senator Burton Wheeler of Ohio, labor leader John L. Lewis, famed aviator Charles Lindbergh, *Readers' Digest* editor DeWitt Wallace, and several congressmen for propaganda purposes in order to influence U.S. foreign policy.[21] Attorney General Clark felt the charges made in the report, which was confidential material within the Department of Justice, were unsubstantiated and could damage the reputations of innocent people. He refused to release it. Determined to make the report public, Rogge leaked information to columnist Drew Pearson, who included excerpts in his column. In addition, Rogge quoted directly from the report in a speech he delivered on October 22, 1946, at Swarthmore College. In the exchange of letters that resulted, Rogge claimed that Clark had given him permission to make public any evidence he obtained about the case. Tom Clark emphatically denied giving permission, and charged that Rogge had told him he would not use the report in speeches and had agreed that it would be "highly unethical" to do so.[22]

On October 25, Clark fired Rogge, stating "It appears that you willfully violated the long-standing rules and regulations of the Department of Justice."[23] The firing created a furor in some quarters, especially after popular news commentator Walter Winchell tore into Clark on his weekly radio broadcast. Within the next four days, Clark received 26,000 letters protesting the firing. "Oh, boy," my father mused in an interview years later, "he [Walter Winchell] really gave me the devil about Rogge!"[24]

Despite the controversies and the dramatic change in our lives, my parents succeeded in maintaining a normal home environment. We had moved from the house we rented on the outskirts of the city to an apartment closer to downtown Washington. Since the government provided the attorney general with a car and chauffeur, we no longer owned a car, but public transportation was excellent and convenient. The bus stopped right in front of the apartment building, and the streetcar only a block away. Walking and public transportation were my favorite modes of travel, for the car and chauffeur that the government provided were a source of great embarrassment to me, a young girl who did not want to be different from her friends in any way. A seventh grader, I could walk to the Holton-Arms School, only three blocks away on S Street. I loved the school and, despite the car and chauffeur, was happy with our new life. I also appreciated the special opportunities that I was experiencing, such as attending the Supreme Court session when my father argued the United Mine Workers case. I was very nervous for my father as he presented the government's case, and was especially disturbed when Justice Felix Frankfurter questioned him. Mother was amused when I confided to her afterward that I didn't like Justice Frankfurter. My opinion changed with maturity.

The United Mine Workers case was the culmination of an ongoing conflict between the union's dynamic leader, John L. Lewis, and President Truman. It also reflected the difficult months of adjustment after World War II, when labor unrest increased significantly. Several industries were threatening to strike, and coal miners had been on strike for several weeks. At that time, coal was used for 95 percent of all locomotives, 62 percent of electrical power, and 55 percent of industrial energy.[25] In May 1946, while 400,000 coal miners were on strike, a nationwide railroad strike became imminent. If coal miners and railroad workers struck simultaneously, the country would be paralyzed.

Truman's dislike for Lewis dated back to the days when Lewis testified before the Truman Committee.[26] The labor leader's flamboyant style was not admired by the no-nonsense president, and Truman viewed the coal strikes that had occurred during World War II almost as a form of treason. As negotiations to prevent a railroad strike and end the coal strike floundered, his frustration turned to anger. On May 24, 1946, he called a special meeting of the cabinet, "not to solicit their ideas but to tell them what he was going to do."[27] He announced that he would call out the army to break the railroad strike if strikers did not return by 4 p.m. the next day; and, in addition, he would draft all striking workers into the army if national security were at stake. The latter announcement stunned the group into silence. Finally, Attorney General Clark questioned the constitutionality of such a move. Truman replied, "We'll draft them and think about the law later."[28]

My father quickly put his concerns in writing: "The Draft Act does not permit the induction of occupational groups and it is doubtful whether constitutional powers of the President would include the right to draft individuals for national purposes." Others voiced opposition, but Truman would not budge. Despite severe doubts about the legality of the legislation, Attorney General Clark, Assistant Solicitor General George Washington, and three other Department of Justice lawyers stayed up all night to draft a bill for the president to present to Congress the next day.[29] On May 25, 1946, at 4 p.m., a grim President Truman appeared before a packed House of Representatives. As the president spoke, Les Biffle, the secretary of the Senate, handed him a note informing him that the coal strike had been settled. Truman announced the news, and Congress erupted with cheering. Nevertheless, Truman continued his speech and asked for "temporary emergency" legislation that would allow him to draft strikers. The bill passed overwhelmingly in the House but was killed in the Senate, largely through the efforts of Senator Robert Taft. The defeat was unimportant, for the crisis was averted and the questionable legislation was no longer needed.

The crisis ended, but only temporarily. Six months later, on the eve of national elections, Lewis demanded renegotiation of the contract that he and Secretary of the Interior Julius Krug had signed in May, and ordered coal miners to strike. Presidential advisers were divided on how to handle Lewis. White House assistant John Steelman and Secretary of Labor Lewis Schwellenbach opposed confrontation, advising the president to reopen negotiations. White House aide Clark Clifford argued adamantly for a tough stand against Lewis, and was supported by Secretary of the Interior Krug and Attorney General Clark. The latter group prevailed, and subsequently Truman directed the attorney general to take Lewis to court and get an injunction to stop the strike. Clark succeeded in doing so. Lewis, however, ignored the court order. Clark then requested that the judge cite Lewis for contempt of court. Judge T. Alan Goldsborough found the United Mine Workers and Lewis guilty of contempt and imposed the incredibly high fine of $3.5 million against the union and $10,000 against Lewis.

Lewis appealed to the Supreme Court, and on January 15, 1947, the government presented its case. Tom Clark opened the proceedings by describing Lewis's refusal to obey the court order as "an insult" to the nation and an invitation to "mob rule." He also argued that "surely Government has the authority and the power to defend itself against destruction from within—as it has the duty to defend the country from destruction without."[30] In March 1947, the Court voted 7–2 in favor of the government. It also reduced the amount of the union's fine to a more reasonable $700,000, but maintained the $10,000 fine against Lewis. The Truman administration exulted in its victory!

During a 1948 presidential campaign speech for Truman, Tom Clark cited the victory, but made a slip of the tongue when he said that Truman had "taken down Joe Louis," the great heavyweight boxing champion. Truman responded quickly: "You give me too much credit, Tom. It wasn't Joe, it was John Lewis that I stopped in Federal Courts."[31]

## CHAPTER 9

# Juvenile Delinquency and the Freedom Train

Attorney General Tom Clark . . . has embarked on one of the most unusual crusades ever undertaken by a cabinet officer.

*Boston Post*, February 7, 1946

E ACH NEW ADMINISTRATION is swept into a powerful stream of current issues that must be dealt with immediately, and individual cabinet members inherit, rather than select, most of the controversies that face them. Opportunities for choice do exist, however, and the independent projects that cabinet members undertake often reveal a great deal about their priorities and characters. Tom Clark initiated two major projects as attorney general: a campaign against juvenile delinquency and the Freedom Train.

My father's concern about crime began when he was assistant attorney general of the Criminal Division, where he learned a great deal about the problem and developed strong opinions on how to handle it. After he became attorney general, he expressed his views in a memo to President Truman:

As an aftermath of the stresses of the war, we are threatened with a crime wave even more vicious and widespread than that which occurred after the first World War. We can meet this threat, first of all, by concerted effort toward the achievement of prosperity and a high standard of living for all our people. Honest and well-paid employment must be made available to all. Secondly, we must, each of us as a matter of patriotic duty, so conduct ourselves as not to encourage any form of violation of law.[1]

While he regarded crime in general as a serious problem, my father's main focus was on juvenile delinquency. This concern came about because of FBI statistics, personal experiences, and his genuine affection for young people. The statistics were alarming. Seventeen-year-olds were arrested more often than members of any other age group. Fifteen percent of all murders, 32 percent of thefts—including 62 percent of automobile thefts—and 30 percent of rapes in the country were committed by those younger than twenty-one.[2] And these crime rates occurred at a time when drugs were not a significant factor! Disturbed by the statistics, my father decided to visit a juvenile correctional institution in the District of Columbia, the National Training School for Boys. He was appalled by the conditions there: crowded housing, the intermingling of first offenders and repeaters, and a general lack of supervision.

My father was also deeply moved by the plight of an acquaintance who was a prominent munitions manufacturer. The man's seventeen-year-old son had been arrested for theft and faced a jail sentence. The father felt that he and his wife were to blame for their son's behavior: both were deeply involved in their work, and the son was unsupervised a great deal of the time. In talking to my father, he pleaded that he should be punished, not his son. "I am the person who is really at fault," he declared.[3]

Once aware of the problem, Tom Clark did not need prodding. He went into action, stressing that "now is the time to turn our efforts, like the proverbial Chinese doctor, to prevention rather than cure," and initiated an aggressive strategy to address the problem of juvenile crime. He firmly believed that "law enforcement in a democracy should rest in the community where it is administered . . . by thoroughly trained, up-to-the-minute, non-partisan controlled local police."[4] He adopted as a model the Brooklyn Plan, a successful community-based program that placed first-time juvenile offenders on probation so that they could avoid prosecution and the stigma of a court record. He also advocated extending the maximum age that youth are protected by the Federal Juvenile Delinquency Act from eighteen to twenty-four years old. Juveniles required special attention, he declared: "The erring youngster from 18 to early 20's must be given every opportunity for rehabilitation so that he may take his place with our useful citizens of tomorrow. He needs more specialized attention and a very different kind of treatment than the adult offender."[5]

On September 28, 1946, Tom Clark announced the formation of a panel on juvenile delinquency composed of twenty-eight prominent federal, civic, and religious leaders, including Father Flanagan of Boys Town and Mrs. Paul Rittenhouse, director of the Girl Scouts of America. The panel concluded that an attack on teenage crime must come from all fronts—the home as well as community, state, and federal agencies. To achieve this goal, a three-day national conference for the prevention and control of juvenile delinquency was planned for October 21–23, 1946. The conference addressed nine categories of crime, and was organized into panels of people from a variety of backgrounds. Each panel had to develop a report with recommendations on how to deal with a specific type of crime. The reports were published and distributed to appropriate groups throughout the country.

On February 17, 1946, a *Boston Post* article described my father's commitment to fighting juvenile delinquency: "There are extremely interesting and potentially powerful personalities entering into the limelight as the first year of the Truman administration nears its close. One of these is Attorney General Tom Clark, who has embarked on one of the most unusual crusades ever undertaken by a cabinet officer—that of trying to solve our very serious juvenile delinquency problem in America from the top level of the government."[6]

To ensure that the campaign against crime did not end with the conference, the attorney general established a new, temporary position with the cumbersome title of executive secretary of the Continuing Committee of the National Conference on the Prevention of Juvenile Delinquency. He appointed a bright, energetic young woman named Eunice Kennedy, whose older brother, future president John F. Kennedy, was a congressman at the time, to fill it. The *American Weekly* featured a picture of the attorney general with Ms. Kennedy and described her as "the smartest young woman executive in Washington" with a "tough job but an easy boss."[7] Eunice's responsibilities included serving as the liaison between Attorney General Clark and the committee on juvenile delinquency, and assisting states, cities, and local organizations in developing programs to prevent youthful lawlessness. Her first project, which resulted from a meeting with a group of sportswriters, was an athletic program that she hoped would be adopted by communities nationwide. Eunice's assistant in the program was a young man named Sargent Shriver. He would later become her husband—an unanticipated personal benefit resulting from her work on juvenile delinquency. Tom Clark's association with Eunice Kennedy was a happy one, and was appreciated and remembered by the Kennedy family.

Tom Clark did not just delegate responsibility for the fight against juvenile crime. He was deeply involved himself, and spoke as often as three times a week throughout the country while launching the campaign. He persuaded the *Washington Post* to contribute the profits from its Third Annual Celebrity Golf Tournament to projects for juveniles in the

District of Columbia. Bob Hope, Bing Crosby, Sam Snead, and Arthur Godfrey were among the golfing celebrities who raised $34,000 for the project, which was described in the program for the event as "inspired by Tom Clark's fight for safe and healthy activities for young people."[8]

Attorney General Clark and his staff also answered thousands of letters, many from young men and women who had been in trouble with the law. The young people he came in touch with sensed his affection for them and his belief in their ability to become productive citizens if given the opportunity. Each year at Christmas my father visited the National Training School for Boys. He received the following letter from Roger James Kahler, a resident of that institution, after one of his annual Christmas visits:

Dear Sir,

I would like, first of all, to tell you how much I really appreciated your seeing the boys up here at the National Training School. It meant a lot to all of us. You see sir, the boys up here think that maybe some of the people on the outside think that they are bad and that they don't care to think about them. But sir, you show all of us that people really do have an interest in us all.

Every Christmas, each and every one of us look forward to your coming and visiting us. You've given us something here, no one could ever do. You've helped us, and you're as a "father" to all. As for my honest opinion, sir, I don't believe there will be another man as great and as helpful as you.[9]

My father's concern for juvenile delinquency and his strategy for dealing with it reflected his love for young people and his belief in rehabilitation. In addition, he was an optimist who believed deeply that this country was a land of opportunity with a unique system of government.

Another major initiative that he undertook—the Freedom Train—was related to the battle against juvenile crime. Its purpose was to give people of all ages an opportunity to learn about our country's heritage.

Here comes the Freedom Train,

> You better hurry down,
> Just like a Paul Revere,
> It's comin' into your home town.
> Inside the Freedom Train,
> You'll find a precious freight,
> Those words of liberty,
> The documents that made us great.
>
> Irving Berlin, "The Freedom Train Song"

My father recalled how impressed he had been as a boy when the Liberty Bell came through Dallas, and credited that experience with inspiring his idea for the Freedom Train, which he saw as a way to "reawaken in the mind and the heart of the American people, a greater appreciation of our American heritage."[10] The project was cosponsored by the newly formed American Heritage Foundation and the Department of Justice. I can remember the Freedom Train quite clearly. The red, white, and blue train consisting of seven cars contained a moving exhibit of 131 documents of American history, including the U.S. Constitution, the Bill of Rights, and the Declaration of Independence. The train traveled 33,000 miles to 300 communities in 48 states, providing Americans with the opportunity to see the founding documents of the United States. Thirty-six carefully selected marines guarded the precious cargo and often doubled as tour guides.[11]

I was unaware at the time of the controversy that the Freedom Train created. Criticism came from diverse sources. Political partisanship was a major charge. The train's travels coincided with congressional hearings and debate over the Marshall Plan. The Truman Doctrine and the UN Charter were among the documents exhibited. Some thought the project was a ploy to rally support for the Truman administration's foreign policy by stirring up people's patriotism. Congressman Clare E. Hoffman, a Michigan Republican, complained: "It's quite obviously a build-up for 1948 [the presidential election]."[12] Hoffman invited the attorney general to appear before the House Expenditures Committee to explain the purpose of the Freedom Train and how it would be financed. Tom Clark, appearing before the committee on June 19, 1947, testified that the Freedom Train was "privately financed and free from political partisanship." Its purpose, according to Clark, was to combat lawlessness and subversion and to reawaken "a greater appreciation of our American heritage."[13]

Clark's response did not satisfy everyone. A letter to the editor supporting Congressman Hoffman's claim of partisanship appeared in the *New York Times* on June 26, 1947. The writer, describing the project as a "political junket," complained that the exhibit omitted Alexander Hamilton completely but included frequent mentions of Thomas Jefferson. The letter continued, "While the literature is replete with the highly inaccurate term 'democracy' it conspicuously omits the word 'republic.'"

Another outspoken critic of the Freedom Train was an organization called the National Blue Star Mothers of America, whose leaders distributed letters claiming that the Freedom Train threatened the American way of life: "Christianity, as well as our American Republic and way of life as we know them, is imperiled by the drive toward world government by way of the so-called United Nations which is being furthered by carefully-planned celebrations in this city this week. . . . What irony that the Declaration of Independence would be used as a means for negating that very National Statehood which it once made possible."[14] As mentioned earlier, the Blue Star Mothers would later also oppose Tom Clark's appointment to the Supreme Court.

The letter attacked the American Heritage Foundation as a "fly-by-night, dummy organization" and suggested that it was controlled by the Anti-Defamation League and B'nai B'rith. At the other end of the political spectrum, the communist newspaper the *Daily Worker* called the Freedom Train "a huge propaganda cover-up" for capitalism.[15]

African American leaders viewed the Freedom Train with cynicism. When Tom Clark argued that the Freedom Train was needed to fight "foreign ideologies," Walter White of the National Association for the Advancement of Colored People (NAACP) cited a recent case in which white men accused of lynching a black man were freed. White exclaimed that he was "not as much worried over the threat of foreign ideology as over the situation inside the United States."[16] Langston Hughes expressed skepticism in a poem entitled "Freedom Train." The following stanza from the poem voices his concerns:

> Who's the engineer on the Freedom Train?
> Can a coal black man drive the Freedom Train?
> Or am I still a porter on the Freedom Train?
> Is there ballot boxes on the Freedom Train?
> Do colored folks vote on the Freedom Train?
> When it stops in Mississippi will it be made plain
> Everybody's got a right to board the Freedom Train?
> Somebody tell me about this Freedom Train!

Paul Robeson spoke eloquently for many black Americans: "I want freedom itself, not a freedom train. It will take much more than a Freedom Train to make negroes believe that freedom for them is more than a word."[17] Robeson also expressed fear that in southern states blacks would not be allowed on the train to view the documents. This possibility brought forth a statement from the American Heritage Foundation that "no racial or religious segregation of any kind would be tolerated at any exhibition of the Freedom Train held anywhere."[18]

Tom Clark's own words may have caused some to view the Freedom Train as a Cold War device that would be used by zealots to promote militant patriotism. When announcing that the train would begin its journey on the 160th anniversary of the signing of the Constitution, Clark declared that "a positive and demanding need has arisen in our country for emphasizing the blessings of the American heritage" and that the Department of Justice had "shocking evidence of disloyalty to our government."[19] He also declared that "our form of government is attacked from within by those who believe in a foreign ideology. There is no place in America for those who believe in the totalitarian force of a foreign power."[20] Such ideologies, he continued, must be "swept away," but, he added, "We shall not sweep them in the fashion of witch hunts."

The Freedom Pledge, which accompanied the train, was signed by more than two million people, and there were programs held that included mass recitations of the pledge. The words of the pledge:

> I am an American, a free American;
> Free to speak—without fear,
> Free to worship my own God,
> Free to stand for what I think right,
> Free to oppose what I believe wrong,
> Free to choose those who govern my country.
> This heritage of Freedom I pledge to uphold
> For myself and all mankind.

Although the pledge was an ecumenical homage to liberty, some were reminded of Hitler's youth movement and the Nazis' tactics used to arouse patriotism.

Demonstrations did occur during the Freedom Train's travels, but they were not due to zealous patriotism or racial discrimination. When the train traveled to New York City's Grand Central Station, a pacifist group called the Committee for Amnesty for All Objectors to War and Conscription picketed and demanded full pardons for the nine hundred conscientious objectors held in federal prisons since World War II. The committee did not actually oppose the Freedom Train, but complained that amnesty proclamations granted by former presidents were omitted from the exhibit. A spokesman for the group stated, "The continued punishment of conscientious objectors is inconsistent with the spirits of the documents shown on the Freedom Train. The idea of the train is excellent."[21]

The demonstrations were not new to my father. Conscientious objectors picketed in front of the Department of Justice for several years after the war ended, and on the occasions that I accompanied him to his office, there were usually one or two pickets at the entrance. My father always greeted them courteously, and they responded in kind.

Pressure to grant a general amnesty to conscientious objectors came from a number of organizations and some prominent citizens, including Eleanor Roosevelt and Charles P. Taft, president of the Churches of Christ in America. My father opposed that policy, however, on the grounds that a general amnesty would compromise the integrity of the Selective Service Act at a time when men were still being drafted. In addition, men whose refusal to serve was based on something other than religious grounds would also be released. On December 18, 1945, he made the following recommendation to President Truman:

> I have concluded . . . that the most appropriate and feasible way of dealing with the imprisoned conscientious objectors is to establish as a general policy that such of them as are over the age of twenty-six, and hence not subject to induction, and who have served a third of their sentence, shall be immediately eligible for general pardon. This means only that hereafter the conditions under which paroles will be granted to conscientious objectors will be the same as those under which paroles are granted to any other prisoner. Under this policy the Parole Board would promptly consider the cases of all conscientious objectors who fall into this category and after screening them to ascertain that imprisonment resulted from violations based on conscience, rather than on other motives, would parole them.[22]

President Truman agreed with the Attorney General's recommendation, and on December 23, 1946, issued Executive Order 9814, establishing the Amnesty Board, which was to determine whether clemency should be granted in each case.

The demonstrations had little effect on the success of the Freedom Train, which was greeted with great fanfare wherever it traveled. Communities throughout the nation held parades, pageants, and rallies in its honor. Newspapers promoted its arrival in their cities, and schoolchildren participated in programs honoring it. More than three million people viewed the historic documents. On its peak day, 14,615 people boarded the train. The poorest attendance occurred on a stormy day in New Jersey when only 6,049 hardy souls braved the weather to see it.[23] The greatest problem was handling the large number of people who came to view the documents. Although the train was open from 10 a.m. to 10 p.m. seven days a week, and children under twelve were not admitted, the crowds were so large, and the time needed to carefully view the materials so lengthy, that many were turned away.

Although Congress passed, and President Truman signed, a bill allowing the National Archives to continue operating the train, funding for the project was omitted from the budget. The Freedom Train's last hurrah occurred on January 16, 1949, as people gathered at the train's site for the opening ceremonies of the presidential inaugural celebration. The exhibit was open to the public throughout the festivities, and the train was then put to rest.

By any account, the Freedom Train was a major success. Millions of Americans came to see the historic documents on display, and the main purpose of the train—to reawaken "a greater appreciation of our American heritage"—seemed to be fulfilled. The success of its second purpose—"to awaken the country to the peril facing the world"—has been more difficult to assess.

## CHAPTER 10

# Civil Rights

## OPENING A NEW ERA

It is my purpose to protect human rights and civil liberties whenever they are infringed.

Tom C. Clark, 1946

INDIVIDUAL LIBERTIES ENJOYED SIGNIFICANT GAINS and suffered
serious threats during the years that Tom Clark served as attorney general. Success in the realm of racial discrimination foreshadowed the
Supreme Court's landmark *Brown* decision and the start of the civil rights
movement of the 1960s. Without question, under Harry Truman's leadership, more was done to end racial discrimination than at any time since
Abraham Lincoln was president. Tom Clark was a key player in this effort,
which was not surpassed until Lyndon Johnson launched his Great Society programs almost twenty years later.

Before appointing him attorney general, President Truman made it
clear to Tom Clark that civil rights were a priority: "When I conferred
with Clark regarding his appointment, I expressed to him my ideas of how
I wanted him to run the Department of Justice. I emphasized to him the
need to be vigilant to maintain the rights of individuals under the provi-
sions of the Bill of Rights. . . . I emphasized this so much that Tom Clark
thought I was "hipped" on the subject—and I was."[1]

Truman and Clark seemed unlikely candidates for initiating a civil
rights movement, nor is that what they had anticipated doing when they
began to battle discrimination. Racism was ingrained in the national
fabric at that time, and both men grew up in areas of the country where
it was strongly entrenched. Although Missouri, unlike Texas, was a border
state during the Civil War, it was also a slave state with southern sympa-

thies. Truman's beloved mother was strongly pro-South and disliked Abraham Lincoln intensely. Tom Clark's southern ties were even stronger: his parents were from the Deep South, and his paternal grandfather was killed in battle while fighting for the southern cause. Despite their backgrounds, both men were dedicated to the principle that all people are equal before the law, and both had remarkable capacities for personal growth.

The timing was right for a breakthrough in civil rights. The Great Depression and World War II had consumed Franklin Delano Roosevelt, and although he and his wife, Eleanor, were advocates of racial equality, little was done to advance civil rights during his administrations. The Roosevelts did, however, bring the issue to the public's attention and shattered precedent by inviting African Americans to the White House. This action, viewed as radical at the time, resulted in vitriolic criticism from some quarters. The criticism did not daunt Eleanor Roosevelt, and she continued to fight for racial equality. In a famous incident, she and Secretary of the Interior Harold Ickes arranged for African American singer Marian Anderson to perform on the steps of the Lincoln Memorial after the Daughters of the American Revolution (DAR) barred her from Constitution Hall. Small cracks in the wall of racism began to appear during the Roosevelts' years in the White House, and these cracks were widened significantly during the Truman administration.

World War II was an important factor in bringing the issue of racism to the forefront. African Americans were needed for manpower, and large numbers took jobs that had once been denied them. Racial tensions grew as whites and blacks competed for jobs and housing, and in 1943 a riot in Detroit left thirty-four people dead—twenty-five of whom were black.[2] Incidents of virulent racism occurred. A young black sergeant was pulled from a bus in Batesburg, South Carolina, and then beaten and blinded by police. He had received an honorable discharge from the army a few hours before. When Truman learned of the crime, he contacted his attorney general. Clark acted quickly and forcefully by bringing criminal charges against Lynwood Lanier Shull, the Batesburg chief of police. Such an action may seem ordinary in today's world, but in 1946, bringing criminal charges against a prominent southern police chief was a drastic move. Sadly, an all-white jury found Shull innocent of the charges after deliberating for thirty minutes.[3]

In another incident, two African American men, one a veteran who served in the Pacific during World War II, and their wives were lynched by a group of twenty white men in Monroe, Georgia. The perpetrators of the crime, angry because one of the victims had been released on bond after being accused of stabbing his white employer, shot at least sixty bullets into the four men and women and then tossed their bodies into nearby bushes. The lynching of soldiers hit a raw nerve with Harry Truman, whose World War I service was a life-changing experience for him.[4] The impact of these heinous acts on the president was enormous. Outraged, Truman ordered the attorney general to use every resource of the Department of Justice to investigate the crime. Attorney General Clark immediately ordered a federal investigation of Ku Klux Klan activities in seven states.[5] He also sent a letter to U.S. attorneys throughout the nation:

> The civil rights of minorities in this country were never in greater danger than at this time. It is my purpose to protect human rights and civil liberties, whenever they are infringed, to the full extent and intent of the Constitution and of statutory provisions. . . . It is my desire that you immediately devote special attention and investigation protection of all Americans in their civil liberties, regardless of race or color.

In addition, he brought in the FBI:

> The probe is being carried on in the tradition of the FBI—with dispatch, efficiency and determination. The full facilities of the Department of Justice are behind this investigation. This crime is an affront to decent Americanism. Only due process of law sustains our claim to orderly self-government. I call upon all our citizens to repudiate mob rule and to assist the authorities to bring these criminals to justice.[6]

Twenty FBI agents were assigned to the case, 2,790 people were interviewed, and 106 witnesses were presented to the grand jury. Yet despite the evidence, no indictment was handed down.[7] The failure to indict was largely due to uncooperative local law officials and citizens. This lack of local support and cooperation continually frustrated the Department of Justice's efforts to deal with civil rights cases.

In 1939, then–attorney general Frank Murphy attempted to strengthen the federal role by establishing the Civil Rights Section as part of the Department of Justice's Criminal Division. But with only seven lawyers and a limited number of laws with which to work, the section had little teeth. No new civil rights laws were enacted when the Civil Rights Section was formed. Those that were in force had been passed during the decade that followed the Civil War and had been seriously weakened over the years as Congress repealed important sections. Existing laws were vaguely worded and failed to clearly designate which rights were protected under federal law. Tom Clark described the Department of Justice's frustration in a speech to the Chicago Bar Association in June 1946: "Every day my Department receives numerous complaints from groups, individuals, and even State officers, concerning violations of personal rights—2699 alone in the first half of the present fiscal year. The great majority reveal on their face that no Federal jurisdiction is present. In comparatively few instances do we have authority to investigate and prosecute."[8]

Action was needed, and on December 5, 1946, President Truman issued Executive Order 9808, establishing the President's Committee on Civil Rights. Its purpose was to assess the status of civil rights in the country and "to inquire into and to determine whether and in what respect current law-enforcement measures and the authority and means possessed by Federal, State, and local governments may be strengthened and improved to safeguard the civil rights of the people."[9] The committee was told to report its findings to the president in writing and to make recommendations for addressing the weaknesses that it uncovered.

The committee's report, *To Secure These Rights*, published in 1947, was a remarkable document that could have been used as a blueprint for ending racial discrimination. It called for eliminating "segregation based on race, color, creed or national origin, from American life." It was also an indictment of the state of civil rights in this country and expressed mild criticism of the FBI, angering director J. Edgar Hoover: "There is evidence in the civil rights case files in the Department of Justice that the Bureau [FBI] has sometimes felt that it was burdensome and difficult to undertake as many specific civil rights investigations as are requested. Moreover, investigations have not always been as full as the needs of the situation would warrant."[10] Walter White, head of the NAACP at that time and a highly respected African American leader, described the report as "the most consequential and specific document of its kind in American history."[11]

Putting the committee's recommendations into effect was not an easy task, despite President Truman's full support. On February 2, 1948, the president delivered a major address on civil rights before Congress. He proposed a "Civil Rights Act of 1949" that would implement the committee's recommendations. Attorney General Clark and Department of Justice lawyers were deeply involved in developing the proposed legislation, and Tom Clark lobbied hard for its passage. He presented an analysis of the bill to Congress, describing its purpose and giving a rationale for each of its sections: "The purposes to be accomplished by this bill are purposes which this nation has sought to achieve since its founding. We have always had the ideal and so long as we seek to realize it we are a healthy, vigorous nation. Great gains have been made, but greater gains will be made if this bill is enacted. The bill does not purport to solve every problem and cure every evil; it does, however, represent a great forward step toward the goal of full civil liberties for all."[12]

Title I of the legislation called for the establishment of a permanent Commission on Civil Rights in the executive branch of the government and a Joint Congressional Committee on Civil Rights. In his analysis, Clark used President Truman's words to describe the purpose of these two groups: "This Committee [the Joint Congressional Committee on Civil Rights] should make a continuing study of legislative matters relating to civil rights and should consider means of improving respect for and enforcement of those rights. . . . [The Joint Congressional Committee and the Commission on Civil Rights] together should keep all of us continuously aware of the condition of civil rights in the United States and keep us alert to opportunities to improve their protection."[13]

The proposed legislation mandated the reorganization of the Department of Justice's Civil Rights Section into a full division with its own assistant attorney general. It strengthened existing laws and empowered federal district courts to act in cases in which local authorities had failed to protect the rights of individuals. It prohibited segregation in interstate and foreign commerce. Segregation in interstate transportation had been declared unconstitutional by the Supreme Court in 1946 in *Morgan v. Virginia*, a case brought by the NAACP and argued by Thurgood Marshall. Enforcement was difficult, however, and segregation continued. Segregation in local transportation was considered outside the scope of federal control and was not challenged until Rosa Parks refused to move to the back of a bus in Montgomery, Alabama, on December 1, 1955. The proposed Civil Rights Act of 1949 also guaranteed minorities' voting rights in primary, general, and special elections. My father had come a long way since Bill McCraw's race for Texas attorney general in 1934, when neither he nor McCraw spoke out against the Texas Democratic Party's decision to prohibit African Americans from voting in its primary.

One recommendation made by the President's Committee on Civil Rights but omitted from the bill was compensation for Japanese Americans who were interned during World War II. In a separate action, the federal government took one step toward providing compensation for the victims of internment. In 1948, after lobbying by the Japanese American Citizens League and support from the Department of Justice, Congress unanimously passed the Japanese American Evacuation Claims Act. It was a small but important acknowledgment of a grievous injustice.

The attorney general's analysis ended with the following quotation from *To Secure These Rights*:

The argument is sometimes made that because prejudice and intolerance cannot be eliminated through legislation and government control, we should abandon that action in favor of the long, slow, evolutionary effects of education and voluntary private efforts. We believe that this argument misses the point and that the choice it poses between legislation and education as to the means of improving civil rights is an unnecessary one. In our opinion, both approaches to the goal are valid, and are, moreover, essential to each.

It may be impossible to overcome prejudice by law, but many of the evil discriminatory practices which are the visible manifestations of prejudice can be brought to an end through proper government controls.[14]

The Civil Rights Act of 1949 never passed. Some of its measures were included several years later in a watered-down version—the Civil Rights Act of 1957—that brought about the reorganization of the Civil Rights Section into a Civil Rights Division and established the Commission on Civil Rights. It also gave the Department of Justice the right to bring suit on behalf of African Americans denied the right to vote. Only ten suits were filed in the three years following the passage of the act, and it wasn't until the Civil Rights Act of 1964, an act my father felt had its roots in the failed Civil Rights Act of 1949, that significant legislation was enacted and enforced.

In 1948, President Truman issued two executive orders that took important steps toward ending segregation. The first opened up federal employment to African Americans, and the second integrated the armed forces. Both orders were highly controversial and were politically courageous, since they came less than four months before a presidential election.

That Tom Clark, a Texan whose father had argued that Negroes could never have social equality with whites, had become Truman's right-hand man in the battle against racial discrimination was clearly established when he and Solicitor General Philip Perlman filed a historic amicus curiae brief, entitled *Prejudice and Property*, in *Shelley v. Kraemer*, a Supreme Court case that involved restrictive racial covenants. These covenants were clauses in housing contracts that prohibited the owner from selling the property to people of color or to adherents of certain religions. Basically, sales were limited to white Christians. The federal government was not involved in prosecuting the case, but through *Prejudice and Property* took a strong public stand opposing this blatant form of discrimination. The brief has been described as "the Department of Justice under Attorney General Clark at its intellectual best with its uncompromising and legally compelling rejection of restrictive covenants."[15] The text of the brief was forceful and clear: "Actual segregation, rooted in ignorance, bigotry and prejudice, and nurtured by the opportunities it affords for monetary gains from the supposed beneficiaries and real victims alike, does exist because private racial restrictions are enforced by courts. These covenants are injurious to our order and productive of growing antagonisms destructive of the integrity of our society. Inadequate shelter, disease, juvenile delinquency are some of the major evils directly traceable to racial restrictive covenants."[16]

The Supreme Court agreed, and on May 3, 1948, Chief Justice Fred Vinson handed down a decision reversing that of the lower court and declaring restrictive covenants in housing unenforceable because of the Fourteenth Amendment's equal protection clause. Although the clause did not apply to private parties—and so the restrictive covenants were not unconstitutional—it did prohibit the government from supporting or defending these clearly discriminatory, racially based covenants.

Perhaps the most remarkable aspect of the Truman administration's civil rights efforts was that they were done independently, without the political or social pressures that were to develop by the 1960s. They were also unpopular with a majority of voters. A Gallup poll conducted in March 1948 found that 82 percent of those polled opposed Truman's civil rights program.[17] Harry Truman knew that making civil rights a priority would hurt him politically, but he saw it as a moral issue and was determined to do the right thing, regardless of the repercussions. My father characterized the president's actions in the following way: "[Truman] had a faculty that no one else had—any of the Presidents that I know of, and that was of forgetting the decision as far as the effects of it on his political life or on his image."[18]

While the president was achieving important gains in the area of civil rights, however, another issue loomed—the Cold War. It dominated the country's attention, and the president's handling of it was generating a great deal of criticism directed at both him and his attorney general.

## CHAPTER 11

# Cold War Fever

## NATIONAL SECURITY VERSUS INDIVIDUAL FREEDOM

> You cannot lose sight of the constitutional questions which
> inevitably arise in attempting to curb the activities of those with
> whom we disagree and whose actions we deplore.
>
> Tom Clark, 1948

BY THE LATE 1940S, an issue had emerged that would dominate the country's foreign and national security policies for decades to come: the Cold War. As attorney general, my father found himself in the middle of a historic battle to protect the nation from communist subversion without sacrificing the civil liberties that are guaranteed to people in a free society. It was not an easy task!

The threat of communism had been an issue for many years, and reached a height with the "Red Scare" that occurred soon after World War I. In response to the perceived danger to the country, Attorney General A. Mitchell Palmer established the Justice Department's Intelligence Division for the purpose of hunting down radicals, and appointed twenty-four-year-old J. Edgar Hoover to head it. The rampage of arrests and deportations that resulted—known as the Palmer Raids—became infamous, regarded by most historians as a "wholesale violation of civil liberties."[1] The Red Scare ended, but the specter of communism continued, and in 1938, Congressman Martin Dies of Texas, chairman of the House Committee on Un-American Activities (a special investigating committee), claimed that "there are not less than two thousand outright Communists and Party-liners still holding jobs in Washington."[2] The rhetoric subsided during World War II when the USSR and the United States were allies, but even during the war years, communism remained a political issue. In the 1944 election campaign, the Delaware Republican Committee placed full-page advertisements in local newspapers such as the *Georgetown Sussex Countian* with headlines implying that the Democratic Party was unable or unwilling to deal with the issue: "Save America, Vote Republican," one ad read.

With the advent of the Cold War, the anticommunist movement once more gained momentum, and the special committee formed in 1938 became the permanent House Un-American Activities Committee (HUAC), chaired by Democrat Edward J. Hart of New Jersey. After the Republicans gained control of Congress in 1946, J. Parnell Thomas (also of New Jersey) became chairman. During the 1946 congressional elections, the Republican National Committee announced that the electorate's choice was between "Communism and Republicanism."[3] It charged that the Truman administration was "soft on communism" and that the government was riddled with communists.

Democrats attempted to discredit these accusations and, at the same time, to convince the public that they too were concerned about the threat of communism and were dealing with the issue effectively. It was in this context that Tom Clark gave a speech before the Chicago Bar Association on June 21, 1946, entitled "Civil Rights: The Boundless Responsibility of Lawyers." Two-thirds of the speech dealt with individual rights and described problems that the President's Committee on Civil Rights would address a year later. But the final third of the speech overshadowed everything that had come before. The attorney general shifted into an assault on radicals, both communist and fascist, describing them as "one of the greatest dangers, in my opinion, to civil liberties of our fellow citizens." He became more specific, citing the infiltration of labor unions:

We know that in the Black Bible of their faith they [communists and fascists] seek to capture important offices in the labor unions, to create strikes and dissentions, and to raise barriers to the efforts of lawful authorities to maintain civil peace.

I am told that in the councils of many labor unions, wherein deliberations are screened from the public, identical tactics staged with acute parliamentary skill are used to disconcert and disrupt proceedings, in the hope that the communists or fascists, or both—for I see no difference in them— may achieve final power. . . . No country on earth, and no government, can long endure this vicious attack. I say to you that they are driving law enforcement in this country to the end of its patience.[4]

Lawyers were targeted next:

The high responsibility of the practice of law demands that we view the present with open eyes so that we may not be blind to the future. . . . I do not think there is anyone more subject to censure in our profession than the revolutionary who enters our ranks, takes the solemn oath of our calling, and then uses every device to further the interests of those who would destroy our government by force, if necessary.

I do not believe in purges because they bespeak the dark and hideous deeds of communism and fascism, but I do believe that our bar associations, with a strong hand, should take those too brilliant brothers of ours to the legal woodshed for a definite and well-deserved admonition.[5]

An uproar followed. The National Lawyers Guild denounced the speech and called for Clark to resign unless he changed his policies:"The Attorney General's address is an insult to the legal profession. It seeks to intimidate lawyers into abandonment of their calling, namely the vitalization of democracy through a defense of democratic rights. . . . It invites a witch-hunt against labor unions and their members. . . . It seeks to set in motion a purge of lawyers who serve minority groups."[6] The Civil Rights Congress called the speech "a threat to American democratic principles, a call to witch-hunting and lynch rule, and a step towards fascism in America that must be challenged."[7]

Just a month after the speech, and adding fuel to the fire, Attorney General Clark, at the request of J. Edgar Hoover, asked President Truman to "reaffirm" a directive, issued by President Roosevelt in 1940, that allowed wiretaps when national security was involved. In his memo to the president, my father cited the following paragraph from Roosevelt's directive:"You are therefore authorized and directed in such cases as you may approve, after investigation of the need in each case, to authorize the necessary investigating agents that they are at liberty to secure information by listening devices directed to the conversation or other communications of persons suspected of subversive activities against the Government of the United States, including suspected spies."[8]

Roosevelt's directive was not intended to apply to domestic radicals but to military or foreign espionage threats, and my father emphasized to the president that wiretaps would be used with restraint: "While I am reluctant to suggest any use whatever of these special investigative measures in domestic cases, it seems imperative to use them in cases vitally affecting the domestic security, or where human life is in jeopardy."[9] Neither my father nor the president foresaw that this renewal would result in the significant expansion of wiretapping by the FBI.

As Election Day drew closer, the attorney general became increasingly defensive about the communist issue. In a radio speech on October 9, 1946, he accused Republicans of fearmongering and of exaggerating the danger for political purposes:

Those who control the machinery and the medium of the Republican Party nationally and in many States would have you believe that the great Democratic Party—the party of Jefferson and Jackson and Wilson and Franklin Delano Roosevelt and Harry Truman—has surrendered itself to Communists. . . . I am the Attorney General of the United States and the chief law enforcement officer of the Federal Government. It has been my responsibility to investigate and maintain a constant check on all subversive groups in the United States. I know who the Communists are and what they are doing and what they plan to do. . . . What breeds communism is the avarice and greed of a selfish minority that seeks to deprive the vast majority of men and women of an opportunity to achieve security, of an opportunity to work at a decent job for decent wages, under conditions of labor commensurate with human dignity and to enjoy a fair share of the wealth they create. . . . It is counted good Republican campaign strategy to drive fear into the hearts of the people. Inasmuch as the country, despite the alarms of the Republican press, is enjoying full prosperity and full employment, they have selected the issue of Communism as the one which they hope will drive good Americans—through fear—into the arms of their party. . . . The issue of Communism has been exaggerated and distorted by the Republican Party for political purposes. . . . It is so clear to me as to be beyond doubt that we face no danger of Communism in the United States so long as we assure the American people of an opportunity to make orderly progress toward social goals.[10]

It isn't possible to know whether the issue of communism was responsible for the outcome, but the 1946 election was a disaster for the Democrats. The Republicans took control of Congress for the first time since Herbert Hoover was president, and two freshmen congressmen—Joseph McCarthy and Richard Nixon—would make anticommunism their battle cry. The 1946 results convinced the Democrats that further action on the issue of communism was essential, and on November 25, 1946, President Truman issued Executive Order 9806, creating the President's Temporary Commission on Employee Loyalty. The commission was made up of members from various government agencies and was chaired by the Department of Justice representative, A. Devitt "Gus" Vanech, who was special assistant to the attorney general. The commission was assigned the tasks of examining existing security standards and procedures within the federal government, investigating persons who were employed by or seeking a position with the federal government, and removing from office or disqualifying from employment any disloyal or subversive person. The commission was required to submit a written report to the president, with recommendations for changes to the existing system used to deal with subversion.

The commission's report, issued in March 1947, stated that no uniform system existed for dealing with subversives within the government. It recommended that loyalty review boards be established within each agency and department and within the Civil Service Commission. Applicants for federal jobs and current federal employees should be investigated. If an investigation resulted in dismissal, the employee could appeal to the loyalty board of the appropriate agency or department. If that appeal failed, the employee could appeal to the Civil Service Commission's loyalty review board. The employee would be given a summary describing the nature of the charges against him or her and would be allowed to choose a defense lawyer, but could be suspended while the appeal was being considered. Removal from office would be justified when "on all the evidence reasonable grounds exist for belief that the person involved is disloyal to the Government of the United States." Evidence that supported proof of disloyalty included sabotage, the unauthorized disclosure of classified documents or information, performance of duty that served the interests of another country rather than those of the United States, and membership in or affiliation with any organization or movement designated by the attorney general as totalitarian, fascist, communist, or subversive.

J. Edgar Hoover was especially unhappy with the first draft of the commission's report, which recommended that each department, rather than a central agency, have the responsibility of investigating its employees. Hoover wanted the FBI to be designated the principal investigative body, and in a memo to the attorney general, he suggested that the FBI might not participate in the program unless given this responsibility: "I want you to know that this Bureau is perfectly willing to withdraw from this field of investigation rather than to engage in a tug of war with the Civil Service Division."[11]

Tom Clark supported Hoover in a memo sent to President Truman on October 23, 1948: "From my experience in this field, there is no question that the handling of all phases of domestic intelligence, counterintelligence, sabotage and subversion should be made the function of the

Federal Bureau of Investigation."[12] Hoover and Clark prevailed, and the final version of the report designated the FBI as the central investigative body for the program.

The commission's report became the basis of the Federal Employee Loyalty Program, which was initiated with Executive Order 9835 on March 22, 1947. The most controversial provision of the program involved the attorney general, who was directed to compile a list "of each foreign or domestic organization, association, movement, group or combination of persons which the Attorney General, after appropriate investigation and determination, designates as totalitarian, fascist, communist or subversive, or as having adopted a policy of advocating or approving the commission of acts of force or violence to deny others their rights under the Constitution of the United States, or as seeking to alter the form of government of the United States by unconstitutional means."[13]

The idea of a list of subversive organizations was not new. Attorney General Biddle published one in 1943 after FDR issued an executive order dealing with the subversive activities of government employees during World War II. Biddle's list was the starting point for the expanded one that Attorney General Clark developed. In a memo to Seth Richardson, chairman of the Loyalty Review Board and a prominent Republican lawyer, Clark emphasized the limitations of such a list:

> I wish to reiterate, as the President has pointed out, that it is entirely possible that many persons belonging to such organizations may be loyal to the United States; that membership in, affiliation with or sympathetic association with any organization designated, is simply one piece of evidence which may or may not be helpful in arriving at a conclusion as to the action which is to be taken in a particular case. Guilt by association has never been one of the principles of our American jurisprudence. We must be satisfied that reasonable grounds exist for concluding that an individual is disloyal. That must be the guide.[14]

Tom Clark released the list of organizations determined subversive on December 4, 1947. The list included a wide-ranging group of ninety-one organizations, some of which were schools. Publication of the list brought a barrage of criticism from all sides. The Ku Klux Klan, one of the listed organizations, responded angrily: "This is purely an arbitrary matter of Clark's department setting itself up as Czar of this country."[15] The anticommunist publication *Counterattack* complained that the list failed to include 143 communist-front organizations—a later edition of the list added 6 of the 143. The National Council of American-Soviet Friendship, the Joint Anti-Fascist Refugee Committee, and the International Workers Order filed suits against the government after failing to obtain a hearing at which they could present evidence against their inclusion in the list.

Civil libertarians were especially alarmed. The American Civil Liberties Union expressed extreme concern: "The greatest threat to civil liberties lies in the power given the Attorney General to designate, after investigation, organizations for blacklisting."[16] Eleanor Roosevelt, in a letter to Truman written on November 13, 1947, expressed the fears of many who saw the loyalty program as a threat to individual liberties. After recommending that the makeup of the Loyalty Review Board include more women and fewer lawyers, the former first lady expressed her personal views: "My own reaction is anything but happy. I feel we have capitulated to our fear of Communism, and instead of fighting to improve Democracy, we are doing what the Soviets would do in trying to repress anything which we are afraid might not command public support, in order to insure acceptance of our own actions."[17]

The president responded to Mrs. Roosevelt on November 28 in a lengthy letter defending the loyalty program:

I have told the Civil Service Commission, the members of the Loyalty Review Board and the Press that I did not wish this inquiry to become a "witch hunt," but rather to establish what I think is the truth, that the overwhelming number of civil servants in the United States are not only faithful and loyal, but devoted patriots. It is, I think, contrary to American tradition to inquire into the political or philosophical view of anyone, and I think that is why all of us feel a certain repugnance to this program, but I became convinced that it was necessary not because as you say "we were trying to repress anything we were afraid might not command public support," but because there were indications of a small infiltration of seriously disloyal people into certain sensitive parts of the government.[18]

My father strove to ease these fears. When interviewed by journalist Doris Fleeson, he was emphatic: "No witch hunts, I'm no A. Mitchell Palmer."[19] He was well aware that the power given the attorney general to label organizations subversive had the potential for abuse, and so he sought to be as fair and thorough as possible when determining which groups should be listed. He vowed "to set up a yardstick for judging organizations, before compiling the most complete dossier possible on those considered suspect." In an interview years later, Philip Perlman, the solicitor general at the time the list was being compiled, described the procedure that was used: "I was there when the work was done on that list by Clark. He took all the names of the organizations from all the reports of the FBI and he distributed them to about thirty lawyers in the Department of Justice. All those thirty lawyers were supposed to have read the reports on all those organizations in order to advise him which ones, in their opinion, based solely on these reports should go on a list."[20] All information, along with the standards for evaluation, was then delivered to the Boards of Appeal for their consideration. They could accept an organization's inclusion on the list, reject it, or order hearings for further investigation.

Many perceived the attorney general's list and the loyalty program as a cave-in to HUAC. Initially, Republican leaders greeted the program with begrudging approval, but the enthusiasm of Carroll Reece, chairman of the Republican National Committee, was guarded: "If the President's order means what I hope it means—a real effort to drive out those subversive termites who have been using positions of power and influence under the present Administration to undermine our form of government—then I am glad the President, however belatedly, has adopted this important part of the program supported by the Republican party and its candidates in the 1946 campaign."[21]

Even this minimal approval was short-lived, however, and Republican members of HUAC continued to criticize the administration's handling of communist subversion. Its chairman, Congressman J. Parnell Thomas, clashed with Attorney General Clark over his refusal to allow the committee access to FBI files, and wrote a letter to President Truman, complaining, "You and your Attorney General have attempted to obstruct and thwart our pursuits of the *facts*."[22] The letter declared that HUAC would "expose the participants in this communist conspiracy whether they be Government employees, scientists, diplomats, labor leaders, or movie stars." The attorney general voiced his frustration: "Again and again I have requested the critics of the President's program to name any communists in the executive branch of the government.... They have failed to uncover one communist presently working in the federal government."[23]

Unbeknownst to my father, the Republicans, especially those on HUAC, had an ally in FBI director J. Edgar Hoover. Hoover had never fully supported the Federal Employee Loyalty Program, which he considered weak and only a slight improvement over existing programs. On March 26, 1947, just a few days after the program was made public, Hoover testified before HUAC. His willingness to testify was unusual, for in the past he had refused to appear before congressional committees, except for the Appropriations Committees, because he felt he might jeopardize FBI investigations. But Thomas had informed Hoover that the hearing was going to be "a full dress denunciation of Communism" and that Hoover could use the occasion as a sounding board—"a grand opportunity"—to say anything he wanted to say.[24] Hoover accepted the invitation. His testimony was a tirade against communism, a veiled condemnation of the Truman administration's handling of that problem, and an endorsement of HUAC.

HUAC members were delighted! They considered the speech a denunciation of what they considered liberals' indifference to the communist threat. It was the beginning of a special relationship between HUAC and Hoover. On one occasion, HUAC chairman Thomas commented that "the closest relationship exists between this committee and the FBI. . . . I think there is a very good understanding between us. It is something, however, that we cannot talk too much about."[25] The reason for secrecy was that Hoover was bypassing the attorney general and dealing directly with HUAC members, especially Richard Nixon.

My father was unaware of the covert communication between the FBI and HUAC. He had been a strong supporter of Hoover, and his papers at the Truman Presidential Library contain numerous notes congratulating the director on various jobs well done. But their relationship began to suffer as differences developed over the handling of subversion. In an interview in 1973, my father stated: "I think that it's fair to say that Mr. Hoover had an overriding passion to protect the FBI in every circumstance and in the area of—where we began to fall out—was in the area of security—Communist infiltration. Edgar Hoover had a "yen" on Communism. He spent about half of his appropriations on it. I used to kid him that he thought there was a Communist under every government desk, including mine."[26]

Hoover's obsession with communism was surpassed only by his dedication to the FBI and his sensitivity to any criticism of it. He sometimes resented constraints put upon his agents and was not always pleased with the subsequent repercussions, which, in some cases, he blamed at least partially on my father. The *Amerasia* case may have been a turning point in the two men's relationship. *Amerasia* was an obscure, left-wing diplomatic journal with a readership of fewer than 2,000 people. Its issues focused on Asia, especially China. China was in the midst of a power struggle between Chiang Kai-shek and Mao Tse-tung, and *Amerasia*'s editors were sympathetic to Mao. In February 1945, *Amerasia* published an article based on a secret British report that had been leaked to its editors. British intelligence was angry and lodged a complaint. It was suspected that the source of the leak was the Office of Strategic Services (OSS), the predecessor to the Central Intelligence Agency (CIA), and a complaint was sent to that agency. The OSS reacted by illegally breaking into *Amerasia*'s offices, where the agents discovered and took dozens of classified documents. Many of the documents were critical of Chiang Kai-shek and opposed his leadership—exactly the kind of information that *Amerasia* would find helpful in building a case for its viewpoint.[27]

In June 1945, six members of the *Amerasia* staff were arrested and charged with espionage on behalf of the Chinese communists. But the government's case was weak, and relied on documents that OSS agents had obtained through illegal entry. In addition, the FBI had illegally tapped the home phones of Philip Jaffe, editor of *Amerasia*, and had broken into the homes of other staff members. My father was unhappy when he learned of the FBI agents' actions: "I told Hoover that I thought this was wrong, that we would have to dismiss charges. He was furious. That probably started the deterioration of our friendship."[28]

Despite my father's reaction, the government prosecuted the *Amerasia* officials. The results were disappointing. James McInerney, chief of the Criminal Division's Internal Security Section, described the documents submitted as evidence as being "of innocuous, very innocuous character . . . a little above teacup gossip."[29] When the case was brought before the grand jury, only three of six *Amerasia* officials were indicted, and they were charged with "unlawful possession of government documents." There was no charge of espionage, for the offenders had never communicated with China or any other nation. Hoover was disappointed with the proceedings, and upset because the case reflected poorly upon the FBI and its tactics.

Another highly publicized case that produced mixed results for the Department of Justice and the FBI involved sixteen board members of the Joint Anti-Fascist Refugee Committee. All were convicted of contempt of Congress after refusing to provide HUAC with the organization's records. Several prominent people, including the novelist Howard Fast and Dr. Edward R. Barsky, a New York surgeon who had operated a hospital for the International Brigade during the Spanish Civil War, were in the group. But the most notorious member was Gerhart Eisler, a communist who claimed that he was a European antifascist and "a victim of witch-hunting hysteria in this country, instigated and encouraged by the Un-American Activities Committee."[30] Out on bail, Eisler escaped the country by boarding a Polish ship and fleeing to Great Britain. The attorney general asked Britain to extradite Eisler, but the British courts denied the request. Eisler soon immigrated to East Germany, where he became a member of the People's Council of the Soviet Zone of Germany. He never returned to the United States. Eisler's escape and the failure to extradite him were embarrassments to the Department of Justice, and the media made the most of the criticism that resulted. The attorney general bore the brunt of it, but the reputation of Hoover's FBI was also marred.

The prosecutions involving *Amerasia* and the Anti-Fascist Refugee Committee were the first of what became a deluge of investigations into subversion. The summer of 1948 witnessed the most sensational and controversial cases. First came the Judith Coplon fiasco. Coplon, a respected employee in the Department of Justice, had been promoted to positions of responsibility. In 1945, she was assigned to the Foreign Agents Registration Office within the department's Internal Security Section, where she had access to FBI reports on diplomats and suspected Soviet spies. In 1948, during a routine loyalty check, the FBI became suspicious of Miss Coplon and began an investigation that eventually uncovered a plot worthy of a spy novel. Coplon was passing classified documents to her lover, Soviet spy Valentin Gubitchev. The two frequently met in New York City, where Gubitchev worked for the United Nations. FBI agents followed Miss Coplon to New York City several times, and eventually caught her in the act of passing the documents. Gubitchev and Coplon were arrested, tried, and convicted of espionage. Gubitchev was deported to the Soviet Union, and Coplon was sentenced to ten years in prison. Her lawyers appealed the case on grounds that the FBI had acquired the evidence through unauthorized wiretaps and arrested her without first obtaining a warrant. Hoover sent a memo to my father urging him to declare a mistrial or seek a contempt of court citation. He argued that the appeals court might require FBI files opened for public scrutiny, thereby exposing informants and endangering national security. Hoover even sent a copy of his memo to the president, but no action was taken. Hoover's fears were realized. Raw FBI files became public and for the first time citizens got a glimpse of the extent of FBI intrusion into private lives. The Court of Appeals overturned the conviction, and Judith Coplon never served a day of her sentence. Years later Hoover described the Coplon case as one of the greatest disasters in the history of the FBI.[31]

A more successful prosecution was that of eleven members of the Communist Party for violating certain articles within the Smith Act, legislation passed in 1940 that prohibits persons from knowingly and willingly participating in activities designed to overthrow the government by force. Even this success was marginal, for the men were convicted not of espionage, but of "conspiracy to advocate" and to teach communism—vague charges at best, and ones widely criticized by civil libertarians. The trial was controversial. Many felt that Judge Harold Medina showed bias against the defendants throughout the trial and that his charges to the jury virtually ensured conviction.[32] The case was appealed, but the court of appeals upheld the conviction in a decision handed down by distinguished jurist Learned Hand. A few months later the U.S. Supreme Court upheld the lower court's conviction in *Dennis v. United States.* Justices Hugo Black and William O. Douglas dissented. Tom Clark, by then an associate justice on the Supreme Court, did not participate because of his involvement with the case while attorney general.

The most dramatic testimonies of 1948 came from Elizabeth Bentley and Whittaker Chambers, former spies for the Soviet Union. Both Chambers and Bentley claimed that they received classified government documents in the 1930s from Harry Dexter White, a former assistant secretary of the treasury whom Truman had appointed U.S. representative to the International Monetary Fund, and Alger Hiss, a former assistant secretary of state. White testified before HUAC, denying that he had ever been a communist. A few days after his testimony he died of a heart attack, and the investigation ended. The committee turned its total attention to Alger Hiss. One highly publicized piece of evidence used against Mr. Hiss was the so-called "pumpkin papers." The "papers" were actually reels of microfilm, supposedly containing classified government documents that Hiss had passed on to Chambers. Chambers claimed that fifteen years earlier he had hidden the microfilm in a pumpkin on his farm. He took Congressman Richard Nixon to the farm, along with photographers, and retrieved the hidden film. The discovery of the pumpkin papers was front-page news and convinced many of Hiss's guilt. My father made the following comments on the pumpkin papers in a 1972 interview:

Indeed I didn't know anything about the pumpkin papers until after they had come out in the press. . . . He [Richard Nixon] was on the Committee of Un-American Activities and I remember he at first said he wouldn't give us the so-called pumpkin papers. But when Judge John Knox told him he'd have to hold him in contempt, why then he gave them to us. There wasn't anything in them. The pumpkin papers consisted of photographic material. Microfilm. It was all blank—the whole thing. It was in a little container, and Mr. Chambers had contended that he had dropped it for safekeeping down a well [an air well] in his apartment.

I think the whole pumpkin affair was a concoction of Nixon and Chambers. . . . Mr. Nixon was down in the Caribbean, and he called Mr. Snyder who was then Secretary of the Treasury, and the Coast Guard was in his Department. Nixon asked if he could get a lift to Miami and they either furnished him with a boat or a helicopter or something; anyway, he got into Miami and then flew up and met Chambers over in the latter's garden. They took the film out of the pumpkin, you know, sort of smacked of a publicity stunt in the beginning. Then when it shows up exposed and there's nothing on the film, why it certainly indicated that it was a hoax— certainly no proof of any overt acts.[33]

My father's recollection of the pumpkin papers was somewhat faulty. There were actually five rolls of film—two containing documents dated 1938 had already been developed and examined by the FBI; two contained information on how to use devices such as fire extinguishers, life rafts, and chest parachutes; and the fifth roll was blank. His conclusion, however, as far as the value of the microfilm, was accurate—no incriminating evidence was found. Alger Hiss was convicted of perjury and served five years in prison. Once released, he spent the rest of his life trying to clear his name. But the case remains controversial, and there are staunch believers in his guilt and in his innocence.

Elizabeth Bentley, a former Soviet spy whom the press dubbed the "Red Spy Queen," appeared eight times before congressional committees and named approximately eighty people in the government who, according to her, were part of the communist underground. Only two of the accused were indicted, for she had little documentation to support her charges, and much of her testimony proved to be untrue or inaccurate. The exceptions were Julius and Ethel Rosenberg. The information she gave led to their trials, convictions, and executions.

Despite the continuing investigations, congressional pressure on my father to do more was unrelenting. He testified before HUAC many times, and on February 5, 1948, he appeared before the committee to inform its members of the different laws that the Justice Department could use in its battle against subversion, and to request new legislation. He attempted to placate committee members by stating that HUAC and the Truman administration shared the same goals, but at the same time, he warned them that the Communist Party was not illegal and that constitutional rights had to be guarded:

My views on all forms of totalitarianism, and particularly on Communism, are known to you. I feel sure they are identical with your own. . . . We may say, I think, that you in the Congress and we in the Department of Justice are laboring in neighboring vineyards and that we have the same motives and the same purpose in view. But in your deliberations with regard to legislation you cannot lose sight of the constitutional questions which inevitably arise in attempting to curb the activities of those with whom we disagree and whose actions we deplore.

... Membership in the communist party is not enough. In prosecutions against individuals we have to do more than prove that persons are members of the party. ... In other words it is necessary to prove that it is a party which advocates overthrow of the Government by force or violence.[34]

The attorney general then described the existing laws that the government could use in its pursuit of communist subversion. His main emphasis was on deportation, and he requested new legislation that would strengthen the Espionage Act and make the deportation of aliens easier. He also recommended that Congress amend the Alien Registration Act to require that all aliens verify their addresses with the registration authorities each year.

My father continued to defend the Federal Employee Loyalty Program, describing its achievements in a speech before the Jewish War Veterans on September 18, 1948. By that time, every federal employee had been fingerprinted and all name checks had been completed. Name checks involved examining the personnel file of each employee in search of derogatory information. It was a huge undertaking. The files of 2,110,521 employees had been stamped "No disloyalty found." The government had completed 5,421 investigations, and 54 employees had been removed from their positions in the government. Less than one-half of 1 percent of federal employees warranted investigations, and none of those investigated were found to be communists.[35] Tom Clark was proud of the effort:

And despite all those "witch hunt" stories that appeared back in 1947, a few days ago I was much pleased to hear from President Luther C. Stewart of the National Federation of Federal Employees, which includes thousands of Government workers, that neither he nor his union had received a single complaint on the conduct of the loyalty program.

This is a great tribute to the FBI, the Civil Service Commission, and the Loyalty Boards that have conducted this program. We cannot emphasize too much that the loyalty boards in each Government agency, as well as the regional ones located over the country, have a dual mission in their trial of cases. They must protect the country against any disloyal employee. But they must also protect an employee who may be unjustly accused.[36]

My father gave credit to the FBI for its part in implementing and enforcing the loyalty program, despite his differences with its director. Hoover was still an icon in the 1940s, and the fact that the FBI was keeping secret files on many respected and unsuspecting Americans was unknown at that time. My father was shocked when he learned, while still attorney general, that a file had been established on him.

The existence of the file came to light during a Senate investigation of the infamous Kansas City vote-fraud case that plagued the Truman administration for several years. The case involved the 1946 Democratic primary in Kansas City, Missouri. The incumbent congressman, Roger C. Slaughter, had clashed with Truman over domestic policies, and Truman endorsed his opponent, Enos Axtell, in the primary. Axtell also had the backing of the Pendergast machine, the Democratic Party political organization that controlled Kansas City during the 1930s and '40s and had been responsible for Truman's first entrance into politics, in 1922. Soon after the election results showed Truman's candidate the winner, election officials were notified of voting discrepancies, so the state began an investigation. A significant amount of data was gathered and turned over, along with the ballots, to U.S. Attorney Sam Wear's office, where it was placed in a vault. The evidence was examined, and Wear concluded that it did not support calling in a federal grand jury. But the newly elected Republican prosecutor disagreed, and impaneled a Jackson County grand jury, which subsequently returned indictments against seventy-one people, including a state representative, minor county officials, precinct captains, and election officials. Most were Democrats.

Five days before the trial was scheduled to begin, thieves broke into the county courthouse, where the evidence was being kept, blew the door off the vault, and stole the documents. An uproar followed. The freshman Republican senator from Missouri, James Kem, called for a Senate investigation, and the Senate Judiciary Committee appointed a subcommittee made up of two Republican senators, Homer Ferguson of Michigan and William Langer of North Dakota, and one Democrat, Pat McCarran of Nevada.

The FBI file on Tom Clark was set up after the Senate subcommittee investigation began, and any derogatory information that the FBI received on him was put into it.[37] My father would not have learned of the file's existence had it not been for William Rogers, legal counsel for the Senate subcommittee. Rogers, who later served as secretary of state under Eisenhower and as attorney general under Nixon, was given permission to examine the FBI files on the Kansas City case after my father finally agreed to a compromise with Senator Ferguson. Rogers was allowed to view the files at the Department of Justice in a private room set up for that purpose. Rogers discovered the file on my father and told him about it. When my father confronted Hoover, the director claimed to have no knowledge of the file, blaming his assistant Mickey Ladd. Since Ladd had died by that time, it was difficult to learn the truth of the matter.

My father expressed his anger:

One of the things—it was really outrageous—he had investigated—unbeknownst to me—investigated my former law partner [Bill McCraw]. I had not been practicing law since 1934 with my law partner and this was in about 1948. [They investigated McCraw] to see if there wasn't some connection between him and the ballot boxes disappearing. I can't imagine such a thing. . . . He had nothing to do with the Kansas City vote frauds, but they were reaching out hoping to involve him. Then another untoward thing that was in the file was a copy of the Kansas City Star [unpublished] and it said, "Clark Rebuked" or something . . . It had some derogatory headline. It was a story based on Mr. Ferguson's report that he intended to make on behalf of the Committee when his Republican colleague [Senator Langer] on the Committee joined it. However, his colleague did not join but filed his own report which was favorable to me. But Mr. Ferguson had leaked the report to the Star believing his colleague would join and the Star had set it up all ready for delivery when Mr. Ferguson had to call them to tell them to hold it. . . . Later the SAC [FBI special agent in charge] sent a copy of the newspaper article to Hoover with a note saying: "I know you'll be pleased to see what the Kansas City Star is going to say."

He [Ferguson] had "a pipeline to the FBI. . . . he was getting reports before I got them; before they were announced. . . . He was very, very vitriolic. . . . I think he went out of his way to destroy me."[38]

Because of the continuing controversy over the Kansas City vote-fraud case, the attorney general ordered the FBI to conduct a full investigation. Still, Republicans continued to attack Clark, and in a raucous session of the committee on June 6, 1947, Senator Kem accused him of thwarting the FBI's investigation and trying to "whitewash" the case. My usually easygoing father flushed and retorted angrily: "There has been no effort to whitewash. I think it is very unbecoming of you, Senator, to indicate that I would attempt a whitewash. My record as attorney general is a good one. I have prosecuted some of the most powerful people and corporations in this country, including two former Congressmen. For you to say this is a whitewash is uncategorically untrue and I deny it."[39]

Senator Kem persisted, claiming that it appeared there had been "dereliction of duty on the part of the Attorney General of the United States Tom Clark in failing to prosecute the guilty persons."[40] Clark insisted that the case was not prosecutable under federal law and that it was appropriate for the state to take the lead, as it had done. A crowd of spectators jammed the hearing room as word got out that Senators Ferguson and Kem were "loaded" for Clark. The two men saw my father's testimony as a way to "capitalize on the Kansas City snarl and President Truman's association with the Pendergast machine."[41] They accused my father of obstructing the FBI investigation, but Hoover supported my father: "[The Attorney General] has not in any way taken any action to prevent any investigation being conducted to its logical conclusion."[42] The statement apparently rankled Ferguson, who responded, "It doesn't change my mind a bit."

• • •

Did Tom Clark strike a balance between national security and individual freedom? Scholar Bernard Wiecek has concluded that he did: "Clark retained a sense of proportion, denouncing the excesses of McCarthyism while energetically defending the administration of Republican charges of being 'soft on communism.'"[43]

Some did not agree with Wiecek's assessment. Civil libertarians were convinced that both the attorney general's list of subversive organizations and the loyalty program in general were serious threats to civil liberties. On the other side of the political spectrum, right-wing conservatives felt that Harry Truman and his attorney general had failed to deal with the communist threat that they viewed as jeopardizing national security.

The conservatives' attacks on my father were clearly political. The 1948 presidential election was looming, and the Republican campaign was focused on two major issues: communism and corruption. J. Edgar Hoover was among those who were dissatisfied with the Truman administration's anticommunist policies. Although in the past he had maintained a relatively neutral position regarding politics, he was more than an impartial observer of the 1948 presidential contest. He wanted Truman out of office and was actively—and secretively—sending Thomas Dewey information helpful to his campaign. In an interview years later, Hoover's assistant William O. Sullivan described the FBI's involvement: "The FBI helped Dewey during the campaign itself by giving him everything we had that could hurt Truman, though there wasn't much. We resurrected the president's former association with Jim Pendergast—and tried to create the impression that Truman was too ignorant to deal with the [emerging] Communist threat. We even prepared studies for Dewey which were released under his name, as if he and his staff had done the work.... No one in the bureau gave Truman any chance of winning."[44]

They were in for a surprise!

## CHAPTER 12

# The 1948 Presidential Election

Harry Truman will be nominated as the Democratic Party's presidential candidate ... and will be elected in the November election.

Tom Clark, 1948

THE YEAR 1948 WAS ONE TO REMEMBER! The state of Israel was formed; the armed forces were integrated; India achieved independence; Mahatma Gandhi was assassinated; the Berlin airlift began; the Kinsey Report on male sexuality was published; and one of the most surprising elections in the country's history was held.

The presidential election would have a great impact on my family. My father was certain that Harry Truman would be victorious, but Mother and I, like most people, were skeptical. My father was a hopeless optimist, we thought, or was putting on a brave front. As a fifteen-year-old adolescent, I was not seriously affected by most of the controversies that swirled around the nation and my father, but the presidential election was another matter. Harry Truman's defeat could mean returning to Texas and therefore leaving close friends and a school I loved. Mother hoped for a Democratic victory, but would also have been happy to return to Texas. She had welcomed the move to Washington, D.C., as an opportunity for my father, but admitted years later that had she known we would never return to Dallas, she would have "cried her eyes out." But she always said she could be happy anywhere as long as the four of us were together, and I know that she loved her life in Washington. She described her feelings in notes written to me: "I had never been ambitious, but I must say I enjoyed, for a time, all of the attention we—or I was getting. No one had ever noticed me much but I suddenly became that cute little Mrs. Clark.—[I] got orchids, flowers and we were deluged with invitations. Fortunately we both realized that it was the position, not us. We had seen the McCraws after he was defeated [for governor of Texas] and how hurt they were."

Both my parents kept their perspectives, never letting the attention and flattery that a prestigious position can bring go to their heads. Mother was always supportive of my father, but was not ambitious and tended to underestimate herself. Her gracious, warm personality made her popular with any group and a definite asset to my father's career. J. Edgar Hoover was among those who admired her, and on one occasion said that the smartest thing Tom Clark ever did was to marry her. Mother loved the remark, but I always wondered whether it might have been double-edged: a compliment to Mother but a dig at my father.

Despite uncertainties about our future, the summer of 1948 was a happy one. Uncle Bob and his family had rented a beach house in Margate, New Jersey, and we often spent the weekends visiting them there. It was a long, hot drive, and there was sometimes a substantial wait at the ferry, since there was no bridge at that time. Margate was close to Philadelphia, where the Democratic National Convention was scheduled to be held, and I was excited at the prospect of attending with my parents. The Republicans had held a calm, dignified convention in June and nominated Thomas E. Dewey for president and Earl Warren for vice president. It was viewed as a "dreamboat of a ticket," and Clare Boothe Luce declared that Truman was a "gone goose."[1] The Democratic convention was quite a contrast to the Republicans'. The convention hall was beastly hot—no air conditioning—and the Democrats seemed to be in a self-destructive mode. On the right, southern delegates were angry because of the civil rights plank in the party's platform. On the left, Henry Wallace and the Progressive Party felt the Truman administration's policies were threatening the civil liberties of citizens and world peace. In addition, a liberal group that included the Americans for Democratic Action (ADA), Walter Reuther of the United Auto Workers, Hubert Humphrey, the young mayor of Minneapolis, and Franklin, James, and Elliott Roosevelt, sons of FDR, had organized to find a candidate other than Harry Truman. They formed the Draft Eisenhower Committee and wooed General Eisenhower, even though his party allegiance was unknown. The movement died, since Eisenhower was firm in his refusal to be a candidate, but many in the group never gave wholehearted support to the president.

The vice presidential nominee was still an open question; Supreme Court justice William O. Douglas and Senator Alben Barkley of Kentucky were the most likely choices. Tom Clark had also been mentioned as a possibility. A lead editorial in the July 13 issue of the *Philadelphia Inquirer* argued that Clark would be the strongest candidate. The author, describing the convention as "that of a once-great political party tearing itself to pieces," reasoned that the "nomination of Mr. Clark, a Texan who is highly respected in the North as well as in the South, would come as a healing touch to the political wounds caused by the Southern revolt against Truman. It would serve to unify the party and bring confidence where there is now only despair."[2] Tom Clark was not interested: "I'm for whoever the boss wants, so long as it isn't me," he declared.[3] Douglas, Truman's first choice, decided against accepting the position, so the seventy-one-year-old Barkley became the Democratic Party's nominee.

We watched as Sam Rayburn wielded the gavel and controlled the rowdy delegates as only he could. The mood was gloomy, and the only comic relief came when a flock of doves was released from a floral Liberty Bell presented to the president by a national committeewoman. She described them as "doves of peace," but the effect was anything but peaceful, and temporary pandemonium broke out as the doves careened around the convention hall. Despite Rayburn's skills, the convention was also anything but peaceful. There had been a bitter battle over the party platform's civil rights plank. The Truman administration had supported a more moderate statement than the one that liberal Democrats succeeded in passing. Subsequently, the whole Mississippi delegation and half of the Alabama delegation walked out in protest. Senator Richard Russell from Georgia challenged the president for the nomination and received all the southern states' votes. Although his bid failed, Senator Russell accepted his loss graciously and supported the party's ticket. Many of his southern colleagues refused to do so. Mississippi governor Fielding Wright called on southerners to attend a rump convention in Birmingham, Alabama. It was there that the Dixiecrat Party formed and nominated Senator Strom Thurmond for president (Wright was the vice presidential nominee).

The southern split from the party was not a surprise. After appearing at a dinner sponsored by Arkansas Democrats in March 1948, my father became convinced that the Democrats would lose the South. Truman had just proposed his civil rights legislation, and the atmosphere at the event was not friendly. My father offered this description: "You could feel sort of a coolness, you know, the air was so thick you could almost cut it."[4] The program for the evening included a speech by the president on closed-circuit television. Before the program began, a Truman supporter confided to my father that the governor was going to try to prevent the president's television appearance, and if he failed to prevent it, he would organize a walkout. My father thwarted the governor's plan: "I was speaking . . . He [the Governor] wanted me to get through ten minutes before the President was to come on. I kept speaking after the ten minutes and he kept tugging on my coat for me to sit down. I kept speaking until Mr. Truman came on and thus averted a mass exodus of the hall."[5]

My father remained a strong supporter of Harry Truman and campaigned vigorously for him, unlike many Democrats who, certain Truman would lose the election, began to distance themselves from the president. In the weeks before the election, my father made at least twenty-eight campaign speeches and half a dozen radio broadcasts, including some debates with Republicans. Texas was crucial to the Democrats, and the outlook for keeping it in the Democratic camp was bleak. Civil rights and the tidelands case were sore subjects for many Texans, and my father tried hard to mollify them. In several campaign speeches in Dallas during the spring of 1948, he attempted to address these two issues. The tidelands case was especially difficult. The Supreme Court had already ruled in favor of the federal government in *United States v. California*, and the Department of Justice was planning to file suit against Texas and other states claiming ownership of offshore oil. My father described his personal dilemma to a group of Texans. He explained that "no matter how personally uncomfortable" he felt, it was his duty to file suits against all states affected by the Supreme Court decision.[6] The oil industry in Texas was not soothed by his words, and his defense of the administration's civil rights policies was greeted with an equal lack of enthusiasm. My father also defended the Truman administration's efforts to combat communist subversion—another major concern in his home state—and accused the Republican Congress of obstructing his efforts to rid the nation of communists: "I asked the Senate committee way back in February to give me a law so we could pick up alien Communists and jail them for deportation. . . . But I didn't get that law."[7]

My father campaigned throughout the state with other Texans, including Sam Rayburn, Senator Tom Connally, former vice president John Nance Garner, and senator-elect Lyndon Baines Johnson. Johnson, who had just won the Democratic senatorial primary by 87 votes, would forevermore be labeled "Landslide Lyndon." My father also solicited the help of his brother Bob, who had important connections in the state, especially with conservative Democrats. Truman spent four days of his whistle-stop tour in Texas and made twenty-four stops, speaking at each. My father would get out at each stop, mingle with the crowds, and talk to people. It was during the whistle-stop campaign that he got a sense of the shifting momentum and became confident that Texas, and the country, would reelect Harry Truman.

During the weeks before the election, my father traveled extensively.

On October 17, he spoke at a Democratic rally in Salt Lake City, Utah. Afterward, he traveled to Butte, Montana, from there to Denver, and then back to Utah to campaign in Ogden. On October 26, he spoke at a Democratic banquet in Scranton, Pennsylvania. Attendance at the dinner was so much greater than expected that two hundred people were turned away, though they were able to return after dinner to hear the speakers. My father, described as a forceful speaker by the *Scranton Times*, lashed out at the Republican Congress. He accused Republican congressmen of being under the thumb of a "Third House"—lobbyists—and of mishandling problems such as displaced persons, housing, inflation, and labor. He claimed that Republicans were using communism as a "red herring," and mentioned that J. Edgar Hoover had reported that the bulk of the nation's communists lived in California and New York, the home states of Earl Warren and Thomas Dewey. The speech was partisan and confident: "A lot of people are going to be walking the streets on November 3 if they think the Democrats are going to be beaten. They are just beginning to fight."[8]

My parents bought their first television set a few days before the election, and invited a group over to watch as the results came in. The screen was small, and only a black-and-white image was available at that time, but the new technology was an exciting novelty. Unfortunately, our first television set was a disappointment, for it failed to work properly for the big event. After much effort to fix it, the group gave up and went down to Democratic headquarters. By then, things were looking favorable for the Democrats, although commentators such as H. V. Kaltenborn continued to insist that Dewey would win.

It was the next morning before Harry Truman's victory became official. I was jubilant! We would remain in Washington! It didn't occur to me at that moment that four years was a long time for my father to have held the highly stressful office of attorney general. I was not aware that he was receiving lucrative offers to return to private practice, and that he was planning to return to the family law firm in Dallas. It was probable that finally, thirteen years after we moved to Washington, D.C., for a two-year stay, we would return to Texas. My father was not in a rush, however. President Truman had not suggested that he wanted a different attorney general, and their relationship was stronger than ever, reinforced by my father's active support during the campaign.

Timing is everything. As my father used to say, "You have to be at the stop when the bus comes by." During the summer of 1949, the bus came by, Tom Clark was at the stop, and whatever plans were in the offing were totally changed.

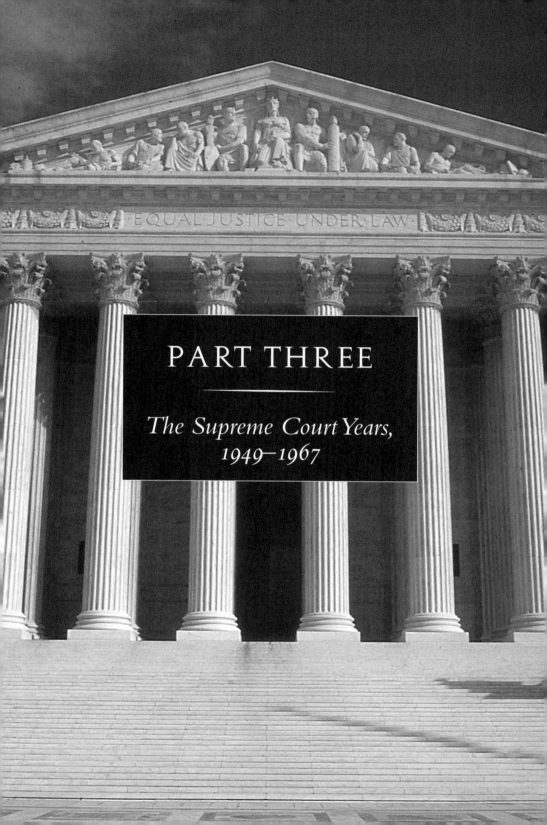

# PART THREE

## The Supreme Court Years, 1949–1967

## CHAPTER 13

# A Controversial Appointment

We have had a great Attorney General for four years, and we will
have a great justice from now on.

Harry S. Truman, 1949

THE REELECTION JUBILATION WAS STILL STRONG on January 30,
1949, when Harry Truman delivered his inaugural address and
called upon the nation to unite: "The tasks we face are difficult. We
can accomplish them only if we work together. Each period of our
national history has had its special challenges. Those that confront us now
are as momentous as any in the past." The speech described what became
known as the Point Four Program—a strategy for building world peace
through four initiatives. The president's program pledged "unfaltering
support to the United Nations and related agencies"; the continuation of
"programs for world economic recovery"; the protection of "freedom-
loving nations against the dangers of aggression"; and "a bold new program for making the benefits of our scientific advances and industrial
progress available for the improvement and growth of underdeveloped
areas." The president was optimistic and idealistic: "On the basis of these
four major courses of action we hope to help create the conditions that
will lead eventually to personal freedom and happiness for all mankind."
Tom Clark continued a strenuous speaking schedule to support and reinforce the president's agenda.

In February 1949, my father, speaking at a celebration of George Washington's birthday, cited the country's commitment to the international
community: "All patriotic citizens realize that there is room for improvement in all things that are human. But our country is not standing still. It is
on the march forward and continues marching in the direction of peace,
liberty and brotherhood under the leadership of that great American, Harry

S. Truman. . . . Today we continue to forge ahead . . . steadily advancing the cause of individual freedom and human dignity. And this, not for ourselves but for peoples everywhere."[1] A few days later, he spoke again, focusing on the potential of technology. Atomic energy, telecommunications, computers, and television were all in their infancy, but the Truman administration understood both their positive and negative potentials, and my father's words are as appropriate and meaningful today as they were in 19 49: "The technology of this modern age—this wonderful challenging age—must advance and serve humanity, not wreck it. . . . Builders, not destroyers, Americans will not fail a world yearning for harmony and peace."[2]

On June 30, 1949, the fourth anniversary of his appointment as attorney general, Tom Clark published a summary of the Department of Justice's activities during his four-year tenure and recorded the accomplishments of each division. The Criminal Division and the FBI received the lion's share of the report because of their activities in handling crime, civil rights, national security, and the communist threat, but the report cited impressive achievements for other divisions as well. The Tax Division, for example, had waged an effective war against tax evaders. Department of Justice lawyers prosecuted 744 cases and obtained 719 convictions—a 96 percent success rate.[3] The Antitrust Division had a record that Tom Clark was especially proud of. He had, in fact, established himself as an exceptional trustbuster, despite initial speculation that antitrust efforts under his leadership would be less rigorous than those under his predecessor. That assumption proved false. My father expressed his commitment to antitrust soon after taking office:

> I believe that I state the deep conviction of all of us when I say that lasting prosperity can best be achieved by the American system of free enterprise . . . Monopoly whether domestic or international in scope is the greatest threat to our continued prosperity. As quickly as we can we are completing the removal of war-time controls over American business. In the near future we shall return to the American free economy system. But we must not allow the removal of government regulation to be supplanted by private monopolistic regulation. It is our duty to see that the door of opportunity remains open.[4]

According to the report, the average number of successful antitrust prosecutions for previous attorneys general had been 42, whereas the figure for Tom Clark was 160.[5] As attorney general, Clark challenged the practices of some of the country's most prominent corporations, including the American Can Company, the A. B. Dick Company, Alcoa (the Aluminum Company of America), and Paramount Pictures. The Paramount case went all the way to the Supreme Court. The antitrust charges arose because Paramount and eight of the largest movie producers controlled both the production of films and their distribution. The government claimed that these studios' distribution system constituted a monopoly that was unfair to small independent theater owners. The Antitrust Division sought a "divorcement" that would sever the connection between the production of films and their distribution to various theaters. The lawsuit had been filed by the government in 1938, had gone through the courts, and was appealed to the Supreme Court in 1947. During the spring of 1948, Attorney General Tom Clark argued the case before the Supreme Court. The Court ruled in the government's favor, reversing a decision by the federal district court of New York City. In February 1949, the Department of Justice accepted Paramount's proposed plan for separating its production activities from the distribution of films. *U.S. v. Paramount Pictures, Inc.* was the third of the three cases that my father argued before the Court as attorney general, joining *U.S. v. California* (the tidelands case) and *U.S. v. John L. Lewis and the United Mine Workers.* He was successful in all three.

As the summer of 1949 progressed, the hectic work pace that my father seemed to thrive on continued, despite his likely resignation. It was not in his nature to slow down, and he was still deeply involved in his work. His secretaries, Grace Stewart and Alice O'Donnell, shared his workaholic values and exemplified the characteristics he sought in his staff. Both were exceptionally hardworking, intelligent achievers in their own right. They were dedicated to their jobs and to their boss. In an interview years later, Mrs. Stewart, who was appointed a district judge after my father joined the Supreme Court, gave the following description of what it was like to work for Tom Clark:

> Well it was work, I'll tell you. He was a hard worker and had no patience with people who didn't do their job. He gave us a lot of leeway, but we worked for him just completely. Everybody had the greatest respect for him. If there was something he wanted, we did it. You knew when he meant business. We knew if he made a request, he wanted it. He generally wanted it yesterday. . . . I frequently rode home in the car with him when he had a government car and chauffeur, and I tell you from the moment we got in till I got out of it he would give me about twenty instructions. . . .
>
> He tried to be helpful to those who didn't have the same opportunities he'd had. Oscar [Bethea] was the first chauffeur, I think. If the chauffeurs ever had any complaints, they knew who to go to. They went right to him, and he'd take care of it. He'd work it out if it was possible.

I tell this story: They had a private elevator that came up to the assistant attorneys general and to the attorney general's offices. He came back from lunch one day, and he had with him a black woman who worked for General Services. She was in her work clothes. He said: "Miss Grace, you know, this lady hasn't had a raise in salary for years. We've got to get her a raise because she needs it."

We had nothing to do with General Services. NOTHING! He patted her on the back, walked toward his office, and said, "Don't worry. Miss Grace will get that raise for you." That was typical! I found somebody over there and got her the raise. He gave the authority so I could call over and use the name of his office. She had waited for him to come in to the private elevator. I'm sure when she spoke to him, he said, "Come on, get on the elevator and we'll go up to the office." So she got on the elevator and walked through the offices. When she went home and told her folks the attorney general got her a raise, they didn't believe it.[6]

The incident tells a lot about my father's compassion for others but also about his high expectations of the people who worked for him. Grace Stewart knew that he meant what he said when he told the woman "Miss Grace will get that raise for you," and she acted accordingly.

By 1949, Tom Clark was the longest-serving member of Harry Truman's cabinet, and there was speculation that he might resign. An article published on May 27, 1949, described him as ". . . indefatigable in his devotion to difficult duty" and as shaping the Department of Justice into a "splendid instrument for public service and national defense."[7] A number of journalists speculated about Clark's future: "His impending resignation to cash in on his standing as a former Attorney General has been repeatedly rumored but flatly denied by Mr. Truman, who is grateful to Clark for substantial help in the last campaign and for sundry other services. . . . The lively Clark family . . . enjoys the Washington whirl, sometimes doing the whirling as host to the Trumans, and has no intention of leaving it any time soon. Of more importance, Clark is determined to go through with his antitrust campaign."[8]

Clearly, the journalist was correct in his assessment of the antitrust "campaign." Antitrust initiatives were continuing, and in the first week of July, Department of Justice lawyers filed charges against E. I. du Pont de Nemours, calling it "the largest single concentration of industrial power in the United States." According to Clark, the du Ponts controlled General Motors and U.S. Rubber through their stock holdings and were responsible for policies unfair to competitors. A *Newsweek* article called the lawsuit the largest since the one that resulted in the breakup of Standard Oil in 1911, and described Clark as "the biggest antitrust man of all times."[9]

The family "whirling" was undoubtedly a reference to the birthday party my parents gave for President Truman on May 8, 1949—his sixty-fifth. It was held at the Anderson House, a grand historical home that had been converted into an elegant party place for Washingtonians. Pianist José Iturbi was a guest, and for forty-five minutes he and Harry Truman took turns playing the piano for the sixty or so attendees. The group loved it. A birthday cake was brought out at midnight, and President and Mrs. Truman stayed on until two—unusually late for them. The party was a big success!

As for the rest of the "lively" Clark family, a major event occurred on April 16, 1949, when Ramsey married his college sweetheart, Georgia Welch. After being discharged as a corporal in the Marine Corps in October 1946, Ramsey had enrolled at the University of Texas in Austin. He and Georgia met and fell in love at the university and married during their senior year. Their wedding, held in Georgia's hometown, Corpus Christi, Texas, was a joyful event attended by members of both families and marking the beginning of a long and happy marriage.

As speculation continued that my father would resign from office, an unexpected event occurred. On July 10, 1949, Associate Justice Frank Murphy died of a heart attack at the age of fifty-nine. His death gave Harry Truman the opportunity to appoint someone of his choosing to the Supreme Court. My father did not anticipate being selected as Frank Murphy's successor. Instead, he immediately developed a short list of possible nominees for the president's consideration. Most of the men on his list were Catholic—Justice Murphy's religion—since there was an unstated tradition at that time that one seat on the Court should be held by a Catholic. But Harry Truman, having already made his decision, did not consult with advisers. When he called my father to his office a few days after Murphy's death, he told him he was considering a "package" appointment—Tom Clark as associate justice and J. Howard McGrath as attorney general.[10]

The choice of McGrath was not surprising, for he had an impressive background. At the time, he was chairman of the Democratic National Committee and a senator from Rhode Island. He had also served as governor of Rhode Island, and as solicitor general from 1945 to 1947. My father and McGrath were good friends. Truman asked my father to think about the package plan and to discuss the possibility with McGrath. Both men approved the package, and Truman announced the appointments on July 29.

Ramsey remembers vividly how he learned of the appointment. He had enrolled at the University of Chicago's law school in the summer of 1949, and he and Georgia were living in a tiny fourth-floor walk-up apartment in the city. He had just returned home from a class taught by Professor Edward Levi when he heard heavy footsteps on the stairs and then a loud knock at the door. When he opened the door, he was startled to see Professor Levi, and wondered whether he (Ramsey) was in some kind of trouble. Levi, a highly respected legal scholar, had known my father when he was Thurman Arnold's assistant in the Antitrust Division (and would serve as attorney general under President Gerald Ford from 1975 to 1977). Levi, panting heavily after climbing four flights of stairs, was obviously excited. "Have you heard the news?" he asked. Ramsey had not. "Your father has been appointed to the Supreme Court!" he retorted gleefully.

Not everyone was as pleased about the appointment as Ed Levi. "Oh No!" moaned an editorial in the conservative *Dallas Morning News*, a reaction that reflected the anger of some Texans over Tom Clark's support of civil rights and his prosecution of the tidelands oil case.[11] The reaction of newspapers from other parts of the country was mixed. Respected *New York Times* columnist Arthur Krock gave a thoughtful assessment:

> The personal traits Mr. Clark has displayed are modesty, loyalty, courtesy in dealings with individuals, and a hard sense of duty which convinced him, a Texan, that he must defy public opinion in that state in the tidewater oil cases. His political philosophy appears to be something to the right of the extreme New Deal and Fair Deal, but to the left of both in his construction of what is a monopoly.... On the whole it is a fair guess that on constitutional questions he will be a moderating influence in the Supreme Court.[12]

Criticism ranged from charges of "cronyism"—Truman, some argued, had appointed a loyal friend rather than the best-qualified person to fill the vacancy—to claims that Clark had mishandled the Kansas City vote-fraud case. Liberals viewed Clark as a threat to civil liberties and an anticommunist extremist, whereas conservatives claimed he had been weak and ineffective in fighting communism. The Blue Star Mothers of America, a conservative group that claimed its goal was the "preservation of Constitutional Republican Form of government," requested the opportunity to testify before the Senate Judiciary Committee in opposition to the appointment: "We must respectfully suggest to you that before considering seriously any such nomination, your investigators should be concerned chiefly with the relations existing between Felix Frankfurter and the Administration, not necessarily because of Frankfurter's Russian birth, but because of his well-known interest in and relations with those composing the personnel of the Kremlin in Moscow. . . . We unequivocally CHARGE TOM CLARK TO BE DEFINITELY OF COMMUNISTIC TENDENCIES."[13]

At the other end of the political spectrum was a group of liberals who strongly opposed the appointment. Former secretary of the interior Harold Ickes expressed his unhappiness in an article entitled "To Tom With Love." Ickes, a strong civil libertarian and an opponent of the Federal Employee Loyalty Program, argued that Clark did not have "the legal learning, the intellectual qualities, or the vision" needed for the position.[14] Henry Wallace, a vice president under Franklin Roosevelt and a presidential candidate for the Progressive Party in 1948, also spoke out: "I trust that every person who believes in and is willing to fight for the Bill of Rights and the Constitution will write and wire the Senate Judiciary Committee to oppose this appointment."[15]

Despite these protests against the nomination, my father enjoyed solid support from Democrats in Congress and from his colleagues at the Department of Justice. One of the most eloquent tributes came from Solicitor General Philip Perlman. In a letter to President Truman, Perlman wrote:

> We who have been in close contact with Attorney General Clark in recent years are sure he will make a great Justice! His long training in the handling of legal problems, his calm, judicial temperament, his personal experience with people in all walks of life, his intense feeling of obligation on behalf of those less fortunately circumstanced, his firm adherence to the letter and spirit of the Constitution, and his great and limitless store of common sense combine to assure him of a place among the great Justices in the history of this Nation. He has won our everlasting affection and esteem. This kindly, forthright citizen, eager to maintain the best and greatest traditions to which he falls heir, cannot fail.[16]

My father received a touching tribute from the federal Bureau of Prisons, an agency that was part of the Department of Justice, in the form of a photo album with letters from the wardens of federal prisons all over the country. The letters expressed congratulations on the appointment, but regret that he would no longer be attorney general. One from the director of the Bureau of Prisons was typical:

We are, Mr. Justice, extremely proud of the accomplishments that the Prison Service was able to make during the time you were our Chief. Many of these we owe to the fact that somehow you were able to make your own philosophy of good will, friendliness, and brotherhood reach to the furthermost parts of our far-flung service. Also, as the booklet will indicate, we are indebted to you for the many practical ways you found to implement these and for your steadfast adherence to sound administrative practices in dealing with our service.[17]

A letter from the superintendent of the National Training School for Boys, an institution that benefited from my father's project to combat juvenile delinquency, shows the special relationship that Tom Clark established with those involved in that field and the high regard they felt for him: "Selfishly, we received the news [appointment to the Court] with misgivings, because we have all felt the security of your friendship, enthusiasm and leadership during the past four years. We were under the impression that former Attorneys General did not know that this School existed. Your annual Christmas Day visit, with the pleasure of encountering your warm, generous personality on that most important day in the boys' year, always took away the sadness with which we had previously been confronted."[18]

The Senate Judiciary Committee began hearings on Tom Clark's appointment on August 9, 1949. Senator Tom Connally led the confirmation effort; Lyndon Johnson, a senator for less than a year but already a force within the Senate, handled the opposition; and Senator Richard Russell of Georgia took charge of procedural matters. On the first day of the hearings, more than seventy endorsements were read from lawyers, judges, educators, clergymen, and labor leaders from throughout the country. Four past presidents of the American Bar Association were among Tom Clark's supporters, and it appeared that confirmation would move quickly and smoothly. The second day, when the opposition had its turn, was a sharp contrast to the first. My father's old nemesis O. John Rogge, representing the Progressive Party, was the first to testify, and was followed by Fowler V. Harper, a spokesman for the National Lawyers Guild; Carol King, the lawyer who had represented Gerhart Eisler; Elizabeth Gurley Flynn, an official of the Communist Party USA; and representatives from the Civil Rights Congress, the Committee for the Protection of Foreign Born, and the National Council of the Arts, Sciences and Professions. Most of these groups had been placed on the Attorney General's List of Subversive Organizations.

Their opposition focused on two related issues: the loyalty program and civil liberties. O. John Rogge, the first to speak, gave lengthy testimony, beginning with charges that the loyalty program and extensive use of wiretapping by the FBI were threats to the civil liberties of citizens and totally unnecessary. In an exchange with Rogge, Senator Homer Ferguson, an avid anticommunist and outspoken opponent of my father's appointment, expressed disbelief at these charges, and found himself in the awkward position of defending Tom Clark: "Wait a minute now. This is what you would do if you were Attorney General of the United States? You are criticizing the Attorney General of the United States in connection with the loyalty program? When you have something here that is vital to the security of America, you say that you would assume everybody was loyal, and therefore nothing would be done about disloyalty?"[19]

The discussion deteriorated into a debate between Rogge and Ferguson on loyalty and communism, causing another committee member to exclaim that they'd be there until Christmas if this were allowed to continue. Rogge finally moved on to other subjects, but got into trouble again when he resurrected the 1936 Texas Senate subcommittee investigation. Republican senator William Langer challenged him on that issue:

Langer: Do you not know that at that time (when Clark was confirmed as Assistant Attorney General) this committee went into the greatest detail on this matter of the $60,000 or $70,000 a year salary?
Rogge: I am not aware of that, Senator.
Langer: At Mr. Clark's insistence? And that he furnished the Judiciary Committee the name of every single client who paid him more than $500 a year?[20]

The exchanges with Ferguson and Langer virtually destroyed Rogge's testimony.

It is difficult to understand the objections of some African American leaders to the appointment on the basis that Tom Clark was anti-Negro. They seemed to ignore a couple of salient facts: Clark was the first attorney general to file an amicus curiae brief—in *Shelley v. Kraemer*—opposing racial discrimination in public housing contracts, and as president of the Federal Bar Association in 1944, he insisted that Negroes be admitted as members. Yet William Patterson, spokesman for the Civil Rights Congress, contended, "The nomination of this man must be an indication to Negro Americans of a perilous future."[21] Many of the complaints Patterson made were historical conditions that existed before my father was born and for which he bore no responsibility. Patterson's lengthy testimony opposing my father was undermined by the announcement that both Robert Silberstein, the president of the liberal National Lawyers Guild, and Thurgood Marshall, then a lawyer for the NAACP, endorsed the appointment. In addition, committee chairman Patrick McCarran displayed an award given to Tom Clark by the District of Columbia Branch of the NAACP. The document read: "For giving actual expression to the practical idealism of our Constitution—that in a true Democracy there be no denial of equality, liberty and Justice to any American."[22]

The opponents had their day, but to no avail. The committee voted 9–2 to forward the nomination to the full Senate, despite the objections of Ferguson, who described himself as "hot under the collar" because the committee had refused to call Clark to testify.[23] Ferguson berated my father on the floor of the Senate for an hour and a half, and was joined by Senator Robert Taft. Taft, a newcomer to the issue, expressed outrage that the committee had failed to force Clark to testify. Finally, the appointment was presented to the full Senate, and Tom Clark was confirmed, 73–8.

He was sworn in on August 24, 1949, by Chief Justice Fred M. Vinson in a ceremony held at the White House on a portico next to the Rose Garden. It was a sunny, sweltering August day with approximately 300 people attending, including family members and friends, many who had traveled from Texas. Senators Tom Connally and Lyndon Johnson, Speaker of the House Sam Rayburn, Vice President Alben Barkley, and President Truman were also present. The president spoke warmly of Tom Clark: "We have had a great Attorney General for four years, and we will have a great justice of the Court from now on."[24]

And so it was official—Tom Clark became the eighty-sixth man, and first (and so far only) Texan, to serve as an associate justice of the United States Supreme Court.

## CHAPTER 14

# A Period of Adjustment

The responsibilities are much greater now.

Tom Clark, 1953

THE SUPREME COURT WAS STILL ENJOYING its summer recess when Tom Clark was sworn in as an associate justice, and the new term would not begin until the first Monday in October. It was a good time to get away, so the day after the swearing-in, we left for Santa Monica, California, where Uncle Bob and his family were vacationing. Mother and I persuaded my father to travel by train—a mode of transportation that we both enjoyed and that gave us the opportunity to stop off in Chicago to visit Ramsey and Georgia. Knowing my father's restless nature, we predicted that he would never make the return trip by train and would find some excuse to fly home.

It seemed the perfect vacation. My father loved the beach—it was the one place where he could relax totally, and he was happy taking walks, lying in the sun, and occasionally dipping in the ocean. Unfortunately, sunny California was cloudy and cool when we arrived, and remained that way. It was the first time in memory that my father had time on his hands, and it was a situation he did not enjoy. Mother described his reaction: "After four years as attorney general and being busy every minute, he was at loose ends. It took everyone in the family to keep Tom busy. He couldn't sit still for a minute." A tragic event suddenly ended our vacation and my father's restlessness. On September 10, Associate Justice Wiley Rutledge suffered a massive stroke and died at the age of fifty-five. Mother's and my prediction that my father would never return home by train came true, for he returned to Washington immediately—via the airlines—to attend Justice Rutledge's funeral.

Tom Clark's life as an associate justice had begun, and he received a warm and cordial welcome from all members of the Court. In fact, no one was happier about his appointment than Chief Justice Fred Vinson. Soon after the appointment was announced, a cartoon by Gib Crockett appeared on the front page of the *Washington Evening Star* showing Vinson gazing contentedly at a photograph of Tom Clark. The caption read: "Thank heavens he's good-natured!"[1] Vinson was in his third year as chief justice—a period known for conflict among its members. It was understandable that he hoped for a good-natured colleague to fill Frank Murphy's seat. My father believed Vinson discussed the appointment with the president and probably recommended him for the position.

My father and Fred Vinson first met when our family moved to Washington, D.C., in 1937. Vinson was a congressman from Kentucky at the time and a good friend of Speaker Sam Rayburn. Later, he and my father served together in Harry Truman's cabinet—Vinson as secretary of the treasury—and became good friends. Vinson was a regular, and my father an occasional, member of Harry Truman's poker group. Vinson left the cabinet in 1946 when Truman appointed him chief justice following the death of Harlan Fiske Stone. Scholar William Wiecek describes Vinson as having "an extraordinary record of achievement," having served as a congressman, a judge on the U.S. Court of Appeals for the District of Columbia, and in several positions in the executive branch of government including secretary of the treasury.[2] My father praised the president's selection in glowing terms during a speech given on June 27, 1946, in Vinson's home state of Kentucky:

Almost in the moment in which I speak, the mere appointment of Fred Vinson to the chief justiceship has already given the whole country, in a troubled hour, a wave of comfort. . . . In a disturbed instance when the tempers of men had been worn raw, the appointment by President Truman acted like the balm of Gilead. This is the gift from Kentucky to the people of America. . . . Few men have risen to the Supreme Court amid anything like the universal paean of praise that met the announcement of the Vinson appointment.[3]

But Vinson joined the Court at a difficult time—a *New York Times* article described the opening of the Court's 1946 term as "the tensest . . . in all of the 157 years of the tribunal's life."[4] The causes of dissension were complex, but a major issue involved Associate Justices Robert Jackson and Hugo Black. The conflict began when Justice Black failed to recuse himself from a case involving the Jewell Ridge Coal Corporation and the United Mine Workers. Black's former law partner was counsel for the

United Mine Workers, and Jackson was angry that Black had remained in the case. The Court ruled in favor of the UMW in a 5–4 decision—Black voting with the majority and Jackson with the minority. Later, while in Germany presiding over the Nuremberg Trials, Jackson made a public statement about the case that Black considered a "gratuitous insult."[5] It was known that Jackson wished to be chief justice, and rumors spread that Black had threatened to resign if the president selected him to replace Stone. My father later expressed his views on the controversy: "Well of course Black had been on the bench then for some nine years, and so you can't just keep staying out of cases forever. . . . I didn't think there was much foundation to Bob's blast, but it caused the President some troubles. . . . So we had to try to figure out who would be the best peacemaker."[6]

Truman concluded that he should not appoint a sitting justice as chief justice, and quickly decided upon a friend, Secretary of the Treasury Vinson. Vinson seemed eminently qualified for the position. He had served in all three branches of the government, and was known for his congenial personality and ability to work with others. My father supported Vinson:

> I was for Vinson too. . . . And, I think one of the motivating forces was the fact that there was a rift—a public rift—on the Court. . . . Frankly, I'm in favor and I had always thought that the President should promote within the Court, but this was an exception because of this rift which had been aired publicly. So, I would say that Vinson was appointed largely on account of his warm friendship with the President, and the president's knowledge of him being able to bring about understanding among competing forces and the necessity of trying to bring the Court a little higher respect from a public standpoint.[7]

Justices of the Supreme Court are typically independent, assertive individuals, and the Vinson Court was made up of some of the strongest personalities in the history of that institution—among them were Hugo Black, Felix Frankfurter, William O. Douglas, and Robert Jackson. Despite Vinson's reputation as a conciliator, he had failed to bring harmony to the Court after three years as its nominal leader.

Ironically, in an interview given years later, my father described the justices' relationships in a way that contrasted sharply with his earlier description and with the public perception at that time: "When I came to the Court I never heard of any animosity between any of the Justices. Indeed, Justice Black and Justice Jackson were more Chesterfieldian than any of them, and certainly all of the justices evidenced not only hospitality but respect for each other, although they were from various backgrounds and geography. I never saw any ill-will or animosity. They treated each other as equals. There was no evidence of any Justice having any animosity towards another. There were differences of opinion, of course."[8]

He did acknowledge that Felix Frankfurter may have felt some animosity toward Vinson, and recalled an incident during which the two men almost clashed physically. It occurred during discussion of a case at the justices' weekly conference. Frankfurter had the habit of standing and walking around, as if lecturing, when talking during a conference—probably a remnant of his years as a professor at Harvard. One Saturday while "lecturing" his colleagues in this manner, he made a remark that Vinson took as a personal insult. Vinson rose from his chair at the conference table and started toward Frankfurter. My father, who was sitting between the two men, quickly pushed his chair back, blocking the chief justice. Vinson stopped and withdrew, and Frankfurter sat down. My father concluded:

I don't think there would have been any "free-for-all," but the Chief was sort of making towards Felix and when I pushed my chair back, it was sort of a blockade. He withdrew a little bit, and then quieted down, and Felix sat down. He [Vinson] never showed any temper other than that while I was there. And I think everyone had a very warm feeling towards Chief Justice Vinson. It may be that Justice Frankfurter had some animosity. He never expressed it to me. I officed next door to him for years. He and I were very close friends. I am a great admirer of Felix. I think he was terrific, although we often differed.[9]

Although my father revered the Court and was not part of any discord that may have existed, he found adjustment to his new life difficult. The fast-paced, high-pressure schedule of an attorney general suited his energetic and gregarious nature, and, in contrast, the quiet, scholarly atmosphere of the Supreme Court seemed monastic. Besides the dramatic change of pace, my father also felt the enormous responsibilities of his new office: "The responsibilities are much greater now. As attorney general I could refer a law case to a member of the staff, but in this court the justice must study every case and be prepared to give his best judgment because it is the final say for the people appearing before it."[10]

Tom Clark was not the first to find adjustment to the nation's highest bench challenging. Earl Warren described the change from being governor of California to becoming chief justice "a painful transition."[11] Associate Justice Robert Jackson, another former attorney general, told my father that he had asked Chief Justice Charles Evans Hughes how long it took him to adjust to the Court's environment, and Hughes had replied, "About three years."[12] Jackson said it had been closer to five for him, and I suspect my father's timetable was similar to Jackson's.

Perhaps the fact that he dealt with four cases involving Texas that first year also contributed to his discomfort. Just as he immediately found himself in conflict with his native state on the tidelands case when he became attorney general, he found himself ruling against Texas four times during his first term on the Court. All four cases concerned civil rights, and two, *Sweatt v. Painter* and *McLaurin v. Oklahoma State Regents*, were important precursors to the landmark *Brown v. Board of Education*. Both cases involved segregation in graduate schools, but the petitioners' circumstances were very different. Heman Sweatt had been denied entrance to the University of Texas Law School on the grounds that the Texas Constitution required separate schools for white and black students. At a hearing before a district court in Travis County, Texas, it was ruled that Sweatt must be admitted to the University of Texas Law School or to another state law school of equal quality. Since no such law school existed for blacks, the state immediately undertook organizing one. The new school, established in Austin, consisted of four rooms—an entrance hall, two small classrooms, and a bathroom. Sweatt refused to enroll in the newly formed Negro school, claiming he would not receive an education equal to that obtainable from the established all-white law school.

In the case of *McLaurin v. Oklahoma State Regents*, George McLaurin, a sixty-eight-year-old black teacher, had initially been denied admission to graduate school at the University of Oklahoma. A three-judge court held that the state must provide him with graduate-level education, and subsequently the university admitted him. But McLaurin was isolated from other students. He was required to sit at a desk in an alcove separate from the regular classroom; he ate alone in an area removed from the rest of the cafeteria; and he was assigned a special desk on the mezzanine of the university library. McLaurin claimed that this degrading and discriminatory treatment prevented him from obtaining an education comparable to that of white students. The issue in both cases was whether the doctrine of "separate but equal" resulted in true equality.

In April 1950, before the cases were discussed in conference, Tom Clark circulated a memo to the other justices:

> I hesitate to state my views prior to conference, but in these cases I think my convictions, based in part upon my experience in Texas, might be helpful to the Court.
>
> . . . I will not recite all the reasons underlying my conviction that segre-

gated education is unequal education. . . . But we know that the facilities are unequal all through the South. . . . My question, then is "how" to reverse [*Plessy v. Ferguson*, the 1896 case that found the "separate but equal" doctrine constitutional] not "whether" or "why." There is fear that a flat overruling of the Plessy case would cause subversion or even defiance of our mandates in many communities. Intimidation, threats and riots are envisioned. A long and terrible step backward is forecast if we go too far forward with legal doctrines at this time. . . . I believe those fears are relevant in resolving Constitutional issues of this type and of this magnitude. I would share those fears should we begin holding, today or tomorrow, that swimming pools may not be segregated; or should we decide that the fourth grade in schoolhouses in Mississippi must be open to Negro and white alike. But I feel confident that those fears are groundless should we rule that there can be no segregation in the college or graduate schools. There will be no defiance by the school administrators. Negroes now attend the University of Texas Medical School, the Oklahoma Law School, the Arkansas Medical and Law Schools.

I am in accord with the suggestion that we limit our opinion to graduate schools. I do not suggest, however, that we write an opinion reaffirming *Plessy* to all but graduate schools. I would not sign an opinion which approved *Plessy*.

I join, then, with the proposal that we reverse this case upon the ground that segregated graduate education denies Negroes the equal protection of the laws. I repeat that I would not approve *Plessy* in any manner. We have before us just two cases. Both concern graduate schools. Perhaps the fundamental legal reason for limiting discussion to graduate schools is that we should avoid decision of Constitutional questions in advance of the strict necessity for that decision.[13]

The memo clearly states Tom Clark's belief that *Plessy* had to be reversed, but also reveals his caution regarding how best to do it. In 1950, he was not ready to tackle the "separate but equal" doctrine beyond the graduate-school level:

How will I vote when the swimming pool and grammar school cases arise? I do not know; that is irrelevant. Should they arise tomorrow I would vote to deny certiorari, or dismiss the appeal, so that we would not be compelled to decide the issues.

I join with those who would hold that whatever the present validity of *Plessy v. Ferguson* there is no square ruling in this court that separate graduate education is equal education within the meaning of the Fourteenth Amendment; and that for the reasons outlined above, the petitioner Sweatt should be admitted to the University of Texas Law School and the discrimination against McLaurin at Oklahoma ended.[14]

The Court voted unanimously in favor of the petitioners in both cases and for the first time, in *Sweatt v. Painter*, ordered a black student admitted to an all-white institution—a major achievement![15]

Two other cases did not deal with the "separate but equal" doctrine but with other forms of racial discrimination. In *Cassell v. Texas*, Tom Clark voted with the majority in a case that overturned the murder conviction of a black man because of racial discrimination in the selection of the grand jury. The fourth case, *Terry v. Adams*, involved a Texas county's system for barring blacks from voting in the Democratic Party primary. Since Texas was a one-party state at that time, the Democratic primary was tantamount to the general election. In 1944, the Supreme Court ruled in *Smith v. Allwright* (a suit originating in Harris County, Texas) that it was unconstitutional for states to deny African Americans the right to vote in the primaries of political parties. Fort Bend County, Texas, however, concocted a way to bypass that ruling through a group known as the Jaybird Democratic Association. The Jaybirds held meetings at which they endorsed candidates for county offices. These meetings were in reality preprimaries, but since their association was a private club, the Jaybirds were able to prohibit blacks from participating. The candidates endorsed at these all-white meetings then entered the Democratic primary, usually unopposed. The Texas Court of Appeals had ruled in favor of the Jaybirds, but a majority on the Supreme Court, including Tom Clark, reversed the lower court's decision. In his concurring opinion, my father wrote:

> To be sure, the Democratic primary and the general election are nominally open to the colored elector. But his must be an empty vote cast after the real decisions are made. And because the Jaybird-indorsed [sic] nominee meets no opposition in the Democratic primary, the Negro minority's vote is nullified at the sole stage of the local political process where the bargaining and interplay of rival political forces would make it count.
>
> The Jaybird Democratic Association device, as a result, strikes to the core of the electoral process in Fort Bend County. Whether viewed as a separate political organization or as an adjunct of the local Democratic Party, the Jaybird Democratic Association is the decisive power in the county's recognized electoral process.[16]

Detractors who insisted that Tom Clark's appointment to the Court would have disastrous repercussions for African Americans should have been comforted by these decisions written during his first term as an associate justice. Tom Clark, the grandson of a Confederate officer killed during the Civil War, had grown far beyond his southern-based background and would continue to do so.

A scholarly article appearing in a 1951 issue of the *Indiana Law Journal* offers an insightful analysis of Tom Clark's first term on the Court. I'm certain my father would deny that his presence on the Court eased the existing tensions between its members, but that is what the author, Professor C. B. Dutton, suggested. He concluded that the justices were more in accord after my father joined the Court because the number of 5–4 decisions during my father's first year dropped dramatically—from thirty-six during the 1948–1949 term to two during 1949–1950.[17] Dutton also noted that Clark had been "scrupulous about disqualification," recusing himself from 101 cases.[18] The figure seems high, but justices who are former attorneys general have inevitably been involved in a large number of cases that will eventually appear before the Court, and so they must recuse themselves from those cases to avoid any perception of bias or conflict of interest.

One highly publicized case that my father withdrew from was *Dennis v. U.S.*, which upheld the perjury convictions of Communist Party leaders who had been prosecuted while he was attorney general. There was much speculation whether Tom Clark would recuse himself from the case. His law clerks, Larry Tolan and Percy Williams, apparently thought he would participate, and in a memo to him argued that the convictions should be reversed because the jury was made up of government employees and the trial was unfair. They felt his vote might be decisive, but their effort was in vain, for my father recused himself and a majority of justices upheld the conviction.

Dutton observed that though many had predicted Justice Clark would shift the Court's balance to the conservative side, it was difficult to put him into a strictly conservative or liberal slot. Clark wrote thirteen opinions for the majority, a respectable number for a new justice. He did not write any dissenting opinions. An examination of his decisions, according to Dutton, led to four basic conclusions. First, Tom Clark was a "federalist," who came down on the side of federal laws if they conflicted with state laws. This conclusion may have surprised those who had followed my father's career, for as recently as 1947 he had described himself as a states'-rights supporter: "The Federal Government should enter the local field only when the unlawful action is clearly a federal offense or where local law enforcement breaks down. I am a great believer in States' rights. The best government is that closest to the people."[19]

But his experience as attorney general made him realize that states were sometimes unable or unwilling to protect the rights of individuals, and that awareness produced Dutton's second conclusion: Tom Clark believed the federal government should take responsibility for protecting civil rights when the states fail to do so. The third conclusion—that Tom Clark was not antiblack—should have been evident before he joined the Court, and was clearly supported by his votes in *Sweatt, McLaurin,* and other opinions dealing with civil rights.

In the article's fourth and final conclusion, Dutton noted that Tom Clark voted with Chief Justice Vinson most of the time, and to Dutton, this meant that Clark looked to Vinson for leadership. While I believe it was more a case of two people with similar backgrounds seeing things in similar ways, it is true that many justices new to the Court tend to have a mentor. Justice Harry Blackmun and Chief Justice Warren Burger, for example, were known as the "Minnesota Twins" for the first few years Blackmun served as associate justice, yet they frequently took opposite sides after Blackmun became more experienced.

Whatever influence Vinson, or any other justice, may have had on him initially, by 1952, Tom Clark was comfortable with his role as a justice, and he clearly established his independence in *Youngstown Sheet and Tube v. Sawyer.* Presidential power was the issue. The Korean War was in process—an undeclared multinational war backed by the United Nations. At the same time, steelworkers and steel companies were in an altercation over benefits and wages. A strike loomed. Truman believed that a steel strike during the war would have a devastating effect on the country and create a serious national emergency. After lengthy negotiations failed to produce an agreement, Truman announced on April 8, 1952, that he was ordering Secretary of Commerce Charles Sawyer to seize the steel plants. The steel companies were stunned, and the press's reaction was overwhelmingly negative. The liberal journal the *Nation* declared that the president had exaggerated the crisis and overstepped the constitutional powers of his office. Though known to be at the other end of the political spectrum, the *New York Daily News* took a similar, though more strident, stand. Its lead editorial, headlined "Truman Does a Hitler," also argued that the president had no authority to take over the mills and should have consulted Congress.[20]

Steel companies took the issue to the federal district court of Judge David A. Pine and succeeded in getting an injunction against the seizure. The government immediately appealed to the Supreme Court, and the justices agreed to review the case. Oral arguments were held on May 12,

1952, and speculation about the outcome was rampant. A majority believed the Court would uphold the president's power to seize the steel plants, a conclusion partly based on the makeup of the Court—five Roosevelt and four Truman appointees. Views on the issue were not strictly based on party allegiance. Some Republicans, such as Senator Everett Dirksen, expressed the view that the president had the power to seize the steel mills. Legal scholars argued both sides of the issue. One who supported the president's power to seize the mills suggested that constitutional protections could be relaxed even in periods before and after a war.

The Court's decision came as a surprise. By a 6–3 vote, the justices declared that the president's action was unconstitutional. Truman and his colleagues were shocked and distressed. The justices' differing opinions must have made the decision especially difficult to accept. Amazingly, all of the justices who composed the majority—Black, Douglas, Frankfurter, Jackson, Burton, and Clark—wrote separate opinions. In a session that lasted two and a half hours, each presented a unique reason for his decision. Judicial scholar Carl Swisher remarked that "because of the diversity [of the justices' opinions] the only thing we can assert with confidence is that in some degree the enhancement of the power of the presidential office has been restrained."[21]

My father's opinion differed sharply from those of the other members of the majority. He argued that the president had the authority to seize the mills, but was obligated to use an option established by Congress—the Taft-Hartley Act—before employing the more extreme measure:

> The Constitution does grant to the President extensive authority in times of grave and imperative national emergency. In fact, to my thinking, such a grant may well be necessary to the very existence of the Constitution itself.... In describing this authority, I care not whether one calls it "residual," "inherent," "moral," "implied," "aggregate," "emergency," or otherwise. I am of the conviction that those who have had the gratifying experience of being the President's lawyer have used one or more of these adjectives only with the utmost of sincerity and the highest purpose.
>
> ...Where Congress has laid down specific procedures to deal with the type of crisis confronting the President, he must follow those procedures in meeting the crisis.[22]

Vinson, joined by Minton and Reed, strongly defended the president, and commented while delivering his dissent that Justices Clark's and Jackson's views had changed drastically since they were attorneys general. The press picked up on the same point, putting my father on the defensive and eliciting the following comment: "The press pointed out that as Attorney General I had advised Senator Thomas that the inherent powers of the President were very great but as a Justice had stricken down the President's seizure of the steel mills. My reply was that when writing the Senator I was Attorney General; now I am a Justice! Still these self-reversals haunt you and arouse disagreeable comment."[23]

The general public's reaction to the decision was extremely favorable. Although he had previously defended the president's use of power, scholar Edward S. Corwin viewed Tom Clark's reasoning as the most sensible approach to the issue: "Only Justice Clark . . . guided by Marshall's opinion in the early case of *Little v. Brown*, had the courage to draw the appropriate conclusion."[24]

We continue today to debate the powers of the president, especially in times of undeclared war. *Youngstown Sheet and Tube* clearly placed a limit on those powers, and history has come down on the side of the justices who voted that the seizure of the steel mills was unconstitutional. The decision also shows that by 1952, Tom Clark was relying wholly on his own judgment and was not influenced by Chief Justice Vinson or by his association with the president. He established himself as his own man on the Court—an independent thinker, not an ideologue, who did what he thought was right based on the specific case at hand. Arguably, the greatest tribute my father received concerning the steel case came from a colleague who was not known for extending compliments lightly—Felix Frankfurter. In a handwritten letter to my father, Frankfurter expressed his views on the significance of the case "to thoughtful people who are fairly called 'liberals'—New Dealers and Fair Dealers. [The decision] vindicated and restored their faith in law. They feared our Court was just like Hitler's court, Stalin's court and Peron's court, merely a political agency of the government. And you, more than anyone else, proved the Court's independence."[25]

But Tom Clark's decision in *Youngstown Sheet and Tube* came with a personal price, for it had a negative impact on his relationship with a man he revered—Harry S. Truman.

My father would not admit that a change in the friendship had occurred. His affection for Harry Truman never wavered, and though he knew that some people around Truman were angry with the outcome of the case, he refused to believe that the president shared their animosity:

> Some of his [Truman's] people have talked to me and they were very much disturbed over it. They didn't like it at all. I talked to the President many,

many times since that time, and once not too long before his death. At no time did he mention it.... I think he knew that in my heart I'd done what I thought was the correct thing for me to do under my oath. He was not going to criticize me for that. Some of these people seemed to think that he was disturbed about it, but I rather doubt that. Some people tried to visit some reprisals on me, but they never did come about....

I just called the case as I saw it, and I rather think that I was trying to be what I'd call a constitutionalist, if you had to have a tag. And that would be that I tried to interpret the Constitution in the light of the necessities of the time. It's not a document that was written in a vacuum, and the framers did not put it in a straitjacket; and those who have the function and duty to interpret it should interpret it in the light of the necessities of the period in which it evolved. And if the necessities of the State require a decision in favor of the state, why so be it. Certainly in that case the rights of the individual companies should prevail, and that's the way I voted.[26]

During the years following *Youngstown Sheet and Tube*, my father and Truman were together many times, and the decision was never mentioned. I remember my father returning home one day a few months after the opinion was handed down, and announcing to Mother and me that he had just "bumped into the Boss"—a reference to the president. Their meeting was cordial, and my father beamed as he recalled it. Many others who saw the two men together were unaware of any tension between them. Jim Knox, my father's law clerk during the 1961–1962 term, recalled the apparent warmth that characterized their relationship: "The Justice was close to former President Truman who visited the Justice several times during the October 1961 term. It was obvious that any disappointment the President may have had with some of Justice Clark's earlier decisions had long since been forgotten. There was a great warmth between these two great men."[27]

In April 1972, just eight months before Truman's death, my father visited him at the hospital in Kansas City. The doctor limited the visit to five minutes, but the president was enjoying the conversation and wanted my father to stay longer. For almost forty-five minutes they talked about everything from poker to world affairs. In November 1972, civil rights groups honored the president with an award for his accomplishments in that field. The rapidly failing president was unable to attend the presentation, so my father was asked to accept it for him.

Despite these cordial encounters and an outward appearance of warm friendship, some closest to the president have recorded a different view of the impact of *Youngstown Sheet and Tube* on Truman. They say that the president reacted emotionally to the unfavorable decision and took it as a personal rebuke. While not specifying a specific justice, Truman's own words seem to support their assessment: "Packing the Supreme Court simply can't be done. . . . I've tried it and it won't work. . . . Whenever you put a man on the Supreme Court he ceases to be your friend. I'm sure of that."[28]

Whatever changes in the friendship may have occurred on Truman's part, my father's feelings toward the president remained constant. After Truman died on December 26, 1972, Tom Clark expressed the high esteem and deep affection that he felt for the former president:

> He had a profound effect upon my life, and I'm grateful for the opportunity to have been able to, not only serve with him, but be his friend over the years. I deeply appreciate the many, many things he did for me—not only from the standpoint of appointments he gave me, but also from a standpoint of giving me the privilege of associating with him and knowing him intimately and having some of his personality rubbed off on myself. One thing that we don't have now [in 1972] but he certainly did have, and that is integrity with the people. They believed in him—there wasn't any gap in credibility. . . . They knew that when he said what he was going to do, "come hell or high water" it was going to be done. That's why he's going down as one of the great Presidents—I'd say one of the five greatest.[29]

## CHAPTER 15

# Investigation Mania

The courts must be kept free from public controversy.

Tom C. Clark, 1953

H ARRY TRUMAN'S EMOTIONAL REACTION TO *Youngstown Sheet and Tube* may have been exacerbated by the circumstances he was experiencing as president. The early 1950s were an exceptionally difficult time for Truman. China entered the Korean War and our troops were in retreat; the firing of General MacArthur for insubordination created a storm; McCarthyism was at its height; and the president's approval rating sank to an all-time low. The early 1950s were difficult for my father as well. The 1952 election was looming, and the Republicans, still reeling from their unexpected defeat in 1948, were determined to win at any cost. They launched a campaign to discredit the Truman administration by leveling charges of corruption and of mishandling the communist threat. Tom Clark, though out of political office for more than two years, became a target.

The trouble began in the fall of 1951 when a subcommittee of the House Judiciary Committee, while investigating misconduct on the part of officials in the Bureau of Internal Revenue, expanded its search to include the Department of Justice's Tax Division, headed by Assistant Attorney General Theron Lamar Caudle. The subcommittee, chaired by Democratic congressman Frank Chelf, sent President Truman information on Caudle that it considered incriminating. Truman fired Caudle, citing "outside activities incompatible with the duties of his office," but adding that as far as he knew, Caudle had done nothing illegal.[1] As attorney general, Tom Clark had recommended Caudle to Truman for appointment as assistant attorney general, and consequently he was immediately brought into the controversy as questions were raised about his reasons for the recommendation.

The reasons were valid. Tom Clark was assistant attorney general of the Criminal Division when he first met and worked with Caudle, a U.S. attorney in North Carolina with an outstanding reputation and a progressive record on civil rights. After my father became attorney general, he felt that Caudle was a good choice to succeed him as assistant attorney general of the Criminal Division. Caudle had the strong backing of North Carolina's two senators, and his record as a progressive southerner made him an especially attractive candidate for the position. Two years later, in 1947, my father transferred Caudle to the Tax Division.

After the Caudles moved to Washington, our families became close. Mother and Mrs. Caudle belonged to the same canasta club and saw each other frequently. Rose Caudle, the second of the Caudles' four children, became one of my best friends. I spent most of the summer of 1946 with the Caudles while my parents were in Europe for the Nuremberg Trials. During the following school year, I often walked or rode the bus to their house after school to play spud or touch football with the gang of kids that lived around them. I loved going to their home, which was always lively and somewhat disorderly—a sharp contrast with my own, which was especially quiet since Ramsey had joined the marines and I was virtually an only child.

Lamar Caudle was a big man, exuding warmth and charm, even to a twelve-year-old girl. "Sweet thing," he would greet me with his booming, baritone voice and thick southern drawl. Everyone who knew him believed in his honesty but, at the same time, acknowledged that he was naïve and trusting to a fault. Neither these characteristics nor his experience in small-town North Carolina prepared him for the potential pitfalls of the nation's capital, and he became friendly with people who were perceived to be taking advantage of his position in the government. Appearances can be everything, and his association with some of these people led to his downfall. One highly publicized incident involved a mink coat that Mrs. Caudle purchased through a friend, Joseph Landau, a tax lawyer who had official business with the Department of Justice's Tax Division. She paid for the coat with money she inherited from an aunt, but newspapers jumped on the incident, implying that the coat was a bribe for favors to be done by her husband.

Another incident could have caused my father problems had he not been extremely judicious about his associations. The Caudles were struggling to make ends meet on an assistant attorney general's salary, so when the opportunity arose to invest in oil property that was estimated to bring in two hundred dollars a month, Mr. Caudle took advantage of it. Mrs. Caudle, after describing the investment to Mother during one of their canasta club get-togethers, suggested that she and my father invest in the oil properties. My parents were also on a tight budget and found living on a cabinet member's salary difficult. Additional income would have been helpful, and Mother wanted to take advantage of what seemed like a good opportunity. My father discussed the investment with Caudle but felt further investigation was necessary. The man offering the properties was from Texas, so my father asked his brother Bob to check into his background. Uncle Bob discovered the man was known as a "big-time gambler," and that was enough for my father. He turned down the opportunity to invest, despite Mother's protests. My father had turned down other seemingly harmless offers and had returned many attractive gifts during his years as attorney general in order to avoid any appearance of impropriety, and Mother sometimes felt that he was unreasonably cautious. She changed her mind when the Caudle investment became a news item, and was portrayed as a "shady" deal. Sadly for the Caudles, the purchase of the oil property not only was used against Mr. Caudle, but also proved to be a poor investment financially.

In February 1952, the subcommittee of the House Judiciary Committee held lengthy hearings, and its main witness was Lamar Caudle. Caudle was devastated by Truman's dismissal. "My heart is broken!" he declared in emotional testimony.[2] In his desire to clear himself, he denied any wrongdoing and suggested that if he had erred, it was only because he was following the orders of his superiors—Tom Clark and Howard McGrath.[3] He hinted at possible impropriety on my father's part in the *Amerasia* and Kansas City vote-fraud cases—both still controversial despite thorough investigations that had found no evidence of illegality. Up to that point, Attorney General Howard McGrath had supported Caudle, but McGrath became increasingly frustrated with the way the issue was being handled, and pressured by the subcommittee, he resigned. James McGranery, who served as the assistant to the attorney general under my father for one year before being appointed a federal judge, became attorney general.

Subcommittee members had clashed with McGrath, and so they welcomed McGranery as someone who could usher in a "new attitude of helpful cooperation."[4] Initially, McGranery opposed another congressional investigation, and on July 2, 1952, while testifying before the subcommittee, expressed that view: "It would be difficult for me to understand why another committee of the Congress of the United States would devote its valuable time to going over the same ground that was so thoroughly exhausted by two of its predecessors and to resurrecting charges which were conclusively established to have been wholly without foundation in fact and inspired wholly by political considerations."[5]

Despite this strong statement, two months later McGranery ordered an FBI investigation of my father and Herbert Bergson, Assistant Attorney General of the Antitrust Division. My father gave the following account of his first encounter with the new FBI investigation:

> McGranery was Attorney General, and they had the FBI, Edgar [J. Edgar Hoover], call me one day and said he had a memorandum from the Attorney General, that wanted me to be interviewed and that he's going to send up a fellow named Hood who was the SAC. They have Special Agents in Charge of the various cities.... And so he came with another FBI man— usually they travel in pairs ... They asked me some of the most asinine questions I ever heard of in my life. They had taken every case, every antitrust case, and tried to figure out something that was wrong with it or if I'd interfered with it when I was Attorney General.[6]

The investigation began with an examination of allegations that Tom Clark had accepted money to facilitate the paroles of four convicted gangsters. Since my father had no part in granting the paroles and learned of them through the newspapers, the allegations were quickly dismissed. The investigation finally focused on two cases—one concerning the liquor industry, the other the movie industry. The liquor case involved four major liquor companies, known as the Big Four: Seagrams, Schenley, National, and Hiram Walker. The Antitrust Division, after investigating possible antitrust violations from 1943 to 1945 under Attorney General Biddle, had concluded there wasn't sufficient evidence to warrant prosecution. After the war, a second investigation was undertaken, and the same conclusion was drawn. One Department of Justice attorney, however, Ernest Branham, was unhappy about the decision not to prosecute, and although he admitted he had no proof, stated that he believed there had been a "fix."[7] His complaints and accusations apparently led the FBI to investigate possible mishandling and misconduct by Clark and Bergson.

Of the twenty-seven Justice Department lawyers interviewed by the FBI, all but Branham stated forcefully that the investigation of the case had been carried out with no interference from anyone in the department. Holmes Baldridge, who served in the General Litigation Section of the Antitrust Division for twelve years, concluded his interview with the statement that the Department of Justice was "as clean as a whistle," and he knew of no irregularities at any time, in any case. The following statement, made by one attorney, was a typical response to FBI interrogations: "I did not at any time receive any instructions, either direct or by inference, from Tom Clark or Herbert Bergson or anyone else to soft-pedal or mishandle the investigation. On the contrary, I got the impression there was a conscientious effort to see if it could be prosecuted successfully."[8]

In the movie industry case, Schine Chain Theatres had been prosecuted, convicted, and ordered to divest itself of a number of its theaters. Controversy developed over the settlement negotiated for divestiture. One government lawyer, Philip Marcus, convinced that the penalties were too light, suggested that favoritism was being shown because the Schine lawyer, Irving Kaufman, was a friend of Tom Clark. Sigmund Timberg, who was involved in the negotiations as chief of the Judgment and Judgment Enforcement Section of the Antitrust Division, refuted Marcus's claim. He stated that neither Clark nor Bergson had interfered with negotiations in any way and that on several occasions the attorney general had supported his decisions over the objections of Kaufman.[9] Robert Wright, the Antitrust Division's attorney in charge of the Schine case, stated, "During the trial and throughout his work on the [case] he never encountered any efforts on the part of anyone in the Department to suppress his activities or retard the normal prosecution of the case."[10] Twenty-three lawyers besides Marcus were interviewed, and all stated that the case was handled properly.

The FBI investigation cut a wide swath and, in the spirit of beating a dead horse, once more dredged up the Texas subcommittee investigation of 1936. An FBI agent even went to Dallas to interview my father's former law partner Bill McCraw! The House subcommittee worked closely with the FBI and requested a comparison of its files on the case with those of the Department of Justice files. One file contained a letter from Hoover to Senator Homer Ferguson, dated June 18, 1947, supporting my father: "In the years the present Attorney General Tom C. Clark has been associated with the Department of Justice, I have had the opportunity of working with him in innumerable cases, and I am glad to state that he has not in any way taken any action to prevent any investigation being conducted to its legal conclusions."[11]

By this time, my father had been on the Court for almost four years. The subcommittee of the House Judiciary Committee was chaired by Republican congressman Kenneth Keating, who requested that my father appear before the subcommittee. My father refused, citing the separation of the three branches of government:

Dear Mr. Keating:
I wish to acknowledge the invitation of your subcommittee to appear and furnish any information in my possession regarding my official activities as Attorney General, particularly in respect to seven cases. . . .

Your invitation involved a principle of great importance: the preservation of the independence of the three branches of the Government. As with the Executive and Legislative branches, our Constitutional system makes the Judiciary completely independent. This complete independence from the Executive and Legislative branches is necessary for the proper Administration of justice. . . . The subcommittee should agree that the courts must be kept free from public controversy. In order to discharge their high trust, judges have scrupulously maintained, as is clearly the duty of the office, a dignified retirement from the strife of public affairs and partisan politics. . . .

In view of the above considerations I must forgo my personal inclination to appear before your subcommittee. . . .

Sincerely yours,

Tom C. Clark[12]

My father then attached a summary of the seven cases that the subcommittee had inquired about, and described his involvement in each. Still, Republican members of the subcommittee were not satisfied. Keating called Clark's refusal to testify "unthinkable" and an "escape" from responsibilities.[13] A number of newspapers were also critical. "Anything Sacred about Clark?" one newspaper's editorial exclaimed.[14] The *Washington Times Herald*, never a friend of Democrats, headlined an editorial "The Impeachment of Mr. Justice Clark."[15]

Besides the Keating subcommittee and FBI investigations, two other congressional investigations that affected my father were being conducted, both on the issue of communism. The inquiries were conducted by HUAC, then under the chairmanship of Congressman Harold Velde of Illinois, and by the Senate Internal Security Subcommittee, chaired by Senator William E. Jenner of Indiana. A crisis occurred in November 1953 when Velde, without consulting Democratic members of the committee, issued subpoenas to former president Truman, former secretary of state James Byrnes, and Associate Justice Tom Clark. The subpoenas were the result of a scathing speech by Attorney General Herbert Brownell in which he accused Truman of appointing an alleged Communist spy—Harry Dexter White—to the International Monetary Fund in 1946. When Brownell gave his speech, both White, who was an assistant secretary of the treasury at the time of the appointment, and Fred Vinson, the secretary of the treasury and White's boss at that time, were dead. My father was drawn into the issue after Lamar Caudle testified that he had given Attorney General Clark an FBI report indicating that White had communist connections. Caudle claimed that he had "begged and pleaded" with Clark to stop White's confirmation.[16] He was apparently unaware that White had already been confirmed.

Truman and Byrnes immediately refused to appear before the committee, despite the subpoenas. My father also refused after consulting with all members of the family and with two former colleagues: Peyton Ford, a former deputy attorney general, and Philip Perlman, a former solicitor general. My father's two law clerks, Ellis McKay and Ernest Rubenstein, were assigned the task of researching the legal aspects of the situation, and they, along with Ramsey, who had flown up from Dallas to help in any way he could, scoured files from the attorney general years that were stored in the Supreme Court basement. No relevant material was found. Everyone agreed that my father's appearing before HUAC would create a political circus, and so advised him against doing so. A letter declining the invitation to appear was prepared, and McKay, Rubenstein, and my father's secretary, Alice O'Donnell, walked from the Supreme Court to the Capitol to deliver it. In the letter, my father again cited the importance of the separation of powers and of keeping the judicial branch out of politics. He also offered to respond in writing to any questions committee members might have. Public response to the subpoenas was negative. A large majority felt that HUAC had overreacted and. overstepped its boundaries in issuing the subpoenas. No further action was taken and the matter was dropped.

None of the investigations found any wrongdoing on the part of Tom Clark. The House Judiciary subcommittee's report was not published until July 6, 1954. It cleared my father but criticized his refusal to testify. It also included a vague accusation suggesting that Clark "was responsible for some of the conditions the subcommittee has found most worthy of criticism."[17] The report was sympathetic to Lamar Caudle: "Every member of the Subcommittee and its staff who observed Caudle and his testimony over a long period shares in the opinion that he is an honorably-motivated man. This does not rule out his shortcomings; he was weak and the naïve code of a country lawyer did not serve him well in the corrupting sophistication of the Washington he knew. . . . But Caudle never sold himself for riches or for power. And in every instance where the choice was clearly black or white, Caudle's choice appears to have been impeccably correct."[18]

The statement that "every member" shared the same view was not totally accurate, for Representative Byron Rogers, a Democrat from Colorado, filed dissenting opinions and charged that the report was "shot through with half truths, innuendoes and examples of the smear techniques so abhorrent to fairness. . . . The committee for days permitted

Caudle to relate every suspicion, rumor and gossip in Washington. He blamed everyone but Caudle."[19]

Looking back, I am amazed at my father's ability to handle this stressful period. He remained as upbeat and optimistic as ever, and the ongoing investigations, with the accompanying sensationalized news coverage, did not distract him from his work on the Court or from his involvement with the family. Mother found the situation more difficult. She was upset by the bad publicity and the unfair charges. She felt that my father had sacrificed wealth and a much easier life for public service, and was being rewarded with ingratitude and slander. Ramsey and I were minimally affected. Ramsey was practicing law in the family law firm in Dallas, establishing himself as a successful and highly respected young lawyer. The family was thrilled when he and Georgia had their first child, Ronda, on February 17, 1952.

I was a freshman at Wellesley College in the fall of 1951, when the events that triggered the investigations occurred. I was angry about the investigations, which I viewed as purely political, and was concerned about the Caudle family. Rose and I had drifted apart, not because of any conflict between us, but because we attended different schools and our busy lives took us in different directions. While still in high school, I had met and fallen in love with Tom Gronlund, a handsome Naval Academy midshipman, and by the spring of 1952, we were planning to marry. Our wedding took place on August 7, 1953—at the height of the investigations—but the controversy did not detract in any way from the celebration. Unlike most fathers of the bride, my father was actively involved with the arrangements. He and I discussed the guest list, and the question of whether we should invite the Caudles arose. By this time, events and Mr. Caudle's testimony implicating my father had caused a break in their friendship, and the Caudles' attendance at the wedding would have been awkward. With his usual wisdom and lack of bitterness, my father said that of course I should invite them: they were my friends, and what had happened did not change that. The Caudles were invited, but did not attend the wedding. Instead, they sent a warm and loving letter of congratulations.

I remember the good times and warm friendship that I enjoyed with the Caudles and am still angry when I recall what happened to them. Despite the subcommittee's conclusion that Caudle was an honest man, the Department of Justice under Attorney General Brownell reopened the case in 1956, charging him and Matthew Connelly, Truman's appointments secretary, with attempting to block the prosecution of a St. Louis shoe manufacturer, Irving Sachs, who had been charged with tax evasion. The grand jury deliberated for two months before issuing indictments.

Caudle and Connelly were tried separately, and the Caudle trial was, at best, bizarre. The prosecution had completed its side of the case, but the defense was still presenting its evidence when the judge presiding over the case committed suicide. Rather than having a mistrial declared, another judge was brought in. The new judge simply read the record of what had taken place, and based his instructions to the jury on his reading of it. Graham Morrison, a former assistant attorney general and a close friend of Lamar Caudle, attended the trial, and felt that the judge's instructions were virtually an order to convict.[20] Caudle was convicted and sentenced to two years in prison. When released on parole after six months, he described himself as a political prisoner. Even those who were involved in removing Caudle from office were outraged. Charles Murphy, Truman's former special assistant who had advised Truman to ask for Caudle's resignation, considered the indictments and convictions of Caudle and Connelly "one of the worst cases of political persecution that I ever heard of. It appears to me that the Eisenhower administration, at least the Attorney General, came into office with the purpose of doing everything he possibly could do to discover and make some kind of case of wrongdoing against the Truman administration."[21]

President Lyndon Johnson pardoned Lamar Caudle in 1965. Caudle expressed appreciation, but his life had been destroyed. He was not only ruined professionally and financially, but, most tragically, his family was devastated. The death of Mrs. Caudle in 1958 was a direct result of the investigations and conviction. The children's lives were permanently scarred. Despite the differences that had developed between him and Caudle, my father agreed with the many people who felt that Caudle had been a victim of politics and that the resulting miscarriage of justice would remain a black spot on this country's political history.

For my father, however, the investigations that had plagued him for more than two years finally ended. He emerged from them stronger than ever, and, as my brother Ramsey predicted, the accusations and attempts to smear his good name were soon forgotten. Ironically, as the fifties proceeded and cases concerning national security and communism predominated, Tom Clark would become a favorite of many of his former detractors.

*Tom Clark in Boy Scout uniform,
age fourteen, 1913 or 1914.*

*Tom Clark in
his Bryan Street
High School
graduation
photo, Dallas,
1917.*

*Tom Clark,*
*University of*
*Texas graduate,*
*1922.*

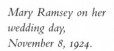

*Mary Ramsey on her*
*wedding day,*
*November 8, 1924.*

Tom C. Clark, Jr.,
age four, and William
Ramsey Clark, age
two, 1930.

Mimi,
Mary
Clark, and
Ramsey, 1934.

*Mimi, Mary Clark, Tom Clark, and Ramsey at home after Clark's appointment as attorney general, June 1945.*

*Tom Clark in the kitchen with his mother, Virginia Falls Clark, summer 1945.*

*Attorney General Clark, Secretary of the Treasury Fred Vinson, and President Harry Truman at an American Newspaper Women's Club reception, January 11, 1946. Photo by Harris & Ewing.*

*J. Edgar Hoover testifying before a Senate Judiciary subcommittee, June 5, 1947. Left to right: Senator James P. Kem, subcommittee chairman; Tom Clark; D. M. Ladd, assistant director of the FBI; and FBI director J. Edgar Hoover. The man in the foreground is unidentified. Photo by Acme Photo.*

*Tom Clark dancing with Mimi, Inaugural Ball, January 20, 1949. Photo by Acme Telephoto.*

*Tom Clark being sworn in as an associate justice by Chief Justice Fred Vinson, August 24, 1949.* Left to right: Dean Acheson, Tom Clark, Harry Truman, Fred Vinson, and Postmaster General Jesse M. Donaldson.

*On the White House lawn following Tom Clark's swearing-in as a Supreme Court justice.* Left to right: Ramsey Clark, Georgia Clark, Mimi, Tom Clark, Mary Clark, Robert L. Clark, August 24, 1949.

*Chief Justice Fred Vinson kisses the bride, Mimi Clark Gronlund, August 7, 1953. Probably the last picture taken of Vinson. Photo by Wide World Photos, Inc.*

*Justices of the U.S. Supreme Court, 1964.* Back row: *Byron White, William Brennan, Potter Stewart, and Arthur Goldberg.* Front row: *Tom Clark, Hugo Black, Earl Warren, William O. Douglas, and John Harlan.*

*Tom and Mary Clark on their fortieth wedding anniversary, Reception Room, Supreme Court Building, November 8, 1964.*

*Ramsey Clark, Tom Clark, Georgia Clark, Mimi Clark Gronlund, Mary Clark, and Tom Gronlund, Supreme Court Conference Room, November 8, 1964.*

*Justice Clark swearing in his son Ramsey as attorney general, March 11, 1967. Left to right: President Lyndon Johnson, Tom Clark, Ramsey Clark, Vice President Hubert Humphrey, Thurgood Marshall.*

*Tom Clark and Ramsey Clark, 1967.*

*Tom Clark at seventy.*

## CHAPTER 16

# A Delicate Balance

The problem of balancing the State's interest in the loyalty of those in its service with the traditional safeguards of individual rights is a continuing one.

Tom Clark, *Slochower v. Board of Higher Education* (1956)

EACH SUPREME COURT SESSION deals with cases that reflect the issues of that particular time, and during the 1950s, when the Cold War dominated the country's attention, the justices faced a virtual flood of cases pitting national security against individual freedoms. In 1957, for example, 41 percent of the decisions handed down dealt with that conflict.[1] Tom Clark, who as a former attorney general was responsible for controversial policies that strove to control subversion during the early years of the Cold War, frequently, with some important exceptions, came down on the side of the government in these decisions.

Many of the appeals heard by the Supreme Court during the 1950s involved prosecutions based primarily on the Smith Act (officially, the Alien Registration Act of 1940), which made it a criminal offense "to knowingly or willfully advocate, abet, advise, or teach the duty, necessity, desirability, or propriety of overthrowing the Government of the United States or of any State by force or violence, or for anyone to organize any association which teaches, advises or encourages such an overthrow, or for anyone to become a member of or to affiliate with any such association." One major issue that emanated from these appeals concerned the constitutionality of loyalty oaths. During the 1951–1952 term, the Court dealt with several cases challenging loyalty oaths required by states, and in most cases it upheld the states' positions. In one example, *Gerende v. Election Board*, the justices upheld a Maryland law requiring candidates for office to first take an oath that they were not attempting to overthrow the government nor were knowingly members of organizations pursuing that goal. Just two months after *Gerende*, my father wrote and handed down the majority opinion in another loyalty-oath case, *Garner v. Board of Public Works of Los Angeles*. His opinion found constitutional a California loyalty oath barring from employment anyone who had belonged, within the previous five years, to an organization that "advised, advocated or taught, the overthrow, by force, violence or other illegal means, of the Government of the United States."[2] The decision was based on the assumption that members of the organization were aware of its goals when they joined it, and, if they were not aware, that Los Angeles officials would give them another opportunity to take the oath. The decision was not unanimous—Justices Black and Douglas dissented, and Frankfurter and Burton concurred in part and dissented in part.

Since Tom Clark was not an ideologue but judged each case on its merits, a year later, in December 1952, he was part of a unanimous Court that came to an opposite conclusion from those in *Gerende* and *Garner*. *Wieman v. Updegraff* was about a state loyalty oath in Oklahoma, but the state, unlike the city of Los Angeles in *Garner*, failed to determine whether employees who belonged to an organization on the attorney general's list were aware of its subversive goals. Furthermore, if they claimed that they were not aware of a subversive goal, the state did not allow them another chance to take the oath. In his opinion, Tom Clark declared, in terms that are relevant today as we face comparable problems, that democratic principles must be upheld:

> During periods of international stress, the extent of legislation with such objectives [loyalty as a requirement for public office] accentuates our traditional concern about the relation of government to the individual in a free society. The perennial problem of defining that relationship becomes acute when disloyalty is screened by ideological patterns and techniques of disguise that make it difficult to identify. Democratic government is not powerless to meet this threat but it must do so without infringing the freedoms that are the ultimate values of all democratic living . . . The legislature is therefore confronted with the problem of balancing its interest in national security with the often conflicting constitutional rights of the individual. . . .
>
> But membership may be innocent. A state servant may have joined a proscribed organization unaware of its activities and purposes. In recent years, many completely loyal persons have severed organizational ties after learning for the first time of the character of groups to which they had belonged.[3]

The unanimous opinion was considered remarkable because it was written by a justice known for his conservative views on national security. My father's argument pleased civil libertarians especially, and he received a complimentary letter from Richard Barnes Kennan, the secretary of the National Commission for the Defense of Democracy through Education:

> It was a most heartening and encouraging experience to read the opinion you wrote in the Oklahoma Loyalty Oath case. . . . The steadily narrowing circumscription of freedom of thought thru fear techniques is a blow at the unique elements that have served to place our nation in a position of leadership in the world today. It was a very stirring experience to have the Supreme Court render such a timely and important decision for the cause of freedom.[4]

Civil libertarians must have been disappointed in another 1952 decision, *Adler v. Board of Education of City of New York*. In that case, the justices ruled on New York's civil service law, the Feinberg Law, which denied employment to anyone belonging to an association on the state Board of Regents' list of subversive organizations. But unlike the loyalty oath at issue in *Wieman*, the law applied only to members of an organization who were aware of its purpose. A majority of the justices, including Tom Clark, ruled in favor of the state in a 6–3 decision, with Justices Black, Douglas, and Frankfurter dissenting.

Fred Vinson was still chief justice when these decisions were handed down, but by 1954, as the stream of cases involving communist subversion continued, the makeup of the Court changed significantly. Earl Warren became chief justice after Vinson's death, and he presided over arguments in another case involving subversion, *Emspak v. U.S.* The defendant, Julius Emspak, testified before HUAC during its investigation of communist infiltration of labor unions. He answered numerous questions willingly until interrogators sought information about specific individuals and their possible membership in the Communist Party. Emspak refused to answer, invoking the Fifth Amendment, which protects against self-incrimination, and the First Amendment, which guarantees freedom of speech, including the right to criticize the government. Emspak's defense failed, and a lower court convicted him of contempt of Congress. The case reached the Supreme Court in October 1953, a month after Chief Justice Vinson died, and took a virtual roller-coaster ride before a final decision was reached.

The outcome illustrated the beginning of a new direction for the

Court under the leadership of Earl Warren. When the case was first argued, Associate Justice Stanley Reed wrote what at that time was the majority's opinion, which affirmed the lower court's ruling by a vote of 6–2. The new chief justice voted with the majority; Associate Justice William O. Douglas did not vote. Justice Hugo Black, unhappy with the decision, moved to have the case reargued. His motion carried, and the case was reargued in April 1955. When the justices met in conference to reconsider the case, Chief Justice Warren opened the discussion with the announcement: "I have changed my mind from last year."[5] Justice Douglas joined him, making the vote 5–4, still in favor of upholding the lower court's conviction. The count changed again after Justices Burton and Clark switched to the Warren group. My father was a strong defender of all the amendments that make up the Bill of Rights, including the Fifth. He changed his vote after rethinking Emspak's right to refuse to testify, as guaranteed by the Fifth Amendment. The conviction was reversed by a 6–3 vote.

Another example of my father's support of the Fifth Amendment came in *Slochower v. Board of Higher Education of New York City*. At issue was the constitutionality of New York City's charter, which required that any employee using the Fifth Amendment to avoid answering questions be discharged from office and ruled ineligible for employment. Harry Slochower, an associate professor at Brooklyn College, an institution run by New York City, denied being a member of the Communist Party but used the Fifth Amendment to avoid answering certain questions. He was summarily discharged from his position and given no opportunity for a hearing. In a 5–4 decision, the Supreme Court reversed the lower court's conviction. The dissenting justices were Reed, Minton, Burton, and John Harlan, who had joined the Court after the untimely death of Robert Jackson. Tom Clark wrote the opinion for the majority, upholding Slochower's invocation of the Fifth Amendment and reversing the conviction. His decision stated that Slochower had been denied due process of law:

> The problem of balancing the State's interest in the loyalty of those in its service with the traditional safeguards of individual rights is a continuing one. . . .
>
> . . . We must condemn the practice of imputing a sinister meaning to the exercise of a person's constitutional right under the Fifth Amendment. . . . The privilege against self-incrimination would be reduced to a hollow mockery if its exercise could be taken as equivalent either to a confession of guilt or a conclusive presumption of perjury.[6]

*Wieman, Emspak,* and *Slochower* clearly illustrate that Tom Clark, although typically described as a conservative who came down on the side of the government, could not be tagged with any ideological label.

Another important change in the makeup of the Court occurred in 1956 when Associate Justice Sherman Minton retired and President Eisenhower appointed William J. Brennan to fill the vacancy. Brennan would prove to be a significant presence on the Court and would reinforce the new direction begun under the leadership of Earl Warren. My father often found himself on the opposite side of Brennan and Warren, and a series of decisions inadvertently made him a temporary hero to ardent anticommunists. The case that caused the greatest uproar was *Jencks v. U.S.* (1957). Clinton Jencks was a former president of the International Union of Mine, Mill and Smelter Workers. The Taft-Harley Act required that union members file a statement affirming that they were not members of the Communist Party. Jencks did so, but during an FBI investigation, informants indicated otherwise, and Jencks was indicted for perjury. Testimony during the trial revealed that the informants had provided the FBI with written statements about Jencks, and his defense attorney requested that the judge be allowed to review these papers to determine whether they were consistent with oral testimony given during the trial. Government lawyers objected to revealing classified FBI files, and the lower court refused Jencks's request. The case was appealed to the Supreme Court.

Early deliberations by the justices did not suggest the controversy that *Jencks* would produce. All members of the Court, including Tom Clark, agreed that the FBI files should be made available to the judge.[7] The main issue was whether all the documents should be submitted or only those that the government considered relevant. Tom Clark and Harold Burton felt that the latter procedure should be followed. Warren assigned the case to Brennan, who differed from that approach. He argued that the documents should be available not only to the judge but to all involved parties. Frankfurter expressed misgivings but went along with Brennan. My father had agreed that the judge should receive the materials, but to hand them over to the defendant as well was more than he could tolerate. This decision clearly struck a nerve after his years as attorney general, when he protected sensitive FBI files and refused to turn them over to congressional committees. A 6–2 opinion was handed down on June 3, 1957, overturning Jenck's conviction unless the requested documents were forthcoming and made available to everyone involved in the case. Harold Burton issued a brief dissenting opinion, but Tom Clark delivered a stinging dissent in terms that contrasted sharply with his usually discreet, tactful style:

Even the defense attorneys did not have the temerity to ask for such a sweeping decision. . . .

Unless the Congress changes the rule announced by the Court today, those intelligence agencies of our government engaged in law enforcement may as well close up shop, for the Court has opened their files to the criminal and thus afforded him a Roman holiday for rummaging through confidential information as well as vital national secrets.[8]

My father's angry words made newspaper headlines and became a rallying call for anticommunists. An uproar ensued, and conservative members of Congress moved quickly to pass legislation that would bypass the decision. Two months later, the Jencks Act was passed. It modified but did not overturn the decision. Tom Clark's views prevailed, however, since the act allowed only judges access to classified files and made them responsible for giving relevant documents to defendants.

The controversy over Jencks was an embarrassment for the Court, and Frankfurter felt he was at least partially to blame. In a note to Brennan, he wrote: "I do justifiably blame myself regarding Jencks, for I can say with complete confidence that if the majority opinion had contained what I wanted to put into it, there would have been no Clark opinion to help kick up a rumpus. Without the Clark dissent there would have been no rumpus."[9] In response, Brennan accepted responsibility and expressed concern for the unanticipated criticism of the Court: "The regrets should not be yours but wholly mine, because you suggested not once but several times that something be done to answer Tom's approach. I confess to considerable concern over the summer that I may have been the instrument (and in my first year) for demeaning the standing of the Court."[10]

Brennan never expressed any unhappiness about the Jencks dissent to my father, and when I asked him in a 1981 interview whether he had been angry with my father, he gave the following unequivocal response: "Never! I mean, we put on quite a show, and you feel some fervor involved, but in personal relations—never. His and mine were just so close. We sat next to each other, and I announced the decision, and your dad announced his dissent. As far as the courtroom was concerned, you'd think we were at each others' throats. Afterwards, we went out to lunch— as always."[11]

In contrast to Brennan's reaction, Frankfurter was clearly upset. Soon after the Jencks decision was handed down and the unfavorable publicity was at its height, my father confided in Mother and me that "Felix" hadn't spoken to him for almost a week. My father was also uncomfortable with the praise he was receiving from far-right conservatives. On his way home from the Court one day, he was sitting in the car, waiting for the traffic light to change, when another car pulled up beside him. The driver motioned to get his attention. It was Senator Joseph McCarthy. "Great decision, Mr. Justice," the senator proclaimed, "we appreciate your fine work." My father chuckled ruefully when relating the incident: "Makes me wonder if I made the right decision," he mused.

The uproar over *Jencks* had not subsided two weeks later, when four controversial opinions reversing lower-court convictions were handed down. June 17, 1957, became known as "Red Monday" because all four cases concerned alleged communists. Tom Clark did not participate in one case, *Service v. Dulles*, because it involved the *Amerasia* case, which he had presided over as attorney general, but he dissented in the remaining three cases. Two, *Watkins v. U.S.* and *Sweezy v. New Hampshire*, involved the investigatory powers of Congress. The plaintiffs in both cases had refused to answer questions about colleagues when testifying before HUAC. John Watkins, a union vice president, responded to inquiries about his own activities with the Communist Party, but refused to answer questions about associates who might have been communists in the past, claiming that the questions had nothing to do with the investigation. A lower court convicted him of contempt of Congress. The Court's decision reversing the conviction was based on "fundamental fairness" and the committee's responsibility to tie the questions to the stated purpose of the inquiry.[12]

In *Sweezy v. New Hampshire*, Paul Sweezy, a university professor who described himself as a "classical Marxist" but not a communist, refused to answer questions about his associates in the Progressive Party. Sweezy had been investigated by Louis Wyman, the attorney general of New Hampshire, who had a reputation as an anticommunist extremist. A major issue was whether the Court had the right to intervene in the state's activities. Clark, joined by Burton, wrote that the Court could intervene only if an individual's constitutional rights under the First Amendment were superior to the right of the state to pursue possible subversives. Clark and Burton felt that an individual's rights were not superior, but a majority of the justices disagreed.[13] The lower court's ruling was struck down, and limitations were placed on the state's investigatory powers.

The most controversial of the four Red Monday cases was *Yates v. U.S.* Oleta O'Connor Yates was a leader of the Communist Party in California. She and thirteen other communist leaders were accused of organizing the party for the purpose of overthrowing the government. They denied the charge, but were convicted and given the maximum sentences allowed by law. Their appeal challenged the Smith Act, which made illegal not only membership in the Communist Party, but also the organizing of any group with the goal of overthrowing the government. Eight of the nine justices ruled that advocating overthrow was not enough; there had to be evidence of action or planned future action rather than mere words. Five of the defendants were freed, and new trials were required for the remaining nine. Tom Clark was the lone dissenter. His notes, written after the majority opinion was distributed to the justices, were adamant: "Majority seems to think [it] must find articles in *People's World* (a Communist party publication) advocating forcible overthrow—absurd! Knocks out organizing count of indictment. . . . Too bad—hope government will not be discouraged."[14] In his dissent, Clark pointed to precedent—*Dennis* (1949), in which the court upheld the convictions of eleven communists who had been prosecuted under the Smith Act. Tom Clark felt that the two cases were virtually the same and that the Court should not reverse itself. He also understood that the *Yates* decision was a death knell for the Smith Act.

Reaction to the four Red Monday cases covered the political spectrum. The *St. Louis Post-Dispatch* cheered the decisions: "The Bill of Rights is stronger because of these four decisions." The *Washington Post* proclaimed that "the Court had "reasserted its guardianship of individual liberty which was long overdue." At the other end of the spectrum, the headline of a *Chicago Tribune* editorial read "Major Service for Reds," and the *New York Journal-American* described Red Monday as "Communists' Greatest Victory."[15]

A flurry of anti–Supreme Court legislation erupted in Congress. The most serious threat to the Court's power was sponsored by Senator William E. Jenner, a Republican from Indiana. He, along with Senator John Marshall Butler of Maryland, introduced legislation that would have prohibited the Court from considering five types of cases that involved subversion. While the bill was being debated, anti-Court members passed five other bills that reversed specific decisions related to communism. The seriousness of the situation was expressed by legal scholar Walter Murphy: "If Jenner-Butler or all or most of the House bills were enacted into law the resurgence of judicial power would come crashing down."[16] The efforts to undermine the Court continued for a year, but were finally defeated by liberals in Congress under the effective leadership of majority leader Lyndon Johnson.[17]

As the McCarthy era ended and concern over communism mellowed, appeals involving that issue decreased significantly. My father's experience as attorney general clearly influenced his views on national security, and he continued to support the government in a majority of national-security cases. There were notable exceptions to that support. In 1957, during the same term in which *Jencks* and the Red Monday cases were decided, he agreed with the majority in *Schware v. Board of Bar Examiners* that the state of New Mexico could not prohibit someone from taking the state's bar exam simply because he was a former member of the Communist Party. Initially, my father had leaned toward dissent, but changed his mind. When he finally decided to join the majority opinion, he wrote a note to Justice Black, the author of *Schware*:

Dear Hugo—Brace yourself! Don't fall from your chair! For in #92, *Schware*, I agree! TCC[18]

He remained a consistent supporter of the Fifth Amendment, and in 1965 voted with the majority in *Albertson v. Subversive Activities Control Board*, another case that involved violation of the protection provided by that amendment.

The justices undeniably had strong feelings about certain cases, but even if there was disagreement between them, personal relationships were rarely affected. Ellis McKay and Ernest Rubenstein, who clerked for my father during the 1953–1954 term, said they never heard my father say anything negative about another justice, though they cited an incident in which they felt criticism would have been appropriate. The occasion dealt with an opinion that Felix Frankfurter was writing for the majority. My father had objected to certain language in it, and said he would join the majority only if changes were made. Frankfurter agreed and my father joined the majority. When the final text came out, the changes in language had not been made. The law clerks were angry, but my father made no comment or criticism.[19] A year later, another law clerk reported somewhat differently: "By the 1955 term, he [Tom Clark] had begun to shed any awe in which he had originally held Frankfurter; a number of times he made mildly deprecatory comments about him and his desire to run everything."[20] Despite these differences, Frankfurter, known for his sometimes prickly personality, and my father enjoyed a friendly relationship and mutual respect. My father spoke warmly of him: "He and I were very close friends. I am a great admirer of Felix. I think he was terrific, although we often differed."[21]

In 1981 interviews with Justices William Brennan, Byron White, and Potter Stewart, I asked each about Tom Clark's relationships with other members of the Court.

Justice Stewart:

Oh, they were very, very amicable and cordial—very friendly. There was a great deal of mutual respect. Your father was a great personal friend of Chief Justice Warren, although professionally many times they did not agree. But that didn't affect one bit their personal friendship. One of the things that lawyers learn, any lawyer, let alone any member of this court, is that professional differences really don't have much to do with personal relationships.

Justice White:

. . . he was very friendly, asked if there was anything he could do to help me, to make it easier, and he invited me to come around to chat any time I felt like it. And he was always very solicitous of any suggestions I might have. . . . I used to see him quite a bit downstairs in the first aid room. There's a place down there where justices can go and have a little mild exercise. Bicycles, things like that. I used to see your father there with some regularity and have a chat with him. We always had a good time. . . . Your father had a marvelous sense of humor, and, as you know better than I, hardly ever forgot anything he ever experienced.

William Brennan, describing a close relationship with my father:

We hit it off immediately. He was wonderful to everybody. I was impressed with the extent to which he tried to make me feel comfortable. He taught me something and that is to help someone new feel comfortable. It's quite a frightening experience to come here [the Supreme Court] for the first time.

Undoubtedly, my father felt great respect and affection for his colleagues on the Court. On one of the two or three occasions that he played golf with President Dwight Eisenhower, the president expressed his disappointment in Warren and Brennan. Eisenhower may have assumed that he had a sympathetic ear in Tom Clark, but he was mistaken. When commenting on Eisenhower's remark, my father made the following statement: "I think Brennan and Chief Justice Warren are two as distinguished judges as we've ever had on the Supreme Court, and I think they'll go down in history as contributing as much as any justice who ever sat there. I really believe that Warren will be equal to, if not ahead of, [John] Marshall."[22]

Clearly, the issue of national security versus individual freedom, which frequently placed Tom Clark on the opposite side of cases from Warren and Brennan, was waning by the 1960s. In studying Tom Clark's opinions in these cases, scholars will inevitably differ on whether he succeeded in addressing "the problem of balancing" these two important needs. Ironically, however, the most significant case of the fifties, and the one that had the greatest impact on the country, dealt with a totally different area of the law.

## CHAPTER 17

# The Brown *Decision and Civil Rights*

We don't have any army to enforce our opinions.

Tom Clark

T HE FIFTIES HAVE TYPICALLY BEEN VIEWED as a bland decade during which a "silent" generation conformed to the norms of the day. But as the late author David Halberstam wrote, stirrings beneath the placid surface would explode during the following decade and bring about dramatic changes in the country.[1] Civil rights was foremost among these changes, and the Supreme Court, through the landmark decision *Brown v. Board of Education*, a catalyst for achieving them.

Although it was not universally recognized, Tom Clark had established himself as a champion of civil rights before *Brown* was decided. His development into a civil rights advocate was gradual but began early—perhaps starting when he witnessed a lynching at age nine. Eight years later, his choice of the topic "modern slavery" for his speech as Bryan Street High School's class orator suggests that he was sensitive to the plight of black Americans and felt that they remained in a form of slavery. His views expanded more when, as a young lawyer, he represented a number of impoverished African American clients, such as Charlie Ellis, whose case is described in Chapter 4. In 1944, as president of the Federal Bar Association, he insisted that African American lawyers be admitted as members of that association. And there can be no doubt that President Harry Truman was a powerful influence on his development. Under Truman's direction, he was deeply involved in writing and lobbying for the proposed Civil Rights Act of 1949. He was the first attorney general to file an amicus curiae brief in a civil rights case (*Shelley v. Kraemer*). Justice

William O. Douglas once commented that "[Tom Clark had] the indispensable capacity to develop so that with the passage of time he grew in stature and expanded his dimensions."[2] Nowhere was this characteristic seen more clearly than in the field of civil rights. The man from Texas whose father felt that the white and black races could not mix and whose mother refused to visit the Lincoln Memorial became a dedicated civil rights supporter. Once my father became an associate justice, his decisions in cases such as *Sweatt v. Painter* and *Cassell v. Texas* illustrated his growth and should have indicated how he would vote on the issue of segregation.

Then, in 1953, major changes occurred in the Clark family and on the Supreme Court. In the case of our family, my marriage, at the age of twenty, meant a transition to an empty nest for my parents and the start of a new life for me. I met Tom Gronlund in the fall of 1949, when I was sixteen and he was in his second year at the U.S. Naval Academy. Four years later, on August 7, 1953—just after my sophomore year at Wellesley College—we were married. Initially, my parents, though they liked Tom, were concerned because of my age and were disappointed that I did not finish my education. I assured them that I would do so, but could not say when. There was also concern because Tom was a Catholic. In 1953, marriages between Protestants and Catholics were labeled "mixed marriages" and were viewed negatively by many. The Catholic Church had not yet experienced the "open window" that Pope John XXIII initiated almost ten years later, and it demanded a great deal of the non-Catholic. Some of my Texas relatives felt that my parents should have tried to prevent the marriage, but that would have been totally out of character for Tom and Mary Clark. They respected all religions, believing that religion was an individual choice. My father had been raised in the Episcopal Church, but felt that the wife should determine the family's church preference. He joined Mother's Presbyterian church after they married, and was an active church member during the early years of their marriage, serving as a church elder and teaching a Sunday-school class. He, even more than mother, worried that religious differences could cause problems in our marriage, but both he and mother gave us their full support once our decision to marry was final, and our wedding was a large, beautiful celebration. One of the guests was Chief Justice Fred Vinson, and my wedding album contains a picture of him in the process of planting a kiss on my forehead. I believe it was the last picture taken of the chief justice. A month later, at the age of sixty-four, he died suddenly after a massive heart attack. His death ushered in a new era for the Supreme Court.

There was an immediate outpouring of sympathy. My father was one of the first to visit and bring condolences to Roberta Vinson, the chief justice's widow. President Eisenhower, vacationing in Colorado, immediately returned to Washington to attend the memorial service. Former president Truman also attended the service, describing Vinson as a "great man and a great justice."[3] Tributes poured in from various sources. *Life* magazine reported that Vinson's "firm but conciliatory influence restored the dignity it [the Supreme Court] was losing through the squabbling of the justices."[4] An article in the *American Bar Association Journal* praised Vinson's performance as chief justice: "During his years as Chief Justice he wrote from a brilliant and penetrating mind some of the most important and controversial legal opinions of our time."[5] These opinions included one rescinding Justice William O. Douglas's stay of execution for Julius and Ethel Rosenberg as well as several forerunners of *Brown*—*Shelley v. Kraemer,* banning racially restrictive housing covenants; *Sweatt v. Painter,* ordering the University of Texas Law School to admit a black student; and *McLaurin v. Oklahoma,* requiring that black graduate students have the same rights to the facilities of the University of Oklahoma as white graduate students.

Along with the tributes to Vinson came speculation about who the next chief justice would be. Eisenhower decided quickly, for he had promised the governor of California, Earl Warren, an appointment to the Supreme Court when the first opening occurred, and Vinson's death created that opening.[6] Tom Clark and Warren had known each other briefly in 1941 when both were involved in the Japanese internment. They were on opposite sides of the 1948 election campaign, when Warren ran on the Republican ticket as Tom Dewey's running mate, and their paths did not cross. After Warren became chief justice, they quickly became good friends. The two men were alike in a number of ways. Both were warm, outgoing, unpretentious, and devoted to their families. The Warrens lived at the Shoreham Hotel, located across the Taft Bridge, which spanned Rock Creek Park, and a short walk from our apartment on Connecticut Avenue. My father and Warren often walked to the Court together when the weather allowed.

When Earl Warren arrived on the Court, five segregation cases, combined under the rubric *Brown v. Board of Education,* had already been placed on the Court's docket. The cases had been discussed the previous term, while Vinson was still chief justice, and notes from that 1952 conference reflect conflicted views and the probability of a divided decision. Chief Justice Vinson believed that Congress should take the lead in eradicating segregation. Justice Reed, a Kentuckian like Vinson, felt that within the next twenty years, segregation would be eliminated without a court ruling if the states were allowed to deal with it themselves. Justices Jackson and Frankfurter were torn between judicial precedent—*Plessy v. Ferguson* (1896) had established the constitutionality of "separate but equal"—and personal conviction: both men abhorred segregation. Black (the only justice from the Deep South), Douglas, Burton, and Minton advocated overturning *Plessy*. Tom Clark, whose southern roots were similar to Black's and whose father had declared that "white people will never allow them [Negroes] social equality," seemed ambivalent.[7] He was willing to overturn *Plessy* if the ruling allowed states the time and flexibility to work out effective methods for implementing the decision. But he warned, "It must be done carefully or it will do more harm than good."[8] Frankfurter, who thought a divided decision might be "catastrophic," suggested having the cases reargued.[9] A majority of the justices agreed, and *Brown* was rescheduled for the fall of 1954. When Chief Justice Warren took office, consideration of the segregation cases was moved to December to give him more time to familiarize himself with them.

There was absolute secrecy as far as what transpired as the justices debated the issue, but clearly Chief Justice Warren's leadership brought about unanimity. Justice Reed had begun to prepare a dissent in February, but by April, when arguments were completed, a unanimous decision had been reached. Several of the justices made minor revisions to the draft of the opinion that was circulated. My father, sensitive to the southern reaction, softened the language by changing "[the] education of Negroes was forbidden by law in most Southern states" to "in some states," and "public education had already received wide acceptance in the North" to "had already advanced further in the North."[10] He also requested a change in one of the citations listed in footnote 11. The footnote cited educator and sociologist Kenneth Clark, but referred to him only as "Clark," with no first name or initial. My father, afraid that some would think he was the "Clark" in the footnote, requested that a *K*. be added to the citation.[11] His request was granted.

On the morning of May 17, 1954, my father made a point of passing through his law clerks' office before going to the robing room. As was the custom, only the justices knew what decisions would be handed down that day. Even my father's law clerks did not know that the momentous day was at hand, nor did they know what the ultimate decision would be. As he walked through the office, my father spoke to his law clerks, Ellis McKay and Ernest Rubenstein: "I think you boys ought to be in the courtroom today." He had never before made that suggestion, and they knew that a historic moment was at hand.

Historians in general have not acknowledged the Vinson Court's achievements regarding civil rights, although scholar William Wiecek, referring to *Sweatt* and *McLaurin,* has written that it "blazed ahead in civil rights cases."[12] Despite these cases, a question that continues to be debated is whether the *Brown* decision would have been the same if Fred Vinson rather than Earl Warren had been chief justice. When asked that question, Tom Clark responded unequivocally: "The result would have been the same," he proclaimed in a 1972 interview.[13] When Robert Ireland, the interviewer, pressed the point, suggesting that Vinson may have deliberately avoided dealing with the segregation issue, my father was adamant: "That's all tommy rot, just pure and simple. . . . It's not a question of evading at all. It's just the practicalities of life—common sense. The cases were not really clear-cut. The records were cloudy. They came from the South. We wanted national coverage rather than a sectional one. . . . There was no shuffling of feet, no holding back on the legal question."[14]

My father felt that the momentum for reversing *Plessy* and ending the "separate but equal doctrine" began with *Shelley v. Kraemer* and continued with *Sweatt v. Painter* and *McLaurin v. Oklahoma*—all unanimous decisions handed down during Chief Justice Vinson's tenure. In his opinion, timing rather than the particular Chief Justice was the crucial factor, and by 1954, the time was right for reversal. He could sense the change:

> Well, you know, I could feel the change on the Court. I came in '49 and these cases that came here then, mostly in the area of higher education you could sort of feel the Justices. Those were all unanimous cases [*Sweatt, McLaurin*] and I think it's just a question of cases happened to be timed at that period. . . . We can't go out, you know, like Congress, and pass a law whenever we see something that may be wrong. We have to wait until the case comes here. It's just logical that if the Court is going to find that higher education inherently cannot be segregated in order to have equal quality, why not elementary. So those cases came in droves. So it was I think the justices were more or less ready for it.[15]

Today, it is difficult to imagine that the justices could have done anything other than declare segregation unconstitutional. At the time, however, the issue was not that clear-cut, and almost half the population was unhappy with the decision. My father and, I am sure, all of the justices received hate phone calls and hate mail. One angry phone call denounced my father in personal terms: "The segregation case is an outrage and for you to have joined it is contrary to your upbringing. I'm sure your father has turned over in his grave. . . . I understand you have four granddaughters and I hope each one of them marries a negro."[16]

Some prominent legal scholars and judges were critical, complaining that the decision was based on social science rather than legal precedent. This accusation was based on a footnote to the opinion—footnote 11— listing the publications of several respected social scientists, including Gunnar Myrdal, a Swedish scholar whose book *The American Dilemma* was a strong indictment of racism in this country. The reference to Myrdal hit a nerve, especially with southerners. Tom Clark had opposed using the footnote: "I questioned the Chief's going with Myrdal in the opinion. I told him—and Hugo Black did too—that it wouldn't go down well with the South. And he didn't need it."[17]

A year later, the Court handed down a second decision, known as *Brown II,* which gave instructions on how to implement desegregation. This decision may have been more difficult to arrive at than the original *Brown.* The justices, fully aware of the complexities of ending segregation, wished to give as much support and flexibility as possible to the states. A major issue was whether to order the states to desegregate by a specific date, or to allow them to follow a more general timetable that would pro- vide greater flexibility and acknowledge the different circumstances and levels of difficulty within the states. Their conclusion resulted in the con- troversial "all deliberate speed" clause, introduced by Felix Frankfurter, which unintentionally gave the South the opportunity to delay imple- mentation. As he later recounted, my father had objected to the use of the phrase "all deliberate speed" at the time:

I was very much disappointed in the deliberate speed formula. I believe it would have been much better if we'd just told them: Why don't you start this next fall, or maybe a year from there, in the kindergarten. . . . If you'd start in kindergarten in twelve years you'd have the thing up through high school. . . . But the minute we put it in a general phrase, such as "deliber- ate speed," there were those who wanted to take advantage of that. . . .

We made mistakes; we're human too. We decided that was the way to do it, and we did it. I think it delayed integration for possibly fifteen years at least.[18]

Regardless of these flaws, *Brown v. Board of Education* was a magnificent decision that proved to be a turning point and led to remarkable gains in the battle against racial discrimination in this country. It was not, however, the end of civil rights cases brought before the Court. On December 14, 1964, three decisions were handed down concerning the Civil Rights Act of 1964. Two of the cases, *Heart of Atlanta Motel v. U.S.* and *Katzenbach v. McClung,* claimed that title II of the act was unconstitutional. Title II requires businesses serving the public to open their facilities to minorities:

"All persons shall be entitled to the full and equal enjoyment of the goods, services, facilities, privileges, advantages, and accommodations of any place of public accommodation, as defined in this section, without discrimination or segregation on the ground of race, color, religion, or national origin."[19]

In title II, the definition of a public accommodation includes "any inn, hotel, motel or other establishment which provides lodging to transient guests." In *Heart of Atlanta Motel*, a lower court ruled that title II was constitutional, and ordered the defendants, who operated a segregated business, to comply with the law by renting rooms to African Americans. The case was appealed to the Supreme Court. The defendants argued that Congress did not have authority over local businesses and therefore could not force them to serve African Americans or anyone else they chose to reject. Lawyers for the federal government countered that barring African Americans from the motel interfered with interstate travel and that Congress had the authority, under the commerce clause of the Constitution, to remove such interference. The Heart of Atlanta Motel was in the downtown section of the city and close to major interstate highways. Seventy-five percent of its registered guests were from out of state.[20] Tom Clark wrote the opinion, and his rationale, which produced a unanimous decision, was based on Congress's power to regulate interstate commerce.[21] He affirmed the constitutionality of title II of the Civil Rights Act of 1964 and ruled that the Heart of Atlanta Motel was required to serve African Americans.

The second case, *Katzenbach v. McClung*, was less clear-cut. Ollie McClung was the owner of Ollie's Barbecue in Birmingham, Alabama, which catered to local whites. It provided take-out service to African Americans but would not allow them to use the restaurant's facilities. (Interestingly, two-thirds of its employees were African American.) A district court ruled that the Civil Rights Act was not applicable to the restaurant's operations and that therefore McClung could deny Negroes access to the restaurant. Tom Clark took a different approach. A substantial amount of the food served in the restaurant came from other states. His opinion cited that fact and pointed to evidence of discrimination's negative effect on interstate commerce. Based on Congress's control over interstate commerce, he declared in his opinion for the majority:

> The District Court was in error in concluding that there was no connection between discrimination and the movement of interstate commerce. The court's conclusion that such a connection is outside "common experience" flies in the face of stubborn fact. . . .

The power of Congress in this field [interstate commerce] is broad and sweeping; where it keeps within its sphere and violates no express constitutional limitation it has been the rule of this Court, going back almost to the founding days of the Republic, not to interfere. The Civil Rights Act of 1964, as here applied, we find to be plainly appropriate in the resolution of what the Congress found to be a national commercial problem of the first magnitude. We find it in no violation of any express limitations of the Constitution and we therefore declare it valid.[22]

The third case, *Hamm v. Rock Hill*, did not challenge the constitutionality of the Civil Rights Act of 1964 but questioned whether its protections applied to sit-in demonstrations that occurred before it was passed. A lower court had upheld the trespassing convictions of African Americans who were denied service at the lunch counters of retail stores in South Carolina and Arkansas. (*Hamm* originated in South Carolina; during arguments before the Court, it was combined with a companion case, *Lupper v. Arkansas*.) The men refused to leave the stores after being ordered to do so, and they subsequently participated in sit-in demonstrations. Initially, my father was undecided, but became the swing vote that gave a majority to those who ruled that the Civil Rights Act of 1964 applied to peaceful sit-in demonstrations, and that the convictions should be overturned even though the sit-ins occurred before passage of the act. It was a 5–4 decision, but even those voting to affirm the convictions must have been relieved by the opinion, because there were approximately 3,000 cases on appeal by sit-in demonstrators. The decision made those appeals unnecessary, for it meant that sit-ins were lawful, and so no one who participated peacefully could be prosecuted. The 3,000 pending appeals were dropped, and *Hamm* was the last sit-in case to come before the Supreme Court.[23]

Besides being a strong advocate for civil rights, my father remained a supporter of law enforcement and an independent voice whenever the two issues appeared to be in conflict. One year after the civil rights cases of 1964, he wrote a strong dissent in another civil rights case, *Cox v. Louisiana*. The case involved the conviction of the leader of a demonstration of 2,000 college and high school students who were protesting the arrests of 23 college students from Southern University, a black college, for "illegal picketing." Cox, the leader of the demonstration, which took place across the street from a courthouse, was arrested for "breach of peace" and "picketing near a courthouse," among other charges. His conviction for the latter offense, which was appealed separately from the others, was based on a Louisiana statute that protected courts and judges from disruptive and possibly violent demonstrations. The statute prohibited demonstrations located "in or near" a courthouse for the purpose of influencing court officials. It exempted one group: labor unions. Cox had not asked for or been given a permit to demonstrate, but as the group marched toward the courthouse, the chief of police gave his verbal permission if the demonstrators stayed across the street from the courthouse and limited their time to seven minutes. They failed to stay within those limits, and Cox was arrested. The case went to the Supreme Court, where five justices favored reversing the courthouse-picketing conviction on the grounds that the statute's designation of "near" was too vague, that the exemption for labor unions was discriminatory, and that the arrest, coming after the chief of police had given permission for the demonstration, was "entrapment."[24]

Four justices, Clark, Black, Harlan, and White, disagreed. My father's dissent described the demonstration as "a modern Donnybrook Fair" led by someone who "preferred to resolve the controversy in the streets, rather than submit the question to the normal judicial procedures." He rejected the charge that "near" was too vague, citing the fact that the demonstrators' singing and cheering was clearly heard inside the courthouse and was even responded to by the students who were jailed inside. He also argued, with some sarcasm, that the chief of police's permission to the demonstrators, while a "laudable" attempt to prevent violence, was beyond his legal authority:

> I never knew until today that a law enforcement official—city, state or national—could forgive a breach of the criminal laws. I missed that, in my law school, in my practice and for the two years while I was head of the Criminal Division of the Department of Justice.
>
> I have always been taught that this Nation was dedicated to freedom under law, not under mobs, whether they be integrationists or white supremacists. . . . The contemporary drive for personal liberty can only be successful when conducted within the framework of due process of law. Goals, no matter how laudable, pursued by mobocracy in the end must always lead to further restraints of free expression.[25]

*Cox* dealt with a principle that my father considered basic to our judicial system: the rule of law must be adhered to. In *Cox*, he felt that this principle overrode the civil rights of the petitioners.

An earlier case, *Williams v. Georgia*, exemplified another principle that was dear to Tom Clark: the powers of the Supreme Court are limited. The 1955 decision involved an African American convicted by an all-white jury of killing a white man. He was sentenced to death. He appealed the case, requesting a new trial on the grounds that there were no African Americans on the jury. The Supreme Court of Georgia denied the request, stating that under Georgia law, objection to the makeup of a jury had to be made before the trial began. Six of the justices ruled in favor of the defendant and ordered that the case be remanded (sent back to a lower court for a new trial). Tom Clark wrote a dissent, joined by Justices Reed and Minton, that stressed precedents and the limited power of the Court: "While I, too, am not deaf to the pleas of the condemned, I cannot ignore the long established precedents of this Court. The proper course, as has always been followed here, is to recognize and honor reasonable state procedures as valid exercises of sovereign power. We have done so in hundreds of capital cases since I have been on the Court, and I do not think that even the sympathetic facts of this case should make us lose sight of the limitations on this Court's powers."[26]

• • •

Today, civil rights cases brought before the Supreme Court are more likely to involve women, religious groups, or homosexuals rather than racial minorities. Although problems remain, African Americans have made enormous gains during the more than fifty years since *Brown v. Board of Education. Brown* was the catalyst for these gains. Change was achieved as our founding fathers intended, through a system of government based on a Constitution that is able to adapt to current times and to the needs of the people. Tom Clark summed it up well:

I'd always thought that the Constitution was not written in a vacuum . . . and we ought not to put straitjackets around the amendments. I rather think that there was a definite purpose on the part of the founders, and particularly Madison and those that wrote the Bill of Rights, to couch them in ambiguous words. . . . So that later generations might be able to interpret them to the necessities of their times, not to be bound in this straitjacket that you would be in if they specified with such specificity that you couldn't escape it. . . . They wanted to give you an escape hatch that you could go through. . . .[27]

You see, we don't have any army to enforce our opinions; and we don't have any money to buy ads to run favorable ads in newspapers. The only way we have is logic and the force and common sense of the opinion.[28]

## CHAPTER 18

# Some Troublesome Issues

One fledgling prayer leader in the home is worth a dozen parroters in the schoolhouse.

Tom Clark

T HE 1960S BECAME A DECADE OF UNREST for the country. Complex, diverse issues came to the forefront: crime, the civil rights
movement, and the Vietnam War, to name a few. But for the
Supreme Court, two areas of the law were especially contentious and controversial: censorship of allegedly obscene materials, and the separation of
church and state as that principle applies to prayer in schools. Tom Clark's
participation in these types of cases reveals a great deal about his personal
values and philosophy and his independence as a justice.

A flood of cases involving obscenity and pornography began in the
fifties and continued throughout the sixties and into the seventies. My
father wrote the opinion for one of the earliest and most highly publicized
cases, *Burstyn v. Wilson* (1952), known as "The Miracle." *The Miracle* was a
short film directed by Roberto Rossellini and starring Anna Magnani. The
Catholic Church's censorship board labeled the film "sacrilegious" and initiated a lawsuit in New York to prevent it from being shown. The New York
Court of Appeals banned the film, and the case was appealed to the
Supreme Court. A unanimous Court reversed the lower court's decision,
overturning a 1915 precedent that held movies to be "a business pure and
simple" and therefore not worthy of First Amendment protection.[1] Tom
Clark's opinion reversing that ruling gave the following rationale: "The
basic principles of freedom of speech and the press, like the First Amendment's command, do not vary. Those principles, as they have frequently
been enunciated by this court, make freedom of expression the rule. There
is no justification in this case for making an exception to that rule."[2]

His decision also made it clear that this ruling did not ban all forms of control over films: "Since the term 'sacrilegious' is the sole standard under attack here, it is not necessary for us to decide, for example, whether a state may censor motion pictures under a clearly drawn statute designed and applied to prevent the showing of obscene films."[3]

In a separate concurring opinion, Justice Frankfurter cited a basic problem in determining what is sacrilegious: "But in America, the multiplicity of the ideas of 'sacredness' held with equal but conflicting fervor by the great number of religious groups makes the term 'sacrilegious' too indefinite to satisfy constitutional demands based on reason and fairness."[4]

Reaction to the decision was overwhelmingly positive. The *New York Times* praised it as establishing "freedom of the screen" and stressed its significance: "In short, the Court said that a censor with the power to pass or restrain motion pictures in advance of their public release is clearly unconstitutional—which implies that censor boards must go."[5]

Edward Ennis, a former assistant attorney general, sent the following letter to my father:

Dear Tom,

I have never written a Judge about an opinion and I am not sure of the protocol. But upon reading the text of your clear and concise opinion in "The Miracle" for the whole Court, I feel that it is, and will be recognized as, such a great landmark in the constitutional area of free speech that it is not wrong for me to tell you so.[6]

My father responded with a handwritten note in typically self-effacing style:

My dear Ed,

Yes, we get letters and telegrams on both sides, reflecting democracy at work. It is good to receive these reactions for they tend to keep one's feet on the ground and, perhaps, his head out of the clouds.[7]

But "The Miracle" was not without critics. My father received the following letter from a New Jersey college student:

Your Honor,

I am deeply shocked to hear of the Supreme Court decision upholding the showing of the film, "The Miracle." This decision, I think has given the green light to men in the Movie Industry who have no code of moral ethics whatsoever to unload upon the public sacrilegious and immoral films mocking the various beliefs in Christianity. I cannot understand how men of conscience who are supposed to have good moral character could possibly uphold a film which associates religious belief with drunkenness, seduction, mockery and lewdness. And I don't think this film should be placed behind and protected by the right of Freedom of the Press and Freedom of speech. . . .

If this film is in any way scandalous in the future to the teenage group of our country, I place the entire blame upon the present Supreme Court Justices. It is amazing and deplorable to find just how far the Fear of God has decreased. . . .

Sincerely,
Ronald F. Pelican, College Student[8]

Although even a favorably received decision is not without critics, the ruling on censorship in the case of "The Miracle" was easy for the Court compared to those in the obscenity cases that followed.

Determining a definition of obscenity became one of the most frustrating and divisive challenges that the justices faced. Their views ranged from those of Black and Douglas, who felt that it was impossible to define the obscene and that all materials were therefore protected by the First Amendment, to the personal perspective of Potter Stewart, whose remark "I know it when I see it" became a classic. Tom Clark's decisions in these cases reflected the personal abhorrence he felt for obscenity and pornography.

In 1957, William Brennan, the author of virtually all of the obscenity opinions, produced a definition of obscenity in *Roth v. U.S.* It stated that a work is obscene if "to the average person, applying contemporary community standards, the dominant theme of the material taken as a whole appeals to prurient interest." In addition, his definition required that a work be "utterly without redeeming social importance."[9] Using that definition, six justices, including Tom Clark, ruled against Samuel Roth, a bookseller who published a magazine entitled *American Aphrodite*. The justices declared that his magazine was obscene and therefore not protected by the First Amendment.

The *Roth* definition would be used for the next fifteen years, but not always happily. A 1964 case, *Jacobellis v. Ohio*, illustrates the differing views and inconsistent interpretations of the justices. Nico Jacobellis, manager of a movie theater in Cleveland Heights, Ohio, was convicted of exhibiting a film that the state deemed obscene. In a 6–3 decision, the justices overturned his conviction, using an array of reasons. Altogether, six decisions were handed down—four by the justices in the majority, two by the dissenters. Brennan wrote for the majority, but was joined by only one justice, Arthur Goldberg, and even Goldberg wrote a separate concurring opinion. Justices Stewart and Black also wrote concurring opinions, and Black was joined by William O. Douglas. The three dissenters produced two separate opinions, one by John Harlan, the other by Earl Warren. Tom Clark joined Warren's dissent. In his dissent, the chief justice argued that "community standards," which Brennan had interpreted as "national" in *Roth*, meant local, not national, standards:

> It is my belief that, when the Court said in *Roth* that obscenity is to be defined by reference to "community standards," it meant community standards—not a national standard, as is sometimes argued. I believe there is no provable "national standard," and perhaps there should be none. At all events, this Court has not been able to enunciate one . . . But communities throughout the Nation are in fact diverse, and it must be remembered that, in cases such as this one, the Court is confronted with the task of reconciling conflicting rights of the diverse communities within our society and of individuals.[10]

The lack of consensus on obscenity cases was illustrated again the following year when three were argued before the Court: *Ginzburg v. U.S.*, *Mishkin v. New York*, and the case known as *Fanny Hill* (officially, *A Book Named "John Cleland's Memoirs of a Woman of Pleasure" v. Massachusetts*). The three cases produced fourteen opinions. Tom Clark voted with the majority in the first two cases, which affirmed the convictions of two publishers for distributing obscene materials, but in *Fanny Hill*, despite the chief justice's efforts to persuade him to join the majority,[11] he dissented in a strongly worded opinion: "The public should know of the continuous flow of pornographic material reaching this Court and the increasing problem States have in controlling it. *Memoirs of a Woman of Pleasure*, the book involved here, is typical. I have 'stomached' past cases for almost 10 years without much outcry. Though I am not known to be a purist—or a shrinking violet—this book is too much even for me."[12]

Tom Clark also objected to the "utterly without redeeming social value" rule, which he described as allowing "the smut artist free rein to carry on his dirty business."[13] The force of his argument persuaded Potter Stewart to change his vote and join the dissenters.[14] They were still a minority, however, and the final vote was 5–4.

Charles Reed, my father's law clerk during the term when the three obscenity cases were being decided, made this observation about Tom Clark:

> His vote and reaction to the facts in those cases reflected his upbringing and his set of moral values. Where so subjective a concept as obscenity is involved, there is no way to approach decision making without involving, consciously or not, one's background and experiences. . . . The eighteen law clerks thought to a man that there was no obscenity in either of these cases (*Ginzburg* and *Fanny Hill*). I actually tried to argue the point with the Justice. He rejected it without a qualm. It was evident to me that this was a generational and background difference.[15]

The flood of obscenity cases continued throughout the sixties and into the seventies. During the 1971–1972 term, more than sixty were on the Court's docket.[16] Then in 1972, by a 5–4 vote, a new definition of obscenity established in *Miller v. California* gave greater flexibility to the states. When I interviewed him in 1981, Justice Brennan gave credit to my father for developing the rationale that eventually brought about this change: "Your father came up with an idea whose day didn't come, unfortunately, until after he had left us, until Chief Justice Burger and the others decided it . . . Reliance on local customs and attitudes, that was your Dad's idea that he wrote for himself and Earl Warren in a case called *Jacobellis v. U.S.*"[17] *Miller* established a definition that was clearly rooted in the Clark-Warren dissent: local traditions rather than national standards should be the guide in determining obscenity. As the states became better able to handle these cases, the number of them appealed to the Supreme Court decreased significantly and a troublesome issue became much less of a problem for the justices.

While the obscenity cases produced a great deal of stress for the justices, the controversy surrounding them paled in comparison with that produced by the decisions handed down on the separation of church and state—specifically, the school-prayer cases. Justice Black bore the brunt of the controversy as the author of the first decision, *Engel v. Vitale* (1962). *Engel* struck down a New York board of education requirement that a short prayer, written by board members, be recited at the beginning of each school day. The Court ruled, with only Stewart dissenting, that the prayer was unconstitutional based on the First Amendment's establishment clause: "Congress shall make no law respecting an establishment of religion." After reading the decision, Black made the impromptu comment that "the prayer of each man must be his own."[18]

Reaction to the case was the greatest ever produced by a decision. Hundreds of angry letters poured in. "Court Outlaws God" raged one newspaper. Billy Graham declared that he was "shocked and disappointed."[19] The most extreme reaction came from the South. "They put the Negroes in the schools, and now they've driven God out," asserted Congressman George W. Andrews of Alabama.[20] Another congressman, Mendel Rivers of South Carolina, was especially vitriolic: "I know of nothing in my lifetime that could give more aid and comfort to Moscow than this bold, malicious, atheistic and sacrilegious twist by this unpredictable group of uncontrolled despots."[21] In Congress, scores of constitutional amendments and legislative bills were introduced. Congressman Frank Becker proposed a constitutional amendment that would allow prayers "in any governmental or public school, institution, or place."[22] Many viewed the decision as antireligion rather than as supportive of the separation of church and state, which had always been a foundation of the country. In his memoirs, Earl Warren explained and defended the decision:

> History is replete with evidence of terrible wars between different denominations of the Christian religion. In Philadelphia, in the last century, bloody strife, murder and arson were rampant because of a controversy over whether the Protestant or Catholic Bible should be used in public school devotions. The majority of us on the Court were religious people, yet we found it unconstitutional that any state agency should impose a religious exercise on persons who were by law free to practice religion.[23]

President Kennedy publicly supported the Court and gave a mild rebuke to critics of the decision by stating that there was "a very easy remedy and that is to pray ourselves and I would think it would be a welcome reminder to every American family that we can pray a great deal more at home and attend our churches with a good deal more fidelity, and we can make the true meaning of prayer much more important in the lives of our children."[24]

My father, who voted with the majority, was especially disturbed by the uproar. He had always refused to discuss recently decided cases, but in what has been described as "an unprecedented public speech," he made an exception to defend *Engel*:

> Here was a state-written prayer, circulated by a school district to state-employed teachers with instructions to have their pupils recite it in unison at the beginning of each school day in state-owned buildings. . . . The 14th Amendment to the Constitution, as interpreted by the Supreme Court for

over a score of years, incorporates the prohibitions of the First Amendment against the states—which means that both state and federal governments shall take no part respecting the establishment of religion or prohibiting the free exercise thereof. "No" means "No." This was all the Court decided. Questions of official recognition of a Divine Being or the validity of the inscription on silver coins or currency of "In God We Trust" or public acknowledgment of the fact that the United States is a religious nation—were not involved nor passed upon.[25]

A year later, Chief Justice Warren selected Tom Clark to write the majority opinion for two school-prayer cases that were considered together: *Abington School District v. Schempp* and *Murray v. Curlett.* The cases were a natural continuation of *Engel.* In *Schempp,* the state of Pennsylvania required that at least ten verses from the Bible be read, without comment, at the opening of each school day. The verses were followed by recitation of the Lord's Prayer. Children could be excused from the reading and prayer if their parents submitted a written request. Edward and Sidney Schempp, members of the Unitarian Church, brought suit against the state, contending that the practice violated their children's rights under the First Amendment and that the readings sometimes conflicted with their family's religious beliefs. Edward Schempp testified that he had considered asking that the children be excused from the religious exercises, but decided against it because he was afraid that they might be considered "oddballs" and atheists. The "atheist" label especially disturbed him, since atheism was often linked to communism and conveyed an image of immorality. In addition, if excused, the children would have to stand in the hallway while the readings were conducted, and that in itself was a symbol of "punishment for bad conduct." A three-judge district court ruled in favor of the Schempps, and the state appealed to the Supreme Court.

The circumstances in *Murray* were somewhat different. The Baltimore public schools required that either a chapter of the Bible or the Lord's Prayer be read at the beginning of each school day. William Murray's mother, Madalyn Murray, later Madalyn Murray O'Hair, had arranged for her son to be excused from the readings, but brought suit because she viewed the practice as a violation of the principle of the separation of church and state. Madalyn Murray was an outspoken atheist. Her vociferous advocacy of her beliefs made her despised by many throughout the country and increased the controversy surrounding the case. A Maryland court ruled against her, stating that the religious exercises did not violate the Constitution, and she appealed to the Supreme Court.

The courtroom was packed when Tom Clark read the 8–1 decision from the bench—Justice Stewart was the lone dissenter. In writing his opinion for *Schempp* and *Murray*, my father sought to dispel the perception that the decision was antireligion by stressing the necessity of neutrality on the part of the government. His delivery was patient and persuasive as he made the following points:

> The place of religion in our society is an exalted one, achieved through a long tradition of reliance on the home, the church and the inviolable citadel of the individual heart and mind. We have come to recognize through bitter experience that it is not within the power of government to invade that citadel, whether its purpose or effect be to aid or oppose, to advance or retard. In the relationship between man and religion, the State is firmly committed to a position of neutrality.[26]

The opinion also included suggestions for ways that religion could be appropriately brought into the school curriculum:

> It might well be said that one's education is not complete without a study of comparative religion or the history of religion and its relationship to the advancement of civilization. It certainly may be said that the Bible is worthy of study for its literary and historic qualities. Nothing we have said here indicates that such study of the Bible or of religion, when presented objectively as part of a secular program of education, may not be effected consistently with the First Amendment.[27]

The ruling was expected after the *Engel v. Vitale* decision, and the reaction to it was much less dramatic. The media pointed out that "the voices of a Protestant (Clark), Catholic (Brennan), and Jew (Arthur Goldberg) on the Court spoke up for the Church-state separation in the decision."[28] But there was still criticism, and the issue of school prayer continues to be debated today. Tom Clark consistently defended these opinions, and his words reveal a great deal about his personal views on religion: "There is no better place to develop religion than in the home, at the church and in the Sunday School. In my day it was the job of the parents and the preachers and the Sunday School teachers to inculcate and develop a religious atmosphere among children. What we need is more people doing this and fewer passing the buck onto the public schools. One fledgling prayer leader in the home is worth a dozen parroters in the schoolhouse."[29] The criticism persisted, and Tom Clark was still defending the school-prayer decisions in 1976, a year before he died. His comments at that time stressed his desire to provide options that would not be in opposition to the Constitution: "What I was trying to do was point in another direction that we might go, rather than striking down all directions; I was trying to point out a direction we might follow in an effort to try to reach the same goal but go through a constitutional route rather than an unconstitutional one."[30]

Some may view Tom Clark's decisions on the obscenity cases old-fashioned. Some may consider those on school prayer liberal. The logical conclusion to be drawn from these cases is that Tom Clark was independent and did not fit under any label. He could not be persuaded to change his mind, as his decision in *Fanny Hill* illustrated, when he believed he was right. He had the confidence and courage to publicly support controversial decisions, such as *Engel* and *Schempp*, when he felt they were misunderstood. He stood by personal principles that he believed were supported by the Constitution. He contributed to the Court in important ways because of these qualities.

## CHAPTER 19

# He Made a Difference

The most underrated Justice in recent history.

Bernard Schwartz, *Super Chief*

IN HIS BIOGRAPHY OF EARL WARREN, historian Bernard Schwartz described Tom Clark as "the most underrated Justice in recent history."[1] I cannot explain why historians have neglected my father and failed to fully appreciate his contributions to the Court and to the country. Any careful assessment of Tom Clark as an associate justice would have to conclude that his presence on the Court made a significant difference. He wrote and participated in some of its most important opinions, served as a swing voter able to differ from his colleagues without offending them, and possessed remarkable energy that enabled him, through outside activities, to serve as a virtual goodwill ambassador for the Court at a time when it was experiencing severe criticism.

The 1960s proved to be a time of remarkable productivity and growth for my father. Under his leadership, one of the most significant and controversial cases of the decade was decided: *Mapp v. Ohio*.[2] The 1961 case involved the exclusionary rule, which prohibits the use in court of evidence obtained illegally. In 1914, the Supreme Court ruled in *Weeks v. U.S.* that the Fourth Amendment required federal courts to adhere to the exclusionary rule. The language of the Fourth Amendment is clear: "The right of people to be secure in their persons, houses, papers and effects, against unreasonable searches and seizures, shall not be violated." But *Weeks* applied only to federal, not state, courts, and in 1949, before Tom Clark was on the Court, a precedent was established in *Wolf v. Colorado*, which ruled that states had the right to determine whether to apply the exclusionary rule to cases in their courts. The *Wolf* opinion did not give absolute control to the states; it contained some leeway and room for interpretation, and the issue remained contentious.

Two cases that followed *Wolf* arrived at contrasting conclusions. *Rochin v. California* (1953) involved a case in which police had forcibly extracted narcotic pills from the accused with a stomach pump, and then used them as evidence to convict him on a narcotics charge. The justices voted unanimously to reverse the conviction, declaring that there was a line of behavior in obtaining evidence beyond which law-enforcement officials could not go. Writing for the Court, Frankfurter stressed, "State criminal law may not resort to methods that offend civilized standards." The illegally obtained evidence could not be used in the California state court.

A year after *Rochin*, the justices arrived at a different conclusion in a 5–4 decision in *Irvine v. California*. In this case, police broke into the suspect's home while he and his wife were away and installed a microphone in their bedroom. Conversations overheard and recorded by officers at a listening post were used as evidence against Patrick Irvine and helped convict him of violating state gambling laws. Initially, my father favored reversing the conviction. In a memo seen only by my father's law clerks and Justice Jackson, Tom Clark wrote the following:

> I cannot tolerate this burglary on the part of the police any more than I could that in *Rochin v. California* . . . Shall we, must we, accept lawlessness on the part of the police as a solution to the lawlessness of the criminal? . . . Certainly *Wolf* was not then thought to be a carte blanche for the states in the realm of unconstitutional search and seizure. But today we are asked to return to a hard and fast *Wolf* rule which, if adopted, overrules *Rochin*, *sub silentio*. This is too much for me.[3]

According to his law clerks, Clark took the memo into Jackson's office. Jackson was writing the opinion for the justices in favor of affirming the conviction. There were no witnesses to the conversation that took place, but when my father returned to his office more than an hour later, he announced that he was withdrawing his dissent and voting to affirm the conviction. His vote gave Jackson a majority. No explanation was offered to the law clerks, but my father's concurring opinion—he did not join the one written by Jackson—explains his reasoning:

> Had I been here in 1949, when *Wolf* was decided, I would have applied the doctrine of *Weeks v. United States* (1914) to the states. But the Court refused to do so then, and it still refuses today. Thus, *Wolf* remains the law and, as such, is entitled to the respect of this Court's membership. . . .

In light of the "incredible" activity of the police here, it is with great reluctance that I follow *Wolf*. Perhaps strict adherence to the tenor of that decision may produce needed converts for its extinction. Thus, I merely concur in the judgment of affirmance.[4]

Undoubtedly the argument Jackson used to persuade my father emphasized the importance of the precedent established in *Wolf*—an effective strategy, for Tom Clark did not overrule precedents easily. Earl Warren, on the Court for only two months when *Irvine* was decided, was also influenced by Jackson, and was one of the five justices who voted to affirm the lower court's conviction. Warren later said that if he could change any vote he had cast as chief justice, it would be his vote in *Irvine*.[5]

Seven years after *Irvine*, *Mapp v. Ohio* was argued before the Court. The case involved Dollree Mapp, an African American woman living with her daughter on the second story of a two-family house. Cleveland police, believing that a bombing suspect was hiding in the home, requested that Mapp let them enter and search her house. She immediately called her lawyer, who advised her not to allow the police in unless they had a search warrant. They did not, and Mapp refused to let them enter. The police left, but returned a few hours later, broke down the front door, and entered the home. Mapp asked to see the search warrant. The police waved a piece of paper at her, which she grabbed and stuffed in her blouse. The police forcibly took the paper from her, handcuffed her, and ransacked her house. The paper, or so-called search warrant, was never seen again. In the basement, police found pornographic materials in a trunk—Justice Douglas described the materials as "four little pamphlets and a pencil doodle."[6] Ohio had strict antipornography laws, and a Cuyahoga County court convicted Mapp of possession of "lewd and lascivious" materials. The suspect the police were looking for was not found, nor was any evidence indicating he had been in her house.

The justices initially approached the case from the perspective of the constitutionality of Ohio's antipornography laws. Douglas suggested the exclusionary rule as an alternative approach, but seemed to have little support.[7] Following the conference, however, Justices Brennan, Black, and Clark had lunch together and discussed extending the Fourth Amendment's exclusionary rule to the states. *Mapp* provided that opportunity. Chief Justice Warren had assigned the opinion to my father. When the justices met again and my father presented his first draft, he stressed the right of privacy and personal security provided in the Fourth Amendment, and cited *Weeks*, the 1914 case that established the exclusionary rule at the federal level. The other justices were surprised at the changed approach. John Harlan and Felix Frankfurter were especially unhappy, and argued that the basis for the decision should be the constitutionality of Ohio's antipornography laws rather than the exclusionary rule. They did not want *Wolf* overturned. In a memo written to my father on May 1, 1961, Justice Harlan expressed his concern:

> I am unable to understand why a ground for deciding this case should have been chosen which is not only highly debatable and divisive, but also requires overruling of a decision to which the Court has many times adhered over the past dozen years . . . The upshot of all this is that I earnestly ask you to reconsider the advisability of facing the Court, in a case which otherwise should find a ready and non-controversial solution, with the controversial issues that our proposed opinion tenders. Perhaps you will have gathered from the foregoing that I would not be able to join you in your present opinion.[8]

My father responded on May 4:

> It is true also that *Wolf* has been adhered to in several cases, but in each in which a full dress opinion resulted it was done grudgingly. . . . There is, of course, as in all controversial cases, ground for disagreement. I have a court and therefore my theory at least has support. I think the trouble stems from *Wolf* which . . . enunciates a constitutional doctrine which has no escape clause mitigating against the present inexorable result, i.e., if the right to privacy is really so basic as to be constitutional in rank and if it is really to be enforceable against the states . . . then we cannot carve out of the bowels of that right the vital part, the stuff that gives it substance, the exclusion of evidence. It has long been recognized and honored as an integral part of the equivalent right against federal action. . . . I hope that you will restudy the opinion, John, and find logic and reason in it.[9]

Hugo Black expressed another concern. While agreeing with the outcome of my father's opinion, he questioned the wording, which cited that use of the evidence violated "the right of privacy" as embodied in the Fourth Amendment: "My agreement with your opinion depends upon my understanding that you read *Wolf* as having held, and that we are holding here, that the Fourth Amendment *as a whole* is applicable to the states, and not some imaginary and unknown fragment designated as the 'right of privacy.'"[10]

My father responded that his intent was to apply all of the Fourth Amendment to the case, and so the matter was settled, though Black, rather than joining my father, issued a concurring opinion in which he cited the protection from self-incrimination guaranteed by the Fifth Amendment as well as the exclusionary rule. The vote in *Mapp* was 5–4, with Frankfurter, Harlan, Stewart, and Whittaker dissenting. Writing for the majority, my father cited sections of the *Weeks* decision:

> If letters and private documents can thus be seized and held and used in evidence against a citizen accused of an offense, the protection of the Fourth Amendment declaring his right to be secure against such searches and seizures is of no value, and, so far as those thus placed are concerned, might as well be stricken from the Constitution.[11]

He went on to describe the changed circumstances since *Wolf* (thirty-seven states had adopted the exclusionary rule since that case was decided), the inconsistency that defied common sense, and the destructive effect on a government that permits illegal behavior on the part of its law-enforcement officers:

> There is no war between the Constitution and common sense. Presently, a federal prosecutor may make no use of evidence illegally seized, but a State's attorney across the street may, although he supposedly is operating under the enforceable prohibitions of the same Amendment. Thus, the State, by admitting evidence unlawfully seized, serves to encourage disobedience to the Federal Constitution which it is bound to uphold. . . .
>
> . . . Nothing can destroy a government more quickly than its failure to observe its own laws, or worse, its disregard of the charter of its own existence. . . .
>
> . . . Our decision, founded on reason and truth, gives to the individual no more than that which the Constitution guarantees him, to the police officer no less than that to which honest law enforcement is entitled, and, to the courts, that judicial integrity so necessary in the true administration of justice.[12]

Both Douglas and Brennan wrote congratulatory notes to my father. Brennan was especially effusive:

> Dear Tom:
> Of course you know that I think this is just magnificent and wonderful. I have not joined anything since I came with greater pleasure.
>
> Sincerely,
> Bill[13]

A *New York Times* survey found that *Mapp* was regarded as the "most far-reaching constitutional step of the term," and John Harlan was correct: *Mapp v. Ohio* created a controversy that continues to this day.[14] But despite efforts to overrule it and some success in weakening it, *Mapp* survives. Tom Clark was proud of this landmark decision, and later described some of the influences that led him to feel so strongly about the exclusionary rule and illegal police behavior:

> I am proud of it [the Mapp decision] because the idea of *Mapp* shocked me. When I was a kid I came out of the University of Texas Law School. I went back to Dallas and tried to practice a little law and picked up a few cases and one of them was our cook's. We had a cook—believe it or not—for seven dollars a week. We paid her a dollar a day. That was the going wage for cooks. Her son was a nice little fellow but got into trouble. They found a half-pint of corn whiskey, during prohibition, in his house he had on Elm Street. And they cut open the mattress; they didn't have a search warrant or anything; they just took a knife and cut the mattresses open, took crow bars and pulled the baseboards away from the wall—just a terrible thing for these police officers to do.[15]

Clearly, personal experience influenced my father and helped shape his views on the importance of the Fourth Amendment and the protection it provides citizens against invasive, illegal actions on the part of police. *Mapp* sent a clear message: law-enforcement officials—whether federal or state —must not be allowed to break the law. The decision also showed that by 1961, Tom Clark was willing to overrule a precedent that he felt was incorrect and that he believed the Fourth Amendment protects the "right to privacy," a right that some will argue is not part of the Constitution.

Undoubtedly, some were surprised that Clark, known as a conservative and a strong supporter of law enforcement, would come down on the side of the accused as he did in *Mapp*. They must have been even more surprised a few years later when he wrote the majority opinion for *Berger v. New York*, overturning a 1928 decision, *Olmstead v. New York*, which found that the Fourth Amendment did not prohibit wiretapping. Tom Clark, the former attorney general who had been criticized for allowing the FBI to expand its use of the wiretap, wrote the following:

> We cannot forgive the requirements of the Fourth Amendment in the name of law enforcement.
> This is no formality that we require today, but a fundamental rule that has long been recognized as basic to the privacy of every home in Amer-

ica. . . . It is not asking too much that officers be required to comply with the basic command of the Fourth Amendment before the innermost secrets of one's home or office are invaded. Few threats to liberty exist which are greater than that posed by the use of eavesdropping devices. . . .

. . . Our concern with the statute here is whether its language permits a trespassory invasion of the home or office, by general warrant, contrary to the command of the Fourth Amendment. As it is written, we believe that it does.[16]

My father went on to describe what was required of law-enforcement officers before they could use eavesdropping technology and to explain when it could be used legitimately. *Berger* did not outlaw all wiretapping, but placed restrictions on its use that would help prevent misuse. After my father's retirement, he continued to advocate controls over eavesdropping devices: "The relaxation of the normal protections against wiretapping and eavesdropping is a mistake. We should insist that there is probable cause supporting the use of such devices before they are permitted."[17]

Crime was a major issue in the 1960s, and opinions that supported the rights of the accused, like *Mapp* and *Berger*, were extremely controversial. Two other opinions written by my father, in *Estes v. Texas* and *Sheppard v. Maxwell*, also drew sharp criticism. Both dealt with the rights of the accused and reversed convictions handed down by lower courts. *Estes* was the first case that involved a relatively new technology that had become an integral part of American life—television. The case received enormous publicity because defendant Billie Sol Estes, a Texan known as a wheeler-dealer businessman, was a friend of President Lyndon Johnson. He was convicted of fraud and swindling charges in a Texas court. Texas was one of two states that allowed television in the courtroom at that time, and portions of the trial were televised. According to one account, the environment in the courtroom—twelve cameramen, microphones on the judge's desk, bright lights and a web of wires—"turned the courtroom into a broadcast studio."[18] It was in this environment that Estes was convicted. Texas appellate courts upheld the conviction, and the case was appealed to the Supreme Court on the grounds that Estes did not receive a fair trial because of the television coverage.

Initially, the justices in favor of affirming the conviction were Clark, Black, Stewart, White, and Brennan—a bare majority. Stewart, in his draft opinion for the majority, argued that there was no evidence that television coverage affected the verdict: "On the record of this case . . . we cannot say that any violation of the Constitution occurred."[19]

Warren, in a draft opinion for the four dissenters, saw things differently: "The Court today has not faced up to the facts of this case and has given an unwarranted impression that the presence of television in no way affected the conduct of this criminal proceeding. No fair appraisal of the facts will support this conclusion."[20]

Tom Clark undoubtedly abhorred the circus environment of the Estes trial. His love of law and his dedication to the dignity of the courts had to be major reasons for his switch to the opposite side. His swing vote resulted in a reversal of Estes's conviction. He explained his reasons in a lengthy memo to the justices:

I became disturbed at what could result from our approval of this emasculation by TV of the trial of a case. My doubts increased as I envisioned use of the unfortunate format followed here in other trials which would not only jeopardize the fairness of them but would broadcast a bad image to the public of the judicial process. . . . It appears to me that the perils to a fair trial far outweigh the benefits that might accrue in the televising of the proceedings.[21]

The memo went on to list the major dangers in allowing television in the courtroom.

Some witnesses may be demoralized and frightened, some cocky and given to overstatement . . . Inquisitive cranks might approach witnesses on the street with jibes, advice or demands for explanation of testimony. Witnesses with important information might be reluctant to testify in a televised trial if their testimony would expose them to retribution or to embarrassment and ridicule. . . . Telecasting is particularly bad where the judge is elected. . . . The telecasting of a trial becomes a political weapon which diverts his attention from the task at hand—the fair trial of the accused.[22]

Today, some of Tom Clark's fears seem outdated, for television in the courtroom is no longer a major issue. Television coverage is allowed in many courtrooms, although never in the Supreme Court. Cameras are much smaller and less intrusive than they were in the 1960s, and many believe that the openness results in fairer trials by preventing secrecy and manipulation. Nevertheless, some of his concerns remain relevant. We still see the grandstanding and circus-like atmosphere that television helps create in some of our most flamboyant and notorious trials, and we continue to debate whether television coverage affected the outcomes.

A year after *Estes*, the news media—including television—were again seen as a culprit, this time in *Sheppard v. Maxwell* (1966). Ten years earlier, during a trial that had all the trappings of a media carnival, Sam Sheppard had been convicted of killing his wife. He appealed the conviction twice to state courts of appeal, including the Ohio Supreme Court, and his conviction was upheld both times. On federal appeal, the U.S. Court of Appeals for the Sixth Circuit reversed the conviction, agreeing with the finding of the Ohio Supreme Court that the environment during the trial was "a Roman holiday for the news media."[23] The case gained so much notoriety that it was later made into a television series and a movie, both titled *The Fugitive*, the latter starring Harrison Ford. Once more, the justices, with only Hugo Black dissenting, ruled that outside influences had made a fair trial impossible.

In his opinion reversing the conviction, Tom Clark placed the burden of blame on the trial judge and admonished him on several counts: failure to control the behavior of newsmen in the courtroom; failure to prevent newspapers and radio stations from interviewing prospective witnesses; and failure to curb the release of information, gossip, and inaccurate information to the press by police officers and lawyers. Justice Douglas, who had at first stated he could not vote for reversal, described the opinion as "commendable" and as so persuasive that he joined the majority. Sheppard's conviction was overturned, and a new trial was ordered. Sheppard was acquitted in the second trial, and was later exonerated by DNA testing, which identified a handyman as the murderer.

Despite authoring opinions such as *Mapp*, *Berger*, *Estes*, and *Sheppard*, which favored the victims of crime, Tom Clark remained a strong supporter of law enforcement, and wrote a stinging dissent in one of the most controversial law-enforcement cases ever decided by the Court: *Miranda v. Arizona* (1966). William Brennan described *Miranda* as the *Jencks* of its decade because it became the rallying point for anti-Court critics.[24] The issue involved the right to legal counsel. In a unanimous 1963 decision, *Gideon v. Wainwright*, the Court had ruled that indigents had the right to an attorney. *Miranda* went beyond *Gideon* by adding the requirement that police must inform the accused of the right to counsel before interrogating them. Ernesto Miranda had been convicted of kidnap and rape in Arizona. After his arrest, he was interrogated for several hours without being told of his right to have an attorney present. Miranda confessed to the crime during the interrogation, and his confession was used as evidence at trial, over his objections. He appealed his conviction, citing the Fifth Amendment's protection against self-incrimination. The FBI, known as the country's most effective law-enforcement agency, had for years warned suspects of their rights after arresting them, and the warning was well-known to the public because of its use in a popular television program. The fact that the highly respected FBI followed this practice was a persuasive factor for the five justices of the majority.[25] Tom Clark, however, was not persuaded:

> It is with regret that I find it necessary to write in these cases. However, I am unable to join the majority because its opinion goes too far on too little. . . . Nor can I join in the Court's criticism of the present practices of the police and investigatory agencies as to custodial interrogation . . . Moreover, the examples of police brutality mentioned by the Court are rare exceptions to the thousands of cases that appear every year in the law reports. The police agencies—all the way from municipal and state forces to the federal bureaus—are responsible for law enforcement and public safety in this country. I am proud of their efforts, which, in my view, are not fairly characterized by the Court's opinion.[26]

Public outrage ensued when the reversal of Miranda's conviction was announced in a 5–4 decision. Politicians joined in the outcry; the mayor of Los Angeles, Sam Yorty, declared that the decision placed "another set of handcuffs on the police department."[27] Miranda was retried and again convicted, but the debate over the Court's decision continues today. A few years later, Tom Clark's views on *Miranda* changed, and he admitted that his concerns about its impact on law enforcement had not materialized. Instead, in his opinion, the decision had had a positive effect: "*Miranda* has had more to do with the improvement in criminal justice than all the 500 million dollars that the Federal government spent [in 1970] in this area. . . . Because of *Miranda*, a police officer does not stop investigating when he obtains a confession. He knows that confessions are suspect . . . so he goes on investigating and as a result has sufficient evidence, in most cases even without the confession, to prosecute the case."[28]

Tom Clark continued to support the government in most cases that involved national security, and wrote a vehement dissent in *Keyishian v. Board of Regents*, handed down in 1967, his last year on the Court. *Keyishian* challenged New York's Feinberg Law, which was enacted to prevent subversives from being employed by the state. The law required teachers to sign a certificate stating that they were not members of the Communist Party. Harry Keyishian, who taught at a state university, refused to sign and consequently lost his job. He sued the state, claiming that the Feinberg Law was unconstitutional. A lower court upheld the law, and Keyishian appealed to the Supreme Court. Five of the justices found the law unconstitutional, reversing the lower court. My father disagreed, and in his dissenting opinion, used language as strong as that found in the *Jencks* decision twenty years earlier:

> The majority has, by its broadside, swept away one of our most precious rights, namely, the right of self-preservation. Our public educational system is the genius of our democracy. The minds of our youth are developed there and the character of that development will determine the future of our land. Indeed, our very existence depends upon it. The issue here is a very narrow one. It is not freedom of speech, freedom of thought, freedom of press, freedom of assembly, or of association, even in the Communist Party. It is simply this: may the State provide that one who, after a hearing with full judicial review, is found to have willfully and deliberately advocated, advised, or taught that our Government should be overthrown by force or violence or other unlawful means; or to have willfully and deliberately printed[,] published, etc., any book or paper that so advocated and to have personally advocated such doctrine himself; or to have willfully and deliberately become a member of an organization that advocates such doctrine, is prima facie disqualified from teaching in its university? My answer, in keeping with all of our cases up until today, is "Yes"![29]

• • •

When I interviewed Justice William Brennan in 1982, he stated that one of Tom Clark's most important contributions to the Court was his success in building public support for controversial decisions. To illustrate his point, Brennan referred to the landmark opinion *Baker v. Carr* (1962), known as the "one man, one vote" case. The case involved Charles Baker and a group of Tennessee voters who brought suit by claiming that the state's reapportionment process violated the equal protection clause of the Fourteenth Amendment. By law, Tennessee's reapportionment was to be done every ten years. In reality, it had not been conducted since 1901. The dramatic growth of cities during that sixty-year period meant that despite their diminished numbers, rural voters had significantly greater representation in the state legislature than urban voters. A federal district court ruled that the apportionment procedure was unconstitutional. When the case arrived at the Supreme Court, the justices faced two issues: first, whether the federal district court, or any federal court, had jurisdiction over state apportionment, which had always been a state responsibility; and second, whether Tennessee's procedure for apportionment was constitutional. The second issue was clear-cut: Tennessee's system for apportionment, as implemented, like that of many other states, was blatantly unfair and denied equal representation to urban voters. The issue of jurisdiction was more difficult and divisive. Previously, the Court had refused to get involved in reapportionment cases on the grounds they should be left up to the states.

Two camps formed: Brennan, Black, Douglas, and Warren argued that voting was a basic right that could not be obstructed by the state, and that therefore the federal courts had jurisdiction. Frankfurter, Harlan, Whittaker, and, initially, Clark disagreed. They felt that apportionment was a state matter and that the Court should not intervene. Frankfurter was adamant: the case was political and the Court "ought not to enter this political thicket," as he had first stated in the related case *Colegrove v. Green* (1946).[30] Potter Stewart was undecided and appeared to hold the swing vote. He was lobbied by both sides. In a memo to Stewart, Harlan emphasized the importance of the issue: "From the standpoint of the future of the Court, the case involves implications whose importance is unmatched by those of any other case coming here in my time."[31]

To strengthen the Harlan-Frankfurter argument, Frankfurter suggested that my father search for alternatives that Tennessee voters could use to redress the problem. The suggestion backfired. My father searched extensively for other options, but found none. Tennessee's system did not provide for referendums, initiatives, or any other method that could be used to solve the apportionment issue. He wrote the following to Frankfurter: "I have checked into the record and I am sorry to say that I cannot find any practical course that the people could take in bringing this [fair representation] about except through the federal courts."[32] He apologized to Frankfurter, but explained that he was changing his vote. Brennan was overjoyed when he heard the news: "Your father was sick at home—had the flu or something. He called me up and said: 'Look, I've been trying to dissent . . . but I can't, and I think I'm going to join you.' I remember running out of here [the Supreme Court building], grabbing a car driving out to the apartment and discussing his concurring opinion. That was an enormous contribution to a very difficult field, and he brought along, when he changed, a lot of people who were on the fence."[33]

Once he changed his vote, my father felt the opinion should also address the apportionment issue and include suggestions for possible procedures to achieve fair representation. Had he switched earlier, this might have occurred, but because he had seemed firmly in the Frankfurter camp, Brennan's efforts for a fifth vote were directed solely at Stewart, and Stewart had agreed to join Brennan's opinion only if it limited the ruling to the question of jurisdiction. Brennan felt he had to honor his agreement with Stewart, and so was not willing to expand the decision.[34] Consequently, Tom Clark issued a concurring opinion rather than joining Brennan's. His words reveal his views on Tennessee's apportionment policy and his initial reluctance to intervene:

> We must examine what the Assembly has done. The frequency and magnitude of the inequalities in the present districting admit of no policy whatever . . . It leaves but one conclusion, namely that Tennessee's apportionment is a crazy quilt without rational basis. . . .
>
> Although I find the Tennessee apportionment statute offends the Equal Protection Clause, I would not consider intervention by this Court into so delicate a field if there were any other relief available to the people of Tennessee.[35]

Despite disappointment that the apportionment issue was not addressed, my father's concurring opinion expressed his strong support of the majority's decision:

> Its [the Supreme Court's] decision today supports the proposition for which our forebears fought and many died, namely, that to be conformable to the principle of right, the form of government must be representative. That is the keystone upon which our government was founded and lacking which no republic can survive. . . . In my view the ultimate decision today is in the greatest tradition of this Court.[36]

The importance of a 6–3 decision over a 5–4 decision should not be underestimated. The latter is viewed as tenuous—future cases may deal with the same issue, and one changed vote reverses the decision. *Baker v. Carr*, which Earl Warren once described as "the most important case of my tenure on the Court," was controversial, producing a flood of lawsuits challenging apportionment procedures in states throughout the country.[37] William Brennan believed that Tom Clark's concurring opinion built support for the decision and helped establish "one man, one vote" as an important constitutional principle.

Brennan was not the only justice who understood Tom Clark's ability to bring in public support for decisions. In selecting my father to write the majority opinion for controversial civil rights cases such as *Heart of Atlanta Motel, Katzenbach,* and *Hamm,* Earl Warren exhibited his skill at assigning the responsibility of writing opinions, arguably the most important responsibility of a chief justice. Warren recognized and appreciated the value of Tom Clark's reputation as the Court's strongest supporter of law enforcement and understood that opinions written by Clark, because of his reputation, would have the greatest credibility and public support. Warren used my father's reputation to advantage in a number of cases, including *Estes* and *Schempp*. Warren had already written a lengthy dissent in *Estes*, and could have used it as the majority opinion after my father changed his vote, giving Warren the majority.[38] Instead, he assigned the opinion to my father. Knowing that Tom Clark had more credibility than he in the area of law enforcement and victims' rights, he chose him as the justice who would bring in the greatest public support.

In the extremely controversial school-prayer cases, Tom Clark's reputation as a "man of faith" made him Warren's choice to write the majority opinion for *Schempp*, the second case involving that issue.[39] After the uproar that followed Black's decision in *Engel*, the chief justice sought someone whose opinion might soften the criticism that was sure to follow. He also appreciated my father's public defense of *Engel*. Tom Clark could not eliminate criticism, but his reputation helped mute it and brought support from some undecided observers.

Because of Tom Clark's experience at the Department of Justice, he brought expertise to the Court in the field of antitrust. During his tenure on the Court, he wrote more antitrust opinions than any other justice. In his autobiography, Justice William O. Douglas described Tom Clark's contributions in that area of the law: "In my time, Tom Clark contributed more insight into antitrust problems than any other Justice. His experience in various roles at the Department of Justice were illuminating."[40]

My father also exhibited a talent for understanding and dealing effectively with highly specialized law. His former law clerk Charles Reed described this ability in dealing with three patent-law cases known as the "Trilogy Cases":

> There isn't a more arcane and specialized area of law than patents. The Trilogy Cases are the most significant statements on the patent clause of the Constitution since the mid-1800s *Hotchkiss v. Greenwood* case. He [Tom Clark] has been eulogized by the patent bar for his opinion in these cases. I did the first draft of them (I had degrees in chemical engineering as well as law, and I was a natural choice for doing the work). Although your father went around telling the patent bar that I did the real work, the fact is quite the opposite. I presented a first draft which he promptly tore apart and rewrote himself, with a result far, far better than the one I submitted. . . . He not only quickly came to understand the essence of the Constitutional issue, his handling of it is—in typical Tom Clark fashion—a masterpiece of workable law. He understood, as Douglas and several others did not, the

difference between a beneficial monopoly (a patent is a monopoly—granted to incentivize progress) and a bad one. The opinions in the Trilogy Cases are, I strongly believe, significant accomplishments which are generally unknown outside of the narrow band of the patent bar.[41]

Tom Clark's opinions have been described as "lucid, precise and persuasive" and as exhibiting "a sophisticated command of constitutional construction."[42] A few of his dissents could be described as angry or even harsh, yet according to his colleagues and staff, he rarely offended the justices with whom he disagreed. The one exception that I am aware of was Frankfurter's reaction to the *Jencks* decision. Justice Byron White's words describe my father's gifts of diplomacy and compromise:

> [It was] almost impossible for him to offend anyone. He loved people. He was as tough as nails when it came down to short strokes, but he always managed not to scratch people or offend them. And if he had to differ with them, he differed with a great deal of dignity but also tolerance. So you didn't get mad at Tom. At the same time, if you're going to have five people agree, often one or more or everyone will have to modify their views to some extent. . . . That in itself is quite a tug-of-war, and it's the art of reaching an acceptable compromise. And your father because of his personality and his experience and his abilities was an expert at that. He was very good at it, and that kind of talent is extremely valuable here, like in other contexts.[43]

I received a number of letters in response to a questionnaire that I sent my father's former law clerks in 1994. Their letters were similar in many ways, reflecting the affection and respect they felt for Tom Clark. I believe that my father's relationship with his law clerks was not unlike his relationship with his children. He rarely, if ever, lectured, but taught by example. He was our biggest booster, building our confidence and egos, but at the same time, we knew he expected the best from us. He made us want to live up to his expectations. On the rare occasions when he did criticize us, the impact was great!

Most of the justices chose their law clerks from large prestigious colleges or universities, but Tom Clark felt there should be broader representation, and though he had his share of Harvard, Princeton, and Yale graduates, he also selected from lesser-known law schools, such as the South Texas College of Law, Drake, and the University of Mississippi. He invariably treated them with respect and showed an interest in their personal lives. The law clerks and their families were always invited to Thanksgiving dinner at our apartment, and I recall meeting many of them at this annual event. In his letter to me, Larry Temple described his personal relationship with my father:

> For me, like almost all other law clerks, Justice Clark was a surrogate father or out-of-town father. At the very outset of my tenure with him, the Justice specifically told me that he wanted to know if I ever needed anything.[44]

He also gave the following assessment of Tom Clark's relationship with the other justices, admitting that he might be biased:

> I believe that any secret ballot would have reflected that Justice Clark was the number one favorite of all of the other justices on a purely personal basis. That was the foundation for an outstanding working relationship with the other eight.

Law clerks have unique opportunities to observe how justices arrive at their decisions, and also gain insight into their relationships with their staffs and the other justices. John Nolan, who clerked for my father from 1956 to 1957, considered him "a balance wheel" for the decisions of the Court. When asked about Justice Clark's relationship with his staff, Nolan replied:

> More than outstanding. With everyone in his office, the relationship was close, confidential, and mutually supporting. With his law clerks especially he was more open and candid than any other Justice. He would always take the time to give a detailed account of the conference deliberations on any case in which one of his clerks was interested. We always had access to the book where every vote and whatever notes he might have taken were recorded. He was understanding and sympathetic to any personal need of his staff, no matter how far removed from the work of the Court.[45]

Bob Hamilton, who clerked for my father during the 1955–1956 term, gave a similar assessment:

> Justice Clark was a joy to work for as a twenty-four year old law clerk. He had quite an open mind and listened patiently to our thoughts and comments. He was also always polite, considerate and interested in me and my family.[46]

Hamilton also cited Tom Clark's ability to get to the core of an issue:

My most vivid impression of the Justice's strength was his ability to read a record and digest not only the arguments of the parties but also the factual context in which the dispute arose. He could cut to the heart of an issue. He never had an opinion carved in stone but was practical, used common sense.

Several of his former law clerks cited the humanity that shaped my father's judgments:

He labored long and hard at the Court and I think had many personal struggles within himself in order to formulate what he felt was a "right" posture on a given issue. He was devoted to the Court and its principles but was very much a "humanist." The issues were, of course, extraordinarily complex, but he had an innate ability to reach the real heart of an issue and its effect on society generally.[47]

In his judging, as in everything else he did, Justice Clark was usually first concerned with the decision's impact on people, often its impact on the individual. The Justice was extraordinarily perceptive about everyone he met, and he brought a similar perception and understanding to the people involved in the cases that came before him. The human aspects of cases never escaped him, and he probably understood them better than did other Justices.[48]

They also described him as a pragmatist who was primarily interested in making things work. Former law clerk Charles Reed provided the following analogy:

I see Tom Clark as taking advantage of those justices who were enslaved by some perceived judicial philosophy. Because he was more interested in making things work than in making them fit into a neat framework, he was like a karate expert in competition with a sumo wrestler—he used the weight of such heavily encumbered theorists against themselves. I thought Justice Clark was a pragmatist looking to use the cases to solve problems as they currently existed, but without attempting to build edifices or road blocks for the future.[49]

There has been much conjecture about the role of law clerks in the writing of opinions, especially since the publication of *The Brethren*

(1979), by Bob Woodward and Scott Armstrong. A single sweeping statement cannot be made about the relationship between justices and their law clerks, for they naturally depend upon the individuals involved. In a 1972 interview, my father described what he expected from his law clerks and his perception of what other justices expected from theirs:

> I don't think that the law clerks wrote any court opinions. I was told that Justice Rehnquist wrote some when he was a law clerk. Later he wrote an article about it. I expect that he only wrote memos—not opinions—for Justice Jackson.
>
> As far as I know the opinions were written by justices. It is true that I would write the first draft of an opinion in cases assigned to me and then give a copy to my law clerks. Quite often they might suggest that the opinion might be changed in form but not disposition. As long as I was on the Court no one ever suggested I change my vote. Some of the law clerks might suggest changes in language, make it shorter, or perhaps suggest citations of authority that in their view might be stronger or something similar. They always checked the citations and quotations from authorities. . . .
>
> When we got a dissent, we would discuss it (the law clerks and myself) and I would decide how we should answer it by making changes in the circulated draft. Sometimes the dissent almost demolishes you, so you have to get up an answer to it. Of course you never mention the dissent but you just say "Some claim," or "They say" or something of that order. So, the law clerks were confined, when I was on the Court, to writing memorandums and researching.[50]

Despite his genial, informal manner, Tom Clark expected a great deal from his staff. As one law clerk put it, "He set firm deadlines and you had to produce and deliver in all of those things he expected."[51] But he was also extremely fair, even willing to share the work with the law clerks if he believed they were overburdened. The principal job of the clerks is to review petitions for certiorari (that is, appeals to the Court for reviews of lower-court decisions). Each Monday, the Supreme Court clerk's office distributes these appeals to the justices' offices. The law clerks then examine them and write memos summarizing the cases. One former law clerk provided the following anecdote to illustrate Tom Clark's willingness to share the law clerks' work if he felt it appropriate. One Monday, what a former law clerk described as a "mountain" of petitions was delivered. The justices' conference was the next day, and it was clear that reviewing the petitions in time for the conference would mean staying up all night for the two law clerks. My father, aware of the problem, divided the stack into three parts—one for himself and one for each of the clerks. He took his stack home to work on so that the job would be completed in time and without undue hardship on the clerks. Tom Clark's willingness to help others was apparently well known by the staffs of other justices too. Their tendency to bring their problems to my father sometimes annoyed his longtime, devoted messenger Oscar Bethea. "Why don't they go to their own justices?" he once complained to Mother.

The Court's caseload grew dramatically during the years my father served—from 800 in 1949 to 3,400 in 1967.[52] The justices' conferences sometimes went on until seven or eight in the evening. He usually brought work home with him, and went to the Court most Saturdays and some Sundays. Yet despite this heavy workload, my father became active in outside activities, especially in the efforts to improve the administration of justice. He enjoyed these activities, which took him out of the somewhat cloistered, isolating environment of the Supreme Court and provided a satisfying outlet for his gregarious and action-oriented personality.

His involvement began in the mid-1950s when the American Bar Association's Section of Judicial Administration asked him to serve as its chairman. He accepted on the condition that he start as vice chairman of the section before becoming its chairman: "I don't want to just go in and be chairman; I want to spend some time on the council first and then become chairman."[53] His reaction was typical: he would never agree to be a mere figurehead. If he accepted a position of responsibility in an organization, he would first learn about its needs, assess the possibilities, and then do something about them. He served as vice chairman of the section for one year, 1956–1957, and then became chairman in 1957.

Through his involvement with the Section of Judicial Administration, my father met and worked with many members of the ABA. The relationship between the Court and the ABA became strained during the late 1950s because of several critical reports issued by ABA committees on some Supreme Court decisions. The worst incident occurred at the 1957 ABA convention, which was held in London as a joint meeting with the English bench. The president of the ABA had asked Chief Justice Warren to act as head of the American group, which was attending the convention on what he described as "this historic goodwill mission."[54] Warren accepted, but became furious when the ABA's special committee on communism released a report criticizing fifteen recent Supreme Court decisions that, in its view, aided communism. A few weeks later, Warren resigned from the ABA. In his *Memoirs*, he gave the following explanation for his resignation: "I could no longer belong to an organization of the legal profession which would ask me to lead fifteen thousand of its members overseas on a goodwill mission and then deliberately and trickily contrive to discredit the Supreme Court which I headed."[55]

Tom Clark's relationship with the ABA was not affected by this incident. After he became chairman of the Section on Judicial Administration, he traveled throughout the country, speaking and gathering information on ways to improve judicial administration. He spoke before more than two-thirds of the state trial judges—there were 2,300 in the United States at that time—and was dubbed "the traveling salesman of justice" by legal scholar John Frank.[56] Through these efforts, he not only developed recommendations that revitalized the section, but also became known and admired by a large number of ABA members and state trial judges. He served as a communication link between the Court and these groups. In 1962, the ABA awarded him its highest citation—the American Bar Association Medal. He was only the third justice to have received it at that time.

John Frank described how my father's relationship with the ABA benefited the Supreme Court:

> Clark was perfectly aware that he personally was considerably more popular with some sections of the Bar than was the Court of which he was a part.... Clark repeatedly put his own drawing power on the line in defense of the institution. He regularly brought to his audience "the greetings of my Brethren on the Supreme Court." ... The real good Clark did the Court was simply derivative of his presence, whether physical or as a voice not very far off stage. State judicial criticism of the Supreme Court peaked, particularly in the late 1950s, but it has been progressively harder for judges or bar groups to attack a court of which Clark is a part.[57]

He also forged a relationship between the Court and law schools by participating in moot courts held at law schools throughout the country. In 1967, Percy Williams, a former law clerk, described my father's role in providing a link between the ABA, law schools, and the Court: "Justice Clark has become a principal interpreter to the Bar and the law schools of the Court's function in adjudicating the constitutional rights of the individual, repeatedly voicing his concern with 'the necessity of striking a delicate balance between the rights of the individual and those of the public' and his conviction that 'To establish that right means liberty.'"[58]

During the spring of 2001, I attended a Wellesley College alumnae program that featured Associate Justice Sandra Day O'Connor as speaker. Justice O'Connor, knowing that I was in the audience, told the group that Tom Clark was the first member of the Supreme Court that she had ever met. The occasion was a moot-court competition at Stanford University in which Clark was participating. She, like many law students at that time, viewed Supreme Court justices as remote and somewhat unapproachable. For her, Tom Clark dispelled that image. She was impressed by this warm, unpretentious man, and she remembered, and appreciated, his outreach to law students.

My father rarely discussed cases that had been decided, but on a few occasions he felt so strongly about criticism of the Court that he spoke out. He made the following statement after critics attacked some of the Court's decisions as impediments to state law enforcement: "While I dissented in most of the cases to which they point, I give no credence to this claim. Indeed, the short answer to it is that the rules which the Court has now held applicable to state procedures have been followed by federal law enforcement officers for years, some for half a century."[59]

During the 1960s, the Court was frequently under attack for opinions supporting the rights of the accused, and especially for the school-prayer decisions. "Impeach Earl Warren" bumper stickers appeared around the country. In his article "The Court and Its Critics," written after his retirement, my father wrote the following: "The Supreme Court is suffering its darkest hour at a time when it deserves its most glorious day. . . . The 'crime wave' has placed the advancements made by the Supreme Court in the field of criminal justice in jeopardy."[60] He defended *Mapp, Gideon, Berger*, and *Miranda* by pointing to the fact that these decisions had not caused a decrease in convictions but instead had produced improvements in police work. Furthermore, he wrote:

the adaption of these enlightened rules is within our concepts of the presumption of innocence, fair trial, and proof of guilt beyond a reasonable doubt. . . .

Likewise the relaxation of normal protections against wiretapping and eavesdropping is a mistake. We should insist that there is probable cause supporting the use of such devices before they are permitted.[61]

Tom Clark consistently defended the Warren Court before and after his retirement, and while he and Earl Warren did not always agree, they always enjoyed a warm friendship and mutual respect. When Warren retired from the Court, in 1968, a year after my father's own retirement, my father wrote a tribute that reveals the affection and esteem that he felt for the chief justice:

But selfishly I was glad [about Warren's retirement] because I knew we could put in more time together fishing, swimming, walking, attending spectator sports and just prognosticating as old folks do. And now that he is moving his chambers next to mine and Brother Reed's, we welcome him to the ranks of the retired—an honorable estate—where together we, like the three musketeers, can continue to work, perhaps harder than ever, for a more effective administration of justice. . . . The worth of the United States—in the long run—and the worth of the individuals composing it will be greater for Earl Warren having been the Chief Justice.[62]

Bernard Schwartz's observation that Tom Clark has been "the most underrated justice" has been reversed somewhat, but not rectified. Anyone studying his papers at the University of Texas law library will recognize that he was much more than "the ablest of the four Truman appointees." Professor Henry Abraham, a legal scholar who has written extensively about the Supreme Court, is one of those whose opinion has been altered. In his book *Justices, Presidents, and Senators*, Abraham writes:

Thus, he [Tom Clark] developed and embraced three admirable principles as endemic to the judicial role as he perceived it: 1. that it was essential that justices usually follow precedent 2. that although a Court should overturn "an unsoundly decided" case, it should only be done in the presence of a clear majority—one that could articulate and support the doctrinal basis for the precedent's destruction and the establishment of its successor, and 3. that a justice should do everything feasible to render and maintain the Court's decisions with absolute clarity. With the passing of the years, many of his critics had second thoughts about Tom Clark and gladly acknowledge that here was not only the ablest of the four Truman appointees but a jurist of far above-average capability and performance.[63]

Schwartz's statement that Tom Clark has been "underrated" no longer rings true, for more and more scholars now acknowledge his contributions and recognize him as a justice who made a difference!

## CHAPTER 20

# An Ending and a Beginning

The first day of the new life.

Tom Clark, 1967, on his retirement

TOM CLARK WAS IN HIS PRIME in the 1960s—a productive writer of opinions, a facilitator who enjoyed excellent relationships with his colleagues, and a defender of the Court whose outside activities brought it needed goodwill. Retirement was not in his vocabulary. In 1967, he was a youthful sixty-seven and in excellent health. We did not anticipate that his career as an associate justice was coming to a close. Then the unexpected happened.

The 1960s were a time of momentous change for our family as well as for the country in general. In 1959, my husband, Tom, our two small daughters, and I moved from Chicago, where Tom had just earned a master of business administration from Northwestern University, to Dallas. Tom, who had resigned from the navy in 1956, had accepted a position with Texas Instruments, and I was thrilled that we were returning to my birthplace, where many family members still lived, including my brother, Ramsey, his wife, Georgia, and their two children. None of us foresaw the dramatic change that would occur in Ramsey's career and the impact that it would have on our father's.

Ramsey was nine years old when we left Dallas—six years older than I—and his bond with Texas was much stronger than mine. While Ramsey was still in high school, my father encouraged him to go to an eastern college or to one of the military academies, but Ramsey wanted to return to his home state and attend the University of Texas, our parents' alma mater. He graduated from the university in 1949 and then from the University of Chicago Law School in 1951. After graduation, he joined the family law firm. By 1960, he had been practicing law for almost ten years and had established an outstanding reputation as a young lawyer. My father was surprised when, in the summer of 1960, as the presidential campaign was being waged, Ramsey expressed an interest in joining the federal government. He had never indicated an interest in politics but, like many young people, was inspired by the charismatic John F. Kennedy and was eager to serve the country. My father suggested he get involved in the campaign, but Ramsey declined to do so—he did not enjoy campaigning and was not political by nature.

After Kennedy won the election, the subject of an appointment came up again—specifically, one as assistant attorney general of the Department of Justice's Antitrust Division. My father sought advice from a few friends, including vice president–elect Lyndon Johnson, Speaker Sam Rayburn, and Justice William O. Douglas, who was a close friend of the Kennedys. The competition for political appointments was fierce, but an interview for Ramsey with Attorney General Robert Kennedy was arranged. The interview went well, and the two men hit it off immediately. But the position Ramsey wanted was not available. Instead, he was offered the position of assistant attorney general of the Lands Division. At that time, the Lands Division was a quiet, relatively unknown division that was viewed as a dead end within the department. My father was surprised when Ramsey accepted the offer.

The day before Ramsey's confirmation hearings began, my parents attended a dinner party, and Mother found herself seated next to Senator Kenneth Keating, one of my father's strongest critics during the early 1950s investigations. She was not pleased with the seating arrangement, but always the gracious lady and also a very intelligent one, she overcame her displeasure and conversed pleasantly with the Senator. Aware that Keating would be voting on Ramsey's confirmation, she took advantage of the opportunity to launch into a glowing tribute to her son. The next day, when Keating took his turn to question Ramsey, he began with, "I sat next to your mother last night, and she spoke very highly of you." I don't know how much impact Mother's praise of Ramsey had on Keating, but despite his past antagonism toward my father, he, along with all the senators, voted in favor of Ramsey.

Ramsey left for Washington, D.C., in January 1961, and Georgia and the children followed soon afterward. Selfishly, my enthusiasm for John F. Kennedy's victory diminished somewhat when the full realization that Ramsey and his family were leaving Dallas hit me. Ramsey and I had not lived in the same city since 1945, when he joined the marines and left home. After my family moved to Dallas, we saw each other frequently. Our

families were close and congenial. Our two older daughters enjoyed playing with their cousin Thomas (Tom C. Clark II) and loved their beautiful, handicapped cousin Ronda. Despite my disappointment that Ramsey
and his family were leaving, I was happy for my parents, who were proud
of Ramsey's success and thrilled that one of their children would live close
to them. No one dreamed of the impact that Ramsey's change in careers
would have on my father.

Ramsey quickly gained the respect and friendship of Robert Kennedy
and became a close counselor of the attorney general. Kennedy recognized and appreciated Ramsey's ability to deal with difficult issues, especially civil rights. Ramsey also proved to be an able administrator, an area
in which he had little previous experience. Members of the House Appropriations Committee were amazed when he requested a budget cut for his
division—an unprecedented action, according to committee chairman
John Rooney. Congressman Rooney brought up Ramsey's budget cut a
few weeks later when Justices Black and Clark came before the committee with their budget request for the Supreme Court.

Congressman Rooney began the exchange: "Well, Mr. Justice, we hope
you do as well as your son."

My father, unaware of what had happened, replied, "How's that, Mr.
Congressman?"

"He cut $250,000 off his budget!" Rooney declared.

My father's response began defensively but, in typical fashion, ended
with humor: "I couldn't do that well—our budget is so little . . . only a
million and a half. We couldn't cut that much off. And besides, Ramsey
takes after his mother."

After the tragic assassination of John F. Kennedy, in 1963, Ramsey was
one of the few people who remained close to both Robert Kennedy and
President Lyndon Johnson. My family's ties to the Johnsons went back
many years. My father met LBJ in 1938, when he was a young, newly
elected congressman from Texas. A friendship developed that included the
whole family; it was much more than a professional relationship between
the two men. Mother and Lady Bird became close friends, and I always
appreciated Mrs. Johnson's warmth and graciousness. When I returned
home from camp in North Carolina in 1945, she drove down with
Mother to pick me up. When her niece, who was close to my age, visited,
Mrs. Johnson would often invite me over for an outing of some sort. My
parents also felt close to the Johnsons' daughters, and gave parties for both
Lynda and Luci when they became engaged.

If anything, the friendship became closer after Ramsey joined the government. While LBJ was vice president, he and Lady Bird sometimes

invited my parents and Ramsey's family to join them on Sunday afternoons to make ice cream or go for a swim. There was no official residence
for the vice president at that time, but the Johnsons had purchased The
Elms, the home of Perle Mesta, the renowned hostess and former ambassador to Luxembourg. A favorite family anecdote concerns one of these
occasions, which involved Ramsey's eight-year-old son, Tommy. The
family had spent the day with the Johnsons, and as they left, LBJ asked,
"Tommy, did you have a pretty good time?"

Tommy responded, "This is the second-best time I ever had."

"When was the first?" inquired Johnson.

"When Grandad let me drive the golf cart," was the reply.

In the fall of 1966, Nicholas Katzenbach, who had followed Robert
Kennedy as attorney general, resigned to become deputy secretary of
state. Speculation began immediately about who would succeed him as
attorney general. Ramsey was deputy attorney general at the time, and a
natural choice for the position, but Johnson was still uncertain, and asked
Katzenbach for other recommendations. Katzenbach suggested Clark
Clifford or Maurice Tobin. Johnson also asked Katzenbach whether he
had heard any objections to Ramsey. Katzenbach had not, and said that
civil rights groups wanted Ramsey as attorney general and that both
Senate minority leader Everett Dirksen and majority leader Mike Mansfield supported him.[1]

As soon as Katzenbach was sworn in as deputy secretary of state,
Ramsey became "acting" attorney general. Ramsey recalls a conversation
with the president that occurred soon afterward. "Don't expect to be
attorney general," Johnson declared. "I can't appoint a Texan." In a taped
telephone conversation with Justice Abe Fortas, Johnson expressed the
same sentiment. Fortas said he had talked to Tom Clark about the possibility of Ramsey's appointment and that Clark was "very hopeful" that the
president would offer him the position. LBJ responded that he was concerned that there might be "serious trouble with the Department of Justice when he [Katzenbach] leaves and they see a Texan in there. I think
that has great dangers."[2] Apparently, the president was sensitive to criticism that there were too many Texans in his administration, and was reluctant to add to that number.

Of greater concern to Johnson was the appearance of a conflict of
interest if Ramsey was attorney general and Tom Clark chose to remain
on the Court. Many within the legal profession felt that the elder Clark's
retirement was not necessary. They argued that the solicitor general, rather
than the attorney general, was responsible for arguing cases before the
Court, and Tom Clark could recuse himself from those that his son was

personally involved in. Senator Everett Dirksen was among those who felt it unnecessary for Tom Clark to resign. But Johnson was worried, and wanted to know what Clark would do in the event Ramsey was appointed. Clearly, Ramsey did not want to be the cause of our father's retirement. "Dad is only sixty-seven and loves his work—I don't want him to have to retire because of me."[3] Katzenbach was aware that Tom Clark hoped the president would select Ramsey as attorney general, but did not know whether he planned to retire if that occurred. In discussing the situation with LBJ, Katzenbach gave the following assessment: "He's [Tom Clark's] being a good father and Ramsey's being a good son. They have to work it out."[4] Johnson decided to discuss the issue with Ramsey:

LBJ: "You think you could be attorney general with your daddy on the Court?

Ramsey: "Well I think that other people ought to judge that, but I know that as far as I'm concerned that would not affect my judgment. I don't think it would affect Dad's judgment."[5]

Ramsey also warned the president of negative repercussions if Tom Clark retired: "In the police community and some other conservative areas, dad ranks awfully high . . . For you to replace him with a liberal would hurt you."[6]

The president was not convinced. He had decided that Tom Clark's retirement would be necessary:

If my judgment is that you become attorney general, he [Tom Clark] would have to leave the Court. For no other reason than the public appearance of an old man sitting on his boy's cases. Every taxi driver in the country, he'd tell me that the old man couldn't judge fairly what his old boy is sending up.[7]

My father never discussed Ramsey's appointment or his own retirement with Johnson, but he agreed with the president that he could not remain on the Court if his son became attorney general: "You know judges owe a higher degree of not only duty but of public appearance, I think, than the average person. After all, they judge right and wrong between individuals and between the state and individuals. If they maintain a bad image it's not only going to hurt the judicial process but the whole system of democratic society."[8]

On October 3, 1966, Tom Clark sent the following letter to Chief Justice Warren:

Dear Chief:

Press reports say that the President is considering Ramsey for appointment as Attorney General of the United States. I am not advised as to whether the report has foundation, however I thought that you should know that in the event Ramsey becomes Attorney General it is my intention to retire from the Court.

There was no longer a question of what Tom Clark would do if Ramsey became attorney general. Nevertheless, Johnson waited another four months before appointing him to the position. He apparently had concluded that another Texan in his administration would not be damaging, and he knew that Tom Clark would retire when the current Supreme Court term ended. My father expressed pleasure when Ramsey's appointment was announced: "Mrs. Clark and I are filled with both pride and joy over Ramsey's nomination by the President to become Attorney General. We deeply appreciate the high confidence the President has placed in him."[9]

My father had already announced that he would retire at the end of the Supreme Court term when he gave the oath of office to Ramsey on March 11, 1967. President Johnson spoke briefly at the ceremony, describing Ramsey in glowing terms: "Secure in his knowledge of the law, gifted with a quick mind and keen conscience, he is above all else a courageous man of deep convictions and the moral strength of genuine humility."[10]

Johnson still had not named my father's successor, and numerous names were being bandied about: Secretary of Labor Willard Wirtz; Secretary of the Treasury Henry Fowler; Judge Sarah T. Hughes, who administered the oath of office to LBJ after the assassination of Kennedy; Leon Jaworski, the prominent Houston lawyer who later became the prosecutor in the Watergate hearings; and, of course, Thurgood Marshall. When questioned about who his successor might be, my father would only respond modestly, "Someone will take my place and he will fill my shoes to overflowing."[11] Johnson kept everyone guessing for another four months. He seemed ambivalent about Marshall, even telling him at one point not to expect to go on the Court.[12] When Johnson finally appointed Marshall, my father complimented him on "a great appointment."[13]

If my father regretted giving up his lifetime position on the Supreme Court so that Ramsey could serve as attorney general for two years, he never expressed it. He remained upbeat throughout this period, clearly proud of Ramsey, and his sense of humor still intact. He thoroughly enjoyed the affectionate "roasting" that he received when he attended the annual meeting of the Bar Association of the Seventh Circuit on May 9, 1967. The words were put to the tune of the song "Sonny Boy."

> On my knees please climb, Sonny Boy.
> Though you're thirty-nine, Sonny Boy.
> You've no way of knowing
> I've no way of showing
> What you did to me Sonny Boy.
>
> You were selected
> It was expected
> I'd quit for you, Sonny Boy.
> I lost my tenure
> But who needs it when you're
> Doing so well, Sonny Boy.
>
> You went to law school
> I gave you the nudge
> If you had been a doctor
> I'd still be a judge.
> Since you'll do some hiring
> Now that I'm retiring
> How about a job, Sonny Boy?

Some have described Tom Clark's retirement as "forced," but the decision to retire was an easy one for him. He wanted Ramsey, whom he sometimes referred to in typically self-effacing style as "a block off the old chip," to become attorney general. I truly believe that Ramsey's appointment brought my father more satisfaction and happiness than any of his own remarkable achievements. He was the most unselfish person I have ever known. I never heard them argue, although their views on issues sometimes differed sharply. They not only loved and admired each other, but also were confidants and friends. On December 18, 1967, Ramsey's thirty-ninth birthday, my father presented him with a book and the following note:

Dear Bub:
It is my high privilege—never before had by any father—to give you this volume on the Attorneys General of the United States from Randolph to Ramsey Clark.

This gives me great pride and satisfaction—the more so because you are proving yourself to be America's greatest Attorney General—and you always were the best son any dad ever had.

Affectionately, TCC

On June 12, 1967, Tom Clark sat on the Supreme Court for the last time. Speaking for all the justices, Chief Justice Earl Warren gave the following tribute:

Justice Clark has had a great public career. . . . For eighteen years he has served with distinction on this Court. During these dynamic years he wrote many of the most important opinions of the times. He has been a great companion for us, and he departs with the affection of every member of the Court. We are happy to know that he leaves in the best of health and for a happy reason. We have no idea what he will undertake to do in the future, but we know he will be active and that he will continue throughout his useful years, which we hope will be many, to devote his efforts to the improvement of the administration of justice.[14]

Tom Clark's response expressed some nostalgia for an important era in his life that was ending, but more importantly, and in keeping with his personality, he looked to the future and welcomed his new life:

My eighteen years of service on the Court have been the most rewarding of my public life. To two great presidents I am grateful for giving me this opportunity. First to Franklin Roosevelt for bringing me into the Department of Justice in 1937 and appointing me Assistant Attorney General in 1943; and the more I am indebted to the best client of my life, President Harry S. Truman, for whom I served as Attorney General of the United States. . . . Today our emotions are mixed—happiness with regrets. But it is not the last day of which I speak, it is rather the first day of the new life which we shall continue to dedicate to the public interest. As we enter it— and close our eighteen years here—we call to mind the words of the Court Crier: "God bless the United States and this Honorable Court."[15]

# PART FOUR

*Retirement, 1967–1977*

## CHAPTER 21

# The Great Adventure

He exemplified the finer elements that have gone into the making of America.

U.S. Embassy in Malaysia, 1967

"THE FIRST DAY OF THE NEW LIFE" started with a bang: my parents left for an around-the-world trip the afternoon following my father's last day on the Supreme Court. The trip was funded by a grant from the Department of State's Bureau of Educational and Cultural Affairs. Tom Clark was designated a "United States Specialist" serving on a "goodwill" mission for the country. The purpose of the mission was to exchange information with representatives of other countries and to share ideas about our judicial and legal systems and those of the countries visited. Mother called the trip their "great adventure." No one anticipated the negative impact it would have on my father's health.

The voyage began on June 14, 1967, and was to end ninety days later in Rome. The ambitious itinerary included Tokyo, Hong Kong, Singapore, Malaysia, Australia, New Zealand, Indonesia, Thailand, India, Lebanon, Jordan, Jerusalem, Turkey, Greece and finally Rome. The first leg of the journey was to Los Angeles; there they caught a connecting flight to Hawaii, where they spent the first night. They boarded a flight to Tokyo the next morning, but the plane developed engine trouble less than an hour after takeoff and had to return to Honolulu for repairs. They were off again a few hours later, but were five hours late arriving in Tokyo.

Mother recorded a full schedule in her diary—brunches, luncheons, dinners, speeches, and seminars at every spot they visited. They were treated royally, and were impressed and pleased with the efficiency and thoughtfulness of the State Department officials who handled the trip. The Vietnam War was still raging, but there seemed to be more curiosity about the racial tensions that our country was experiencing than questions about the war. The long hot summer in the United States began with race riots in New Jersey that were the worst since the 1965 Watts riots in Los Angeles. The unrest continued, and in July, President Johnson was forced to send federal troops to Detroit to control the violence caused by riots there.

While on their trip, my parents were virtually unaffected by the problems at home. My father met with the chief justices, justices, and legal and judicial officials of each country, and spoke everywhere on various subjects related to our judicial system. He also spoke on television and radio broadcasts. There were occasional breaks for golf, the beach, and shopping, but the schedule was strenuous by any standard. In Japan, my father attended a roundtable meeting and lecture at the country's Legal Training and Research Institute. His lecture, entitled "Behind the Scenes at the Supreme Court of the United States," described the process that the justices go through in arriving at decisions.[1] They spent some time sightseeing in Japan, and Mother's diary describes a train ride to Kyoto, where they stayed at the Miyako Hotel, one of the most beautiful she had ever been in.

Two days later they were in Hong Kong, dining with that city's chief justice and other judicial and legal professionals. It was a difficult time for Hong Kong residents. My father was briefed by the American consul general on one serious problem—China. Hong Kong was still a British protectorate in 1967, and there was great concern that the British would withdraw and China would take over the city.[2] At the same time, China was unhappy that the British were allowing U.S. warships fighting in Vietnam to use the port, and large anti-British demonstrations were held in both Peking (Beijing) and Hong Kong. There were also bombings in Hong Kong, though because the police were able to control most of the violence, no one had been killed. Still, people were afraid to go out, and many refused to use public transportation. Hong Kong was also suffering a serious drought, and strict water rationing was enforced. Fortunately, these problems did not seriously affect my parents' visit. My father was able to go to the beach; also, he had a suit made by the hotel's tailor. They enjoyed their hotel room, which looked out over the bay, with a view of China in the distance. One night they had dinner with Ambassador John Kenneth Galbraith, the renowned economist, and his wife and two children.

From Hong Kong they traveled to Singapore for a two-day stay, and then on to Kuala Lumpur, Malaysia. In his report on the trip, my father expressed concern about Malaysia's "protective custody" practice—a common procedure in many Southeast Asian countries that allowed specified political officials to arrest people without a warrant simply by declaring them "dangerous to the state."[3] Some political prisoners had been held for two or three years or more without being charged with any crime. Tom Clark was disturbed by the practice, which he regarded as totally unacceptable by U.S. standards, but felt constrained from openly addressing the issue for fear of creating an international incident. Ironically, recently the Bush administration defended similar practices by our country in its war against terrorism.

President and Mrs. Johnson, who were also in Kuala Lumpur, attended a banquet held at the parliament with my parents. The following day, Lady Bird joined my parents for a tour of the country's national mosque, the Masjid Negara, which Mother described as one of the most beautiful buildings she had ever seen. On their last full day in Malaysia, my parents were picked up by a driver and taken to the city of Malaka. The drive took them through beautiful countryside, but Mother was too frightened to fully enjoy the scenery. She described the road's surface as "good," but the road itself was only two-lane, and was used by bicyclists, oxcarts, water buffalo, and pedestrians. The driver sped up hills and around curves at sixty miles an hour or so, terrifying Mother, who was always a nervous passenger and a habitual backseat driver when family members were at the wheel. Mother recorded her terror in her diary: "I kept thinking of Jayne Mansfield, decapitated a few days ago, and that instead of air insurance I should have taken out car insurance!" They survived the experience: "I believe in miracles," wrote Mother, greatly relieved when they reached their destination.

From Malaysia they traveled to Australia, where their itinerary followed a dizzying path from Sydney, Australia, to Auckland and Wellington, New Zealand, then back to Australia and the cities of Melbourne, Adelaide, and Canberra, with a short stop in Tasmania. Mother recorded being exhausted on a number of occasions; she caught up on sleep by taking naps whenever possible. My father rarely admitted to feeling fatigue, but even he succumbed to a nap in Adelaide. He still maintained a packed schedule of daily luncheons, dinners, press conferences, and speeches. It was winter in that part of the world, and the weather was cold and rainy much of the time. Both he and Mother developed colds in Sydney, and on July 27, a doctor was called in. There was still no suggestion of any serious health problem, and that same day they took a seven-hour flight to Djakarta (Jakarta), Indonesia, where they enjoyed warmer weather and continuous activities. Their colds were better, and my father joined in games of croquet and horseshoes with some of the men. Mother described the Indonesians as warm and friendly despite the poverty. It was the poorest country they had visited. President Sukarno lived in opulence in his palace at Bogor, but he had relinquished much of his power to General Suharto and was a virtual prisoner, unable to leave his residence except for short, close-by trips under the protection of guards.

They left for Bangkok on August 2—another seven-hour flight, with stops in Singapore and Kuala Lumpur. The next morning, my father visited the Supreme Court of Thailand and spoke at the Thammasat University that evening. He spoke again at another university the next morning, but returned to the hotel feeling nauseated. Mother insisted that he rest and canceled his afternoon schedule. They planned to attend a dinner in the evening, but at the last minute my father was forced to cancel. They called for a doctor, believing he had picked up some kind of intestinal bug. Mother went on to the dinner without him, but while she was there, my father was taken to a U.S. Army hospital for tests and treatment for "a stomach upset and general exhaustion." By August 5, my father was still hospitalized and feeling worse, not better. His intestinal distress was so severe that he was fed intravenously to avoid dehydration. He called August 6, 1967, the longest day of his life, and Mother felt the same. "Our great adventure has turned into a nightmare!" she wrote. She was feeling ill at that point and said the mere thought of food made her nauseous.

Ramsey was attending the American Bar Association convention in Hawaii, where the American Judicature Society, a national organization dedicated to improving our judicial system, had elected Tom Clark chairman of its board of directors. The society also awarded him its Justice Award for his contributions to improving judicial administration. News of Tom Clark's illness reached the convention on August 8, and Ramsey immediately called him. Mother wrote: "Ramsey's call cheered 'old Pop' up more than anything." Her diary ends abruptly on August 9. I knew nothing of what was going on until I awakened the morning of August 9 to a radio news broadcast reporting that Justice Tom Clark was ill and was being flown home from Thailand on a U.S. military plane. The diagnosis was severe infectious hepatitis. He was taken to Bethesda Naval Hospital, where he remained for more than a week, and was then sent home to recuperate.

By October, he was able to resume a fairly normal schedule, and on November 8, my parents' forty-third wedding anniversary, he and Mother gave a prenuptial party for Lynda Bird Johnson and Chuck Robb. Later that month he visited me and my family in Dallas after the birth of our fifth daughter. Seemingly as energetic as ever, he expressed little concern about his illness. Our family has always blamed the hepatitis on raw oysters that my father ate in Australia. Before leaving the United States, he and Mother had taken all the required shots, including gamma globulin, which is specifically for hepatitis. It failed to give protection, however, for he suffered a severe case that damaged his liver and took a heavy toll on his health. Although at first he appeared to make a complete recovery and continued to be as busy and productive as ever, his health was never the same, and the last ten years of his life were plagued by frequent illnesses.

Despite the abrupt and unfortunate ending to the "great adventure," my father achieved the goals of the mission in the countries he was able to visit. In November 1967, a State Department memorandum assessing Justice Clark's performance as an "American Specialist" was sent to Harry McPherson, special counsel to the president. The memo began:

> The President may be interested to know that reports from Foreign Service posts which Justice Tom C. Clark visited as an American Specialist last summer indicate that his appearances were enormously successful.

The memo then listed comments received from officials in the different countries he had visited. The one from Malaysia is especially illuminating:

> The visit of Justice Clark was an unqualified success. He impressed the audiences to whom he spoke and the distinguished individuals whom he met by the breadth of his legal knowledge, the extent of his experience in government, and, above all, by his humanity. His oratorical range includes the popular, the folksy and the technical, and he is equally effective in all three. In word, manner and being he exemplified the finer elements that have gone into the making of America, and no Malaysian with whom he came in contact can fail to have appreciated something of his quality. Further, the post has never programmed a less demanding, more considerate couple than the Clarks.[4]

A copy of the memo was sent to Ramsey, who forwarded it to my father with a brief note:

Dad—
Sounds like you missed your calling. You should have been a diplomat!

Ramsey

Tom Clark's diplomatic skills were not wasted, however. "The traveling salesman of justice" had simply gone international! He would continue to use these skills as he pursued his goal of improving the administration of justice in our country, and did so in spite of the deteriorating health that was the price of the "great adventure."

## CHAPTER 22

# The Federal Judicial Center

Perhaps the most unretired, retired justice the Supreme Court ever
had.

Judge William V. Redmann, 1986

TOM CLARK NEVER LET AN ILLNESS totally shut him down, and,
despite his bout with hepatitis, as well as Mother's pleas to cut back
his activities, he did not withdraw from any prior commitments and
even accepted an additional one as director of the newly formed Federal
Judicial Center. His directorship was the culmination of many years of
remarkable dedication to improving the U.S. system for the administration of justice.

Tom Clark's commitment to improving the management of the country's courts began during his years at the Department of Justice and was
well established by the time he retired from the Supreme Court. While an
assistant attorney general of the Criminal Division, he became increasingly aware of serious problems with the country's judicial system—over-
loaded courts, a breakdown in procedures for parole and probation, and
legal technicalities that were obstacles to efficiency.[1] As attorney general
he could only play a limited role in addressing these problems, but he supported two important pieces of legislation related to them. The Administrative Procedure Act (1946), still in force, gave federal agencies the
flexibility to 'develop their own rules for implementing new legislation.
The Federal Rules of Criminal Procedure (effective 1946) simplified standards in criminal law and increased consistency within the federal court
system. The new Federal Rules also provided indigents with court-
appointed lawyers at the government's expense, but, unfortunately, Congress failed to budget any compensation for these lawyers. Attorney
General Clark advocated a public-defender system that would address this

issue, but it was almost twenty years later—1964—before court-appointed lawyers received compensation for their work.

As attorney general he also had the important responsibility of recommending to the president names of qualified people to serve as judges. His criteria for the recommendations showed the importance he placed on courtroom experience:

> While I am your Attorney General, it shall be my purpose to recommend to the President for the trial bench those who have had trial experience, those who have had the hard knocks in the courtroom, those who have learned . . . to wrestle with juries, those who have had the practical experience. . . . And when we come to the conclusion that a certain person has those attributes, those qualifications that in our opinion will permit him . . . to allow that simple, everyday, ordinary justice that the litigants in that court deserve, that is the person whom we will recommend to the President of the United States to be made a trial judge.[2]

He had been a member of both the Federal Bar Association and American Bar Association (ABA) before becoming attorney general. From 1944 to 1945, while assistant attorney general of the Criminal Division, he served as president of the Federal Bar Association, and under his leadership, new chapters were organized throughout the country, membership doubled, and, for the first time, African Americans were allowed to join.[3] But it was through his membership in the ABA that he became actively involved in improving the administration of justice. In 1957, the president of the ABA asked him to become chairman of the association's Section of Judicial Administration. He accepted, provided that he could start as vice chairman in order to learn more about the section and its needs. Tom Clark would revitalize the section and expand its activities far beyond any previous level.

My father's views on judicial administration were greatly influenced by the highly respected jurist and educator Roscoe Pound, who in 1906 decried the inefficiencies of the system. Pound's criticism resulted in the ABA's establishment of the unit Tom Clark would later chair—the Section of Judicial Administration. The section's activities were limited to internal ABA programs until 1937, when Arthur T. Vanderbilt became president of the ABA, and Judge John J. Parker chairman of the section. Vanderbilt and Parker worked together to improve standards of judicial administration, and the section was active and productive through most of the 1940s.

Unfortunately, by 1957, when Tom Clark became chairman, the section was at best "semi-dormant," but as vice chairman, he had studied the problem and developed a plan of action.[4] As vice chairman, he contacted the nineteen committees that made up the section and requested a written report from each. Six of the committees never responded. At the section's first meeting, my father praised the accomplishments of the active committees, but then made this critical assessment: "But on the whole the committees have been ineffective. The reason for this seems to be that the committees have not been furnished any yardstick covering their respective functions. For example, three of the chairmen frankly stated that they have never been advised as to what activity their respective committee should promote. It is imperative of course that this be corrected. Furthermore there has never been a meeting of all of the chairmen to confer on our overall programs and to outline their own."[5]

Tom Clark then presented the group with a list of recommendations. He proposed that the section reduce the number of committees from nineteen to eleven, and asked for the authority to define their purposes and activities. He also listed six programs that he felt should be reactivated—or initiated—immediately, and was able to persuade other respected jurists, including three Supreme Court justices, to take leadership positions. Justice Stanley Reed became chairman of the Rules Committee; Harold Burton, chairman of the Post-Conviction Remedies Committee; and William Brennan, chairman of the Committee on Court Congestion. Determined to revitalize the section, my father challenged the Membership Committee to increase the number of members from 500 to 2,500. Ten years later, in 1967, there were 6,000 members.[6]

My father realized the section needed direction and a clear focus, so he appointed another committee to write its charter. The committee produced a short, simple document with four main points that provided a framework for achieving effective justice. The document stated:

Justice is effective when—
    Fairly administered without delay
    With all litigants, indigent and otherwise, and especially those charged with crime,
    represented by competent counsel
By Competent Judges
    Selected through non-political methods based on merit,
    In sufficient numbers to carry the load,
    Adequately compensated, with fair retirement benefits
    With security of tenure, subject to expeditious method of removal for cause,

Operating in a Modern Court System
  Simple in structure, without overlapping jurisdictions or multiple
    appeals
  Businesslike in management with non-judicial duties performed by a
    competent administrative staff
  With practical methods for easing the judicial workload,
  With an annual conference of the judges for the purpose of appraising
    and approving judicial techniques and administration,
Under Simple and Efficient Rules of Procedure.
  Designed to encourage advance trial preparation
  Eliminate the element of surprise,
  Reduce the expense of litigation
  And expedite the administration of justice.[7]

This document was a clear statement of goals for the section, and Tom Clark's efforts to achieve them brought it from a nearly comatose state to one of the ABA's most vital units. Judge David Page, who followed him as chairman of the section, attributed Tom Clark's success "to the enormous amount of time and attention that he gave the problems, the depth of his interest in them, and his wide travels in the cause, always being practically helpful locally as well as nationally."[8] Perhaps the single most important accomplishment of the section was the establishment of the National Conference of State Trial Judges. The purpose of the conference was to give judges an arena in which they could discuss problems and exchange ideas. The national conference spawned numerous judicial seminars and court conferences and laid the groundwork for what became the National College of State Trial Judges. John Frank praised Tom Clark's accomplishments during his year as chairman of the section: "By the end of his year as chairman, the foundation was laid for the American Bar Association's modern activities to improve judicial administration."[9] My father remained involved with the section for another year as an ex-officio member and kept a liaison with it for several years, mainly through his secretary Alice O'Donnell, who later became secretary of the section.

But his quest for efficient justice was far from over. As he left his chairmanship of the section behind, he accepted the chairmanship of another committee that had sprung from it: the Joint Committee for the Effective Administration of Justice. This committee's purpose was to coordinate new educational offerings with other judicial and legal groups, such as the American Judicature Society and the Institute of Judicial Administration. The ABA gave the joint committee a modest budget that enabled it to get started, but a more ambitious undertaking was envisioned by Tom Clark. After approaching several foundations with no success, my father and others obtained a grant of $348,000 from the W. K. Kellogg Foundation to form a permanent college for judges. In 1964, the National College of State Trial Judges opened its doors at the University of Colorado. Tom Clark served as chairman of the college's board of directors, and continued to do so until 1971. Professor Maurice Rosenberg, who served on the college's faculty in 1964 and 1965, believed that the college was "an idea whose time had come," but gave Tom Clark credit for getting it started: "The answer to how it started is easy: Justice Tom C. Clark. More than to anything else, the success of the college is due to his vision, energy and leadership in appreciating the possibilities, planning it, raising funds for it, and mobilizing the talents of such devoted men as Ernest C. Friesen, now of Washington, and Judge Frank Murray of Boston."[10]

The original purpose of the college was to provide training for newly appointed or elected state trial judges. Over the years, it expanded its role, offering continuing-education courses for experienced judges, both federal and state. The rigorous four-week classes were held in the summer. The judges seemed to enjoy as well as benefit from the experience, despite the fact that they worked ten hours a day, five days a week. It was no picnic! The college, now known as the National Judicial College and located in Reno, Nevada, thrives today. In 2005, it offered 95 classes and had an enrollment of approximately 2,700 judges from fifty states and 150 countries.

John Frank described Tom Clark's leadership style as "the hand of iron in the velvet glove. . . . If there were alternate points of view and he had to offend someone by taking sides, he took sides. He was an ambassador of good will only when it did not interfere with being an ambassador of improved judicial administration."[11]

A speech Clark delivered in 1964 at a conference held in his beloved state of Texas clearly illustrates his willingness to speak candidly, even at the risk of offending others. After opening remarks that expressed the affection and pride he felt for his native state, he launched into a harsh critique, describing Texas's courts as "possibly the worst court system of any state in the Union" and declaring that "this horse and buggy court system" had to be modernized.[12] Afterward, my father expressed concern that he had offended some: "I hope I didn't step on any toes, but someone had to say those things."[13] Toes had been stepped on, however. A Fort Worth newspaper published an article headlined "Justice Clark Flails Texas Courts." Some Texans labeled him an "outsider" who had no business criticizing the state's system, and one Houston critic vented his anger at the Supreme Court in general, writing that if Clark was going to criticize Texas's courts, "he should first resign from that foreign-ideology dominated group in Washington."[14] The reaction was not all negative. Leon Jaworski, the prominent Houston lawyer who later became well known as the special prosecutor for the Watergate investigation, was actively involved in the conference, and expressed his appreciation to my father: "The conference was a striking success, and it should give much impetus to a reform movement in Texas. We are most grateful to you for your guidance and invaluable aid."[15]

My father had to conduct most of his off-the-Court activities during the three months the Court was in recess, for the Court's workload was heavy: "When I came here the Court had filings of about 800 a year and the year I left it was around 3400. . . . We worked seven days a week though. The Court has no time limitations. We'd sometimes sit down here until 7 or 8 or 9 o'clock at night. I'd come down practically every Saturday and most Sundays."[16]

Still, my father was able to accomplish what he did for the administration of justice without in any way shortchanging his responsibilities as a Supreme Court justice. He carried at least his fair share of the Court's workload, writing the highest or second-highest number of opinions in eight of his eighteen years on the Court.[17] He could not have accomplished all that he did without an outstanding staff to provide essential support, especially Alice O'Donnell, who was with him throughout his years on the Court and whose quiet, unassuming demeanor belied an exceptional work ethic and remarkable efficiency. My father set the priorities for his office, making it clear to his staff that Supreme Court opinions were number one. He felt strongly that justices had to write the opinions themselves, and he strictly adhered to this principle: "There is one uniform rule: Judging is not delegated. Each Justice studies each case in sufficient detail to resolve the question without leaving any doubt in his mind."[18]

With his impressive reputation as a reformer in the field of the administration of justice, it was natural that in 1968 he would be the prime candidate to serve as the first director of the newly established Federal Judicial Center. President Lyndon Johnson first proposed the center to Congress in 1967, in response to recommendations made the previous year by the Judicial Conference of the United States. According to the recommendations, an organization was needed within the country's judicial system to implement and coordinate programs that would offer in-service education for federal judges and conduct much-needed research. The proposal for the center was included in major legislation dealing with crime, the most pressing issue at that time, so passage was assured and fast.

Chief Justice Earl Warren had led the effort to establish the Federal Judicial Center, and he wanted Tom Clark to serve as its first director: "No person of our nation is better qualified to form such a Center. It is almost as though his entire career had been preparing him for the mission of the Center. . . . The Center under Mr. Justice Clark is guaranteed the finest possible leadership. When in September of 1969 this Center's first director reaches seventy and must retire we can be assured that it will be established on a firm foundation."[19]

There was some doubt initially that my father would accept the position. His health was still a concern, and he wasn't sure that he should take on another major responsibility. Warren continued to urge him to accept, and by the time a small committee of Judicial Conference members approached him with an offer, his health did not seem an obstacle. Having been an advocate of the center, he welcomed the opportunity to serve. He felt strongly that modernization—he preferred that term to "reform"—of the court system was essential:

> In a century which has been characterized by growth and modernization in science, technology and economics, the legal fraternity is still living in the past. We have allowed the maintenance of progress to pass us by. . . . Our failure to act becomes alarming when a competent district judge must admit in his testimony before a Senate committee that unless something new and effective is done promptly in the area of judicial research, coordination and management, the rule of law in this nation cannot endure. When justice is denied to any of our citizens because of faulty administration our failure to act becomes inexcusable.[20]

Tom Clark got off to his usual running start before officially becoming director by contacting every federal judge and requesting ideas on ways to improve the courts. Initially, he worked out of his office at the Supreme Court—retired justices were provided with smaller offices, a secretary, one law clerk, and a messenger. As director of the Federal Judicial Center, he did not receive any compensation other than his pension as a retired associate justice. As the suggestions poured in, my father personally examined each one and placed it into one of the categories that he had established. Alice O'Donnell, who came to the Federal Judicial Center with my father and remained there after he left, eventually becoming coordinator of the Interjudicial Affairs Office, described the early days of his directorship: "The papers started coming in—boxes of them. In the meantime I had hired two secretaries, and we officed them in the justice's chambers where space was already dear. So, you can see we started out with a few handicaps, but nothing we couldn't work with. And, nothing has ever deterred Justice Clark from continuing and finishing something he has started—nothing, ever!"[21]

Finding a home for the center was my father's first task, and he achieved a coup when he succeeded in getting the Dolley Madison House on Lafayette Square. Dolley Madison moved into the house after the death of her husband, former president James Madison, and lived there for the remainder of her life. The house was beautiful and in an excellent location for the center. It had been destined for demolition until the Kennedy administration stepped in and designated it a historic site. One day as my father and Chief Justice Warren were walking to the Court together, they noticed that the Dolley Madison House was both unoccupied and being renovated. My father immediately called the administrator of the General Services Administration, the agency responsible for the use of federal buildings, and convinced him that the Federal Judicial Center was the perfect occupant for the house. The Dolley Madison House remained the home of the Federal Judicial Center for more than twenty-five years, until space needs forced a move to the Thurgood Marshall Federal Judiciary Building.

Under Tom Clark's leadership, the center's activities were aimed at "producing the highest quality of justice in the shortest possible time at the lowest possible cost."[22] His strategy was to complete some "quickies" that would immediately establish the center's credibility and then to identify and start needed long-term projects. As the judges' suggestions poured in, it was clear that the number one complaint was the backlog of cases. Despite the creation of new judgeships by Congress, the number of backlogged cases had continued to increase. Tom Clark, convinced that the problem was one of poor management, used a 1959 report to support his view. According to the report, the backlog could be attributed almost solely to poor administration: "Some courts are doing a superlative job while others are hopelessly enmeshed in outmoded, inadequate, and, at times, amateurish and most unbusinesslike procedures."[23]

A possible reason for the backlog was the use of master calendars versus individual calendars. A master calendar was developed under a central system that assigned a judge to a certain stage of a case, and then moved it on to another judge when that stage was completed. Several judges might handle a single case during this process. With an individual calendar, the judge originally assigned to a case remained with it and was responsible for its scheduling. The Mitre Corporation, a high-tech firm in northern Virginia, offered to study, at no charge to the center, the relationship between the type of calendar used and the number of backlogged cases. Its report concluded that master calendars were part of the problem, but stated that more research was needed. Consequently, the center initiated a project to study the issue in greater depth. Two experienced judges were each assigned 124 cases and a second judge, who was designated as an assistant. One team of judges used a master calendar, the other an individual calendar. At the end of two months, the judges using the individual calendar had disposed of 73 percent of their cases; the judges using the master calendar, only 11.7 percent.[24] This study clearly showed the inadequacies of the master-calendar system and resulted in a massive switch to individual calendars by courts throughout the country.

The calendar study succeeded as a "quickie." Another project that fit that category was the *Judges Bench Book*, a ready reference that my father described as a "how-to-do-it detail account—with accompanying forms —of every stage of the trial process."[25] It was used by judges as they presided over trials, and was in loose-leaf format so that it could be updated easily. The book became a popular and useful source of information for judges, besides serving as another project that helped establish the center's credibility.

The statute creating the Federal Judicial Center charged it to "study and determine ways in which automatic data processing systems may be applied to the administration of the Courts of the United States."[26] The newly developing technologies were a challenging area for the center: computers were still in their early stages, and at that point no one knew how to apply them appropriately to the management of court systems. Tom Clark believed in their potential and was eager to develop a system for using them. Through his leadership, the center contacted several computer firms and began to examine ways that computers could be used to improve the efficiency of the federal courts. One use was implemented quickly, in jury selection. Computers scanned voter-registration information, developed lists of potential jurors from the information gained, and then randomly selected jurors from those lists. There were two major benefits to the new system. First, it greatly expanded the jury pool and gave a better mix of jurors; second, the computerized system saved thousands of dollars because of its remarkable speed and efficiency.

Tom Clark proved to be an innovative administrator. It was clear to him that the center had to be willing to experiment, and he looked outside the federal judicial system to seek expertise from nonlawyers. At the dedication of the center, one of the main speakers supported my father's view by stressing the importance of outside help and a willingness to experiment: "If there is a single thing lawyers and judges need to learn from non-lawyers, it is the value and importance of experimental research in solving administrative problems. This is the unique contribution which can be made to the Center and to the administration of justice."[27]

One innovative project involved working with prison administrators and law school faculty to establish legal-assistance clinics in prisons. These clinics were established in prisons located close to law schools, such as the Emory University School of Law, in Atlanta. Faculty members from the law schools were asked to select advanced law students to work with the lawyers who provided legal services to prisoners. The selected students visited the prisoners and offered advice or consultation. The law school professors supervised the visits, and the Federal Judicial Center coordinated the activities of the law schools with the Bureau of Prisons to ensure effective service. The clinics were helpful to wardens, who cited improved discipline and fewer applications for appeal as benefits of the program. They also improved prisoners' morale.

Another major responsibility of the Federal Judicial Center was to develop continuing-education and training courses for judges and their staffs. My father had extensive experience in this area through his successful efforts to establish the National College of State Trial Judges. He was an inveterate lifelong learner himself, and the plan he helped develop was both ambitious and practical:

> The older judges will conduct three-day seminars on substantive topics such as antitrust, litigation, patents and admiralty. Court of Appeals judges will attend sessions on opinion writing and other subjects relevant to the appellate process. The clerks of the District courts are to receive training in management techniques, data processing, and the use of modern business machines in record keeping, etc. The probation system needs help and the Center is organizing a complete training course which it hopes to inaugurate this year for over 600 probation officers. Likewise, the referees in bankruptcy are meeting in September at which time their program will be finalized.[28]

Tom Clark never avoided difficult projects, and one that illustrates his tenacity and powers of persuasion was a study on judges' use of their time. The time study was not popular with judges—they complained that they didn't have time for such an undertaking. But my father wouldn't take no for an answer. He contacted each judge by telephone, wrote long notes to many, and persisted until more than two-thirds of them had agreed to participate. Alice O' Donnell remarked, "No other man in the federal system could have gotten the judges to do this," and described the time study as "enormously helpful in projecting the needs of the court[s] well into the future."[29]

The director of the Federal Judicial Center is required to resign at the age of seventy, so in September 1969, my father announced his resignation. When asked what he considered his most significant achievement during the two years he served as director, he replied: "I would say that our greatest contribution was in building up the image of the Center in the eyes of the public, the Congress and the judges. This was aided greatly in obtaining the Dolley Madison House as its home; and second, in enlisting the support of the judges for the Center as an education tool for judges, by judges and of judges. As a result the Center is considered today as the top judicial education operation in the world."[30]

Once more the family, especially Mother, hoped that with his tenure as director of the Federal Judicial Center ended, my father would cut back on his activities. We knew, however, that cutting back was simply not in Tom Clark's nature. He continued to bounce back from the increasingly frequent illnesses that he was experiencing, and remained, as another judge testified years later, "perhaps the most unretired, retired justice the Supreme Court ever had."[31] Consequently, we were not surprised, knowing his love of a challenge, that at the age of seventy—just two months short of his seventy-first birthday—he would launch a new career, one that was still dedicated to the goal he strived for as director of the Federal Judicial center: "History teaches that a civilization is judged by its system of justice. We shall strive to make ours the most effective in man's memory."[32]

## CHAPTER 23

# Riding the Circuits, Championing Reforms

Someone's got to ride herd on the lawyers.

Tom C. Clark, 1972

A NEWSPAPER ARTICLE WRITTEN IN 1973 captures in colorful terms Tom Clark's remarkable work schedule: "When he is not sitting on assignment as a Federal Court of Appeals justice or District Court judge in one part of the country or another, he is making speeches, participating in study groups and committees, or writing articles. His calendar is as cluttered as a Manhattan subway car; he is as much in demand as the most fetching co-ed on campus. The white-haired, bow-tied gentleman from Texas is level-headed, unpretentious and downright witty. He's sort of a judicial Will Rogers."[1]

The range of my father's activities was truly staggering. Among his papers I found a list of sixteen committees he served on in 1970, and he was chairman of at least two of them. The committees were for groups that included, among others, the Boy Scouts of America, the National Park Foundation, the Federal Bar Association (Ethics Committee), the American Bar Association (Special Committee on Evaluation of Disciplinary Enforcement), and the Presidential Commission for Human Rights (Committee of Lawyers). In addition, in 1970 he became the first president of the American Academy of Judicial Education, a position he held for several years. Along with these numerous activities, in 1970, less than a year after he resigned as director of the Federal Judicial Center, he launched a new career as a trial judge. He would continue to serve as a trial judge for the remainder of his life—the only justice to sit on federal courts in all of the country's eleven circuits.

My father's experience as a trial judge began in San Francisco after his friend Chief Judge George B. Harris of the U.S. District Court for the Northern District of California solicited his help with a crowded court docket. His first case involved a tax refund, and he opened the trial in his typically informal, self-effacing manner: "It's the first time I've had the privilege and pleasure of sitting as a trial judge. I'll appreciate it if the jury and counsel will understand I may be a little slow in these things until I catch on."[2] He immediately got down to the business at hand, announced the schedule for the session, and cut the court's traditional two-hour lunch break to ninety minutes. I'm sure he considered even a ninety minute break too long, but understanding that a drastic change in what had been the norm would not be advisable, he softened the announcement with a bit of humor: "I only had twenty minutes on the Supreme Court," he explained, "and, as you can see, I got a little heavy."[3]

Anyone who thought Tom Clark would regard sitting as a trial judge a step down from the Supreme Court did not know him. He took on his new duties as he did everything—with total commitment. He understood and appreciated the importance of lower courts and expressed that view publicly: "In the last analysis the nation's law is made in the trial court. Only a trickle of cases reaches the Supreme Court and are decided there. Ninety-five percent of all trial court decisions are never appealed."[4] One journalist covering a trial that was held on a snowy day in Chicago described him as working the lawyers and jurors hard and "delving into the facts of the car/train crash as if it were the thorniest constitutional entanglement to come before the Supreme Court."[5]

Although he truly enjoyed sitting as a trial judge, my father was frequently disappointed with the lawyers who appeared before him. He had no patience with lawyers who came to trial insufficiently prepared, and voiced strong criticism of them: "During the past eighteen months I have had the privilege of sitting from time to time in the United States District Court for the Northern District of California at San Francisco. I found that few of the cases I tried were properly prepared. Indeed, in most of them I was obliged to recess for discovery to be conducted and documents to be organized."[6]

While he felt that a high percentage of trial lawyers were lax in preparing cases, he cited one important exception: female lawyers, who were still a small minority in the legal profession: "Someone has to ride herd on the lawyers. Most cases come to trial unprepared. . . . The men come in here carrying a little file they have just looked at out in the hall. . . . Women are really devoted. They know the facts. . . . They know the case from A to Z

. . . They're not nearly so set in their ways . . . If they tell you they'll furnish you something, they furnish it. They don't forget."[7]

His experiences in the courtroom brought him new perspectives on
the legal profession and produced two major concerns: law school curricula and professional ethics. He bemoaned the small number of law students attracted to criminal law, and challenged lawyers to work toward
improving the country's system of justice by spending time in the courtroom as prosecutors or public defenders. "Money isn't everything," he
declared, as he described court congestion, urging lawyers to "take some
leave and help move cases out of the courts."[8] He challenged the country's law schools to address the problem of attracting students to serve as
trial lawyers and to develop a more practical curriculum:

We need to bring the law schools closer to the courts. We can't teach the
lawyers who are out in practice—they think they're the greatest. You could
never tell them to go back to school.[9]

The training of competent advocates is essential to the continuing health
of the adversary system and the law school is the logical place to begin
such training. For nearly a century, legal education has focused almost
exclusively upon the development of intellectual and analytical skills while
neglecting instruction in practical "lawyering." This has prompted one law
professor to note that "today's law school graduate is far better prepared to
assume the bench of the highest appellate court than to draft a will, nego-
tiate a contract, try a case, form a corporation, write a statute, settle a dispute or do any of the other myriad tasks required of attorneys." Although
perhaps an overstatement, this observation, nevertheless, recognizes that
our law schools must reevaluate some aspects of their curricula.[10]

Equally important to preparing lawyers for the courtroom, and equally
neglected, was the need to establish effective disciplinary procedures for
wayward lawyers and to ensure that law schools imbued students with a
strong sense of professional ethics. My father's concern with the ethics of
the legal profession can be traced back to 1967, when he accepted the
chairmanship of the ABA Special Committee on Evaluation of Disciplinary Enforcement. ABA president Orison S. Marden described how he
solicited my father for chairmanship of the special committee:

Promptly on learning of the retirement plans of Mr. Justice Tom C. Clark,
I waited upon his doorstep, hat in hand, in the hope of persuading him to

assume the directorship of this important work. It was grossly unfair to ask this of Justice Clark as he had given so much of his time and energy over the past decade to the work of the organized bar but I overcame the pangs of conscience and made the request. Needless to say, his acceptance filled me with joy and gratitude and I know that lawyers all over the country share these sentiments.[11]

The nine-member committee—all lawyers—became known as the Clark Committee. It was given the following charge: "To assemble and study information relevant to all aspects of professional discipline and to make such recommendations as the Committee may deem necessary and appropriate to achieve the highest possible standards of professional conduct and responsibility."[12]

The committee's first task was to develop a questionnaire that would help determine how derelict lawyers were being disciplined, since little attention had been given to that issue and reliable data was virtually nonexistent. My father participated fully in examining the data that was gathered, even though he was recovering from hepatitis at the time and had been ordered by his doctor to rest. His idea of rest was to read the questionnaires: "I have been reading the papers. . . . I don't have much to do since the doctors say I have to go to bed every afternoon for three hours."[13]

The information gathered from the questionnaires provided the basis for the Clark Report, published in 1970 and officially entitled "Problems and Recommendations in Disciplinary Enforcement." The report was a scathing critique of the legal profession's disciplinary practices. Its use of the word "scandalous" immediately got the attention of the media and, consequently, of lawyers:

> After three years of studying lawyer discipline throughout the country, this Committee must report the existence of a *scandalous situation* that requires the immediate attention of the profession. With few exceptions, the prevailing attitude of lawyers ranges from apathy to outright hostility. Disciplinary action is practically nonexistent in many jurisdictions, practices and procedures are antiquated, many disciplinary agencies have little power to take effective steps against malefactors.[14]

Among the problems cited in the 200-page document were the following: "a majority of states did not take disciplinary action against attorneys convicted of federal income tax violations"; "even after disbarment lawyers . . . [were] reinstated as a matter of course"; "lawyers failed to report violations of the ethics code or criminal law to disciplinary authorities"; "lawyers would not cooperate in disciplinary proceedings against other lawyers but instead would use their influence 'to stymie the proceedings'"; "state disciplinary agencies were undermanned and underfunded, many having no staff whatever for the investigation or prosecution of complaints."[15] The Clark Report contained specific recommendations for each problem that it cited. It advocated that a centralized disciplinary agency be formed within each state to report directly to that state's supreme court.

While some were embarrassed and some angered by the publicity that the report generated, it was a call to action that was heeded. In August 1970, the ABA unanimously approved the Clark Report's recommendations, and efforts to implement them began. My father traveled all over the country to speak in favor of the recommendations, and wrote articles supporting their implementation. His efforts, along with those of others, were largely successful, for several years later the ABA conducted another study on professional ethics, which concluded: "Revolutionary changes had occurred because most states had implemented many of the changes prescribed by the Clark Report. . . . [The] Clark Report . . . reshaped lawyer discipline in the United States."[16]

Members of the Clark Committee worked closely with another ABA special committee on a subject related to disciplinary procedures: professional ethics. Through that association, my father became concerned about the image of the legal profession and its ethical commitment: "He [an unscrupulous lawyer] worships false Gods—winning his cases regardless and making big fees."[17] The Watergate scandal greatly heightened that concern, for virtually all of the participants in that break-in were lawyers. My father felt that public respect for lawyers was at an all-time low and that action to regain that respect was essential. He warned of serious consequences if the legal profession failed to improve its reputation: "The oratory should cease. We have been meeting and talking about it [professional responsibility] for fifty years, but the truth is that we have done little to correct the ethical emptiness in our law schools. Congress is now exploring the necessity for regulating the profession. Several state legislatures have done this in the past. . . . We must act quickly and definitively if we wish to retain the right of self-discipline."[18]

Once again, he felt that law schools had to shoulder the responsibility and make professional ethics an integral part of the curriculum. He acknowledged that the task was not easy:

Yet however difficult it may be for academic institutions to come to grips with the most basic sorts of human values such as honesty and a sense of fairness, it is precisely these basic principles which were so lacking in Watergate and which are so sorely needed in the world. Our law schools, it seems to me, must shoulder the burden of teaching "honesty" because there is simply no one else to do the job. The sad fact of the matter is that integrity is the sort of virtue that once more or less reliably developed through the joint socializing influences of the church, the family, schools and peer groups. For a number of reasons, however, the first two contributors to this process have drastically diminished in importance in this country, and no other force has arisen to take their place. The burden, therefore, has come to rest on our law schools, and it is one which they must shoulder alone and shoulder well, for the profession's other tools cannot perform the task.[19]

He made the following recommendation: "Let us examine the present courses on professional responsibility offered by the law schools, debate the merits of what is being offered and buckle down long enough to produce a basic program of instruction, revise the offerings to meet any inadequacy that arises and make professional responsibility a required course on the subject in every law school."[20]

Describing the third year of law school as "a squeezed orange," he urged a curriculum change that would give third-year students a combination of professional responsibility and clinical work under the supervision of practicing lawyers. He compared law schools to medical schools, which placed students as interns in hospitals: "They learn more in an emergency room in one night than in a classroom in a whole year."[21] My father also advocated continuing education that focused on professional ethics for practicing lawyers, and hoped the courses would instigate an "ethical renaissance . . . across the land."[22]

The issues that my father and his colleagues pursued are continuing ones, but their efforts brought important changes and significant improvements. Today, virtually all law schools offer courses on professional responsibility and require students to take at least one course on that subject. Furthermore, most states now require law school graduates to pass the Multistate Professional Responsibility Examination before they are allowed to practice law. The "deplorable state of affairs" that Tom Clark described in 1975 no longer exists.

Tom Clark's campaign for reform was not limited to professional responsibility or law school curriculum. He called for methods of selecting judges that would remove politics from the process. Judges should not be elected, he argued, for elections subject them to political influences, costly campaigns, and distractions from their judicial responsibilities. He advocated a plan that had been adopted in a few states, most notably Missouri:

> Judges should, of course, be selected on a merit plan that would remove them from politics. The merit plan presently used in an increasing number of states employs a commission composed of laymen, lawyers and judges selected on a nonpartisan basis. . . . Once appointed and qualified the judge should never be required to thereafter run for his office on a political basis. Instead, at stated intervals, his name should be on a retention ballot allowing the voters to pass on the sole question of whether he should be retained on the bench.[23]

Furthermore, he argued, judges' salaries, which were far below those of practicing lawyers, should be increased, along with the salaries of their staffs.

As a sitting justice, Tom Clark had been known as a staunch defender of law enforcement, but his experiences in trial courts persuaded him that the country's penal system was in serious trouble: "Penal institutions are outdated," he asserted. "Instead of putting money to strengthen the bars and walls we must spend money to rehabilitate those convicted of crimes."[24] He was distressed by the number of young people who were filling our prisons after being sentenced for victimless crimes such as drug possession, drunkenness, and gambling. He urged that laws regulating these types of crimes should be examined. In an article he wrote in 1972, he cited his reasons for supporting the repeal of laws criminalizing marijuana: "The cocktail drinkers and tobacco smokers have the protection of regulation. The former know the content of what they drink, its purity and its proof. The tobacco smoker knows of the nicotine content, but marijuana smokers have no such protection. Quite often the 'grass' they buy is not as represented. There should be license laws controlling the sale of marijuana and indicating the type of the drug sold. If this were done, we would be able to give our undivided attention to the hard drugs, and the dangerous ones."[25]

In addition, he encouraged judges to choose probation over prison sentences whenever possible and to send first offenders to halfway houses, where they could receive vocational training, rather than to prisons—a strategy he hoped would reduce recidivism. At the same time, Tom Clark deplored what he perceived as a growing disrespect for the law, as well as the irresponsibility of citizens who failed to assist victims of street crime: "On this account the people are not doing their job. The common man must become uncommonly interested in the workings of justice and compel himself to become involved. Only in this way can justice be fully served, to the benefit of all."[26]

My father was himself a victim of street crime on December 29, 1975. He and Mother had just returned from a trip, and, that same evening, he walked to a drugstore about three blocks from their apartment to purchase a few items. He rarely carried a large amount of cash, but because he had been traveling, had a little more than one hundred dollars with him. Apparently, two young men observed him as he pulled out his wallet to pay for the merchandise. He did not notice them and walked back to the apartment using the parking-lot entrance in the back of the building. As he approached the door, he was grabbed from behind and a hand reached into the pocket where he kept his wallet. The two men did not hurt him but accomplished the theft and immediately ran away. My father ran after them shouting "Police!" and "Help!" but was unable to catch them—fortunately, in my opinion. The men escaped and were never apprehended. My father never expressed bitterness nor exhibited any signs of paranoia in reaction to the incident. In fact, according to Mother, he reacted with amazing equanimity. When he entered the apartment afterwards, he called out, "Guess what, I've been robbed." He even retained his sense of humor as he told Mother what had happened, concluding that, in the future, he would have to be more "judicious."

The mugging incident occurred a little more than a year before his death. Since his retirement from the Supreme Court and his bout with hepatitis, he had endured gall bladder surgery, walking pneumonia, and frequent, seemingly minor illnesses. But his heart had become the greatest cause of concern. He was experiencing fibrillations, and the medications the doctors prescribed had unpleasant side effects. His remarkable energy never seemed to wane for long, but at times I am sure he continued his work through sheer willpower. Chief Justice Warren Burger threatened to intervene by cutting down the number of times he was scheduled to preside as a federal judge. Mother pleaded with him to "slow down." He always agreed to do so as soon as he could clear his calendar of commitments, but that time never came. He would serve on committees, "ride the circuits," give speeches, sit on moot courts, and champion the reform of the profession he loved to the very end.

## CHAPTER 24

# Some Personal Observations

The most unforgettable character I ever met.

Mary Ramsey Clark

T OM CLARK WAS A RARE COMBINATION: a devoted family man, a high achiever, a lifelong workaholic, and a character! He never lost the "kid" within him and possessed a sense of humor that was sometimes subtle, sometimes silly, and often self-effacing. His friend Rabbi Gershenfeld dubbed him "the Happy Heart." Mother called him "the most unforgettable character I ever met," borrowing the term from the popular *Reader's Digest* column of the same name. To his children and grandchildren, who adored him, he was a lot of fun!

He compartmentalized his personal and professional lives, rarely talking about work at home. No matter how busy he was, he gave us his total attention when we were together, and loved to plan trips to the beach or the mountains, fishing or hunting excursions, and, in his later years, shopping sprees with "his girls." During the war years, when gasoline rationing prohibited automobile trips, the four of us would often play dominoes on Sunday afternoons and listen to one of our favorite radio programs, such as *The Shadow*. My father would entertain us by mimicking the Shadow's sinister laugh. He was frequently our Sunday-morning breakfast cook— silver-dollar-sized hotcakes were his specialty. If we took too long eating, he would get up from the table and start washing dishes while the rest of us finished. Claiming to be "the world's greatest dishwasher," he attacked burned spots on pans with the same gusto that he brought to everything; no spot remained by the time he was through.

It was in California that I, as a little girl, wondered whether my father might have magical powers. Not that I believed, when he said, "Let me put my magic on it," as he prepared to fix a broken toy or repair a household item, that he actually accomplished the task through magic. Nor was I especially impressed by the elaborate hocus-pocus that he developed to turn red lights to green as we sat in the car, waiting for the traffic signal to change. One incident, however, really amazed me. We had been out driving on a rainy California afternoon when we entered a long underground tunnel. "I'm going to put my magic on the rain," my father declared, "and when we come out of this tunnel, it will have stopped." "Impossible!" I thought to myself until, to my amazement, we emerged from the tunnel to a cloudy but dry sky. "How did you do it?" I demanded to know. "Why, I just put my magic on it," he replied innocently.

"The Happy Heart" was an appropriate description. We often knew when he was home from work at the end of the day because we could hear him whistling or humming as he walked down the hallway to our apartment. He greeted whoever was within with warmth and enthusiasm. "No one has such fine girls as I do," he would say, referring to Mother and me. He frequently asked Mother, "Have I told you today what a fine mother you are?" He never preached and was rarely critical, but on the few occasions when he did criticize, the impact was great. Rather than scold, he often used humor to make a point. He frequently improvised his own lyrics to familiar songs and one favorite was about me: "Miss Mil, Miss Mil, you're not a pill," he would sing out. One day, when I undoubtedly had been a pill, I heard him singing a different version: "Miss Mil, Miss Mil, you are a pill." Had my ears deceived me, I wondered? I gave him a penetrating look, but he avoided eye contact and continued humming with just a trace of a smile on his face.

Tom Clark was a flatterer—Mother and I were his "beautiful girls," and my daughters were the GGGs, Gorgeous Gronlund Girls. But Mother and I sometimes questioned his sincerity when he called us his "beauties" even as we sat at the breakfast table with our hair in curlers and no makeup on. He would vehemently deny any suggestion that he was having a little fun at our expense.

The summer after my freshman year in college was the summer of "beauties," and that term was even applied to visitors such as my cousin Bobby Clark and future husband Tom Gronlund, who were frequently with us. We were sitting at the dinner table one evening when my father began to wax enthusiastically about his "beauties." "I have all kinds of beauties," he proclaimed, "old beauties, middle-aged beauties, young beauties." My mother interrupted: "And who," she inquired, looking at least a decade younger than her almost fifty years, "is your old beauty?" I can still recall the startled expression on my father's face and the deafening silence that ensued. "She's got him this time," I thought. But no, he quickly recovered. "Why, I'm the old beauty," he declared. The room erupted with laughter.

He spoiled all of us. Although he would brag about how old his clothes were, especially his shoes, which he kept immaculately shiny, he loved to shop for Mother and for his grandchildren and me. He bought most of mother's evening gowns and kept her stocked with beautiful lingerie. He was especially generous during Christmas 1945, just a few months after he became attorney general. Mother had purchased little clothing during the war years, and he wanted her to have a new wardrobe for their new life. He penned the following poem for Mother, signing it from her "three kids—Ramsey, Mimi, and Tom."

> Hello Mom—are you on the line?
> Well listen while we three opine.
> We want our "Mom" to look as neat
> As any "mom" on any street.
> From her tootsies covered with crocodile fine
> Her calves wrapped in nylon twine
> Her waist circled with silken line.
> Her dresses, suits, and a coat too
> We want tailored like Foo Man Chu.
> And hats galore from duster bonnets
> To dum dum ones without feathers on it.
> But you know better even than we
> Some things we pick you cannot see.
> So why doesn't pretty Mom get hopping
> And go right up and do some shopping.
> You say it's dough you need, our light?
> Well bless your heart, you're surely right!
> So here's a thousand bucks to start on
> We hope it lasts thru to the nylons.
> But if not, you just holler
> You can't tell we may try harder.

(The "dum dum" refers to a funny little hat that was one of Mother's favorites. We liked to tease her about it, and Ramsey dubbed it her "dum dum.")

My parents' marriage was truly a lifelong love affair. Not that they did not have their differences: my father's tendency to be late during their early years together and his erratic driving in the later years were sources of friction. But their differences were always minor, and their devotion to each other was obvious to everyone who knew them.

On the occasion of their third wedding anniversary, Mother gave my father a card with the following note:

Just a little remembrance, sweetheart, to remind you how much the 8th of November means to me. May each of the succeeding years be as full of happiness as the past three and I could wish no more! If I loved you November 8, 1924, I can truthfully say I love you "thrice" more this Nov. 8, 1927, for you have never shown anything but love and consideration for me and each year has made you nearer and dearer to me.

All my love to "sweet Daddy" on this our third anniversary

They were still in love twenty-seven years later, when my father sent Mother the following message on their twenty-seventh wedding anniversary:

It's the twenty-seventh year today! Not long it seems since I walked out of City Temple with you on my arm.

Yes, we have been around since then, but you are more beautiful than ever, if that is possible, more charming, more lovely. And this even though you have had some pretty hard jolts from life's realities. But they say experience teaches slowly but surely—and you have always brought back the sunshine.

And now on the threshold of grandparenthood through your love and constant devotion we are pretty close to "two souls with but a single thought, two hearts that beat as one." May we always be. All my love, Pop

He was a virtual Santa Claus to his grandchildren, but he spent time as well as money on them. It was not unusual to see him pushing a baby stroller on the sidewalks of Connecticut Avenue or taking grandchildren to a nearby park. He may have annoyed some of the other grandfathers in their apartment building, for Mother was told that some wives complained, "If Justice Clark can babysit his grandchildren, why can't you?"

He also stayed in close contact with his Texas relatives, and they often turned to him for assistance. No matter how absorbed in his work, he found time to help them if he could. He assisted a sister who was researching the family tree; he wrote letters of recommendation for a nephew who hoped to join his fraternity, Delta Tau Delta, and for others seeking admission to college or looking for employment. He paid for a niece's trip to Hawaii so that she could meet her husband, who was stationed in Vietnam during that war. He was very close to his brother Bob, a successful lawyer in Dallas and head partner of the family law firm. Uncle Bob died of lung cancer in 1963 at the age of fifty-nine. My father was with him during the last days of his life, giving him support and encouragement, and after Uncle Bob's death, he spent a large amount of time helping settle his estate equitably.

My father was known for the many personal notes he sent, not just to family members but also to friends and acquaintances. He wrote these notes while traveling on airplanes or cars, while watching television at home, or sometimes from the bench of the Supreme Court. He never wasted a moment! The notes were not substantive. They were to thank someone for a kindness, remember a birthday, or extend congratulations for an accomplishment. When a friend or a family member attended a Supreme Court session, he always sent a note of welcome from the bench. The recipients loved these notes. Many saved them and expressed their appreciation of them to our family.

He had some quirks. He could not tolerate "laziness," and his standards were very high. He despised gossip or anything resembling it. If I spoke critically of someone, he had an effective put-down: "That's strange, she spoke very highly of you," he would gently admonish. I would laugh but get the point, and the conversation ended. At times, his distaste for gossip seemed unreasonable. While we were living in California, there were rumors—which proved to be true—that the marriage of President Roosevelt's son James was breaking up. Mother heard the news on the radio and repeated it to my father. He scolded her for spreading gossip. That same evening, my parents went to dinner with Thurman Arnold, my father's boss at that time, and Arnold repeated the same story. My father remained silent. When they returned home, Mother noted that my father had failed to reprimand Thurman Arnold as he had done her.

Both my parents were unfailingly courteous and kind to everyone. One act of kindness on my father's part made the newspapers. He was getting a haircut from "Red" Rothe, a barber used by many dignitaries at that time, including Harry Truman. About halfway through the cut, Red received an emergency phone call. His pregnant wife was on her way to the hospital, and it appeared that the birth was imminent. Outside the barbershop, Oscar was waiting for my father in the car. My father pointed to the car and driver and told the barber to get in—Oscar would take him to the hospital.

"But I haven't finished cutting your hair," said Red.

"Don't worry about that," my father replied. "I'll come back tomorrow and you can finish it. You'd better get going."

According to the newspaper, Tom Clark looked a little odd while sitting on the Court the next morning with his uneven haircut. When, later in the day, he returned to the barbershop for the rest of his haircut, he handed Red a box of cigars. "Here," he said, "it's an old Texas custom."

A great deal of his humor was self-effacing. He delighted in introducing Ramsey as a "block off the old chip." Sometimes, however, it was difficult to know whether he was serious or joking. William Powell, a law clerk who served during the 1957–1958 term, recalled the following incident:

> One morning Justice Clark, Justice Harlan and I arrived in the parking garage [of the Supreme Court] at about the same time, and the three of us entered the elevator together. Although they enjoyed a warm friendship, it is hard to imagine two people more different than Justice Harlan and Justice Clark. Justice Clark was a plain-talking Texan with the accent and the hat to match, while Justice Harlan was in every way Ivy League and Wall Street. As the elevator door closed, Justice Harlan looked over at Justice Clark and said: "That's a fine looking suit, Tom."
>
> "Yeah, it's one of those new wash-and-wear jobs," responded Justice Clark.
>
> In an attempt at light humor, Justice Harlan said: "Did you ever wash it?"
>
> He chuckled, and I am sure thought the conversation was over, but Justice Clark replied: "As a matter of fact, I wore it into the shower out in California last month and nearly ruined the damn thing."
>
> The elevator opened and Justice Clark stepped out.
>
> Justice Harlan's face was blank, not knowing whether his own joke had been topped by another, or whether Justice Clark had described an actual experience so far from his own life style as to defy belief.

I could have assured Justice Harlan that Tom Clark's sense of humor was at work! My father's law clerks provided other anecdotes illustrating my father's sense of humor. Some were rather surprising. Charles Reed recalled an incident when the FBI sent a memo to my father's office to warn him that a marine stationed at Quantico had been overheard saying he was going to get that "blankety-blank Tom Clark." He had been hospitalized with a nervous breakdown, and the FBI sent the memo after he went AWOL. I have no idea what caused the marine's anger. My father was not in his office when the memo arrived, so Miss Alice put it on his desk. A short time later, he returned it with a brief note attached: "If this man asks for an appointment, don't give it to him." Nothing more was said and nothing happened.

One attempt at humor was clearly ill advised and regretted. My father and his law clerk Tom Marten were traveling back to D.C. in the spring of 1977 after a trip to the Eighth Circuit and were changing planes in St. Louis. Airport security was relatively new at that time. My father went through the security system with no problem, but Tom Marten set off the alarm. My father joked: "I told you not to bring that gun, Tom." When the woman at the checkpoint heard the remark, she threatened to call the police. "You'd better call two," my father responded. The woman retaliated, and an FBI agent promptly arrived. The matter was cleared up quickly, but according to Tom Marten, my father was very quiet and subdued for the rest of the flight. Finally, he said, "I should have kept my . . . mouth shut. It wasn't enough to make the first crack, I had to make a second one." There was a long pause before he added: "Let's not tell Mrs. Clark about this."

Tom Marten was my father's last law clerk, serving during the 1976–1977 term. He commented on my father's workload during that last year of his life and on his frequent illnesses:

[During the 1976–1977 term] Justice Clark sat on nine of the eleven circuits. He got sick and couldn't sit on the tenth. He heard about 250 cases . . . and authored about one hundred opinions and orders. He was as busy as any active circuit court judge, in addition to other activities—he rarely declined an invitation to speak—if he was sick he'd ask a law clerk to substitute—and wrote a couple of law journal articles. Illness didn't affect his work much. When he'd return from sitting on a court in a distant circuit he'd have three or four drafts of an opinion ready. He became frailer as the year went by yet they thought he'd continue forever. They'd get the medication regulated and control the problem.

One afternoon in the spring of 1977, after sitting on the D.C. Court of Appeals, my father returned to his office with a stack of briefs about two feet high—the largest number of briefs Tom Marten had ever seen. They discussed the case, known as the Rait case, briefly, and as my father prepared to leave, he called out: "Any last words, Tomas?" Tom Marten replied, "Don't take the damn Rait case." He did, of course, but didn't live to see it resolved.

## CHAPTER 25

# A Life Well Lived

The best man I have ever known.

Ramsey Clark, June 1977

W HAT DROVE TOM CLARK? Certainly not money. If wealth had been a goal, he would have left government service and returned to Dallas, where his two brothers in private law practices were significantly wealthier than he. Instead, he remained in public service, and even after reaching an age when he could have enjoyed a leisurely life, he chose to work as hard as ever despite deteriorating health. Ramsey described his motivation as coming from the belief that "the true joy of life is being exhausted in a cause you yourself deem mighty."[1] Alice O'Donnell, who knew him well after serving as his secretary for more than twenty-five years, gave her perspective: "During his entire federal career he tried to convince his associates . . . that their real rewards would come from a tremendous satisfaction a Government servant receives from a job well done; from knowing that a wrong has been made right; that our country is better because of what is done in Government offices; and that no amount of money can bring the same satisfaction."[2]

He persevered, but the demands of his work were clearly taking a toll. The greatest concern was his heart. Fibrillations—rapid and irregular heartbeats—required medications that produced side effects and had to be adjusted frequently. He was thin, yet in the fall of 1976, doctors told him to lose weight. Mother protested, but he obeyed the doctors, as he usually did. We were all concerned, and even friends and colleagues were urging him to cut back on his workload. Chief Justice Warren Burger jokingly threatened to deny him any more federal-court duties. While he assured Burger that he would "slow down," his schedule showed no signs of it, and his travel commitments were strenuous for a person of any age. His calendar for the fall of 1977 provides a sample:

September 16–18: Williamsburg, Supreme Court Historical Society
September 26–30: Chicago, 7th Circuit Court of Appeals
September 30–October 2: California, National Park Foundation meeting
October 10–13: Minneapolis, 8th Circuit Court of Appeals
October 26–29: Dallas, Metropolitan Court National Conference
November 28–December 2: New York, 2nd Circuit Court of Appeals
December 5–9: Philadelphia, 3rd Circuit Court of Appeals

These trips were not recreational. Most of the time he was presiding all day as a federal trial judge. He had to prepare in advance and then write opinions when the trials were completed. When not sitting as a circuit judge, he was making speeches or actively participating in a program. Despite this hectic schedule, he had the remarkable ability, later described by Chief Justice Warren Burger, "to seem unhurried" amid "fabulous activity."[3]

Tom Clark did not live to fulfill his travel schedule. On May 22, he spoke at the first graduation of Nova University Law School in Fort Lauderdale, Florida. He stressed ethics and urged the graduates to live by a code of "professional responsibility." He advised them that "a good name is to be chosen rather than any other thing" and congratulated the school on the number of women graduates in the class. His sense of humor was still intact. When asked about his health, he replied: "My heart used to flutter a lot around women, but I got so old it flutters even when I'm not."[4] A week later, he spoke to my daughter Julie's eighth-grade class at Longfellow Junior High School in Virginia.

On June 12, 1977, after dinner at home with Mother and a nephew, Sam Clark, my father flew to New York City, where he was scheduled to sit on the Second Circuit Court of Appeals. At the airport, he bumped into newscaster Ed Newman, who offered to carry his briefcase, which was full of briefs. My father declined the offer, admitting that he had been scolded for carrying heavy luggage at his age. "I don't think it will do any harm," he stated. He and Newman sat next to each other on the flight and shared a taxi into the city. Newman said the cab driver was "adventurous" and made him nervous. Tom Clark's advice: "Don't look."[5] My father stayed at Ramsey and Georgia's Greenwich Village apartment, though they were in Tunisia attending a human-rights conference. He called Mother when he arrived at the apartment, as he always did, to let her know he had arrived safely. He worked late into the night, laid out the clothes he would wear the next day, and neatly arranged his papers for court on the marble coffee table in the living room.

Judge Irving Kaufman was not concerned when Justice Clark did not arrive in the courtroom promptly, as he usually did, on Monday morning. New York traffic was always treacherous, and the justice was probably stuck somewhere en route to the courthouse. The judge became alarmed, however, as the minutes went by and still Tom Clark did not appear. He called my father's office in Washington, and was told the justice had flown to New York the night before and was staying at Ramsey's apartment. When there was no answer at Ramsey's, Judge Kaufman immediately sent U.S. marshals to investigate. They entered the apartment and found my father in bed as if asleep. He did not respond to their calls; there was no movement. He had died peacefully during the night of heart failure.

There are moments in one's life that are permanently frozen in time. I was at work on June 13, 1977, when my husband, Tom, called to tell me of my father's death. We had been back in suburban Washington, D.C., for a little more than a year, moving from Buffalo, New York, where I received both the bachelor of arts degree I had promised my father over twenty years previously and then a master's degree in library science. I had been a reference librarian at Northern Virginia Community College for six months and had just had my first evaluation. I was wearing a yellow pantsuit that my father and I had shopped for in celebration of my birthday, just two weeks earlier. I loved my job and was happy when I got the message that I had a phone call. Then my world fell apart. After the initial shock, I thought of Mother. What of her world? Her life revolved around my father. I rushed to the apartment to be with her.

Letters and tributes came pouring in. Chief Justice Warren Burger expressed his respect for Tom Clark:

> He is the only man ever to sit as a judge in every court. His work to improve the system will be his lasting monument. . . . No man in the past thirty years has contributed more to the improvement of justice than Tom Clark.[6]

Justice Lewis Powell mused:

> It is likely that Mr. Justice Clark was known personally and admired by more lawyers, law professors and judges than any other justice in the history of the Supreme Court of the United States.[7]

Justice William Brennan observed:

His great distinction as a judge is the reflection of his conviction that it is wrong to live life without some deep and abiding social commitment.[8]

Justice Thurgood Marshall, who succeeded him on the Court, recalled my father's contributions as attorney general:

Tom Clark is also to be remembered as the first Attorney General of the United States to file a brief amicus curiae in a civil rights case. . . . This was the first brief by an Attorney General in support of civil rights, and it was ordered by a man from Texas.[9]

Justice Byron White described an effective, congenial colleague:

This Texan, a remarkable mixture of practicality and idealism, with a talent for getting things done but getting them done better, was unfailingly cheerful, optimistic and generous.[10]

Justice William O. Douglas expressed admiration:

Mrs. Douglas and I . . . greatly admired Tom Clark for the stand he always took on the independence of the judiciary and his willingness to face every issue in turbulent times as well as in peaceful days no matter how difficult and bothersome they were.[11]

Justice John Paul Stevens extolled his retirement years:

His selfless dedication . . . was exemplified by his career as a "working judge" following his retirement from the Supreme Court. He earned the . . . admiration . . . of the entire federal judiciary by his evenhanded, perceptive and tireless participation in our day-to-day work.[12]

In a letter to my brother, Ramsey, Judge Constance Baker Motley, a distinguished African American jurist, wrote:

He [Tom Clark] never failed to take advantage of an opportunity to promote the idea of equal opportunity for blacks and women in the legal profession in general and as members of the federal judiciary in particular.

Alice O'Donnell described the humanity that characterized everything he did:

Above all, he was a human being. In every position he held the door was open. And through those doors walked everyone, from a messenger or driver up to the Chief Justice.[13]


Tom Clark was buried where he wished to be—in the place of his birth, Dallas, Texas. It was a gray day, cool for Dallas, as a group of family and friends watched the casket lowered into the family plot that held the young son who had died so many years before. The space between them was reserved for Mother, who always said she wanted to be buried between her "two Toms."

Even in our grief, we realized that, once more, my father had been lucky, for he died as he would have wished, like the proverbial cowboy "with his boots on," working to the end, still the "traveling salesman of justice." He had come a long way since he left Texas as a young lawyer in 1937, and he had grown immensely. His dedication to public service was inspiring and his achievements were exceptional. He had made a difference.

But he also achieved exceptional success in his personal life. He was adored by his family and loved and admired by his many friends. In his memorial tribute, Ramsey stated his belief that "Few things more fortunate can come to a man than to have a truly great father." Ramsey was not talking about greatness measured by wealth or power—there are dozens of examples of people, successful in that sense, who have failed to achieve happiness in their personal lives and whose children have been stunted by the shadow of the parent. Tom Clark was a great father, a great husband, a great friend—a man of "brilliant humanity." As my brother Ramsey declared, he was "the best man I have ever known."

# Epilogue

His great distinction . . . is his reflection that it is wrong to live life
without some deep and abiding social commitment.

William J. Brennan, 1977

THE WORLD HAS CHANGED DRAMATICALLY since my father, Tom
Clark, died, more than thirty years ago. Many of the changes would
excite him, some would disturb him, and a few are the results of his
own efforts.

The Supreme Court is a prime example. Even the appearance of the
building has been altered by the installation of protective barriers designed
to prevent a terrorist attack. No more the easy access that I enjoyed as a
young girl. An elaborate security system is now in place and scrupulously
enforced. Tom Clark might think these safeguards necessary, but he would
hate them! The makeup of the Court is totally different and reflects the
drift to the right that the country has experienced during the last three
decades. Tom Clark was viewed as a conservative during his years as a justice—incorrectly, I believe, for his opinions defy any ideological label.
Today, he would be tagged as a liberal, and that, too, would be incorrect,
and for the same reason. But the issues have also changed. The Cold War
is over, but peace has not been attained, and the world is as dangerous
today as it was during Tom Clark's lifetime—perhaps more so. International terrorism has supplanted the fear of communism and concern over
civil unrest. Though it is perhaps unwise to speculate, I have no doubt that
Tom Clark would be appalled by some of the policies that have been
employed in the name of "the war on terrorism" and would view them as
unconstitutional.

The current justices still deal with some of the same issues that were
debated when my father was on the Court—school prayer, individual

rights, national security, and others—but new controversies are now dom-inant. Although civil rights for minorities continue to be a challenge, great progress has been made since *Brown v. Board of Education*. Today, the civil rights of other groups have the spotlight—the rights of homosexuals, especially their right to marry, and the right of women to obtain an abor-tion. Abortion cases had not made their way to the Supreme Court during my father's tenure, but they were on the horizon, and *Roe v. Wade* was handed down just five years after he retired. I was surprised to discover during my research that in 1969 he wrote an article entitled "Religion, Morality, and Abortion: A Constitutional Appraisal." He began the article with a quotation of Indian prime minister Jawaharlal Nehru: "Thought without action is an abortion; action without thought is folly."[1]

The quotation is an apt one for my father, but in the context of the article, he is using it to support his belief that "it is readily apparent at this point that a uniform scheme concerning abortion is highly desirous."[2] He is calling for action, not by the judicial branch of the government— "Courts cannot reach out to reform society"—but by state and federal legislators.[3] The article provides historical background on the abortion issue and cites several cases that support a constitutional basis for the "right to privacy," which he clearly believed was a right under our Constitution. In 1944, in *Prince v. Massachusetts*, the Court ruled against the state of Mas-sachusetts because it had interfered in "the private realm of family life which the state cannot enter." In 1960, in *Bates v. Little Rock*, the Court declared that the state must have a "compelling subordinating interest" before it could encroach upon personal liberty, and finally, in 1965, in *Gris-wold v. Connecticut*, the Court declared unconstitutional a state statute that prohibited the use of contraceptives, on the grounds that it interfered with "an intimate relation of husband and wife."[4] My father drew the follow-ing conclusion from these opinions:

> The result of these decisions is the evolution of the concept that there is a certain zone of individual privacy which is protected by the Constitution. Unless the State has a compelling subordinating interest that outweighs the individual rights of human beings, it may not interfere with a person's marriage, home, children, and day-to-day living habits. This is one of the most fundamental concepts that the Founding Fathers had in mind when they drafted the Constitution. No one will deny that a State has a valid interest in regulating the well-being of its inhabitants, especially when it is dealing with children, who are more susceptible to undesirable influences. We have also seen that the State may not unreasonably interfere with the intimate relations of its inhabitants. When deciding on the constitutional

restraints on a State's interference with individual rights, the vital question becomes one of balancing. It must be determined at what point the State is interfering with individuals and at what point it is exercising valid authority by regulating the well-being of children.[5]

The former law clerk who described Tom Clark as the "balance wheel of the Court" was surely right. "Balance" was what he sought and brought to all his decisions.

New technologies have, without a question, brought about the most dramatic changes to our world. When my father became director of the Federal Judicial Center in 1968, computer technology was still in its infancy. He saw its potential—both positive and negative—and worked toward applying it effectively to improve our judicial system. He would applaud the many advantages we now enjoy because of technology, especially our amazing access to information and unimagined communication capabilities, but he would be concerned about their impact on our culture and the amount of time spent in front of the computer screen by people of all ages.

Some changes that have occurred are simply part of life. In 1977, three siblings—his sisters—were still living; his two children were in early middle age, and his seven grandchildren ranged from nine to twenty-five years old. Today, his surviving family consists of two elderly children, grandchildren who have families of their own, and eleven great-grandchildren. I often think of how much he would enjoy the new additions to our family.

Mother, his beloved Mary, lived to be one hundred and died on June 13, 2002—exactly twenty-five years after the day of his death. Still living in the apartment we had moved to in 1945, she died there, peacefully, in her sleep. She outlived my husband, Tom, who passed away in 2001 after a brief battle with pancreatic cancer, and lived to enjoy the rewards of being a great-grandmother. Her greatest joy during the last few years of her life was her great-grandchildren. We had worried about how she would survive without my father, who had been the center of her life from the beginning of their marriage. But she was more than an exemplary traditional wife, and her children, grandchildren, and great-grandchildren continued to benefit from her unconditional love and wise counsel.

Some have wondered about my father's relationship with my brother Ramsey, even speculating that there may have been conflict and competition between them. I hope the portrayal in this biography puts that speculation to rest, for the two truly admired each other and enjoyed an exceptionally loving relationship. Ramsey's dedication to human rights began before my father's death, and I have no doubt that Ramsey would have my father's unwavering support were he living today. I also believe that my father would be disappointed at the lack of public knowledge and understanding about Ramsey, his accomplishments in the area of human rights, and his efforts to establish justice on an international scale. My father's words, written in 1973, can serve as a description of what Ramsey has tried to achieve: "One of our society's greatest strengths . . . and its strongest tenet is that the feared, the despised and the powerless must be protected equally with the mighty, the rich, and the beloved."[6] A system of justice that does not offer equal rights and protection to everyone is significantly flawed. Ramsey understands this, as did my father, and has fought to make justice for all a reality.

Were my father living today, I believe his greatest disappointment would be in the cynicism and distrust that characterize many Americans' view of the government. He believed in public service and dedicated his life to it. Throughout his career, he exemplified the belief, described by his friend and colleague William J. Brennan, that "it is wrong to live life without some deep and abiding social commitment."[7] He would argue that there are many other fine public servants who have done the same.

Tom Clark's presence is still felt today. Historians, legal scholars, and students use his attorney general papers, located at the Harry S. Truman Presidential Library in Independence, Missouri, and his Supreme Court papers, kept at the University of Texas Law School library in Austin. After his death, my father's former law clerks and other friends established the Tom C. Clark Judicial Fellowship, which is awarded each year by the Judicial Fellows Commission. The fellowship serves as a "living memorial" to my father.

I still feel my father's presence more than thirty years after his passing. His unconditional love, the example he set, and the support that could always be counted on continue to be sources of strength and comfort. I hope I have succeeded in conveying to the readers of this biography a portrait of a dedicated public servant, a devoted family man, and a delightful human being.

# Law Clerks of Justice Tom Clark

| Term | Clerk | Clerk's Law School |
|------|-------|--------------------|
| 1949–1950 | Lawrence Tolan | University of Michigan |
| | Percy D. Williams | Harvard University |
| 1950–1951 | Donald F. Turner | Yale University |
| | Percy D. Williams | Harvard University |
| 1951–1952 | Vester T. Hughes, Jr.★ | Harvard University |
| | Stuart W. Thayer | Yale University |
| | C. Richard Walker | University of Chicago |
| 1952–1953 | Frederick M. Rowe | Yale University |
| | Bernard Weisberg | University of Chicago |
| 1953–1954 | Ellis H. McKay | University of Pennsylvania |
| | Ernest Rubenstein | Yale University |
| 1954–1955 | William K. Jones | Columbia University |
| | John Kaplan | Harvard University |
| 1955–1956 | Robert W. Hamilton | University of Chicago |
| | John E. Nolan | Georgetown University |
| 1956–1957 | Harry L. Hobson | New York University |
| | John J. Crown | Northwestern University |
| 1957–1958 | Robert P. Gorman | Notre Dame University |
| | William D. Powell, Jr. | Southern Methodist University |
| 1958–1959 | Charles H. Phillips | University of Southern California |
| | Max O. Truitt, Jr. | Yale University |
| 1959–1960 | Larry E. Temple | University of Texas |
| | Thomas Cecil Wray | Yale University |
| 1960–1961 | Carl L. Estes II | University of Texas |
| | Malachy T. Mahon | Fordham University |
| 1961–1962 | James E. Knox | Drake University |
| | Burke W. Mathes, Jr. | Harvard University |
| 1962–1963 | Raymond L. Brown | University of Mississippi |
| | Martin J. Flynn | Loyola Law School, Los Angeles |

| 1963–1964 | James L. McHugh, Jr. | Villanova University |
| | James H. Pipkin, Jr. | Harvard University |
| 1964–1965 | Michael W. Maupin | University of Virginia |
| | Shannon Ratliff | University of Texas |
| 1965–1966 | Lee A. Freeman, Jr. | Harvard University |
| | Charles D. Reed | South Texas College of Law |
| 1966–1967 | Marshall Groce | St. Mary's University, San Antonio |
| | Stuart P. Ross | George Washington University |

★Time as law clerk cut short by call to service in Korean War

The following served during Justice Clark's retirement years as he sat on the country's judicial circuits.

| Term | Clerk | Clerk's Law School |
| --- | --- | --- |
| 1967–1968 | J. Larry Nichols | University of Michigan |
| 1969–1970 | Jerry M. Snider | University of Houston |
| 1970–1971 | Theodore L. Garrett | Columbia University |
| 1971–1972 | Taylor Ashworth | University of Texas |
| 1972–1973 | Thomas V. Reavley | Harvard University |
| 1973–1974 | Stafford Hutchinson | University of Texas |
| 1974–1975 | William M. Hannay | Georgetown University |
| 1975–1976 | Thomas D. Corrigan | Case Western Reserve School of Law |
| 1976–1977 | J. Thomas Marten | Washburn University |
| | Thomas D. Hughes IV | Loyola University School of Law, New Orleans |

# Notes

## PROLOGUE

1. Robert E. Baskin, "Tom Clark Retires with Praise from Everyone," *Dallas Morning News*, March 5, 1967.
2. Harold I. Ickes, "Tom Clark Should Say 'No Thanks,'" *New Republic*, August 24, 1949: 11.
3. National Blue Star Mothers of America to Senators Edward Martin and Francis Myers, August 10, 1949, Papers of Tom C. Clark, Harry S. Truman Presidential Library (hereafter cited as Clark AG Papers).
4. "Nightmare!" editorial, *Washington Times-Herald*, July 19, 1949.
5. Lynn Landrum, "Thinking Out Loud," *Dallas Morning News*, August 2, 1949.
6. "Oh, No!" editorial, *Dallas Morning News*, March 3, 1967.
7. Baskin, "Tom Clark Retires."
8. John G. Mackenzie, "Justice Clark, Portrait of a Man," *Lansing (MI) State Journal*, March 12, 1967.
9. John P. Frank, "Justice Tom Clark and Judicial Administration," *Texas Law Review* 46, no. 1 (November 1967): 56.

## CHAPTER 1

1. John William Rogers, *The Lusty Texans of Dallas*, 18.
2. Ibid., 121.
3. Ibid., 117.
4. Ibid., 18.
5. Ibid., 109.
6. Ibid., 199.
7. A. C. Greene, *Dallas, the Deciding Years: A Historical Portrait*, 34.
8. Rogers, *Lusty Texans*, 193.
9. Writers Program of the Works Project Administration, *Texas: A Guide to the Lone Star State*, 139.
10. Greene, *Dallas*, 37.
11. I am indebted to the late Elizabeth Clark Capers, my aunt and the family historian whose research, papers, and scrapbook provided information on the McDowell-Clark family tree and additional family history.
12. Elizabeth York Enstam, *Women and the Creation of Urban Life: Dallas, Texas, 1843–1920*, xv. On Dallas as a cotton center, see Rogers, *Lusty Texans*, 202.

13. Enstam, *Women and Urban Life*, 51.
14. Philip Lindsley, *A History of Greater Dallas and Vicinity*, 2:124.
15. Ellis A. Davis and Edwin H. Grobe, eds., *New Encyclopedia of Texas*, 2:618.
16. "William H. Clark," *Dallas Law Journal* 3, no. 3 (1932): 19.

## Chapter 2

1. Quoted in Darwin Payne, *Dallas: An Illustrated History*, 122.

## Chapter 3

1. Payne, *Dallas: An Illustrated History*, 190.
2. Tom Clark, "Teaching Professional Ethics," *San Diego Law Review* 12 (1975): 254.
3. Nancy MacLean, *Behind the Mask of Chivalry*, xi.
4. Writers Program of the Works Project Administration, *WPA Dallas Guide and History*, 184–185.
5. William McCraw, *Professional Politicians*, 71.
6. Ibid., 176.
7. "Heart Attack Kills Bill McCraw," *Dallas Morning News*, November 9, 1955.
8. Payne, Dallas: An Illustrated History, 209.

## Chapter 4

1. Richard O'Connor, "Dad Joiner Blows the Roof Off Texas," in *The Oil Barons*, 295.
2. Harry Hurt III, "The Dad Joiner Deal," in *Texas Rich: The Hunt Dynasty from the Early Oil Days through the Silver Crash*, 78.
3. Ibid., 81–82.
4. James Howard, *Big D Is for Dallas*, 87.
5. O'Connor, "Dad Joiner," 304.
6. Hurt, "Dad Joiner Deal," 92.
7. Ibid., 94–94.
8. William R. Childs, *The Texas Railroad Commission*, 3.
9. O'Connor, "Dad Joiner," 309.
10. Ibid.
11. Howard, *Big D*, 87–88.
12. O'Connor, "Dad Joiner," 302.
13. Hurt, "Dad Joiner Deal," 88.
14. Ibid., 91.
15. O'Connor, "Dad Joiner," 302.
16. Advertisement for the Bill McCraw campaign, *Dallas Morning News*, May 31, 1934.
17. *Dallas Morning News*, July 13, 1934.
18. Mary Clark Burchfield to the author, October 4, 1981.
19. Dawson Duncan, "Bank Account Here 'Personal Matter,' Clark Tells Probers," *Dallas Morning News*, December 8, 1936.
20. Ibid.
21. Dawson Duncan, "Land Hearing in Recess to Await McCraw," *Dallas Morning News*, February 24, 1938.
22. Ibid.

## CHAPTER 5

1. *New York Times*, March 4, 1937.
2. "Foes of Jefferson Memorial," *Washington Evening Star*, March 22, 1937.
3. "61% of Texans Support Court Plan," *Washington Post*, March 14, 1937.
4. Tom Clark, interview by Jerry N. Hess for the Harry S. Truman Presidential Library, October 17, 1972, 37–38.
5. Tom Connally, *My Name Is Tom Connally*, 193.
6. Tom Clark, interview by Joe B. Frantz for the University of Texas Oral History Project, October 7, 1969, 1.
7. "205 True Bills Returned by Scandal Juries over Louisiana since June," *New Orleans Item*, October 29, 1939.
8. Ibid.
9. "42 Reported Ready to Plead Guilty in Indictments on High Building Costs," *New Orleans Item*, January 5, 1940.
10. "Lumber Bodies Fined $12,000 in Anti-Trust Case," *New Orleans Times-Picayune*, January 22, 1940.
11. "Thousands Arrive for Sugar Bowl," *New Orleans Times-Picayune*, January 1, 1940.
12. John Frank, *The Warren Court*, 83.

## CHAPTER 6

1. Thurman Arnold to Francis Biddle, memorandum, January 17, 1942, obtained through the Freedom of Information Act (FOIA).
2. Jim Rowe to Tom Connally, January 29, 1942, Clark AG Papers.
3. "More Alien Areas Closed," *Los Angeles Times*, February 2, 1942.
4. Quoted in Morton Grodzins, *Americans Betrayed: Politics and the Japanese Evacuation*, 242.
5. Tom Clark, interview by Miriam Feingold for the Earl Warren Oral History Project, University of California, Berkley, June 20, 1976, 148.
6. Clark, interview by Hess, 67.
7. *Los Angeles Times*, February 9, 1942.
8. "Dies Committee 'Tentatively' Urges Removal of Japanese," *Los Angeles Times*, February 9, 1942.
9. *Los Angeles Times*, February 6, 1942.
10. Quoted in John Armor and Peter Wright, *Manzanar*, 44.
11. *Personal Justice Denied: Report of the Commission on Wartime Relocation and Internment of Civilians*, 65.
12. Armor and Wright, *Manzanar*, 44.
13. Quoted in Michi Weglyn, *Years of Infamy: The Untold Story of America's Concentration Camps*, 95.
14. Clark, interview by Hess, 67.
15. Francis Biddle, *In Brief Authority*, 216.
16. Jim Rowe to Tom Clark, February 11, 1942, in the author's possession.
17. Jim Rowe to Francis Biddle, February 12, 1942, obtained through the FOIA.
18. *Los Angeles Times*, February 9, 1942.
19. Henry McLemore, "The Lighter Side," *Los Angeles Times*, February 7, 1942.
20. McLemore, "The Lighter Side," *Los Angeles Times*, February 3, 1942.

21. Quoted in Grodzins, *Americans Betrayed*, 278.

22. Quoted in ibid., 258.

23. Walter Lippmann, *New York Times*, February 12, 1942.

24. Tom Clark, letter to the editor, *New York Times*, February 15, 1942.

25. Quoted in Grodzins, *Americans Betrayed*, 258.

26. Clark, interview by Feingold, 16.

27. Quoted in Grodzins, *Americans Betrayed*, 265–266.

28. Grodzins, *Americans Betrayed*, 265–266.

29. Quoted in Bill Hosokawa, *JACL in Quest of Justice*, 150–151.

30. Clark, interview by Feingold, 9.

31. *Los Angeles Times*, March 2, 1942.

32. Quoted in Hosokowa, *JACL*, 165.

33. Quoted in Paige Smith, *Democracy on Trial*, 175.

34. Quoted in ibid., 174.

35. *Eastland (TX) Telegram*, April 14, 1943.

36. Ibid.

37. Ibid.

38. House Select Committee Investigating National Defense Migration, *Japanese Evacuation from the West Coast*, 77th Cong., 2nd sess., March 19, 1942, 11.

39. Ibid., 15.

40. Tom Clark, preface to *The Bamboo People: The Law and Japanese-Americans*, by Frank Churman, vi.

41. Bernard Schwartz, *Super Chief: Earl Warren and His Supreme Court*, 16–17.

42. William Wiecek, *The Birth of the Modern Constitution*, 361.

43. Tom Clark, epilogue to *Executive Order 9066*, by Maisie Conrat and Richard Conrat.

44. Wiecek, *Birth of the Modern Constitution*, 358.

45. Weglyn, *Years of Infamy*, 31.

46. Quoted in Schwartz, *Super Chief*, 16.

## CHAPTER 7

1. Tom Clark to Francis Biddle, November 14, 1941, Clark AG Papers.

2. Jim Rowe to Tom Clark, December 1, 1941, Clark AG Papers.

3. Lyndon Johnson to Tom Clark, November 17, 1941, Clark AG Papers.

4. Tom Clark, "Parting the Curtains on Paytrioteers," *Everybody's Weekly, Philadelphia Inquirer*, February 13, 1944.

5. Ibid.

6. Tom Connally to Franklin Roosevelt, January 16, 1943, obtained through the FOIA.

7. "Calm Tom," *Newsweek*, June 12, 1944.

8. Clark, "Parting the Curtains on Paytrioteers."

9. Tom Clark to J. Edgar Hoover, July 2, 1943, obtained through the FOIA.

10. J. Edgar Hoover to Tom Clark, July 1943, obtained through the FOIA.

11. Robert L. Clark to Tom Clark, December 5, 1943, in the author's possession.

12. Tom Clark, interview by Hess, 3, 5.

13. Ibid., 23.

14. D. B. Hardeman and Donald C. Bacon, *Rayburn: A Biography*, 292.

15. Tom Clark, speech to the Women's National Democratic Club (Washington, D.C., October 1944).

CHAPTER 8

1. Harry S. Truman, *Memoirs: Year of Decisions*, 30.

2. J. Edgar Hoover, memorandum to Mr. Tolson and Mr. Tamm, June 1, 1945, obtained through the FOIA.

3. Elizabeth Churchill, "Town Talk," *Washington Post*, May 29, 1945.

4. Quoted in Marshall McNeil, "Tom Clark Won Approval of Senators by Frankness," *Fort Worth Press*, June 15, 1945.

5. "Clark of Dallas Takes Oath as Attorney General of U.S.," *Dallas Morning News*, July 1, 1945.

6. Biddle, *In Brief Authority*, 364–366.

7. John Frank to the author, December 23, 1999, in the author's possession.

8. The letters of congratulations quoted in this paragraph and the following ones are archived in the Clark AG Papers.

9. Lewis Cassidy to Tom Clark, July 24, 1945, in the author's possession.

10. Elton Miller, "Clark Announces U.S. Attorneys Must Quit Private Law Practices," *Dallas Morning News*, October 14, 1945.

11. Tom Clark, memorandum to assistant attorneys general, January 30, 1946, obtained through the FOIA.

12. Alex Acheson, "High Honors Accorded Here to Native Son," *Dallas Times Herald*, October 11, 1945.

13. Tom Clark to Harry S. Truman, memorandum, May 1, 1947, papers of Harry S. Truman, Official File, Harry S. Truman Library, Independence, Missouri (hereafter cited as Truman Papers).

14. Tom Clark, interview by Robert Ireland for the Fred Vinson Oral History Project, May 6, 1973, 14.

15. Ibid., 64.

16. Tom Clark, "Administrative Law," *Nebraska Law Review* 25 (March 1946): 84.

17. Tom Clark, "The Office of the Attorney General," *Tennessee Law Review* 19 (Fall 1946): 150.

18. Tom Clark, interview by Hess, 90–91.

19. Tom Clark, interview by Frantz, 20.

20. Allen Duckworth, "Tom Clark's Name Stricken Deliberately as Delegate," *Dallas Morning News*, May 27, 1948.

21. James A. Weschler, "The Story behind Ouster of Rogge," *New York Post*, October 28, 1946.

22. Tom Clark to John Rogge, October 25, 1946, Clark AG Papers.

23. "Clark Ousts Rogge for Speech Linking Americans with Nazis," *New York Times*, October 26, 1946.

24. Tom Clark, interview by Frantz, 20.

25. Louis Stark, "Lewis Put Himself Above U.S., Clark Tells High Court," *New York Times*, January 15, 1947.

26. David McCullough, *Truman*, 493.

27. Ibid., 501.

28. Ibid.

29. Tom Clark, interview by Hess, 96.

30. Stark, "Lewis Puts Himself above U.S."

31. Melvyn Dubofsky and Warren Van Tine, *John L. Lewis*, 470.

## CHAPTER 9

1. Tom Clark to Harry S. Truman, memorandum, "Suggestions for State of the Union Address," December 2, 1946, 2, Clark AG Papers.
2. "Attorney General Clark on the 'Pay-off of Law Violations,'" *San Antonio Evening News,* January 3, 1946.
3. Tom Clark, "Justice in the Reconstruction Period," speech at a meeting of the North Carolina State Bar, October 25, 1946, 13.
4. Ibid., 7.
5. Robert L. Norton, "Tom Clark in Rare Crusade," *Boston Post,* February 17, 1946.
6. Norton, "Tom Clark in Rare Crusade."
7. Watson Crews, Jr., "Eunice and the Kennedy Tradition," *American Weekly,* May 23, 1947, 11.
8. Program, *Washington Post*'s Third Annual Celebrities Golf Tournament, May 18, 1947.
9. Roger James Kahler to Tom Clark, January 5, 1949, in author's possession.
10. Mary Purser Beeman, "New Deal Justice: Tom Clark and the Warren Court," Ph.D. diss., Univ. of Texas, 1993, 47–48.
11. "Freedom Train Tours America," *National Geographic,* October 1949, 529.
12. "Political Aim Seen in 'Freedom Train,'" *New York Times,* June 3, 1947.
13. Lewis Wood, "Freedom Train to Start Sept. 17," *New York Times,* May 23, 1947.
14. National Blue Star Mothers of America, letter distributed to the public, October 24, 1947.
15. "Freedom Train and the Commies," *New York Journal-American,* September 26, 1947.
16. Wood, "Freedom Train to Start."
17. Quoted in the *People's Voice,* September 27, 1947.
18. Quoted in the *New York Times,* September 29, 1947.
19. Wood, "Freedom Train to Start."
20. "Ideology Riddance Foreseen for U.S.," *Oregon Journal,* July 17, 1947.
21. Quoted in the *New York Journal-American,* September 26, 1947.
22. Tom Clark to Harry S. Truman, December 18, 1945, Clark AG Papers.
23. "Freedom Train Tours America," *National Geographic,* October 1949, 529–542.

## CHAPTER 10

1. Truman, *Memoirs,* 235–236.
2. Richard Kluger, *Simple Justice,* 227.
3. Michael R. Gardner, *Harry Truman and Civil Rights,* 18.
4. Ibid., 21.
5. Ibid., 45.
6. Quoted in "Truman Orders Lynchers Found; Voices Horror at Georgia Crime," *New York Times,* July 31, 1946.
7. President's Committee on Civil Rights, *To Secure These Rights: The Report of the President's Committee on Civil Rights,* 124.
8. Tom Clark, "Civil Rights: The Boundless Responsibility of Lawyers," *American Bar Journal* 32 (August 1946): 453.
9. *To Secure These Rights,* viii.
10. Ibid., 123.

11. Gardner, *Truman and Civil Rights*, 63.

12. Tom Clark, "Statement and Analysis by the Attorney General Concerning the Proposed Civil Rights Act of 1949 (HR 4682, S 1725)," 6.

13. Ibid., 16.

14. Ibid., 34.

15. Gardner, *Truman and Civil Rights*, 175.

16. Tom C. Clark and Philip B. Perlman, *Prejudice and Property*, 84.

17. Gardner, *Truman and Civil Rights*, 83.

18. Ibid., 69–70.

## CHAPTER 11

1. Bruce Watson, "Crackdown!" *Smithsonian Magazine* 32 (February 2002), 53.

2. Quoted in David Caute, *The Great Fear: The Anti-Communist Purge under Truman and Eisenhower*, 89.

3. Richard G. Powers, *Secrecy and Power: The Life of J. Edgar Hoover*, 284.

4. Tom Clark, "Civil Rights," 456–457.

5. Ibid.

6. Quoted in "Clark's Speech Denounced by National Lawyer's Guild," *Washington Post*, July 8, 1946.

7. Quoted in "Truman Urged to Remove Clark," *People's Daily World*, July 9, 1946.

8. Clark to Truman, memorandum, May 1, 1947, Clark AG Papers.

9. Ibid.

10. Tom Clark, speech broadcast on radio station WCAU, Philadelphia, Pennsylvania, October 9, 1946, 3, 4, obtained through the FOIA.

11. J. Edgar Hoover memorandum to Tom Clark, October 1948, FOIA.

12. Tom Clark to Harry S. Truman, memorandum, October 23, 1948, obtained through the FOIA and in author's possession.

13. Tom Clark to Seth W. Richardson, November 24, 1947. Clark AG Papers.

14. Ibid.

15. Quoted in Eleanor Bontecou, *The Federal Loyalty-Security Program*, 172.

16. American Civil Liberties Union, "Statement on Loyalty Tests for Federal Employees," April 7, 1846, 6.

17. Eleanor Roosevelt to Harry S. Truman, November 13, 1947, Truman Papers.

18. Harry S. Truman to Eleanor Roosevelt, November 18, 1947, Truman Papers.

19. Doris Fleeson, "Clark Keeping Pledge of No Witch Hunts," *New York Daily News*, April 19, 1947.

20. Philip Perlman, interview by William Hillman and David Noyes, December 15, 1954, Harry S. Truman Presidential Library.

21. "President's Order on Loyalty Hailed," *New York Times*, March 3, 1947.

22. J. Parnell Thomas to Harry S. Truman, September 29, 1948, Clark AG Papers.

23. Quoted in Powers, *Secrecy and Power*, 286.

24. Quoted in Athan G. Theoharis, ed. *Spying on Americans: Political Surveillance from Hoover to the Huston Plan*, 99.

25. Ibid., 274.

26. Tom Clark, interview by Ireland, 65.

27. Harvey Klehr and Ronald Radosh, *The Amerasia Spy Case: Prelude to McCarthyism*, 3–7, 40–42.

28. Curt Gentry, *J. Edgar Hoover: The Man and the Secrets*, 340.

29. Quoted in ibid, 338.

30. Quoted in "Barsky, 15 Others Are Found Guilty," *New York Times*, June 28, 1947.

31. Gentry, *J. Edgar Hoover*, 368.

32. Caute, *Great Fear*, 192–193.

33. Tom Clark, interview by Hess, 187–188.

34. Tom Clark, "Statement before the House Un-American Activities Committee," Washington, D.C., February 5, 1948, 1, 5, and 7.

35. Tom Clark, speech before Jewish War Veterans of the United States, Kiamesha Lake, Monticello, New York, September 18, 1948, 4.

36. Ibid., 5.

37. Tom Clark, interview by Hess, 113.

38. Ibid., 115–118, 210–211.

39. Quoted in David Botter, "Clark Angrily Denies He Sought Missouri Vote Fraud Whitewash," *Dallas Morning News*, June 6, 1947.

40. Quoted in ibid.

41. Quoted in ibid.

42. Quoted in David Botter, "FBI Chief Denies Clark Nipped Quiz," *Dallas Morning News*, June 20, 1947.

43. Wiecek, *Birth of the Modern Constitution*, 430.

44. McCullough, *Truman*, 673–674.

## CHAPTER 12

1. Quoted in McCullough, *Truman*, 629.

2. "Why not Tom Clark for V. President?" editorial, *Philadelphia Inquirer*, July 13, 1948.

3. Quoted in Dick Fagan, "U.S. Attorney General 'Out' as Running Mate," *Oregon Journal*, July 17, 1948.

4. Tom Clark, interview by Hess, 160.

5. Ibid., 161.

6. Walter Hornaday, "U.S. Preparing to Sue Texas for Title to Its Rich Tidelands," *Dallas Morning News*, March 3, 1948.

7. Quoted in "Clark Charges Laxity by GOP in Ousting Reds," *Dallas Morning News*, September 25, 1948.

8. Quoted in "1600 County Democrats Hear Clark Flay Congress," *Scranton (PA) Times*, October 26, 1948.

## CHAPTER 13

1. Tom Clark, speech for Washington's Birthday Patriotic Rally, 14th Regiment Armory, Brooklyn, New York, February 21, 1949.

2. Tom Clark, speech before the Jewish Labor Committee Convention, Atlantic City, N.J., February 25, 1949.

3. U.S. Department of Justice, "State of the Department of Justice, 1945–49," unpublished report, June 30, 1949, 22, Clark AG Papers.

4. Clark to Truman, memorandum, "Suggestions for State of the Union Address," December 2, 1946, Clark AG Papers.

5. U.S. Department of Justice, "State of the Department of Justice, 1945–49," 11.

6. Grace Stewart, interview by author, Washington, D.C., September 12, 1981.

7. "Tom Clark's Fine Record of Service," Tom C. Clark Papers, Tarlton Law Library, University of Texas, Scrapbook No. 11.

8. "Dupont on the Carpet," *Newsweek*, July 11, 1949, 19–20.

9. Ibid.

10. Tom Clark, interview by Hess, 20.

11. Lynn Landrum, "Thinking Out Loud," *Dallas Morning News*, July 30, 1949.

12. Arthur Krock, "In the Nation," *New York Times*, August 2, 1949.

13. National Blue Star Mothers, letter to Senators Edward Martin and Francis Myers, August 11, 1949, Clark AG Papers.

14. Harold Ickes, "To Tom With Love," *Washington Daily News*, August 11, 1949.

15. "Wallace Urges Rejection of Clark," *Daily Worker*, n.d. [July 1949?].

16. Philip Perlman to Harry S. Truman, August 1, 1949, Clark AG Papers.

17. James V. Bennett to Tom Clark, December 14, 1949, in author's possession.

18. Harold E. Hegstrom to Tom Clark, September 19, 1949, in author's possession.

19. Senate Committee on the Judiciary, *Nomination of Tom C. Clark: Hearings before the Committee on the Judiciary on the Nomination of Tom C. Clark, of Texas, to be an Associate Justice of the Supreme Court of the United States*, 81st Cong., 1st sess., August 10, 1949, 70.

20. Ibid., 243.

21. Ibid., 246.

22. Ibid.

23. Quoted in David Botter, "Senate Panel Green Light Given Clark," *Dallas Morning News*, August 12, 1949.

24. "Tom C. Clark Takes Oath as Justice," *Dallas Morning News*, August 25, 1949.

## CHAPTER 14

1. Gib Crockett, cartoon, *Washington Evening Star*, August 2, 1949.

2. Wiecek, *Birth of the Modern Constitution*, 404.

3. Quoted in Diane Fisher Johnson, "Available Vinson," *Supreme Court Historical Society Quarterly* 24, no. 3 (2003): 8.

4. James E. St. Claire and Linda C. Gugin, *Chief Justice Fred M. Vinson of Kentucky: a Political Biography*, 164.

5. Ibid., 158.

6. Tom Clark, interview by Hess, 53–54.

7. Tom Clark, interview by Ireland, 18–19.

8. Ibid., 13.

9. Ibid., 50–52.

10. Barney Thompson, "Justice Tom Clark Follows Busy Schedule," *Dallas Times Herald*, February 4, 1953.

11. Schwartz, *Super Chief*, 25.

12. Tom Clark, "Reminiscences of an Attorney General Turned Associate Justice," *Houston Law Review* 6, no. 4 (1969): 626.

13. Tom C. Clark, memorandum to the conference, *McLaurin v. Oklahoma* and *Sweatt v. Painter*, April 1950, obtained through the FOIA.

14. Ibid.

15. Wiecek, *Birth of the Modern Constitution*, 692.

16. *Terry v. Adams*, 345 U.S. 461, 484 (1953).

17. C. B. Dutton, "Mr. Justice Tom C. Clark," *Indiana Law Journal* 26 (1951): 173.

18. Ibid., 174.

19. Quoted in Paul Hauser, "Clark Favors Action Locally," *Portland Oregonian*, July 17, 1947.

20. Maeva Marcus, *Truman and the Steel Seizure Case*, 178–180.

21. Ibid., 174.

22. *Youngstown Sheet and Tube v. Sawyer*, 343 U.S. 579, 662 (1952).

23. Clark, "Reminiscences of an Attorney General," 62.

24. Marcus, *Truman and the Steel Case*, 220.

25. Quoted in Frances Howell Rudko, *Truman's Court: A Study in Judicial Restraint*, 104.

26. Tom Clark, interview by Hess, 220–221, 217–218.

27. James E. Knox to the author, November 22, 1994.

28. Quoted in Henry J. Abraham, *Justices and Presidents: A Political History of Appointments to the Supreme Court*, 63.

29. Tom Clark, interview by Hess, 226.

## CHAPTER 15

1. Quoted in W. H. Lawrence, "Truman Removes Tax Chief of the Justice Department," *New York Times*, November 17, 1951; see also *Newsweek*, November 26, 1951, 30.

2. Quoted in "Caudle and McGrath Speak up on Justice Department Scandals," *Newsweek*, September 29, 1952, 52.

3. House Subcommittee of the Committee on Ways and Means, *Internal Revenue Investigation: Hearings before a Subcommittee of the Committee on Ways and Means on Administration of the Internal Revenue Laws*, 82nd Cong., 1st sess., September 10, 1951–January 29, 1952, 4.

4. Ibid., 134.

5. Federal Bureau of Investigation, "Report on Thomas C. Clark and Herbert Augustus Bergson: Misconduct in Office," October 3, 1952, 122.

6. Tom Clark, interview by Jerald L. Hill and William D. Stilley, 35–36.

7. FBI, "Report on Clark and Bergson," 79.

8. Ibid., 2.

9. Ibid., 158.

10. Ibid.

11. Hoover to Ferguson, June 18, 1947, Clark AG Papers.

12. Quoted in "Justice Clark Writes Keating Reasons for not Testifying," *Washington Evening Star*, June 17, 1953.

13. House subcommittee, *Internal Revenue Investigation*, 135.

14. "Anything Sacred about Clark," *New York News*, June 16, 1953.

15. "The Impeachment of Justice Clark," *Washington Times Herald*, editorial, August 22, 1953.

16. House subcommittee of the Committee on the Judiciary, *Investigation of the Department of Justice: Report*, 83rd Cong., 1st sess., 1953, HR Rep. 1079, 3.

17. Quoted in "'Mess' in Justice Blamed on Clark," *Washington Daily News*, July 6, 1954.

18. House subcommittee, *Investigation of the Department of Justice: Report*, 312.

19. Ibid.

20. Graham Morrison, interview by Jerry Hess, Washington, D.C., August 1972.

21. Charles Murphy, interview by Jerry Hess, May 19, 1970.

## CHAPTER 16

1. Caute, *Great Fear*, 146.
2. *Garner v. Los Angeles Board*, 341 U.S. 716 (1951), 718.
3. *Wieman v. Updegraff*, 344 U.S. 183, 189, 191 (1953).
4. Richard Barnes Kennan to Tom Clark, December 18, 1952, in the possession of the author.
5. Schwartz, *Super Chief*, 178.
6. *Slochower v. Board of Education*, 350 U.S. 551, 555–557 (1956).
7. Schwartz, *Super Chief*, 226.
8. Quoted in Kim Isaac Eisler, *A Justice for All: William Brennan, Jr., and the Decisions That Transformed America*, 134.
9. Quoted in ibid., 137–138.
10. Quoted in ibid., 138.
11. William J. Brennan, interview by the author, June 19, 1981.
12. Arthur J. Sabin, *In Calmer Times: The Supreme Court and Red Monday*, 155.
13. Ibid., 159.
14. Tom Clark, handwritten marginalia on his copy of the majority opinion, June 5, 1957.
15. Newspaper headlines quoted in Sabin, *In Calmer Times*, 188–189.
16. Sabin, *In Calmer Times*, 402.
17. Ibid., 196.
18. Ibid., 142.
19. Ellis McKay and Ernest Rubenstein to the author, January 31, 1995.
20. Robert Hamilton to the author, July 14, 1995.
21. Tom Clark, interview by Ireland, 52.
22. Tom Clark, interview by Frantz, 8.

## CHAPTER 17

1. David Halberstam, preface, *The Fifties*, IX–XI.
2. William O. Douglas, *The Court Years, 1939–1975*, 245.
3. Quoted in "Chief Justice Fred M. Vinson dies at 63," *Washington Evening Star*, September 8, 1953.
4. "Homage from Two Presidents," *Life*, October 1953, 57.
5. "Chief Justice Fred M. Vinson," *American Bar Association Journal* 39 (October 1953): 921.
6. Earl Warren, *The Memoirs of Chief Justice Earl Warren*, 316.
7. William H. Clark, speech on July 4, 1925, 26.
8. Schwartz, *Super Chief*, 89.
9. Ibid., 78.
10. Ibid., 98.
11. Ibid., 108.
12. Wiecek, *Birth of the Modern Constitution*, 404.
13. Tom Clark, interview by Ireland, 2.
14. Ibid., 9–11.

15. Tom Clark, interview by Duram, March 26, 1972, 16.

16. Tom Clark, interview by Frantz, 21–22.

17. Kluger, *Simple Justice*, 706.

18. Tom Clark, interview by Duram, 19–20, 22.

19. *Heart of Atlanta Motel v. U.S.*, 379 U.S. 515 (1964).

20. Ibid.

21. Schwartz, *Super Chief*, 554.

22. *Katzenbach v. McClung*, 379 U.S. 802 (1964).

23. Schwartz, *Super Chief*, 555.

24. Ibid., 559.

25. *Cox v. Louisiana*, 379 U.S. 559, 588–589 (1965).

26. *Williams v. Georgia*, 349 U.S. 375, 393 (1955).

27. Tom Clark, interview by Duram, 13.

28. Ibid., 9.

## Chapter 18

1. "Text of Clark's Opinion and Excerpts from Concurrences on 'Miracle,'" *New York Times*, May 27, 1972.

2. *Burstyn v. Wilson*, 343 U.S. 495, 503 (1952).

3. Ibid. at 505–506.

4. Ibid. at 528.

5. Bosley Crowther, "The Miracle Happens," *New York Times*, June 1, 1952.

6. Edward Ennis to Tom Clark, May 27, 1952, Tom C. Clark Papers, Tarlton Law Library, University of Texas, Box D176, Folder 3.

7. Tom Clark to Edward Ennis, May 28, 1952, Tom C. Clark Papers, Tarlton Law Library, University of Texas, Box D176, Folder 3.

8. Ronald F. Pelican to Tom Clark, May 27, 1952, Tom C. Clark Papers, Tarlton Law Library, University of Texas, Box D176, Folder 3.

9. Quoted in Schwartz, *Super Chief*, 618–619.

10. *Jacobellis v. Ohio*, 378 U.S. 184, 200–201 (1964).

11. Schwartz, *Super Chief*, 620.

12. *Memoirs v. Massachusetts*, 383 U.S. 413, 441 (1966).

13. Ibid.

14. Schwartz, *Super Chief*, 620.

15. Charles Reed to the author, October 4, 1994.

16. *Wikipedia, the Free Encyclopedia*, s.v. "*Miller v. California*," http://en.wikipedia.org/w/index.php?title=Miller_v._California&oldid=227683174 (accessed September 8, 2008).

17. William Brennan, interview by the author.

18. Gerald T. Dunne, *Hugo T. Black and the Judicial Revolution*, 370.

19. Both quotations are from Schwartz, *Super Chief*, 441.

20. Ibid., 442.

21. Ibid.

22. Jay Alan Sekulow, *Witnessing Their Faith: Religious Influence on Supreme Court Justices and Their Opinions*, 242.

23. Warren, *The Memoirs of Chief Justice Earl Warren*, 316.

24. Quoted in Schwartz, *Super Chief*, 442–443.

25. Tom Clark, "A Supreme Court Justice Speaks of God," in *This Week Magazine, Dallas Morning News*, December 23, 1962, 4–5.

26. *Abington School District v. Schempp*, 374 U.S. 203, 226 (1963).

27. Ibid. at 225.

28. Schwartz, *Super Chief*, 467.

29. Quoted in Ellis M. West, "Justice Tom Clark and American Church-State Law," *Journal of Presbyterian History* 54, no. 4 (1976): 394.

30. Ibid., 395.

## CHAPTER 19

1. Schwartz, *Super Chief*, 58.

2. Bernard Schwartz, *Decision: How the Supreme Court Decides Cases*, 113.

3. Tom Clark, memorandum (unreleased), "*Patrick E. Irvine v. People of the State of California*," February 1954, in author's possession.

4. *Irvine v. California*, 347 U.S. 128, 138–139 (1954).

5. Schwartz, *Super Chief*, 134.

6. *Mapp v. Ohio*, 367 U.S. 643, 669 (1961).

7. Schwartz, *Super Chief*, 393.

8. John Harlan to Tom Clark, memorandum, May 4, 1961, Tom C. Clark Papers, Tarlton Law Library, University of Texas, Box 115, Folder 6.

9. Tom Clark to John Harlan, memorandum, May 4, 1961, Tom C. Clark Papers, Tarlton Law Library, University of Texas, Box 115, Folder 6.

10. Hugo Black to Tom Clark, memorandum, June 15, 1961, Tom C. Clark Papers, Tarlton Law Library, University of Texas, Box 115, Folder 6.

11. *Mapp v. Ohio*, 367 U.S. 643, 648 (1961).

12. Ibid. at 657, 659, 660.

13. Schwartz, *Super Chief*, 395.

14. Ibid., 391.

15. Quoted in Paul Baier, "Justice Clark, the Voice of the Past, and the Exclusionary Rule," *Texas Law Review* 64, no. 2 (1985): 416.

16. *Berger v. New York*, 388 U.S. 41, 62–63 (1967).

17. Tom Clark, "The Court and Its Critics," *Villanova Law Review* 15 (Spring 1970): 525.

18. Gregory Curtis, "TV On Trial," *Texas Monthly*, July 1995, 5.

19. Quoted in Schwartz, *Super Chief*, 546.

20. Quoted in ibid.

21. Quoted in Curtis, "TV on Trial," 8.

22. Ibid.

23. *Sheppard v. Maxwell*, 384 U.S. 333, 356 (1966).

24. Eisler, *Justice for All*, 195.

25. Schwartz, *Super Chief*, 589.

26. *Miranda v. Arizona*, 348 U.S. 436, 499–500 (1966).

27. Schwartz, *Super Chief*, 593.

28. Quoted in Beeman, "New Deal Justice," 204.

29. *Keyishian v. Board of Regents*, 385 U.S. 589, 628–629 (1967).

30. Eisler, *Justice for All*, 168–169.

31. Ibid., 171.

32. Ibid., 174.

33. Brennan, interview by the author.

34. Eisler, *Justice for All*, 175.

35. *Baker v. Carr*, 369 U.S. 186, 254, 258 (1967).

36. Ibid. at 261–262.

37. Schwartz, *Super Chief*, 410.

38. Ibid., 551.

39. West, "Justice Tom Clark," 400.

40. Douglas, *Court Years*, 162.

41. Charles D. Reed to the author, October 4, 1994.

42. West, "Justice Tom Clark," 389.

43. White, interview by the author.

44. Larry Temple to the author, December 22, 1994.

45. John E. Nolan to the author, October 31, 1994.

46. Robert W. Hamilton to the author, July 14, 1995.

47. Marshall Groce to the author, November 1, 1994.

48. Nolan to the author, October 31, 1994.

49. Reed to the author, October 4, 1994.

50. Tom Clark, interview by Frantz, 37–39.

51. Fred Rowe, telephone conversation with the author, October 1994.

52. Tom Clark, interview by Frantz, 5.

53. A. Timothy Warnock, "Associate Justice Tom C. Clark: Advocate of Judicial Reform" (PhD diss., Univ. of Georgia, 1972), 103.

54. Warren, *Memoirs*, 322.

55. Ibid., 325.

56. John P. Frank, "Justice Tom Clark and Judicial Administration," *Texas Law Review* 46 (November 1967): 54–55.

57. Ibid.

58. Percy D. Williams, "Mr. Justice Clark," *Texas Bar Journal* 30, no. 2 (October 22, 1967): 756.

59. Frank, "Clark and Judicial Administration," 55.

60. Clark, "The Court and Its Critics," 524.

61. Ibid., 525.

62. Tom Clark, "Earl Warren: Dedication to the Chief Justice," *Nebraska Law Review* 48, no. 1 (1968): 13.

63. Henry J. Abraham, *Justices, Presidents, and Senators*, 187.

## CHAPTER 20

1. Telephone conversation between Nicholas Katzenbach and Lyndon Johnson, tape no. WH6609.12, September 24, 1966.

2. Telephone conversation between Abe Fortas and Lyndon Johnson, tape no. WH6609.11, August 22, 1966, 8:30 a.m.

3. Telephone conversation between Ramsey Clark and Lyndon Johnson, tape no. K67.01, January 1, 1967, 8:22 p.m.

4. Telephone conversation between Katzenbach and Johnson, tape no. WH6609.12.

5. Quoted in David Alistair Yalof, *Pursuit of Justices*, 88.

6. Quoted in ibid.

7. Quoted in ibid.

8. Tom Clark, interview by Frantz, 28–29.

9. Quoted in "Justice Tom Clark Will Quit Court," *New York Times*, March 1, 1967.

10. "Justice Clark Gives Son Oath," *Dallas Times Herald*, March 11, 1967.

11. Quoted in Martin Weil, "Former Supreme Court Justice Clark Dies at 77," *Washington Post*, June 14, 1977.

12. Juan Williams, *Thurgood Marshall: American Revolutionary*, 330.

13. Weil, "Justice Clark Dies."

14. *Journal of the Supreme Court of the United States*, October Term, 1966, 429.

15. Ibid., 429–430.

## CHAPTER 21

1. Tom C. Clark, "Report of Mr. Justice Clark as American Specialist," October 2, 1967, 4.

2. Ibid., 6.

3. Ibid., 11.

4. Katie Louchheim, acting assistant secretary, Department of State, memorandum, "Performance of Justice Tom C. Clark as an American Specialist," to Harry C. McPherson, Jr., special assistant to the president, November 1967.

## CHAPTER 22

1. Warnock, "Associate Justice Tom C. Clark," 100.

2. Clark, "Office of the Attorney General," 151.

3. Percy Williams, "Mr. Justice Clark," 756.

4. Frank, "Tom Clark and Judicial Administration," 13.

5. Quoted in ibid., 11.

6. Ibid., 12.

7. Louis H. Burke, "Recent Milestones for Effective Justice," address delivered before the Federal Bar Association, San Francisco, April 25, 1968, 7.

8. Quoted in Frank, "Tom Clark and Judicial Administration," 44.

9. Ibid., 14.

10. Maurice Rosenberg, "Judging Goes to College," *American Bar Association Journal* 52, no. 4 (April 1966): 342–343.

11. Frank, "Tom Clark and Judicial Administration," 37.

12. Quoted in ibid., 39.

13. Quoted in ibid.

14. Quoted in ibid.

15. Quoted in ibid., 39–40.

16. Tom Clark, interview by Frantz, 5–6.

17. Frank, "Tom Clark and Judicial Administration," 54n120.

18. Quoted in ibid., 54.

19. Quoted in James A. Gazell, "Justice Tom C. Clark as Judicial Reformer," *Houston Law Review* 15 (1978): 326.

20. Tom C. Clark, "The New Federal Judicial Center," *American Bar Association Journal* 54 (August 1968): 743.

21. Quoted in Warnock, "Associate Justice Tom C. Clark," 271–272.

22. Tom C. Clark, "The Federal Judicial Center," *Judicature* 53, no. 3 (October 1969).

23. Quoted in ibid., 100.

24. Ibid., 100–101.

25. Ibid., 103.

26. Russell Wheeler, "Empirical Research and the Politics of Judicial Administration: Creating the Federal Judicial Center," *Law and Contemporary Problems* 51 (1988): 43.

27. John A. Sutro, "Can the Courts Find Improvement through Science?" address at the dedication of the Federal Judicial Center, November 1, 1968, 18.

28. Clark, "Federal Judicial Center," 103.

29. Quoted in Warnock, "Associate Justice Tom C. Clark," 277–278.

30. Quoted in William V. Redmann, "American Judges on Contemporary Society," *Court Review* 23, no. 1 (Winter 1986): 7.

31. Ibid.

32. Clark, "New Federal Judicial Center," 746.

## Chapter 23

1. Roger M. Grace, "Said to Have Done More Than Any to Improve Judicial System—Tom C. Clark," *Los Angeles Daily Journal*, November 6, 1973.

2. Tom Hall, "Retired Justice Clark Becomes a Trial Judge," *San Francisco Examiner*, July 14, 1970.

3. Quoted in ibid.

4. Glen Elsasser, "Ex-Justice Clark Runs a Firm Court, Rides Herd on Lawyers," *Chicago Tribune*, January 20, 1974.

5. Ibid.

6. Tom Clark, "Judicial Reform in Connecticut," *Connecticut Law Review* 5, no. 1 (1972): 6.

7. Quoted in David Nix, "Outspoken Clark Goads Lawyers," *Tucson Star*, February 21, 1973.

8. "Ex-Justice Clark Urges Lawyers to Help Courts," *Dallas Morning News*, n.d. [September 1973?].

9. Quoted in Nix, "Outspoken Clark Goads Lawyers."

10. Tom Clark, "The Continuing Challenge of Advocacy," *Washburn Law Journal* 16 (1977): 243–244.

11. Quoted in Vincent Johnson, "Justice Tom Clark's Legacy in the Field of Legal Ethics," *Journal of the Legal Profession* 29 (2005): 55.

12. Quoted in Ibid., 47.

13. Ibid., 52n68.

14. Ibid., 6.

15. Ibid., 55–57.

16. Ibid., 40–41.

17. Tom Clark, "Changing Times," *Hofstra Law Review* 1 (Spring 1973): 5.

18. Tom Clark, "Teaching Professional Ethics," 260.

19. Quoted in Vincent Johnson, "Tom Clark's Legacy," 65.

20. Tom Clark, "Teaching Professional Ethics," 259.

21. Vincent Johnson, "Tom Clark's Legacy," 42.

22. Ibid., 57.

23. Gazell, "Tom Clark as Judicial Reformer," 321.

24. "Attorneys Thwart Justice, Contends Thomas C. Clark," *The Dickensonian*, newspa-

per of Dickenson College, Carlisle, Pennsylvania, February 15, 1974.

25. Tom Clark, "Drugs and the Law," *Loyola Law Review* 18, no. 2: 247.

26. "Attorneys Thwart Justice."

## CHAPTER 25

1. Ramsey Clark, address at the Tom C. Clark Memorial Service, Washington, D.C., National Presbyterian Church, June 12, 1977.

2. Alice O'Donnell, "Mr. Justice Clark: Federal Lawyer, Federal Judge," *Federal Bar News*, August–September 1977, 222–223.

3. Chief Justice Warren E. Burger, address at the Tom C. Clark Memorial Service, National Presbyterian Church, Washington, D.C. June 12, 1977.

4. "Justice Tom Clark Speaks at NOVA Law School Graduation," *Miami Herald*, May 22, 1977.

5. Ed Newman, radio broadcast, "Close-up," June 13, 1977.

6. *Docket Sheet of the Supreme Court of the United States* 14, no. 4 (July–September 1977), 8.

7. Ibid.

8. Ibid.

9. Ibid.

10. Ibid.

11. Ibid.

12. Ibid.

13. O'Donnell, "Mr. Justice Clark," 223.

## EPILOG UE

1. Tom Clark, "Religion, Morality, and Abortion: A Constitutional Appraisal," *Loyola University Law Review* 2 (April 1969): 1.

2. Ibid., 4.

3. Ibid., 10.

4. Ibid., 8.

5. Ibid.

6. Tom Clark, "Gideon Revisited," *Arizona Law Review* 15 (1973): 343.

7. Docket Sheet of the Supreme Court of the United States 14, no. 4: 8.

# Bibliography

Abraham, Henry J. *Justices and Presidents: A Political History of Appointments to the Supreme Court.* New York: Oxford Univ. Press, 1974.

————. *Justices, Presidents, and Senators.* Lanham, Md.: Rowman and Littlefield, 1999.

Acheson, Alex. "High Honors Accorded Here to Native Son." *Dallas Times Herald*, October 11, 1945.

Alexander, Jack. "The President's New Lawyer." *Saturday Evening Post*, September 20, 1945.

*American Bar Association Journal.* "Chief Justice Fred M. Vinson." Vol. 39 (October 1953): 901–921.

American Civil Liberties Union. Statement on Loyalty Tests for Federal Employment. Adopted by the board of directors, April 7, 1947.

Armor, John, and Peter Wright. *Manzanar.* New York: Times Books, 1988.

"Attorneys Thwart Justice, Contends Thomas C. Clark." *The Dickensonian*, newspaper of Dickenson College, Carlisle, Pennsylvania, February 15, 1974.

Baier, Paul R. "Justice Clark, the Voice of the Past, and the Exclusionary Rule." *Texas Law Review* 64, no. 2 (1985): 415–417.

Baskin, Robert E. "Justice Tom Clark Retires with Praise From Everywhere." *Dallas Morning News*, March 5, 1967.

Beeman, Mary Purser. "New Deal Justice: Tom Clark and the Warren Court, 1953–1967." PhD diss., Univ. of Texas at Austin, 1993.

Biddle, Francis. *In Brief Authority.* Garden City, N.Y.: Doubleday, 1962.

Bontecou, Eleanor. *The Federal Loyalty-Security Program.* Ithaca, N.Y.: Cornell Univ. Press, 1953.

Botter, David. "Clark Affirmed for High Court." *Dallas Morning News*, August 18, 1949.

————. "Clark Angrily Denies He Sought Missouri Vote Fraud Whitewash." *Dallas Morning News*, June 6, 1947.

————. "FBI Chief Denies Clark Nipped Quiz." *Dallas Morning News*, June 20, 1947.

————. "Senate Panel Green Light Given Clark." *Dallas Morning News*, August 12, 1949.

Brandt, Raymond P. "New Attorney General Is Question Mark despite Eight Years in Capital." *St. Louis Post-Dispatch,* June 3, 1945.

Burke, Louis H. "Recent Milestones for Effective Justice." Address Prepared for delivery before the Federal Bar Association, San Francisco, April 25, 1968.

Caute, David. *The Great Fear: The Anti-Communist Purge under Truman and Eisenhower.* New York: Simon & Schuster, 1978.

*Charlotte (NC) News.* "We're Still Waiting to Hear Clark." June 11, 1953.

Childs, William R. *The Texas Railroad Commission.* College Station: Texas A&M Univ. Press, 2005.

Churman, Frank. *The Bamboo People: The Law and Japanese-Americans.* Preface by Tom Clark. Del Mar, Calif.: Publisher's Inc, 1976.

Churchill, Elizabeth. "Town Talk." *Washington Post,* May 20, 1945.

Clark, Tom. Address delivered over CBS Radio, Washington, D.C., October 9, 1946.

————. Address prepared for delivery at George Washington's Birthday Patriotic Rally, under the auspices of the Civilian Military Manpower Committee. Fourteenth Regiment Armory, Brooklyn, New York, February 21, 1949.

————. Address prepared for delivery before the Fifty-ninth Karnea Assembly, Delta Tau Delta, August 21, 1948.

————. Address prepared for delivery before the Jewish Labor Committee Convention. President Hotel, Atlantic City, N.J., February 25, 1949.

————. Address prepared for delivery before the Jewish War Veterans of the United States, Kiamesha Lake, Monticello, New York, September 18, 1948.

————. Address prepared for delivery before the Women's National Democratic Club, Washington, D.C., October 1944.

————. "Administrative Law." *Nebraska Law Review* 25 (March 1946): 79–84.

————. "Changing Times." *Hofstra Law Review* 1 (Spring 1973): 1–8.

————. "Citizens, Courts, and the Effective Administration of Justice." *Journal of the American Judicature Society* 49, no. 3: 6–13.

————. "Civil Rights: The Boundless Responsibility of Lawyer." *American Bar Association Journal* 32 (August 1946): 453–457.

————. "The Continuing Challenge of Advocacy." *Washburn Law Journal* 16 (1977): 243–249.

————. "The Court and Its Critics." *Villanova Law Review* 15 (Spring 1970): 521–526.

————. "Drugs and the Law." *Loyola Law Review* 18, no. 2: 243–247.

————. "Earl Warren: Dedication to the Chief Justice." *Nebraska Law Review* 48, no. 1 (1968): 6–13.

————. "Fair Play and Decency." *San Diego Law Review* 3 (1966): 1–6.

————. "The Federal Judicial Center." *Judicature* 53, no. 3 (October 1969): 99–103.

————. "Gideon Revisited." *Arizona Law Review* 15 (1973): 343–353.

————. "Judicial Reform in Connecticut." *Connecticut Law Review* 5, no. 1 (1972): 2–10.

————. "Justice in the Reconstruction Period." Address given to the North Carolina State Bar, Raleigh, North Carolina, October 25, 1946.

————. "The Need for Judicial Reform." *Washington Law Review* 48 (1973: 806–810.

————. "The New Federal Judicial Center." *American Bar Association Journal* 54: 743–746.

————. "The Office of the Attorney General." *Tennessee Law Review* 19 (Fall 1946): 150–159.

————. "Parting the Curtain on Paytrioteers." *Everybody's Weekly, Philadelphia Inquirer*, February 13, 1944.

————. "Progress of Project Effective Justice: A Report of the Joint Committee." *Journal of the American Judicature Society* 47, no. 3 (August 1963): 88–92.

————. "Religion, Morality, and Abortion: A Constitutional Appraisal." *Loyola University Law Review* 2 (April 1969): 1–11.

————. "Reminiscences of an Attorney General Turned Associate Justice." *Houston Law Review* 6, no. 4 (1969): 623–629.

————. "Report of Mr. Justice Clark as American Specialist." October 2, 1967.

————. Statement and Analysis by the Attorney General concerning the Proposed Civil Rights Act of 1949 (HR 4682, S 1725).

————. "A Supreme Court Justice Speaks of God." In *This Week Magazine, Dallas Morning News*, December 23, 1962.

————. "Teaching Professional Ethics." *San Diego Law Review* 12 (1975): 249–260.

————. "U.T. Memories." *Texas Law School Forum* 8, no. 23 (December 23, 1967): 1–8.

————. "War Frauds Unit of the Criminal Division." *Federal Bar Association Journal* 5 (May 1944): 135–138.

Clark, Tom, and Philip B. Perlman. *Prejudice and Property: An Historic Brief against Racial Covenants*. New York: Greenwood Press, 1969.

Clark, William H. "Brilliant Address of Great Legal and Historical Value." Delivered at the homecoming and dedication of the new courthouse of Brandon, Mississippi, July 4, 1925.

Clifford, Clark. *Counsel to the President*. New York: Random House, 1991.

Connally, Tom. *My Name is Tom Connally*. New York: Crowell, 1954.

Conrat, Maisie, and Richard Conrat. *Executive Order 9066: The Internment of 110,000 Japanese Americans*. Epilogue by Tom C. Clark. Los Angeles: California Historical Society, 1972.

Crews, Watson, Jr. "Eunice and the Kennedy Tradition." *American Weekly*, May 23, 1947, 11.

Crowther, Bosley. "The Miracle Happens." *New York Times*, June 1, 1952.

Curtis, Gregory. "TV on Trial." *Texas Monthly*, July 1995, 5–8.

Cushman, Clare, and Melvin I. Urofsky, eds. *Black, White, and Brown: The Landmark School Desegregation Case in Retrospect*. Washington, D.C.: Supreme Court Historical Society, 1994.

*Daily Worker.* "Wallace Urges Rejection of Clark," n.d. [July 1949?].

*Dallas Law Journal.* "William H. Clark." Vol. 3, no. 3 (1932): 19.

*Dallas Morning News.* Advertisement for Bill McCraw campaign. May 31, 1934.

———. "Clark Charges Laxity by GOP in Ousting Reds." September 25, 1948.

———. "Clark Flayed by Lawyers." July 8, 1946.

———. "Clark of Dallas Takes Oath as Attorney General of U.S." July 1, 1945.

———. "Dallas Man Urged as U.S. Assistant Attorney General." January 24, 1937.

———. "Ex-Justice Clark Urges Lawyers to Help Courts." N.d. [September 1973?].

———. "Heart attack kills Bill McCraw." November 9, 1955.

———. "Oh No!" Editorial. August 2, 1949.

———. "Texas Subcommittee Failed to Get Bank Accounts." February 24, 1938.

———. "Tom Clark Takes Oath as Justice." August 25, 1949.

*Dallas Times Herald.* "Justice Clark Gives Son Oath." March 11, 1967.

Daniels, Roger. *Prisoners without Trial: Japanese Americans in World War II.* New York: Hill & Wang, 1993.

Davis, Ellis A., and Edwin H. Grobe, eds. *The New Encyclopedia of Texas.* 4 vols. Dallas: Texas Development Bureau, n.d.

*Docket Sheet of the Supreme Court of the United States* 14, no. 4 (July–September 1977): 8.

Douglas, William O. *The Court Years, 1939–1975.* New York, Random House, 1980.

Dubofsky, Melvyn, and Warren Van Tine. *John L. Lewis: A Biography.* New York: Times Books, 1977.

Duckworth, Allen. "Tom Clark Returns Home, Speaks for the American Way." *Dallas Morning News,* October 11, 1945.

———. "Tom Clark's Name Stricken Deliberately as Delegate." *Dallas Morning News,* May 27, 1948.

Dunar, Andrew J. *The Truman Scandals and the Politics of Morality.* Columbia: Univ. of Missouri Press, 1984.

Duncan, Dawson. "Bank Account Here 'Personal Matter,' Clark Tells Probers." *Dallas Morning News,* December 8, 1936.

———. "Land Hearing in Recess to Await McCraw." *Dallas Morning News,* February 24, 1938.

Dunne, Gerald T. *Hugo T. Black and the Judicial Revolution.* New York: Simon & Schuster, 1977.

Dutton, C. B. "Mr. Justice Tom C. Clark." *Indiana Law Journal* 26 (1951): 169–184.

Eisler, Kim Isaac. *A Justice for All: William J. Brennan, Jr. and the Decisions that Transformed America.* New York: Simon & Schuster, 1993.

Eliff, John T. *The United States Department of Justice and Individual Rights, 1937–1962.* New York: Garland, 1987.

Elsasser, Glen. "Ex-Justice Clark Runs Firm Court, Rides Herd on Lawyers." *Chicago Tribune*, January 20, 1974.

Enstam, Elizabeth York. *Women and the Creation of Urban Life: Dallas, Texas, 1843–1920.* College Station: Texas A&M Univ. Press, 1998.

Fagan, Dick. "U.S. Attorney General 'Out' as Running Mate." *Oregon Journal*, July 17, 1948.

Federal Bureau of Investigation. Files on Tom C. Clark, November 18, 1936–June 1, 1945. Obtained through the Freedom of Information Act.

———. "Report on Thomas C. Clark and Herbert Augustus Bergson: Misconduct in Office." October 3, 1952. Obtained through the FOIA.

Ferrell, Robert H. *Harry S. Truman: A Life.* Columbia: Univ. of Missouri Press, 1994.

Finley, Joseph E. *The Corrupt Kingdom: The Rise and Fall of the United Mine Workers.* New York: Simon & Schuster, 1972.

Fleeson, Doris. "Clark Keeping Pledge of No 'Witch Hunts.'" *New York Daily News*, April 19, 1947.

Franck, Michael. "New Life for Lawyer Discipline: The Disciplinary Report of the Clark Committee." *Judicature* 54, no. 9 (April 1971): 384–369.

Frank, John P. "Justice Tom Clark and Judicial Administration." *Texas Law Review* 46, no. 1 (November 1967): 5–56.

———. *The Warren Court.* New York: MacMillan, 1964.

Freeland, Richard. *The Truman Doctrine and the Origins of McCarthyism: Domestic Politics, Internal Security, and Foreign Policy, 1946–1948.* New York: Schocken, 1974.

Fried, Richard M. *Nightmare in Red: The McCarthy Era in Perspective.* New York: Oxford Univ. Press, 1990.

Gardner, Michael R. *Harry Truman and Civil Rights: Moral Courage and Political Risks.* Carbondale: Southern Illinois Univ. Press, 2002.

Gazell, James A. "Justice Tom C. Clark as Judicial Reformer." *Houston Law Review* 15: 307–329.

Gentry, Curt. *J. Edgar Hoover: The Man and the Secrets.* New York: Norton, 1991.

Grace, Roger M. "Said to Have Done More Than Any Other to Improve Judicial System—Tom C. Clark." *Los Angeles Daily Journal*, November 6, 1973.

Greene, A. C. *Dallas, the Deciding Years: A Historical Portrait.* Dallas: Encino Press, 1973.

Grodzins, Morton. *Americans Betrayed: Politics and the Japanese Evacuation.* Chicago: Univ. of Chicago Press, 1949.

Halberstam, David. *The Fifties.* New York: Villard, 1993.

Hall, Tom. "Retired Justice Clark Becomes a Trial Judge." *San Francisco Examiner*, July 14, 1970.

Hardeman, D. B., and Donald C. Bacon. *Rayburn: A Biography.* Austin: Texas Monthly Press, 1987.

Harter, Harry. *East Texas Oil Parade.* San Antonio: Naylor, 1934.

Hauser, Paul, "Clark Favors Action Locally." *Portland Oregonian*, July 17, 1947.

Hornaday, Walter. "U.S. Preparing to Sue Texas for Title to Its Rich Tidelands," *Dallas Morning News*, March 3, 1948.

Hosokawa, Bill. *JACL in Quest of Justice*. New York: Morrow, 1982.

Howard, James. *Big D Is for Dallas: Chapters in the Twentieth-Century History of Dallas*. Austin: Univ. Cooperative Society, 1957.

Hurt, Harry, III. "The Dad Joiner Deal." In *Texas Rich: The Hunt Dynasty from the Early Oil Days to the Silver Crash*. New York: Norton, 1981.

Huston, Luther A. "Clark Is Criticized for His Handling of Justice Agency." *New York Times*, July 7, 1954.

———. *The Department of Justice*. New York: Praeger, 1967.

Ickes. Harold L. "Tom Clark Should Say 'No, Thanks.'" *New Republic*. August 24, 1949, 11.

———. "To Tom With Love." *Washington Daily News*, August 11, 1949.

———. "A Wash-Out Attorney General." Editorial, *San Diego Union-Tribune*, October 2, 1948.

Irons, Peter. *Justice at War: The Story of the Japanese-American Internment Cases*. Oxford: Oxford Univ. Press, 1983.

Johnson, Diane Fisher. "Available Vinson." *Supreme Court Historical Society Quarterly* 24, no. 3 (2003): 8–9.

Johnson, Vincent R. "Justice Tom Clark's Legacy in the Field of Legal Ethics." *Journal of the Legal Profession* 29 (2005): 33–70.

Klarman, Michael J. "It Could Have Gone the Other Way." *Nation*, May 3, 2004, 24–28.

———. "Why *Brown v. Board* Was a Hard Case." *Judges Journal* 43, no. 2 (2004): 7–9.

Klehr, Harvey, and Ronald Radosh. *The Amerasia Spy Case: Prelude to McCarthyism*. Chapel Hill: Univ. of North Carolina Press, 1996.

Kluger, Richard. *Simple Justice: The History of "Brown v. Board of Education" and Black America's Struggle for Equality*. New York: Vintage, 1975.

Krock, Arthur. "In the Nation." *New York Times*, August 2, 1949; December 28, 1951.

Landrum, Lynn. "Thinking Out Loud." *Dallas Morning News*, June 30, 1949.

Larkin, Francis J. "What Judges Need to Learn." *Judges Journal* 27, no. 4 (Fall 1988): 2–5.

Lawrence, W. H. "Truman Removes Tax Chief of the Justice Department." *New York Times*, November 17, 1951.

*Life*. "Freedom Train." September 29, 1947, 49–50.

———. "Homage from Two Presidents." October 1953.

Lindsley, Philip. *A History of Greater Dallas and Vicinity*. Vol. II. Chicago: Lewis, 1909.

*Los Angeles Evening Herald Express*. "Able Tom Clark Named as Head of the War Frauds Bureau." May 19 1942.

———. Editorial. April 7, 1942.

———. "Japanese Problem on the Pacific Coast." Editorial. April 7, 1942.

*Los Angeles Times.* "Dies Committee 'Tentatively' Urges Removal of Japanese." February 9, 1942.

———. "More Alien Areas Closed." February 2, 1942.

MacKenzie, John G. "Justice Clark: Portrait of a Man." *Washington Post.* [In author's personal scrapbook, no date]

MacLean, Nancy. *Behind the Mask of Chivalry: The Making of the Second Ku Klux Klan.* New York: Oxford Univ. Press, 1994.

Marcus, Maeva. *Truman and the Steel Seizure Case.* New York: Columbia Univ. Press, 1977.

McCraw, William. *Professional Politicians.* Washington, D.C.: Imperial Press, 1949.

McCullough, David. *Truman.* New York: Simon & Schuster, 1992.

McIntosh, India. "10,000 Stand in Line to Visit Freedom Train." *New York Herald Tribune,* September 26, 1947.

McLemore, Henry. "The Lighter Side." *Los Angeles Times,* February 3, 1942; February 7, 1942.

McNeil, Marshall. "Tom Clark Won Approval of Senators by Frankness." *Fort Worth Press,* June 15, 1945.

*Miami Herald.* "Justice Tom Clark Speaks at NOVA Law School Graduation." May 22, 1977.

Miller, Elton. "Clark Announces U.S. Attorneys Must Quit Private Law Practices." *Dallas Morning News,* October 14, 1945.

Moncado, Hilario. "Know Your Attorney General." *Moncadian Filipino Federation of America,* Summer 1949.

*Nation.* "*Brown* at 50." May 3, 2004.

National Conference of Metropolitan Courts. "Tom C. Clark, 1899–1977: A Memorial Tribute to its Distinguished Founder," n.d.

*National Geographic.* "Freedom Train Tours America." October 1949, 529–542.

*New Orleans Item.* "205 True Bills Returned by Scandal Juries over Louisiana since June." October 29, 1939.

———. "42 Reported Ready to Plead Guilty in Indictments on High Building Costs." January 5, 1940.

*New Orleans Times-Picayune.* "Lumber Bodies Fined $12,000 in Anti-Trust Case." January 22, 1940.

———. "Thousands Arrive for Sugar Bowl." January 1, 1940.

*Newsweek.* "Calm Tom." June 12, 1944.

———. "Caudle and McGrath Speak up on Justice Department Scandals." September 29, 1952.

———. "Dupont on the Carpet." July 11, 1949, 19–20.

*New York Herald Tribune.* "Clark Says Republicans Distort Communism Issue." October 10, 1946.

———. "Conscientious Objection Demonstrators Clash with Police near Freedom Train." September 26, 1947.

*New York Journal-American.* "Freedom Train and the Commies," September 26, 1947.

*New York News.* "Anything Sacred about Clark?" June 16, 1953.

*New York Times.* "Barsky, 15 Others Are Found Guilty." June 28 1947.

———. "Clark Ousts Rogge for Speech Linking Americans With Nazis." October 26, 1946.

———. "Georgia Mob of 20 Men Massacres 2 Negroes, Wives; One was Ex-GI." July 27, 1947.

———. "Justice Tom Clark Will Quit Court." March 1, 1967.

———. "Political Aim Seen in Freedom Train." June 3, 1947.

———. "President's Order On Loyalty Hailed." March 23, 1947.

———. "Religious Center at Fair Proposed." March 4, 1937.

———. "Testimony Closes at Spy Trial Here." February 14, 1945.

———. "Text of Clark's Opinion and Excerpts from Concurrences on 'Miracle.'" May 27, 1972.

———. "Truman Commutes to Life Terms Death Sentences of Two Spies." June 24, 1945.

———. "Truman Orders Lynchers Found; Voices Horror at Georgia Crime." July 31, 1947.

*New York World Telegram.* "Probers Hit Clark, Caudle for Weak Enforcing Job." July 6, 1954.

Nix, David. "Outspoken Clark Goads Lawyers." *Tucson Star*, February 21, 1973.

Norton, Robert L. "Tom Clark in Rare Crusade." *Boston Post*, February 17, 1946.

O'Connor, Richard. "Dad Joiner Blows the Roof off Texas." In *The Oil Barons: Men of Greed and Grandeur.* Boston: Little, Brown, 1971.

O'Donnell, Alice. "Mr. Justice Clark: Federal Lawyer, Federal Judge." *Federal Bar News*, August–September 1977: 221–223.

———. "Tom Clark's Unique Vision." *Judges Journal* 27, no. 4 (Fall 1988): 6–8.

*Oregon Journal.* "Ideology Riddance Foreseen for U.S." July 17, 1947.

Payne, Darwin. *Dallas: An Illustrated History.* Woodland Hills, Calif.: Windsor, 1982.

*People's World.* "Truman Urged to Remove Clark." July 9, 1946.

Peppers, Todd C. *Courtiers of the Marble Palace.* Stanford, Calif.: Stanford Univ. Press, 2006.

*Personal Justice Denied: Report of the Commission on Wartime Relocation and Internment of Civilians.* Washington, D.C.: Government Printing Office, 1982.

*Philadelphia Inquirer.* "Why Not Tom Clark for V. President?" Editorial, July 13, 1948.

Powe, Lucas A., Jr. *The Warren Court and American Politics.* Cambridge, Mass.: Harvard Univ. Press, 2000.

Powers, Richard Gid. *Secrecy and Power: The Life of J. Edgar Hoover.* New York: Free Press, 1987.

President's Committee on Civil Rights. *To Secure These Rights: The Report of the President's Committee on Civil Rights.* Washington, D.C.: Government Printing Office, 1947.

Redmann, William V. "American Judges in Contemporary Society." *Court Review* 23, no. 1 (Winter 1986): 7–10.

Richardson, T. C. *East Texas: Its History and Its Makers.* 4 vols. New York: Lewis Historical, 1940.

Rogers, John William. *The Lusty Texans of Dallas.* New York: Dutton, 1960.

Rogge, O. John. *The Official German Report: Nazi Penetration, 1924–1942; Pan-Arabism, 1939–Today.* New York: Yoseloff, 1961.

Rosenberg, Maurice. "Judging Goes to College." *American Bar Association Journal* 52, no. 4: 342–345.

Rudko, Frances Howell. *Truman's Court: A Study in Judicial Restraint.* New York, Greenwood, 1977.

Sabin, Arthur J. *In Calmer Times: The Supreme Court and Red Monday.* Philadelphia: Univ. of Pennsylvania Press, 1999.

*San Antonio Evening News.* "Attorney General Clark on the 'Pay-off of Law Violations,'" January 3, 1946.

Schwartz, Bernard. *Decision: How the Supreme Court Decides Cases.* New York: Oxford Univ. Press, 1996.

———. *Super Chief: Earl Warren and His Supreme Court; A Judicial Biography.* New York: New York Univ. Press, 1983.

*Scranton (PA) Times.* "1600 County Democrats Hear Clark Flay Congress." October 26, 1948.

Sekulow, Jay Alan. *Witnessing Their Faith: Religious Influence on Supreme Court Justices and Their Opinions.* Lanham, Md.: Rowman and Littlefield, 2006.

Smith, Page. *Democracy on Trial: The American Evacuation and Relocation in World War II.* New York: Simon & Schuster, 1995.

Stark, Louis. "Lewis Put Himself Above U.S., Clark Tells High Court." *New York Times,* January 15, 1947.

St. Claire, James E., and Linda C. Gugin. *Chief Justice Fred M. Vinson of Kentucky: A Political Biography.* Lexington: Univ. of Kentucky Press, 2002.

Stone, I. F., *The Haunted Fifties, 1953–1963.* Boston: Little, Brown, 1963.

Sutro, John A. "Can the Courts Find Improvement through Science?" Address at the dedication of the Federal Judicial Center, November 1, 1968.

Tanenhaus, Sam. *Whittaker Chambers.* New York: Random House, 1997.

*Texas Law Forum.* "A Tribute to Mr. Justice Clark." Vol. 8, no. 23 (December 12, 1967): 1–8.

Theoharis, Athan G., ed. *Beyond the Hiss Case: The FBI, Congress, and the Cold War.* Philadelphia: Temple Univ. Press, 1982.

———. *Seeds of Repression: Harry S. Truman and the Origins of McCarthyism.* Chicago: Quadrangle, 1971.

———. *Spying on Americans: Political Surveillance from Hoover to the Huston Plan.* Philadelphia: Temple Univ. Press, 1978.

Thompson, Barney. "Justice Tom Clark Follows Busy Schedule." *Dallas Times Herald,* February 4, 1953.

Truman, Harry S. Inaugural Address. January 20, 1949.

———. *Memoirs: Year of Decisions.* Garden City, N.Y.: Doubleday, 1955.

Trussell, C. P. "Woman Links Spies to U.S. War Offices and White House." *New York Times,* July 31, 1948.

U.S. Congress. House. Committee on Un-American Activities. Statement by Tom Clark, Attorney General of the United States, February 5, 1948.

———. Select Committee Investigating National Defense Migration. *Japanese Evacuation from the West Coast.* 77th Cong., 2nd sess., March 19, 1942.

———. Subcommittee of the Committee on the Judiciary. *Investigation of the Department of Justice: Hearings.* 82nd Cong., 2nd sess., March 26, 1952–June 27, 1952.

———. Subcommittee of the Committee on the Judiciary. *Investigation of the Department of Justice: Report to the Committee on the Judiciary by the Subcommittee to Investigate the Department of Justice pursuant to H. Res. 50.* 83rd Cong., 1st sess., 1953, HR Rep. 1079.

———. Subcommittee of the Committee on Ways and Means. *Internal Revenue Investigation: Hearings before a Subcommittee of the Committee on Ways and Means on Administration of the Internal Revenue Laws.* 82nd Cong., 1st sess., September 10, 1951–January 29, 1952.

U.S. Congress. Senate. Committee on the Judiciary. *Nomination of Tom C. Clark: Hearings before the Committee on the Judiciary on the Nomination of Tom C. Clark, of Texas, to be an Associate Justice of the Supreme Court of the United States.* 81st Cong., 1st sess., August 9–11, 1949.

U.S. Department of Justice. "State of the Department of Justice, 1945–1949." June 30, 1949.

*U.S. News & World Report,* "Chief Justice of a Court under Fire." September 12, 1958, 38–40.

Walsh, Robert K. "Senate Unit Expected to Back Clark after Hearing Critics Today." *Washington Evening Star,* August 10, 1949.

Ward, Artemus, and David L. Weiden. *Sorcerers' Apprentices: 100 Years of Law Clerks at the United States Supreme Court.* New York: New York Univ. Press, 2006.

Warnock, A. Timothy. "Associate Justice Tom C. Clark: Advocate of Judicial Reform." PhD diss., Univ. of Georgia, 1972.

Warren, Earl. *The Memoirs of Chief Justice Earl Warren.* Garden City, N.Y.: Doubleday, 1977.

*Washington Daily News.* "'Mess' in Justice Blamed on Clark." July 6, 1954.

*Washington Evening Star.* "Chief Justice Fred M. Vinson Dies at 63." September 8, 1953.

———. "Clark Charges GOP with Making Capital of Communist Issue." October 10, 1946.

———. "Foes of Jefferson Memorial." March 22, 1937.

———. "Justice Clark Writes Keating Reasons for Not Testifying." June 17, 1953.

*Washington Post.* "Clark's Speech Denounced by National Lawyer's Guild." July 8, 1946.

———. "61% of Texans Support Court Plan." March 14, 1937.

*Washington Times Herald.* "The Impeachment of Mr. Justice Clark." Editorial. August 22, 1953.

———. "Nightmare." Editorial. July 19, 1949.

Watson, Bruce. "Crackdown!" *Smithsonian* 32 (February 2002): 51–53.

Weglyn, Michi. *Years of Infamy: The Untold Story of America's Concentration Camps.* New York: Morrow, 1976.

Weil, Martin. "Former Supreme Court Justice Clark Dies at 77." *Washington Post,* June 14, 1977.

Weschler, James A. "The Story behind Ouster of Rogge." *New York Post,* October 28, 1946.

West, Ellis M. "Justice Tom Clark and American Church-State Law." *Journal of Presbyterian History* 54, no. 4 (1976): 387–404.

Wheeler, Russell. "Empirical Research and the Politics of Judicial Administration: Creating the Federal Judicial Center." *Law and Contemporary Problems* 51 (1988): 31–53.

Wiecek, William. *The Birth of the Modern Constitution: The United States Supreme Court, 1941–1953.* New York: Cambridge Univ. Press, 2006.

Williams, Juan. *Thurgood Marshall: American Revolutionary.* New York: Times Books, 1998.

Williams, Percy D. "Mr. Justice Clark." *Texas Bar Journal* 30, no. 8 (October 22, 1967): 755–756.

*Wilmington Morning News.* "Clark Discusses Anti-Red Drive." March 20, 1948.

Wood, Lewis. "Freedom Train to Start Sept. 17." *New York Times,* May 23, 1947.

———. "Jurists and Lawyers Back Clark; Confirmation by Senate Is Seen." *New York Times,* August 10, 1949.

Writers Program of the Works Project Administration. *Texas: A Guide to the Lone Star State.* American Guide Series. New York: Hastings House, 1940.

———. *WPA Dallas Guide and History.* Edited by Maxine Holmes and Gerald D. Saxon. Denton: Univ. of North Texas Press, 1992 [written in 1940 but not published until 1992].

Yalof, David Alistair. *Pursuit of Justices: Presidential Politics and the Selection of Supreme Court Nominees.* Chicago: Univ. of Chicago Press, 1999.

Young, Evan. "Turning Down the Heat in the Domestic Cold War: Attorney General Tom C. Clark's Crusade against Subversive Activities." Thesis, Department of History, Duke University, April 19, 1999.

## Interviews

Brennan, William J. Interview by the author. Washington, D.C., June 19, 1981.

Capers, Elizabeth Clark. Interview by the author. Dallas, Texas, June 27, 1979.

Clark, Beulah. Interview by the author. Dallas, Texas, June 25, 1979.

Clark, Mary Ramsey. Interviews by the author. Washington, D.C., August 4–11, 1979.

Clark, Ramsey. Interview by the author. New York, September 2–3, 1982.

Clark, Tom. Interview by James Duram for the Dwight D. Eisenhower Library. Washington, D.C., March 26, 1972.

————. Interview by Miriam Feingold for the Earl Warren Oral History Project, University of California, Berkley. San Francisco, California, June 20, 1976.

————. Interview by Joe B. Frantz for the University of Texas Oral History Project. Washington, D.C., October 7, 1960.

————. Interview by Jerry N. Hess for the Harry S. Truman Presidential Library. Washington D.C., October 17, 1972.

————. Interview by Jerald L. Hill and William D. Stilley. Washington, D.C., March 20, 1976. Archived at the Harry S. Truman Presidential Library. Transcript available at http://www.trumanlibrary.org/oralhist/clarktc1.htm.

————. Interview by Robert Ireland for the Fred Vinson Oral History Project, University of Kentucky. Washington, D.C., May 6, 1973.

Morrison, Graham. Interview by Jerry Hess for the Harry S. Truman Presidential Library Oral History Project. Washington, D.C., August 1972.

Murphy, Charles. Interview by Jerry Hess for the Harry S. Truman Presidential Library Oral History Project. May 19, 1970.

Perlman, Philip. Interview by William Hillman and David M. Noyes. Kansas City, Missouri, December 15, 1954. Harry S. Truman Presidential Library, Post-Presidential File, Memoirs—File B.

Stewart, Grace. Interview by the author. Washington, D.C., September 12, 1981.

Stewart, Potter. Interview by the author. Washington, D.C., June 9, 1981.

White, Byron. Interview by the author. Washington, D.C., June 16, 1981.

# Index